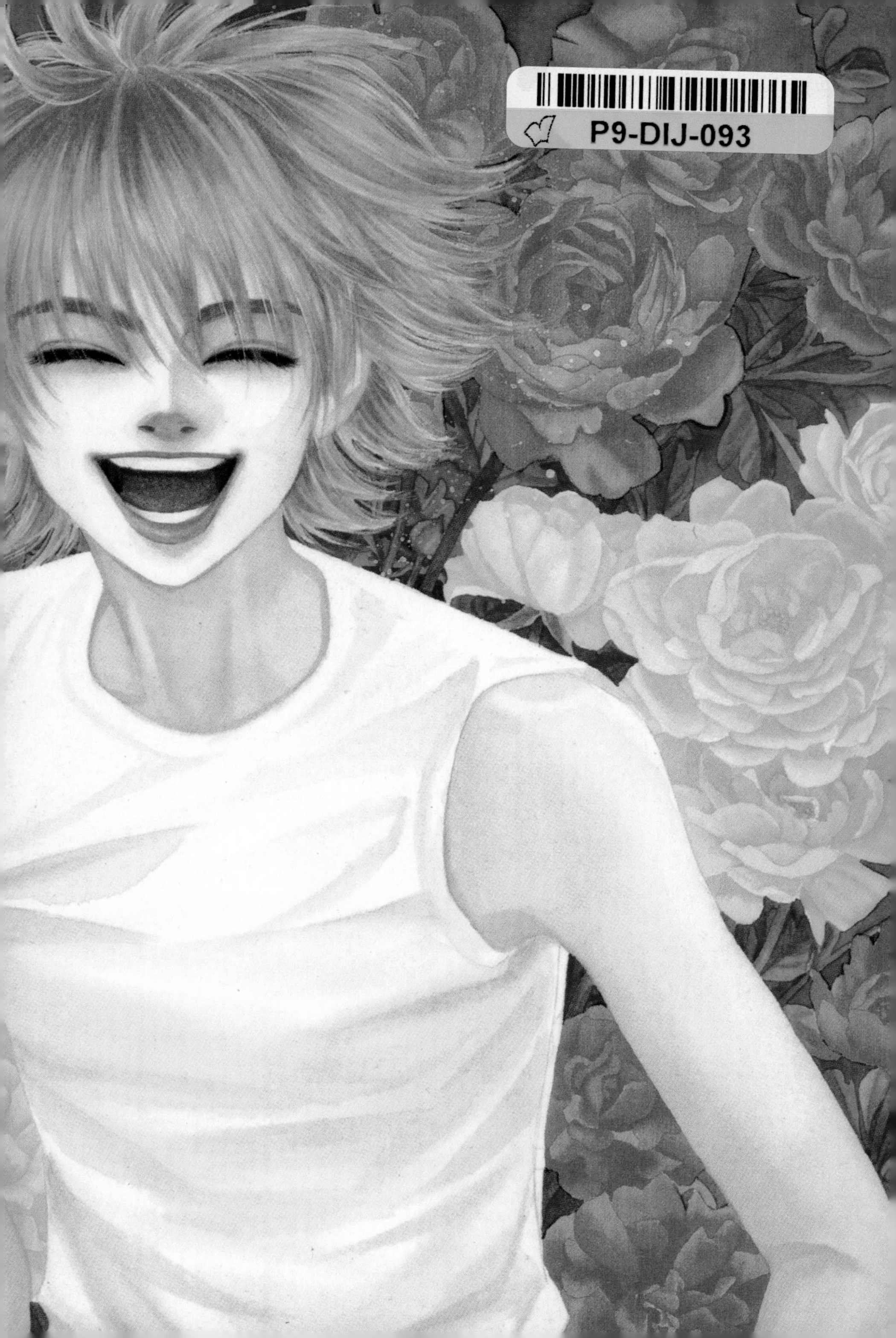

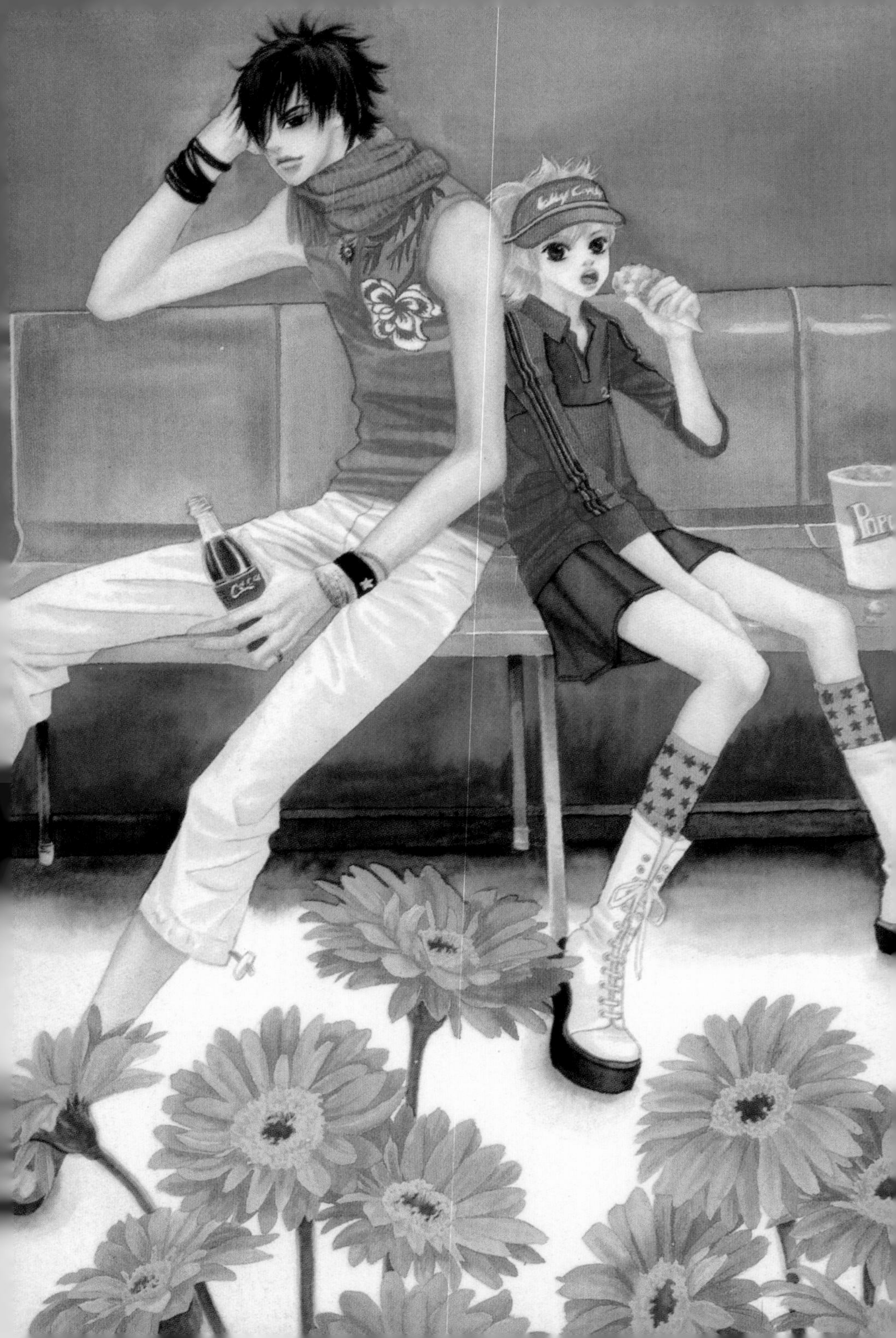

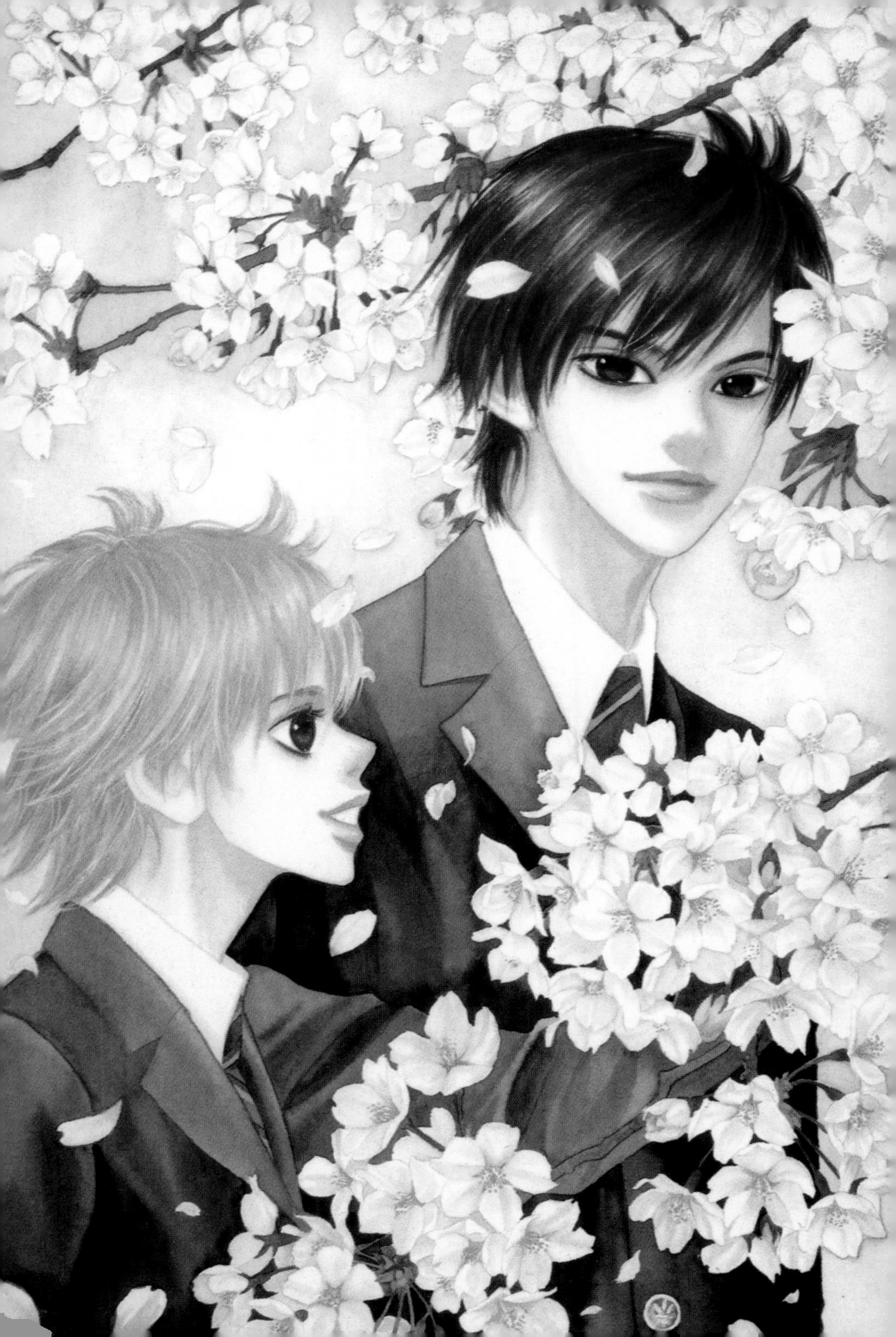

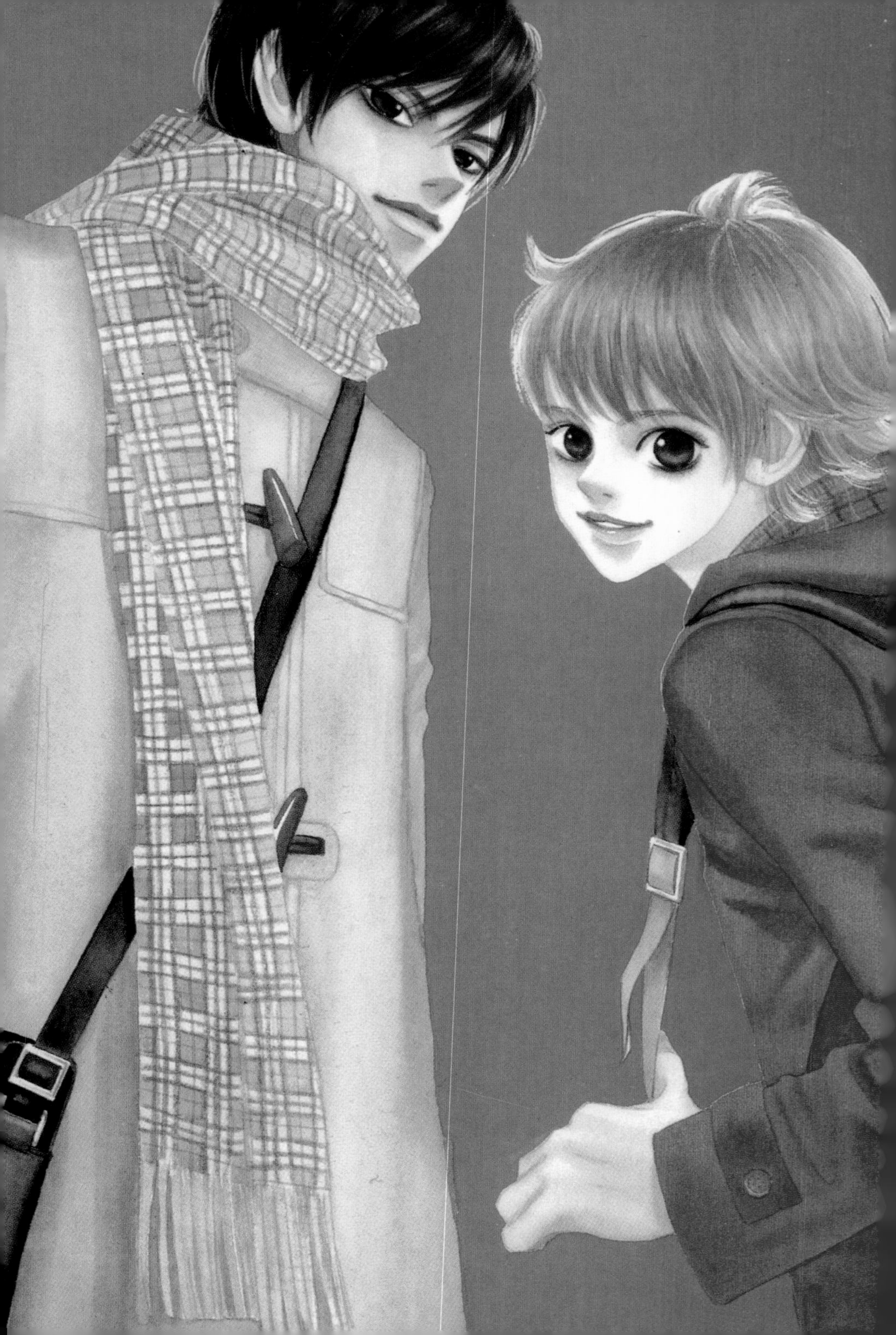

Vol. 1

YoungHee Lee

Yen Press

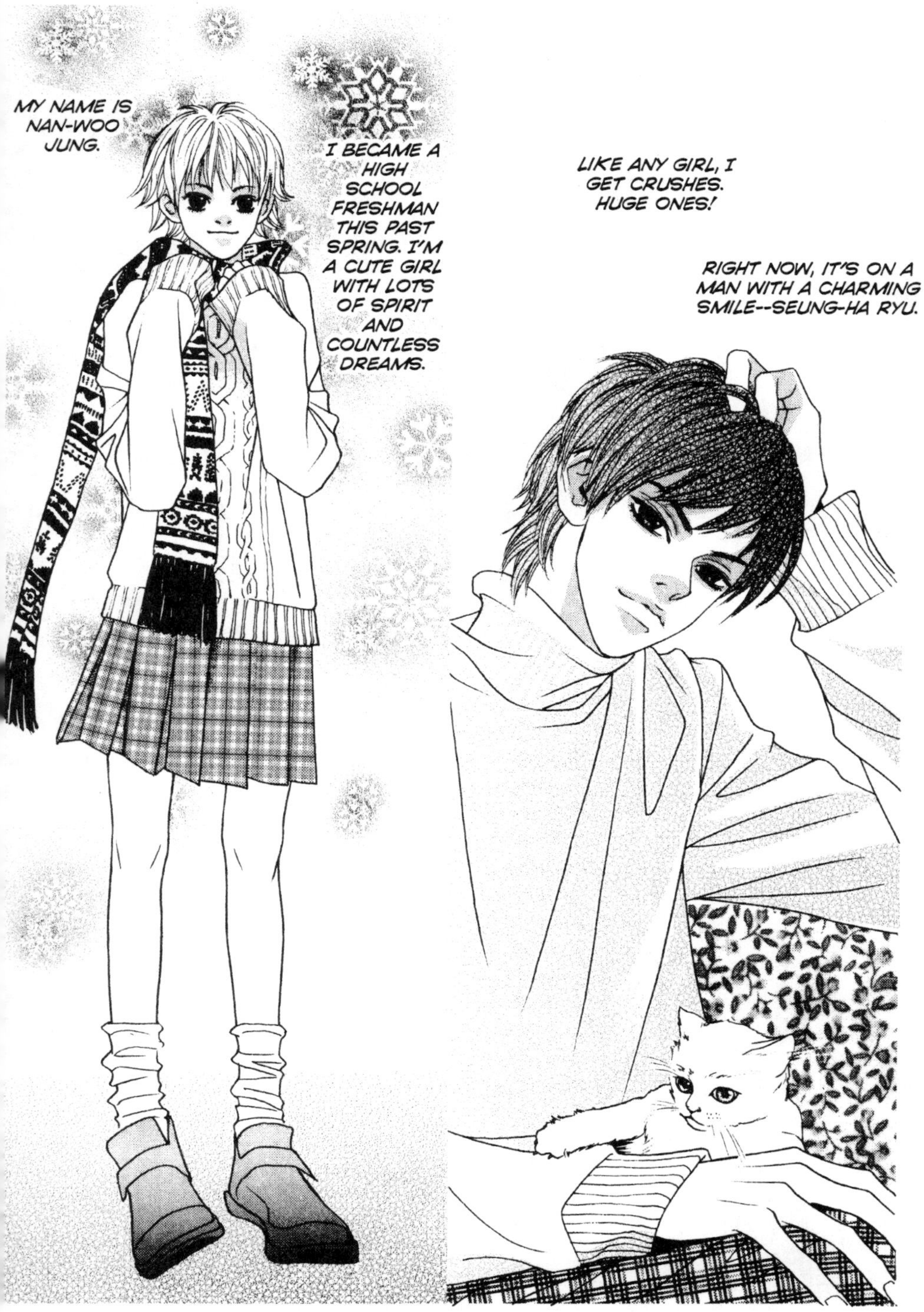
MY NAME IS NAN-WOO JUNG.
I BECAME A HIGH SCHOOL FRESHMAN THIS PAST SPRING. I'M A CUTE GIRL WITH LOTS OF SPIRIT AND COUNTLESS DREAMS.
LIKE ANY GIRL, I GET CRUSHES. HUGE ONES!
RIGHT NOW, IT'S ON A MAN WITH A CHARMING SMILE--SEUNG-HA RYU.

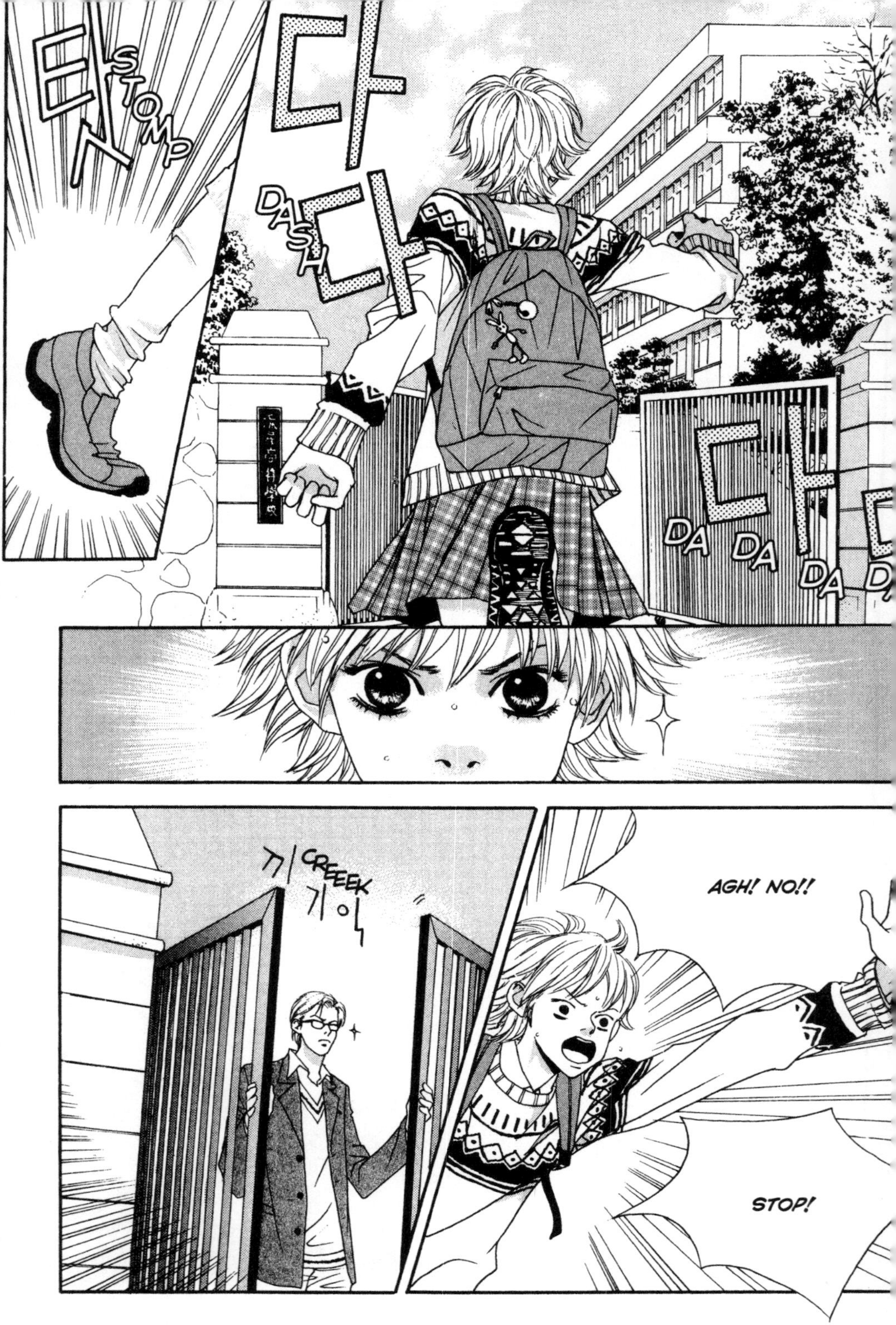
STOMP
다
DASH
다
다
DA DA DA DA
끼이익
CREEEK
AGH! NO!!
STOP!

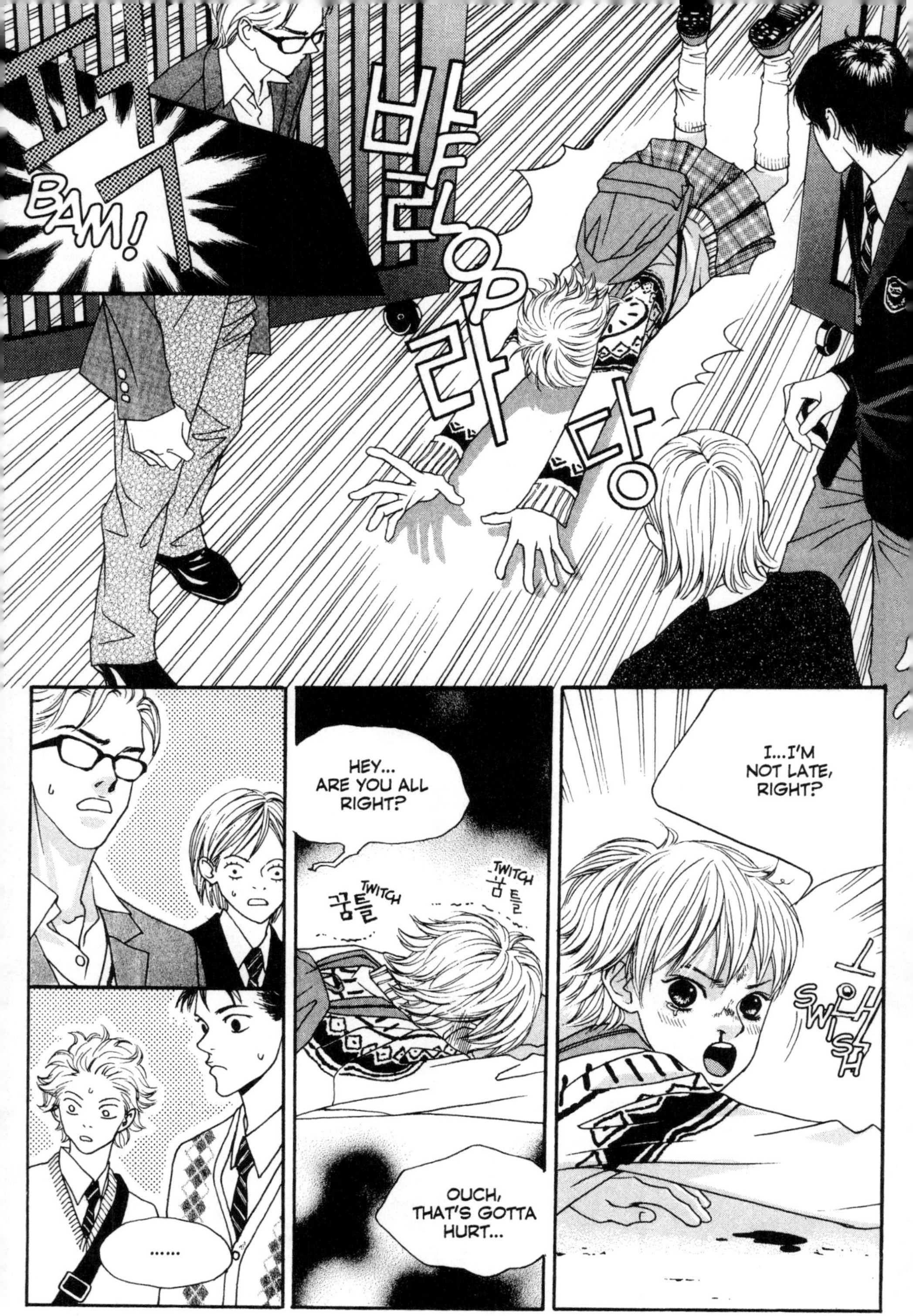
퍽
BAM!
......
HEY... ARE YOU ALL RIGHT?
꿈틀 TWITCH
꿈틀 TWITCH
OUCH, THAT'S GOTTA HURT...
I...I'M NOT LATE, RIGHT?
SWISH

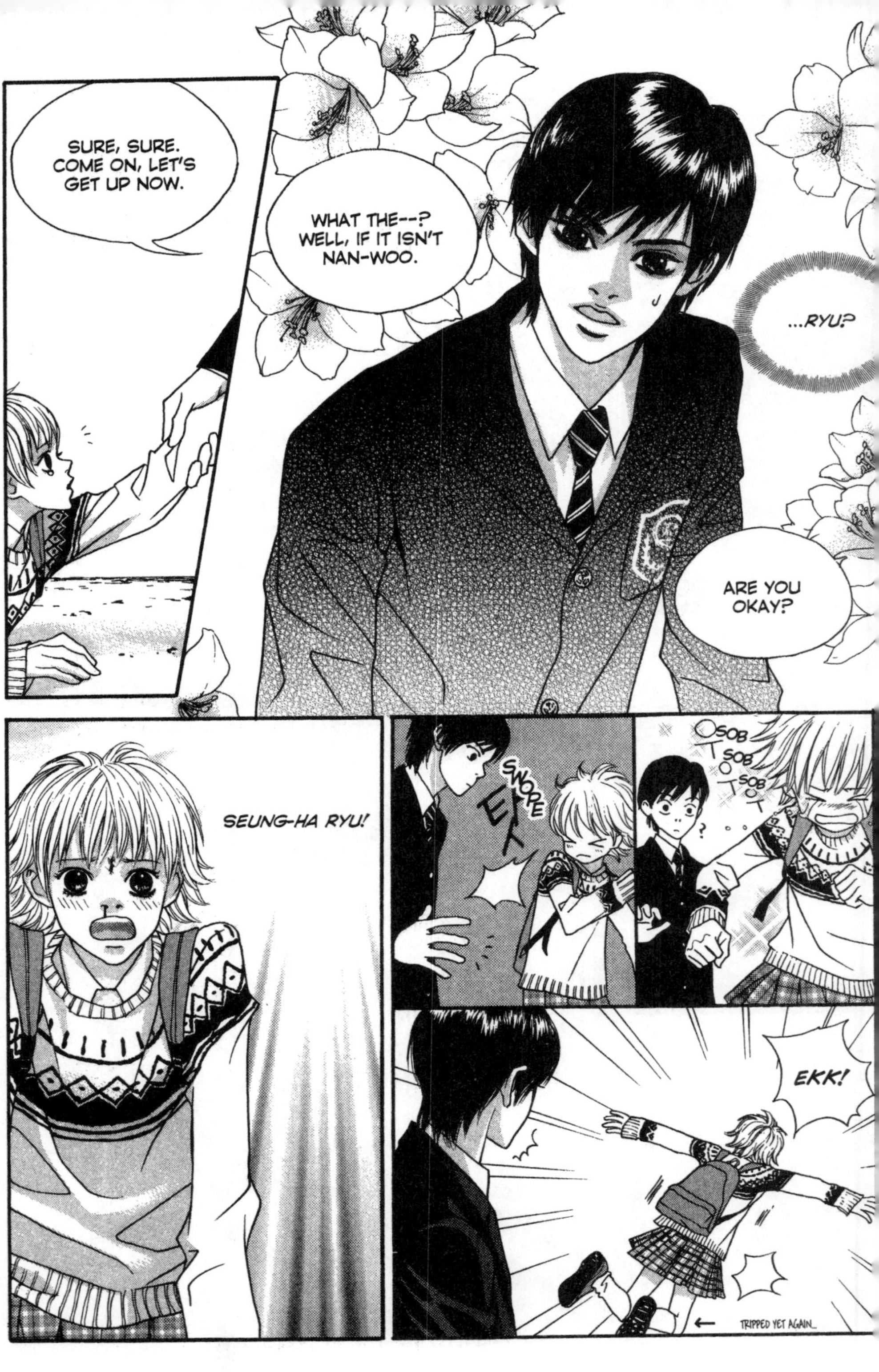
SURE, SURE. COME ON, LET'S GET UP NOW.
WHAT THE--? WELL, IF IT ISN'T NAN-WOO.
...RYU?
ARE YOU OKAY?
SEUNG-HA RYU!
SWOPE
SOB SOB SOB
EKK!
TRIPPED YET AGAIN...

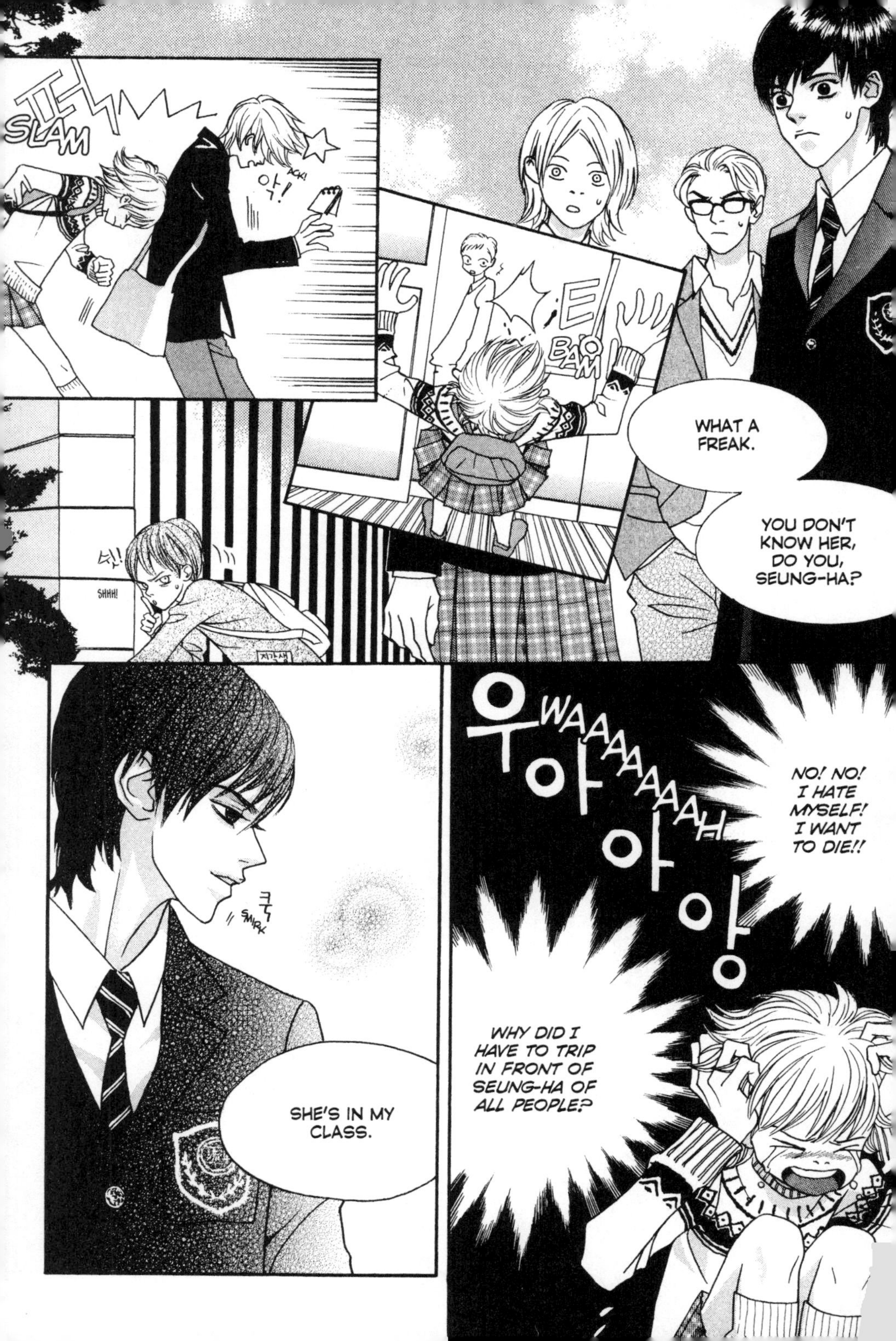

SLAM
악!
ACK!
BAM
WHAT A FREAK.
YOU DON'T KNOW HER, DO YOU, SEUNG-HA?
쉿!
SHHH!
SMIRK
SHE'S IN MY CLASS.
우아아앙
WAAAAAAAAAH
NO! NO! I HATE MYSELF! I WANT TO DIE!!
WHY DID I HAVE TO TRIP IN FRONT OF SEUNG-HA OF ALL PEOPLE?

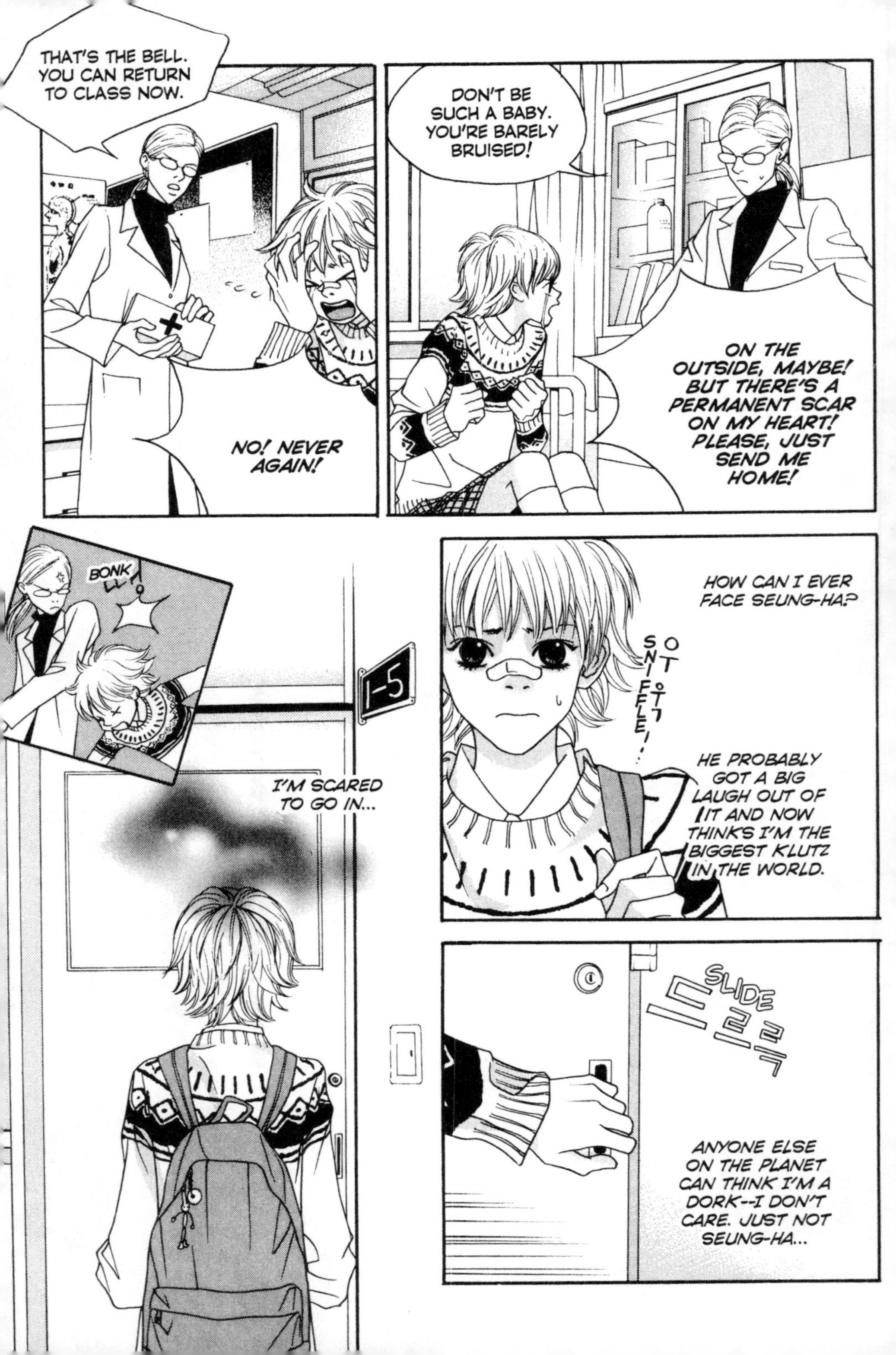
THAT'S THE BELL. YOU CAN RETURN TO CLASS NOW.
NO! NEVER AGAIN!
DON'T BE SUCH A BABY. YOU'RE BARELY BRUISED!
ON THE OUTSIDE, MAYBE! BUT THERE'S A PERMANENT SCAR ON MY HEART! PLEASE, JUST SEND ME HOME!
BONK
1-5
I'M SCARED TO GO IN...
HOW CAN I EVER FACE SEUNG-HA?
SNIFFLE...
HE PROBABLY GOT A BIG LAUGH OUT OF IT AND NOW THINKS I'M THE BIGGEST KLUTZ IN THE WORLD.
SLIDE
ANYONE ELSE ON THE PLANET CAN THINK I'M A DORK--I DON'T CARE. JUST NOT SEUNG-HA...

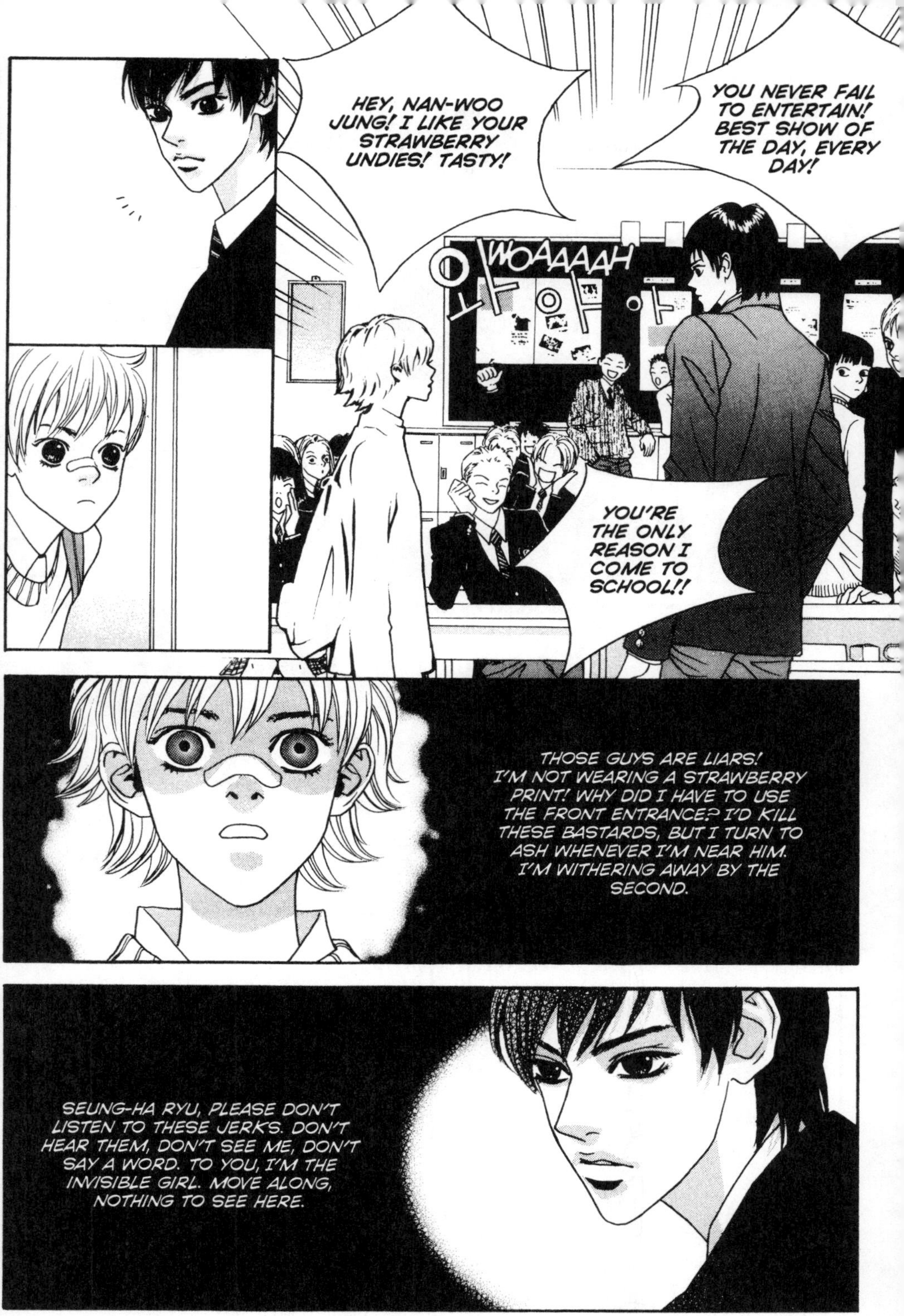
HEY, NAN-WOO JUNG! I LIKE YOUR STRAWBERRY UNDIES! TASTY!
YOU NEVER FAIL TO ENTERTAIN! BEST SHOW OF THE DAY, EVERY DAY!
WOAAAAH
YOU'RE THE ONLY REASON I COME TO SCHOOL!!
THOSE GUYS ARE LIARS! I'M NOT WEARING A STRAWBERRY PRINT! WHY DID I HAVE TO USE THE FRONT ENTRANCE? I'D KILL THESE BASTARDS, BUT I TURN TO ASH WHENEVER I'M NEAR HIM. I'M WITHERING AWAY BY THE SECOND.
SEUNG-HA RYU, PLEASE DON'T LISTEN TO THESE JERKS. DON'T HEAR THEM, DON'T SEE ME, DON'T SAY A WORD. TO YOU, I'M THE INVISIBLE GIRL. MOVE ALONG, NOTHING TO SEE HERE.

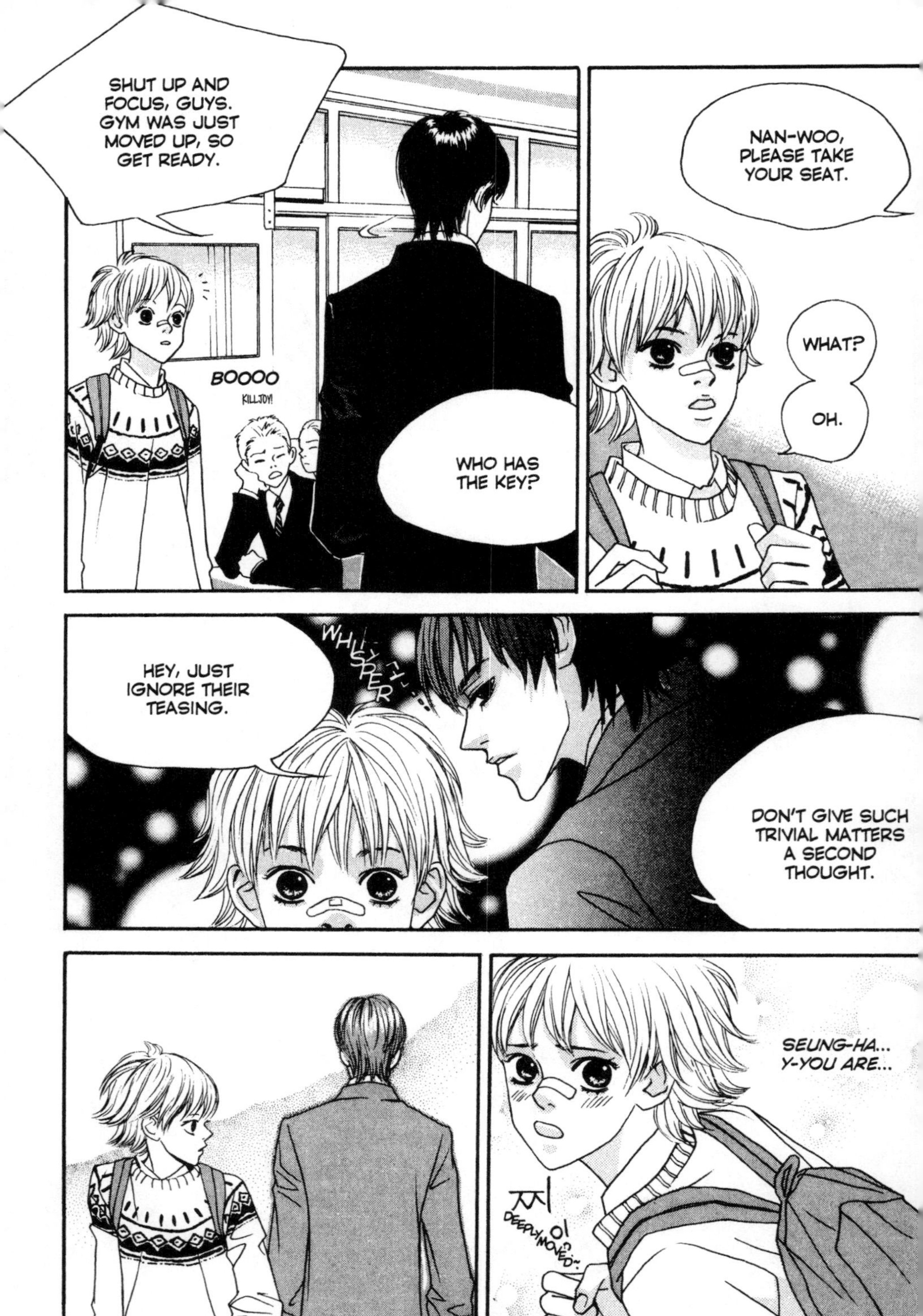
SHUT UP AND FOCUS, GUYS. GYM WAS JUST MOVED UP, SO GET READY.
BOOOO
KILLJOY!
WHO HAS THE KEY?
NAN-WOO, PLEASE TAKE YOUR SEAT.
WHAT?
OH.
HEY, JUST IGNORE THEIR TEASING.
WHISPER
DON'T GIVE SUCH TRIVIAL MATTERS A SECOND THOUGHT.
SEUNG-HA... Y-YOU ARE...
DEEPLY MOVED~

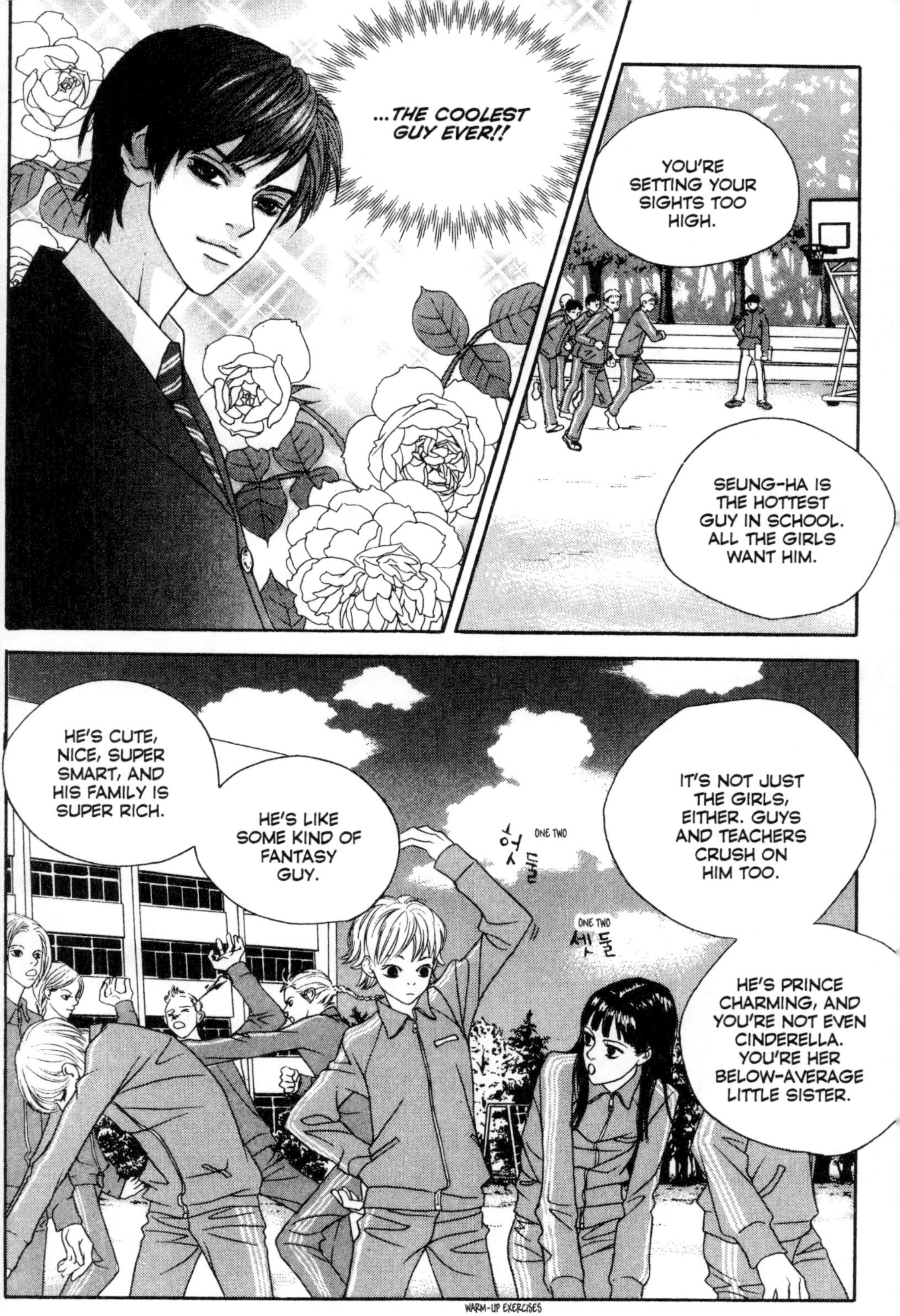
...THE COOLEST GUY EVER!!
YOU'RE SETTING YOUR SIGHTS TOO HIGH.
SEUNG-HA IS THE HOTTEST GUY IN SCHOOL. ALL THE GIRLS WANT HIM.
HE'S CUTE, NICE, SUPER SMART, AND HIS FAMILY IS SUPER RICH.
HE'S LIKE SOME KIND OF FANTASY GUY.
ONE TWO
ONE TWO
IT'S NOT JUST THE GIRLS, EITHER. GUYS AND TEACHERS CRUSH ON HIM TOO.
HE'S PRINCE CHARMING, AND YOU'RE NOT EVEN CINDERELLA. YOU'RE HER BELOW-AVERAGE LITTLE SISTER.
WARM-UP EXERCISES

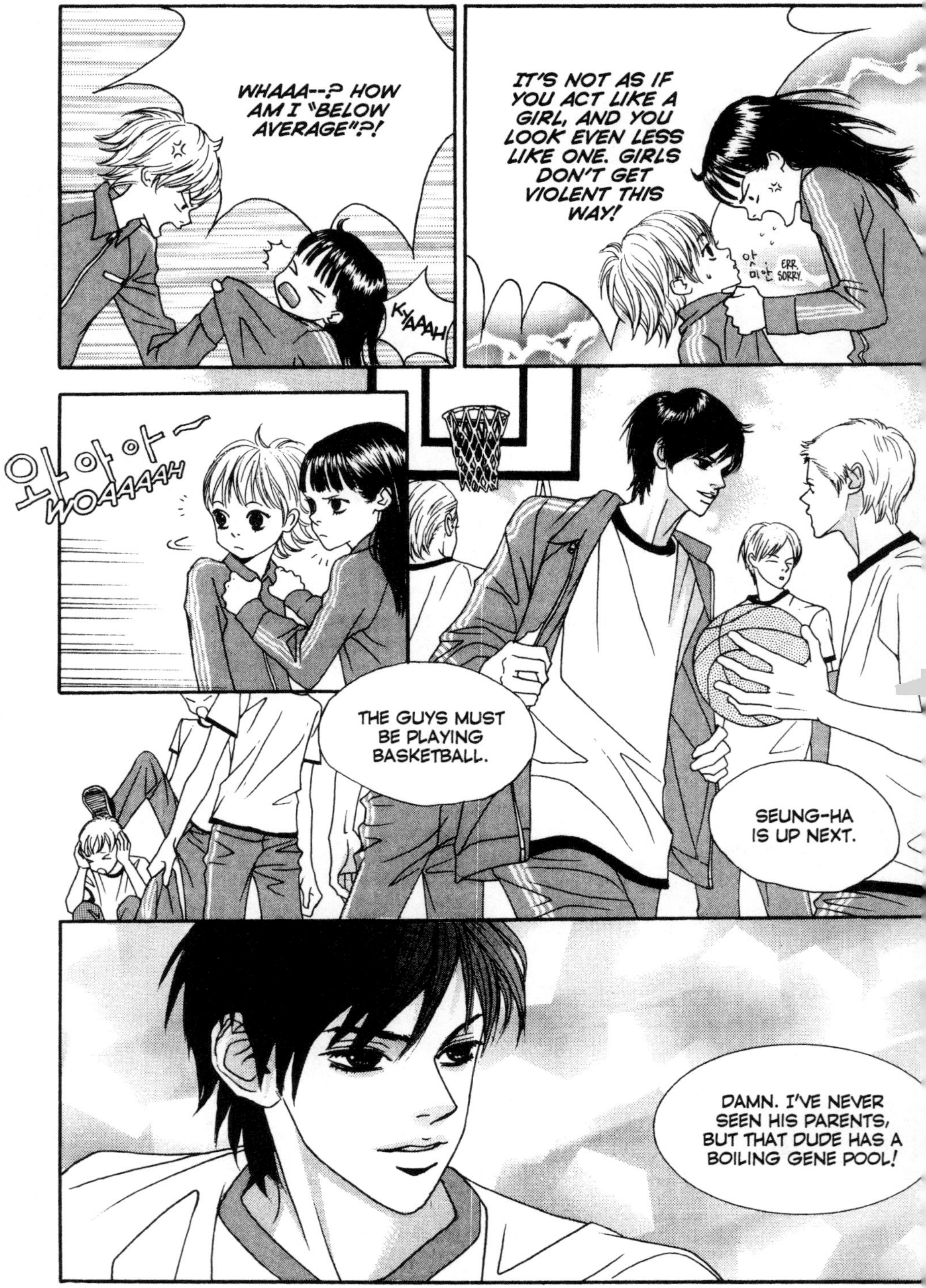
WHAAA--? HOW AM I "BELOW AVERAGE"?!
KYAAAH
IT'S NOT AS IF YOU ACT LIKE A GIRL, AND YOU LOOK EVEN LESS LIKE ONE. GIRLS DON'T GET VIOLENT THIS WAY!
아 미안
ERR. SORRY.
와아아~
WOAAAAH
THE GUYS MUST BE PLAYING BASKETBALL.
SEUNG-HA IS UP NEXT.
DAMN. I'VE NEVER SEEN HIS PARENTS, BUT THAT DUDE HAS A BOILING GENE POOL!

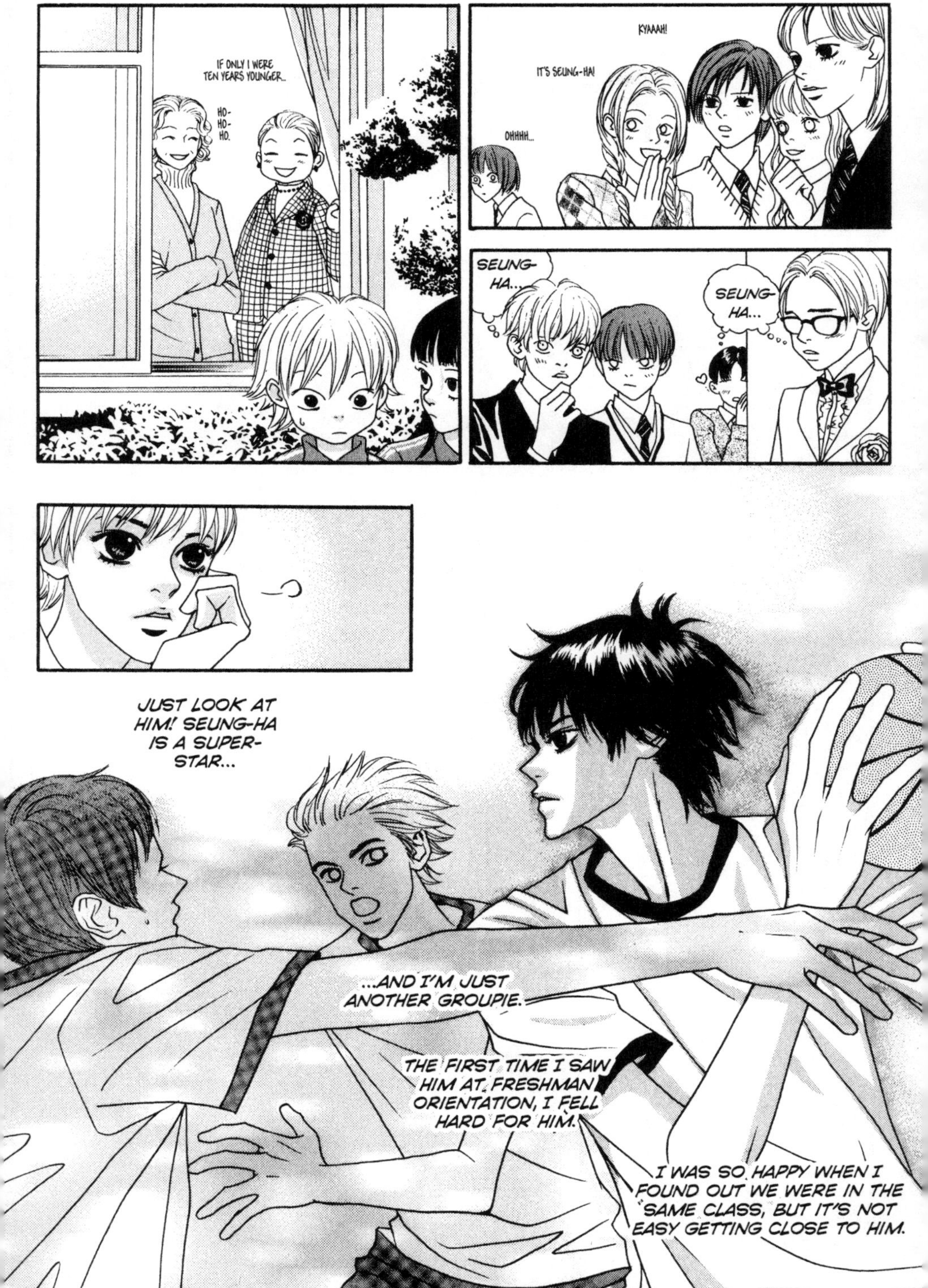
IF ONLY I WERE TEN YEARS YOUNGER...
HO-HO-HO.
KYAAAH!
IT'S SEUNG-HA!
OHHHH...
SEUNG-HA...
SEUNG-HA...
JUST LOOK AT HIM! SEUNG-HA IS A SUPER-STAR...
...AND I'M JUST ANOTHER GROUPIE.
THE FIRST TIME I SAW HIM AT FRESHMAN ORIENTATION, I FELL HARD FOR HIM.
I WAS SO HAPPY WHEN I FOUND OUT WE WERE IN THE SAME CLASS, BUT IT'S NOT EASY GETTING CLOSE TO HIM.

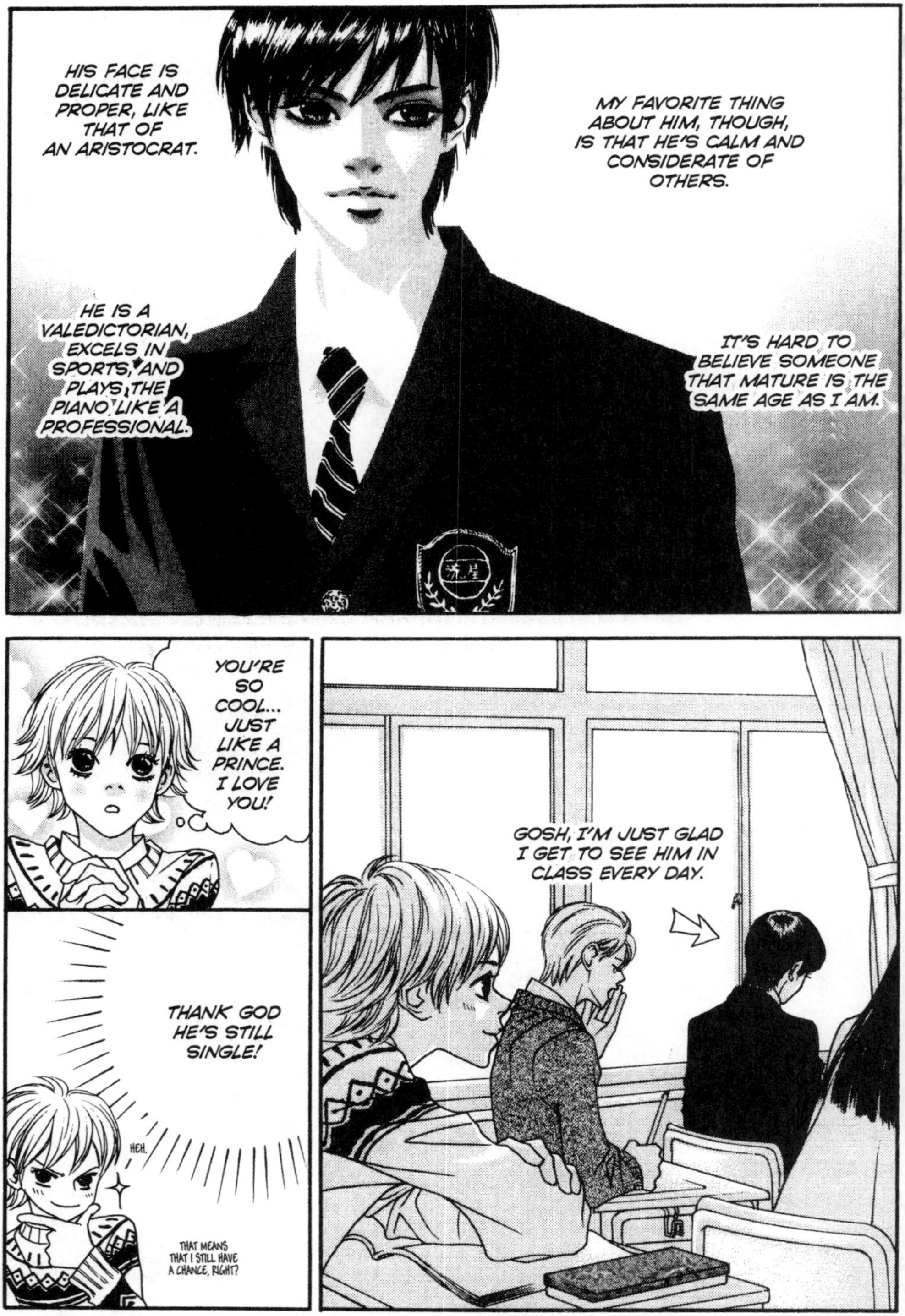
HIS FACE IS DELICATE AND PROPER, LIKE THAT OF AN ARISTOCRAT.
MY FAVORITE THING ABOUT HIM, THOUGH, IS THAT HE'S CALM AND CONSIDERATE OF OTHERS.
HE IS A VALEDICTORIAN, EXCELS IN SPORTS, AND PLAYS THE PIANO LIKE A PROFESSIONAL.
IT'S HARD TO BELIEVE SOMEONE THAT MATURE IS THE SAME AGE AS I AM.
YOU'RE SO COOL... JUST LIKE A PRINCE. I LOVE YOU!
THANK GOD HE'S STILL SINGLE!
HEH.
THAT MEANS THAT I STILL HAVE A CHANCE, RIGHT?
GOSH, I'M JUST GLAD I GET TO SEE HIM IN CLASS EVERY DAY.

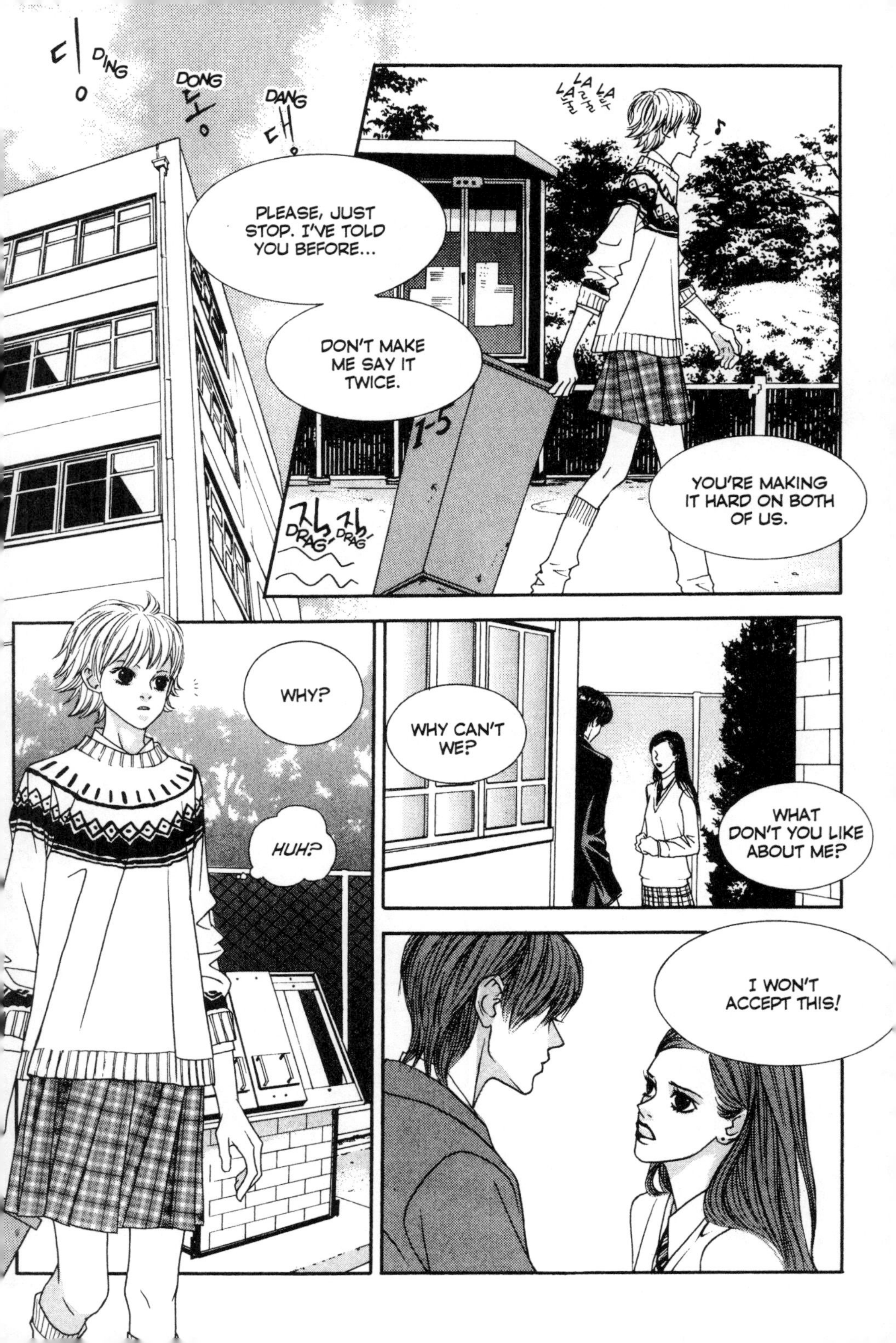
디 DING
동 DONG
댕 DANG
PLEASE, JUST STOP. I'VE TOLD YOU BEFORE...
DON'T MAKE ME SAY IT TWICE.
LA LA LA 랄랄라
1-5
질질 DRAG, DRAG
YOU'RE MAKING IT HARD ON BOTH OF US.
WHY?
HUH?
WHY CAN'T WE?
WHAT DON'T YOU LIKE ABOUT ME?
I WON'T ACCEPT THIS!

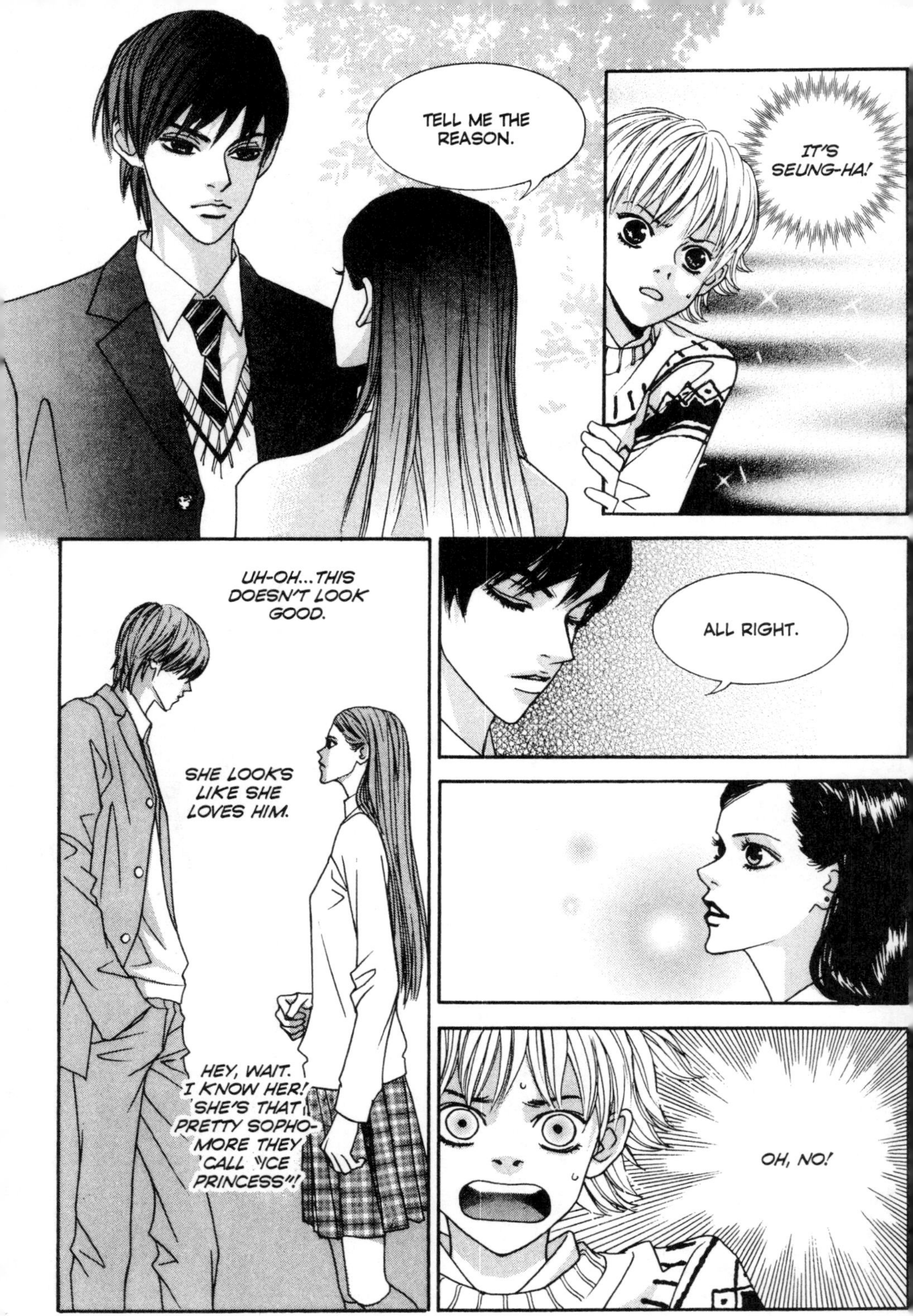
TELL ME THE REASON.
IT'S SEUNG-HA!
UH-OH...THIS DOESN'T LOOK GOOD.
SHE LOOKS LIKE SHE LOVES HIM.
HEY, WAIT. I KNOW HER! SHE'S THAT PRETTY SOPHO-MORE THEY CALL "ICE PRINCESS"!
ALL RIGHT.
OH, NO!

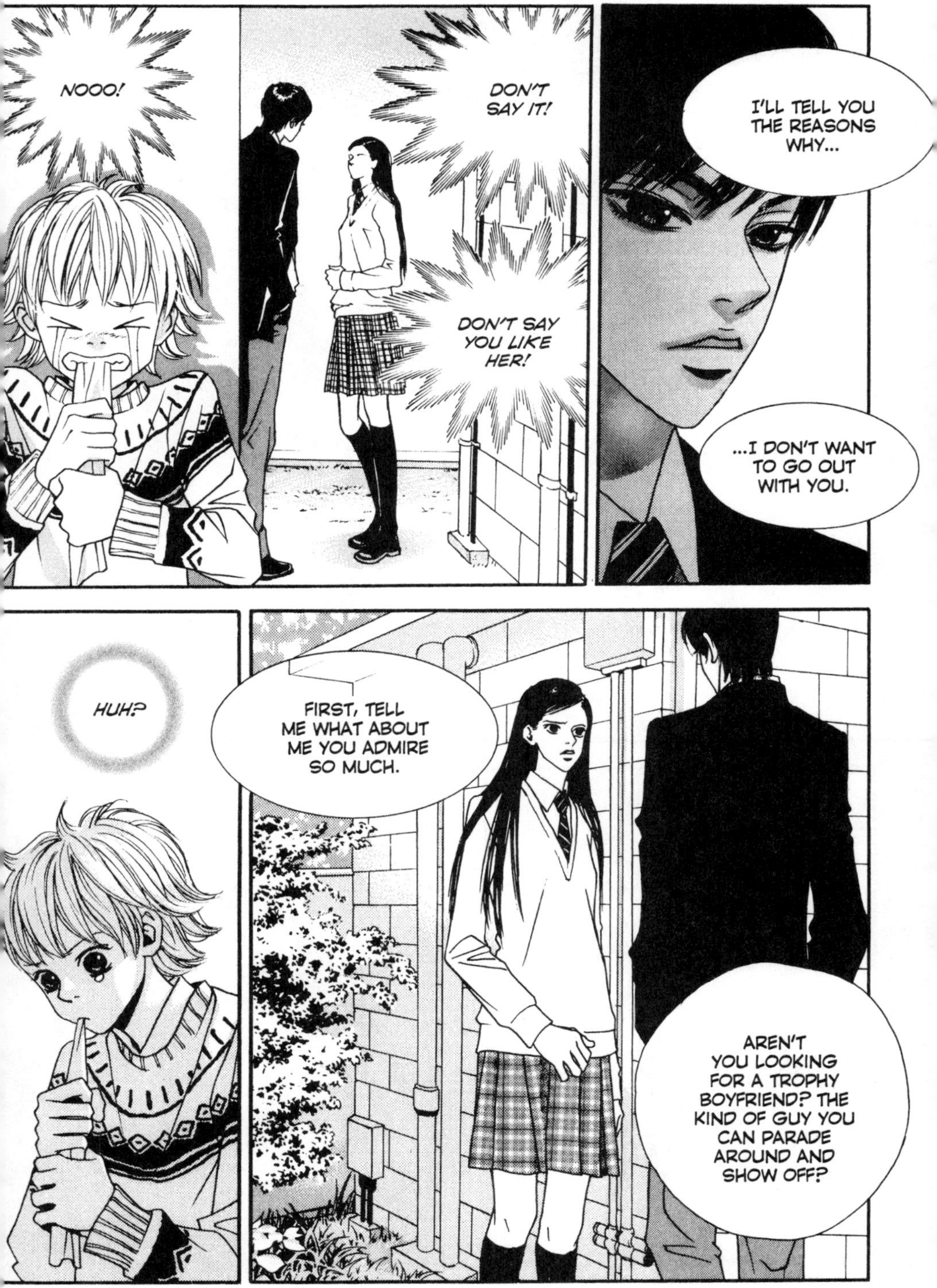
NOOO!
DON'T SAY IT!
DON'T SAY YOU LIKE HER!
I'LL TELL YOU THE REASONS WHY...
...I DON'T WANT TO GO OUT WITH YOU.
HUH?
FIRST, TELL ME WHAT ABOUT ME YOU ADMIRE SO MUCH.
AREN'T YOU LOOKING FOR A TROPHY BOYFRIEND? THE KIND OF GUY YOU CAN PARADE AROUND AND SHOW OFF?

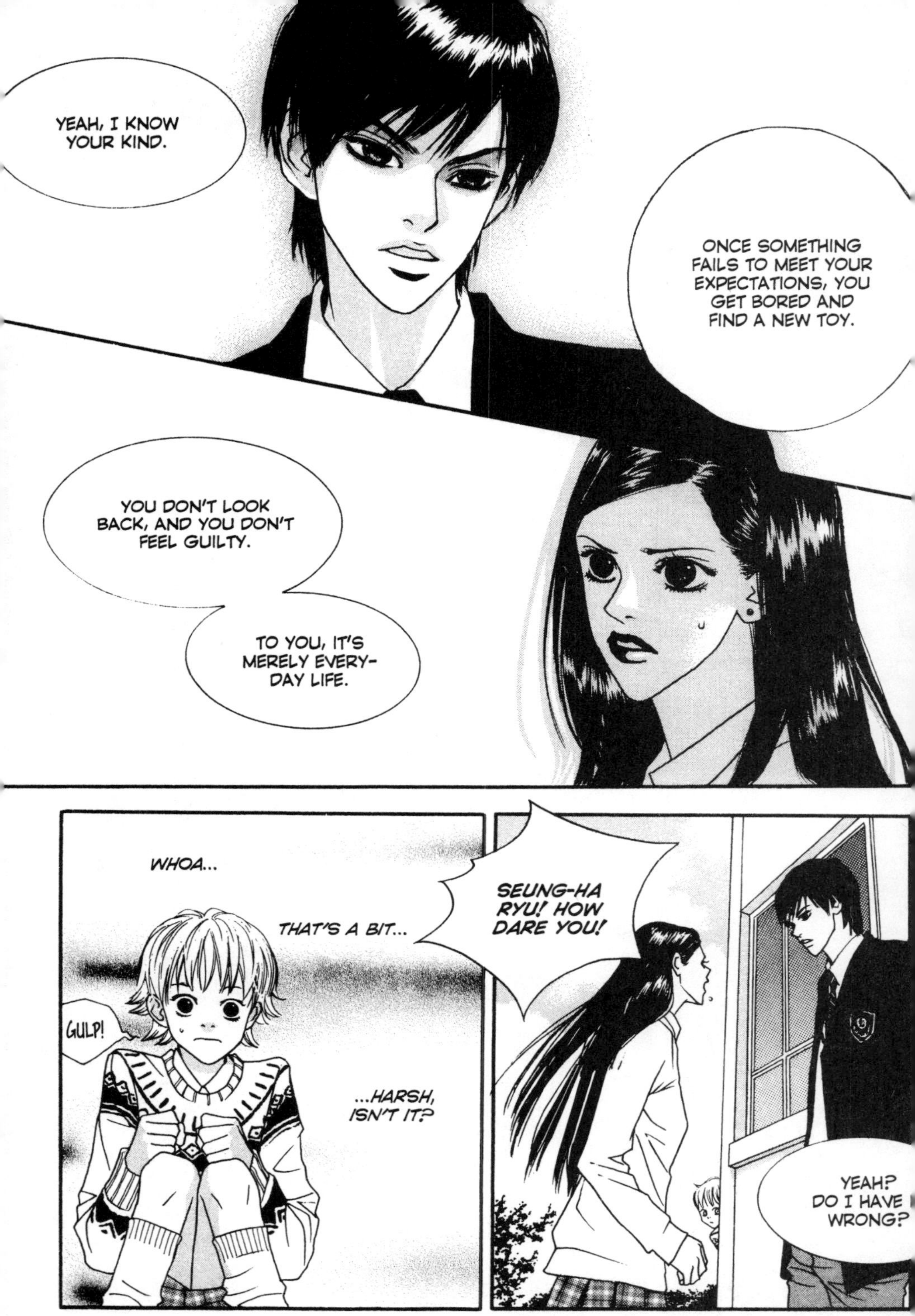
YEAH, I KNOW YOUR KIND.
ONCE SOMETHING FAILS TO MEET YOUR EXPECTATIONS, YOU GET BORED AND FIND A NEW TOY.
YOU DON'T LOOK BACK, AND YOU DON'T FEEL GUILTY.
TO YOU, IT'S MERELY EVERY-DAY LIFE.
WHOA...
THAT'S A BIT...
GULP!
...HARSH, ISN'T IT?
SEUNG-HA RYU! HOW DARE YOU!
YEAH? DO I HAVE WRONG?

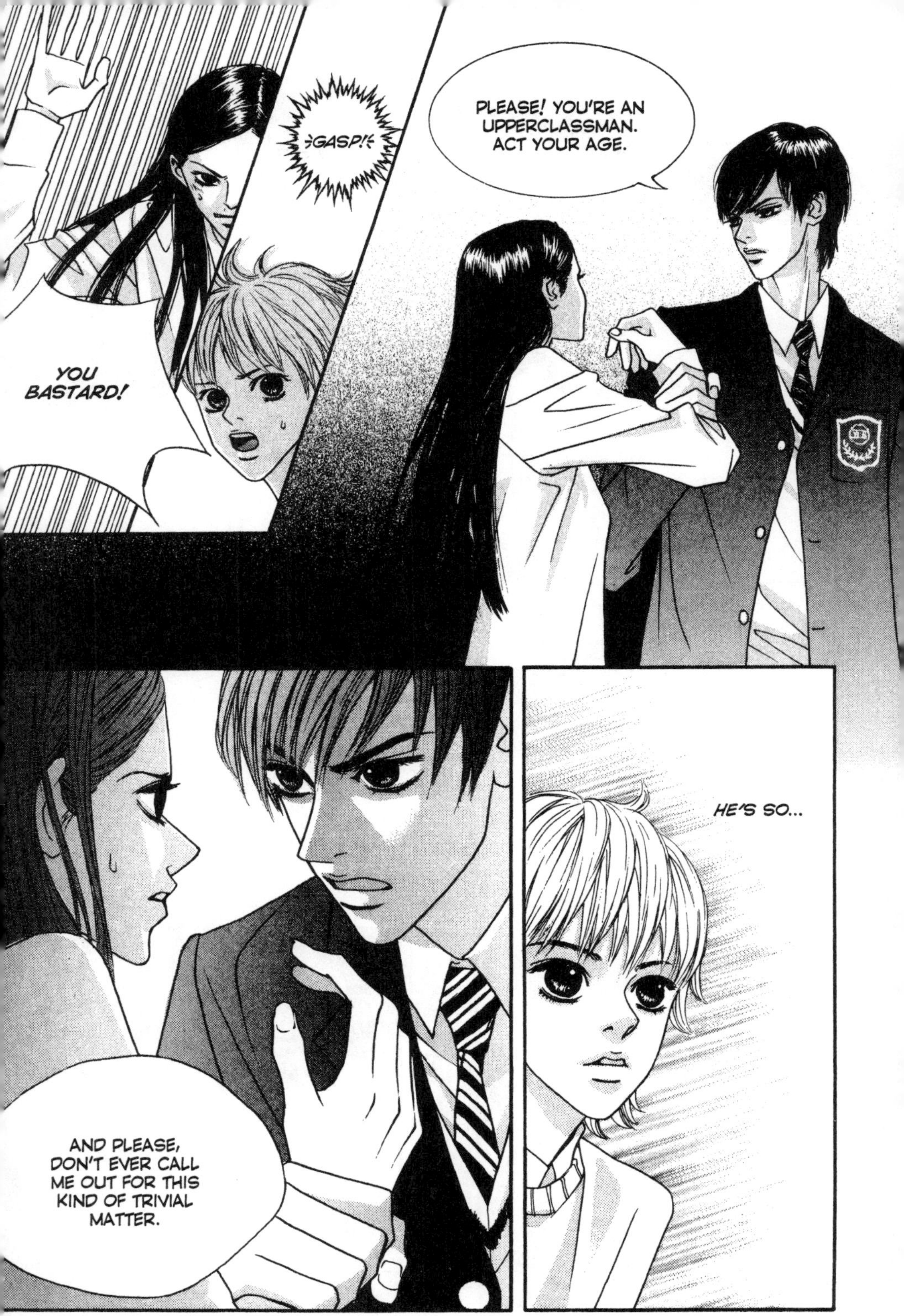
YOU BASTARD!
GASP!
PLEASE! YOU'RE AN UPPERCLASSMAN. ACT YOUR AGE.
AND PLEASE, DON'T EVER CALL ME OUT FOR THIS KIND OF TRIVIAL MATTER.
HE'S SO...

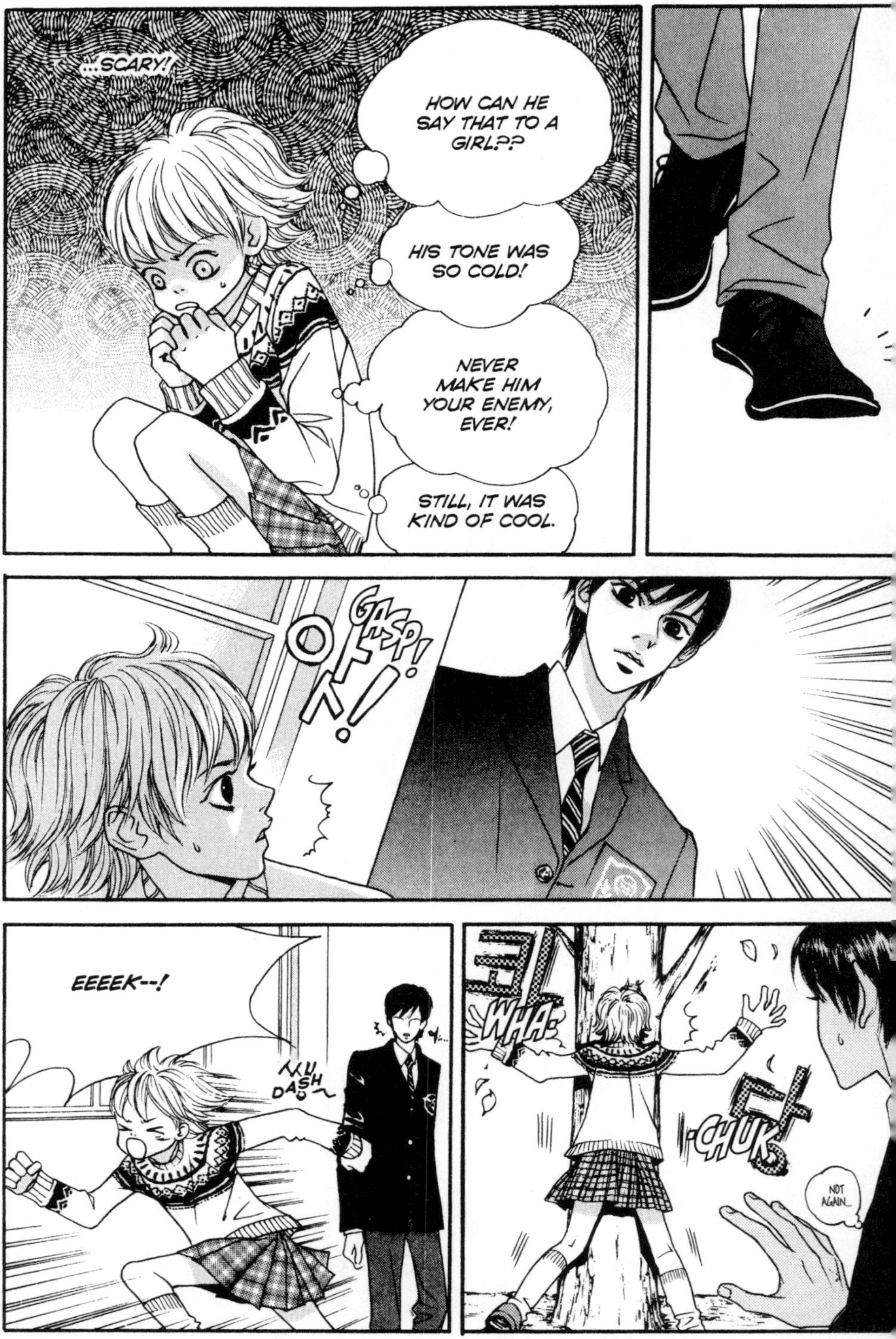
...SCARY!
HOW CAN HE SAY THAT TO A GIRL??
HIS TONE WAS SO COLD!
NEVER MAKE HIM YOUR ENEMY, EVER!
STILL, IT WAS KIND OF COOL.
GASP!
EEEEK--!
DASH~
WHA-
-CHUK
NOT AGAIN...

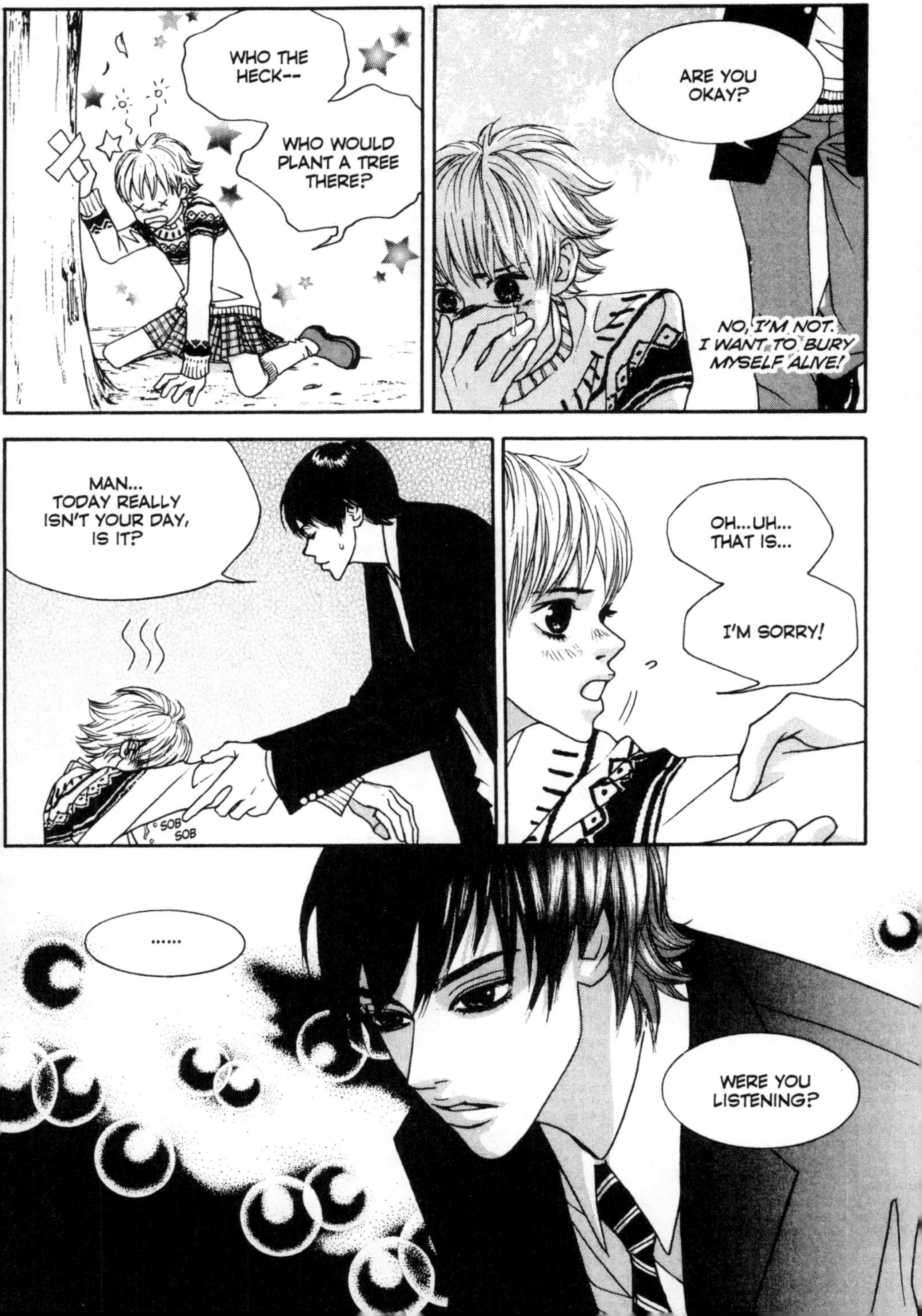
WHO THE HECK--
WHO WOULD PLANT A TREE THERE?
ARE YOU OKAY?
NO, I'M NOT. I WANT TO BURY MYSELF ALIVE!
MAN... TODAY REALLY ISN'T YOUR DAY, IS IT?
SOB SOB
OH...UH... THAT IS...
I'M SORRY!
......
WERE YOU LISTENING?

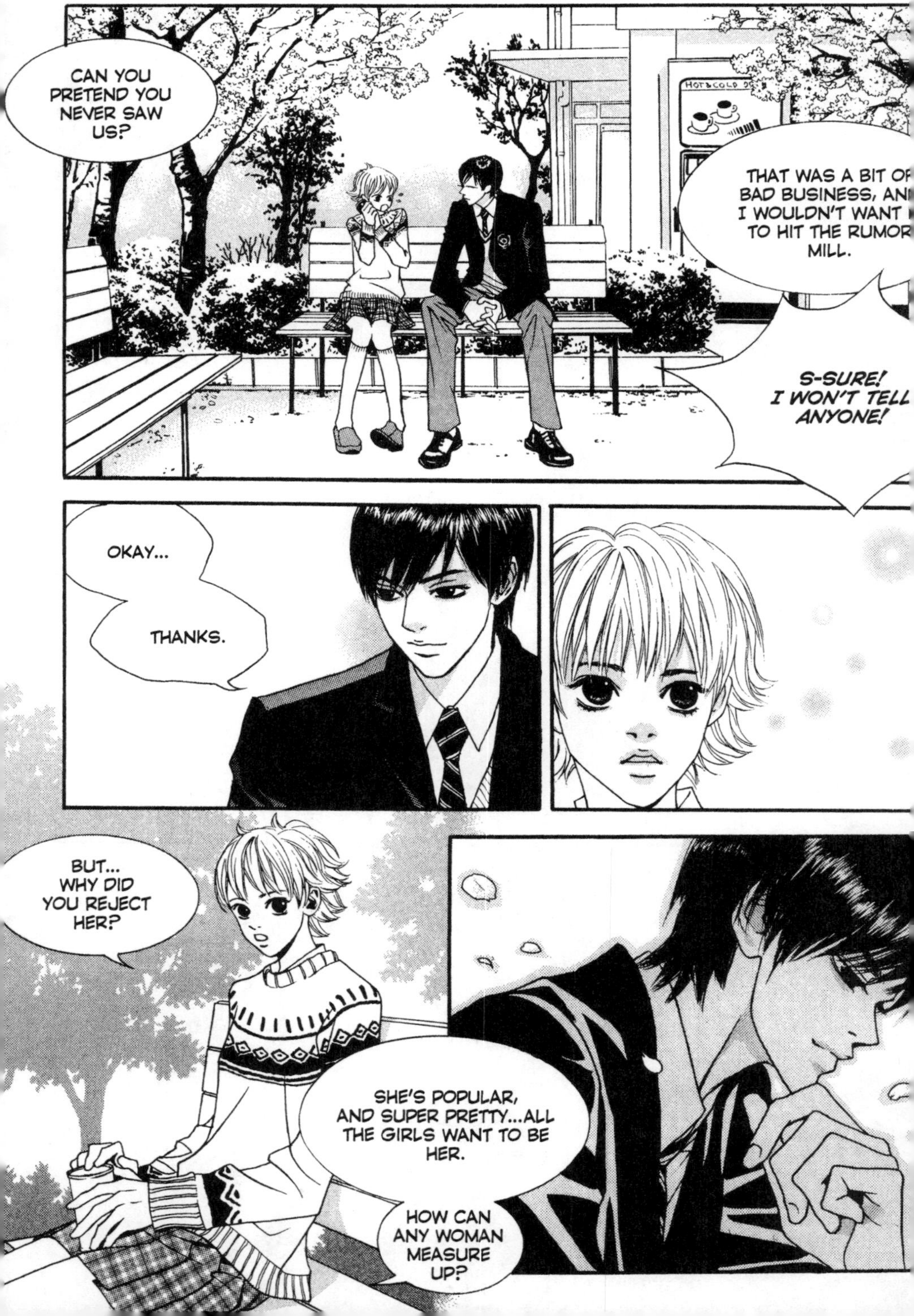
CAN YOU PRETEND YOU NEVER SAW US?
THAT WAS A BIT OF BAD BUSINESS, AND I WOULDN'T WANT IT TO HIT THE RUMOR MILL.
S-SURE! I WON'T TELL ANYONE!
OKAY...
THANKS.
BUT... WHY DID YOU REJECT HER?
SHE'S POPULAR, AND SUPER PRETTY...ALL THE GIRLS WANT TO BE HER.
HOW CAN ANY WOMAN MEASURE UP?

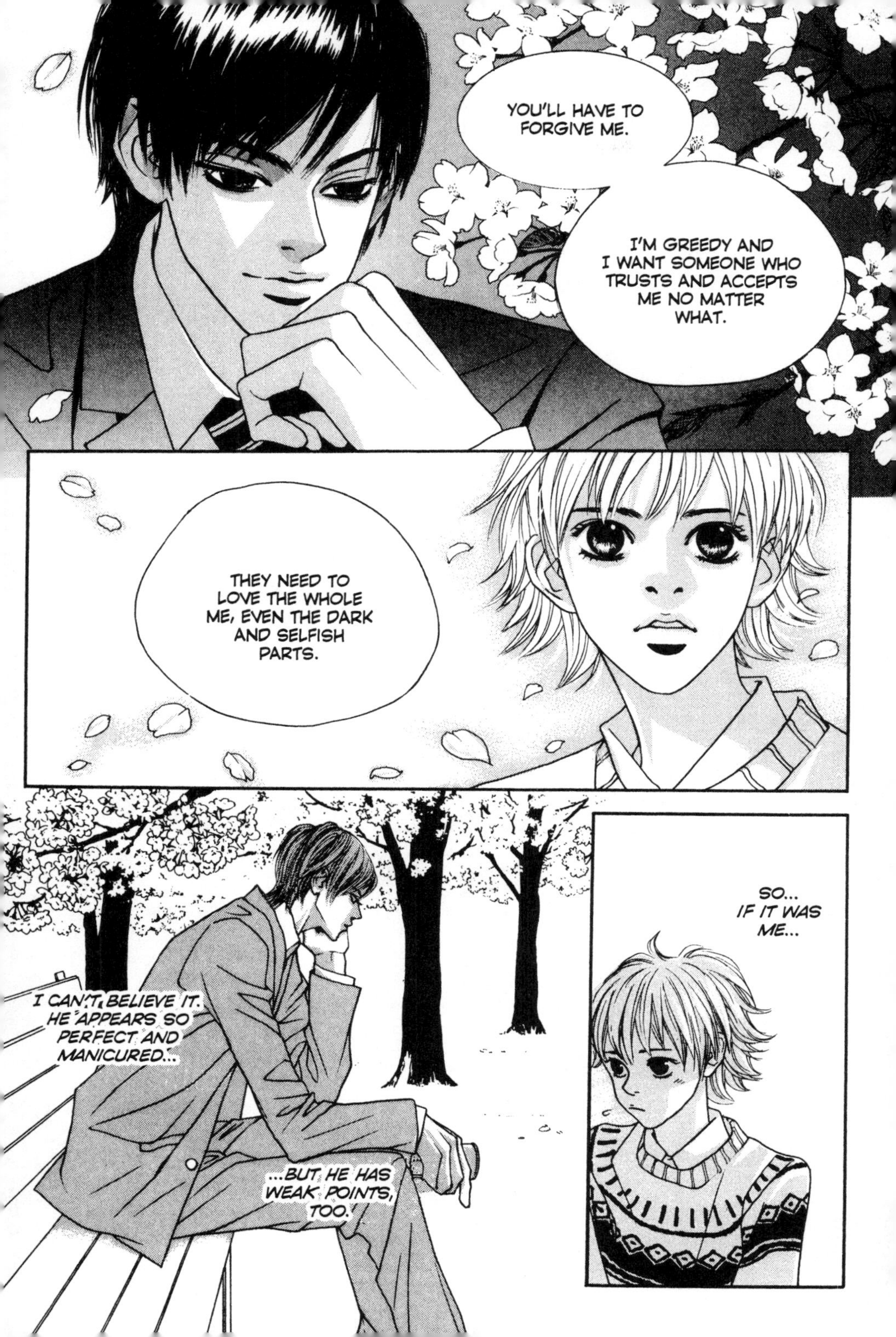
YOU'LL HAVE TO FORGIVE ME.
I'M GREEDY AND I WANT SOMEONE WHO TRUSTS AND ACCEPTS ME NO MATTER WHAT.
THEY NEED TO LOVE THE WHOLE ME, EVEN THE DARK AND SELFISH PARTS.
I CAN'T BELIEVE IT. HE APPEARS SO PERFECT AND MANICURED...
...BUT HE HAS WEAK POINTS, TOO.
SO... IF IT WAS ME...

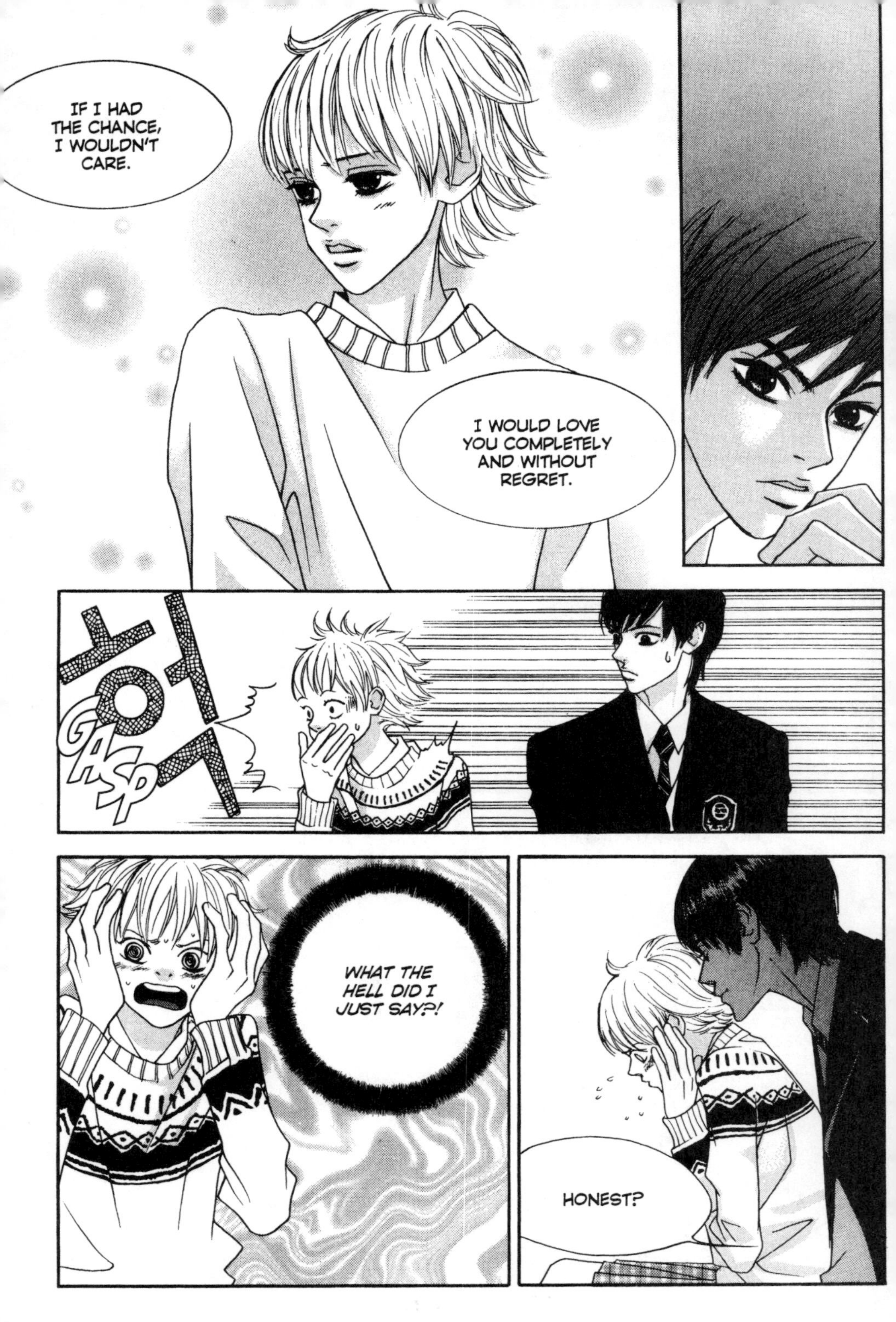
IF I HAD THE CHANCE, I WOULDN'T CARE.
I WOULD LOVE YOU COMPLETELY AND WITHOUT REGRET.
GASP
WHAT THE HELL DID I JUST SAY?!
HONEST?

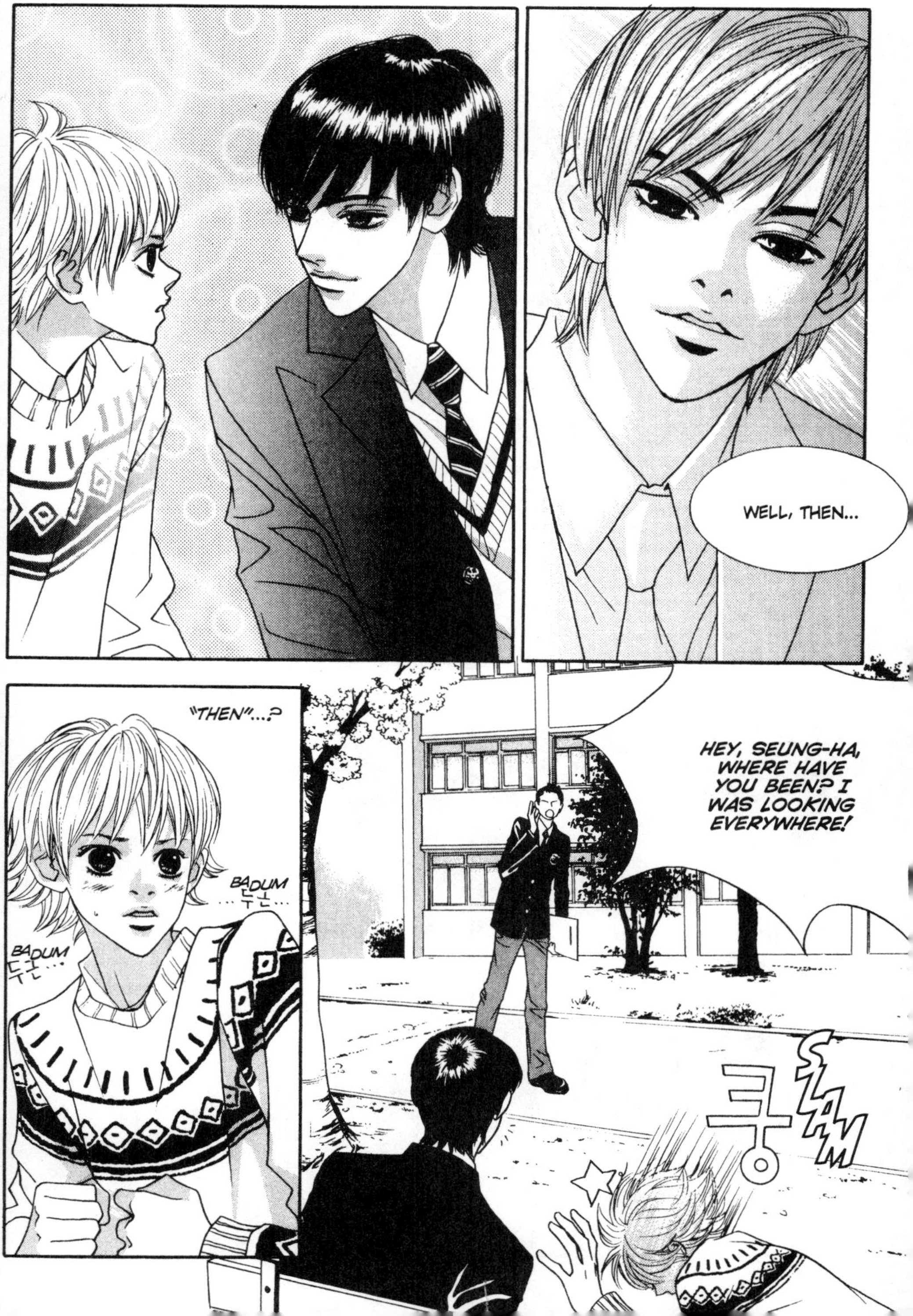
WELL, THEN...
"THEN"...?
BADUM
두근...
BADUM
두근...
HEY, SEUNG-HA, WHERE HAVE YOU BEEN? I WAS LOOKING EVERYWHERE!
쿵
SLAM

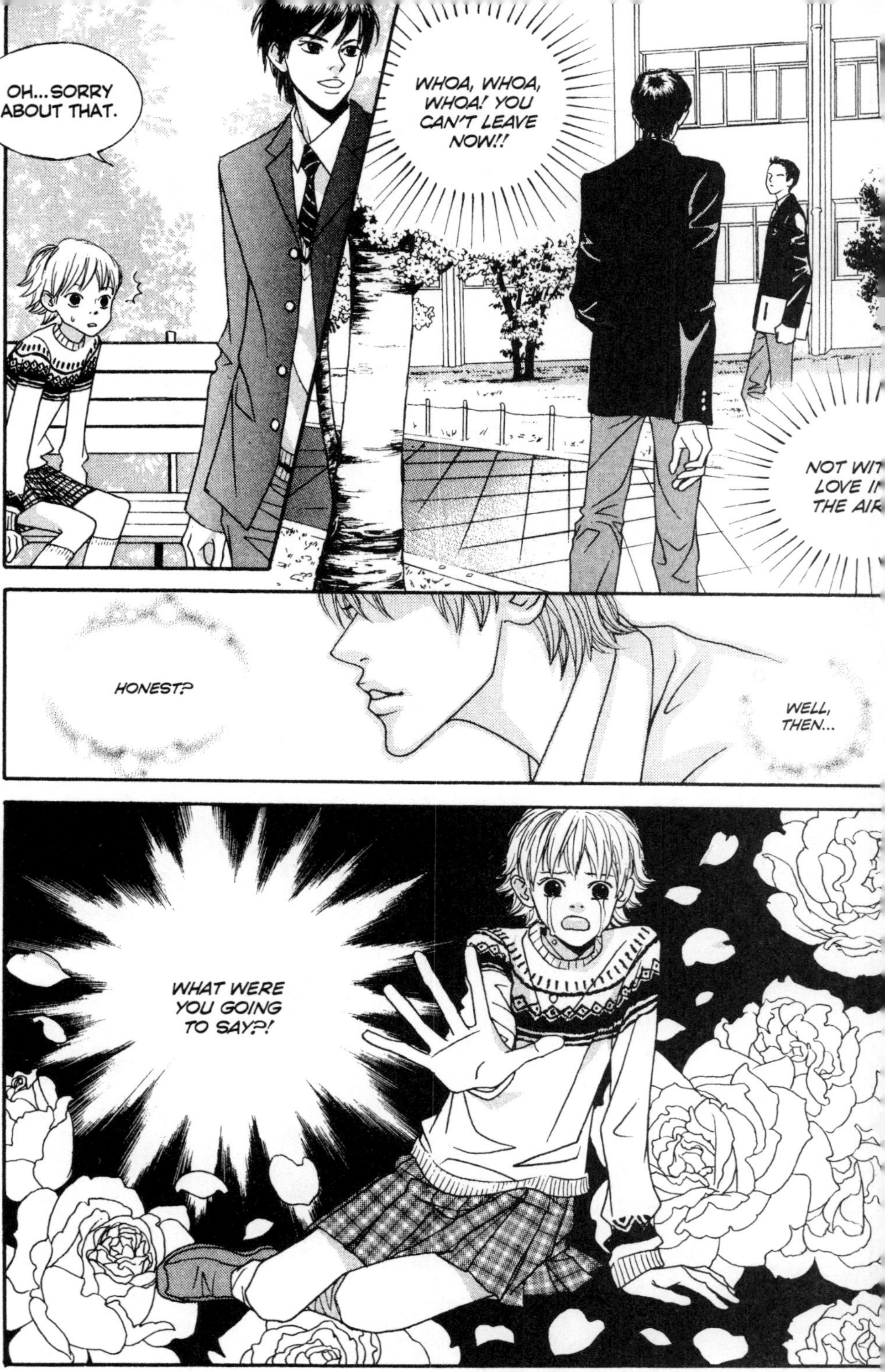
OH...SORRY ABOUT THAT.
WHOA, WHOA, WHOA! YOU CAN'T LEAVE NOW!!
NOT WIT LOVE II THE AIR
HONEST?
WELL, THEN...
WHAT WERE YOU GOING TO SAY?!

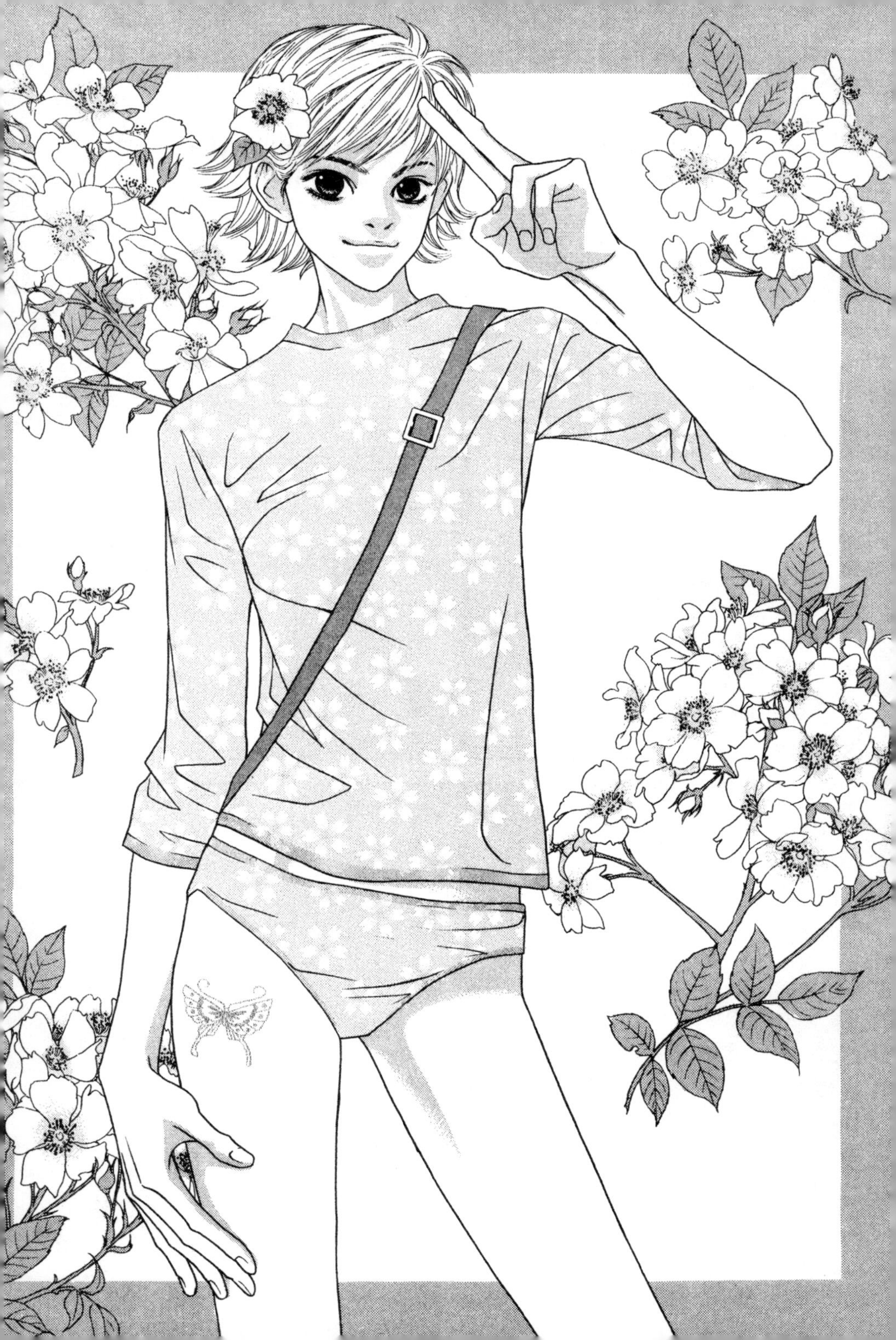

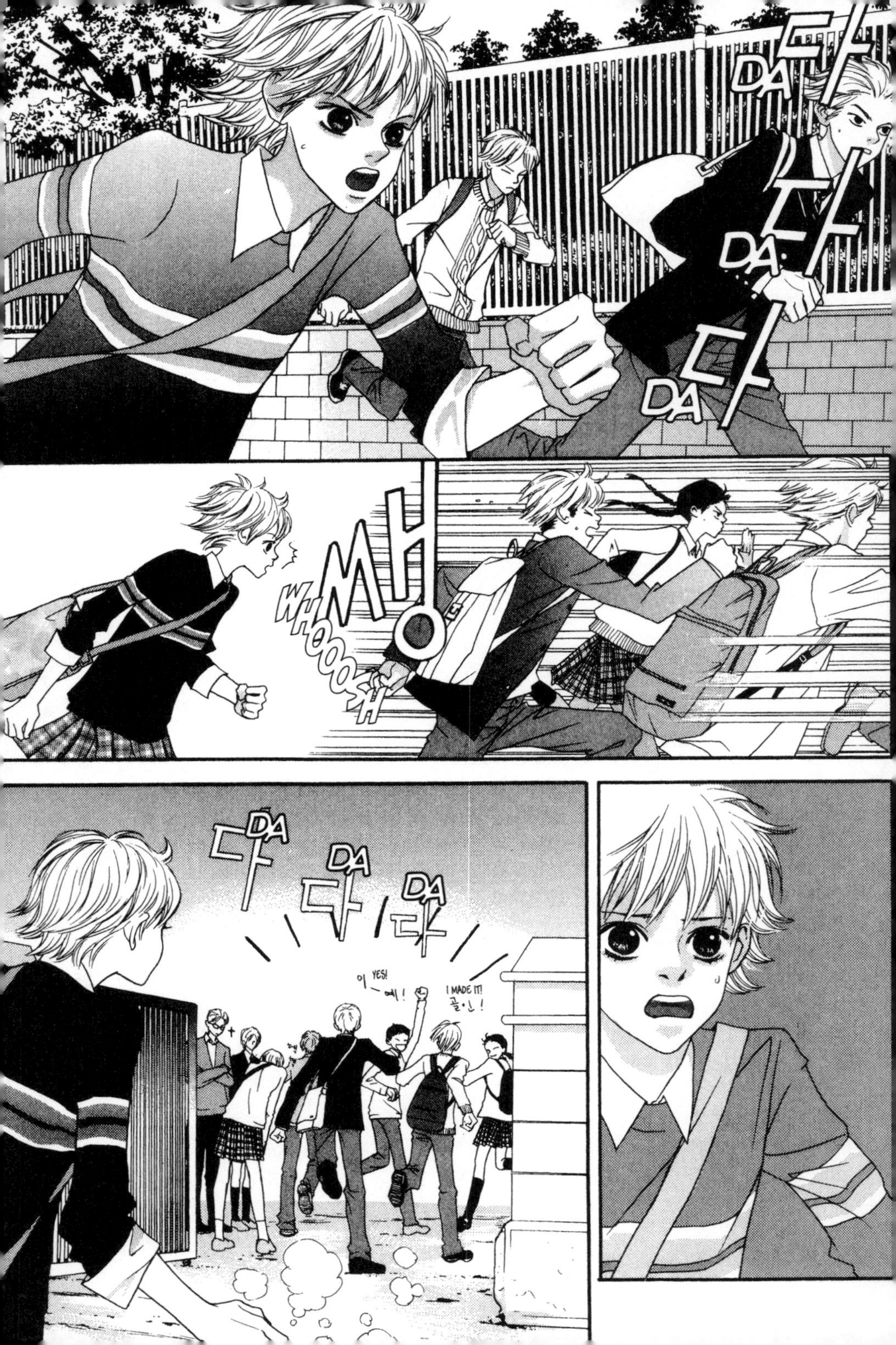

다 DA
다 DA
다 DA
WHOOOOSH
다 DA
다 DA
다 DA
YES!
이-예!
I MADE IT!
골인!

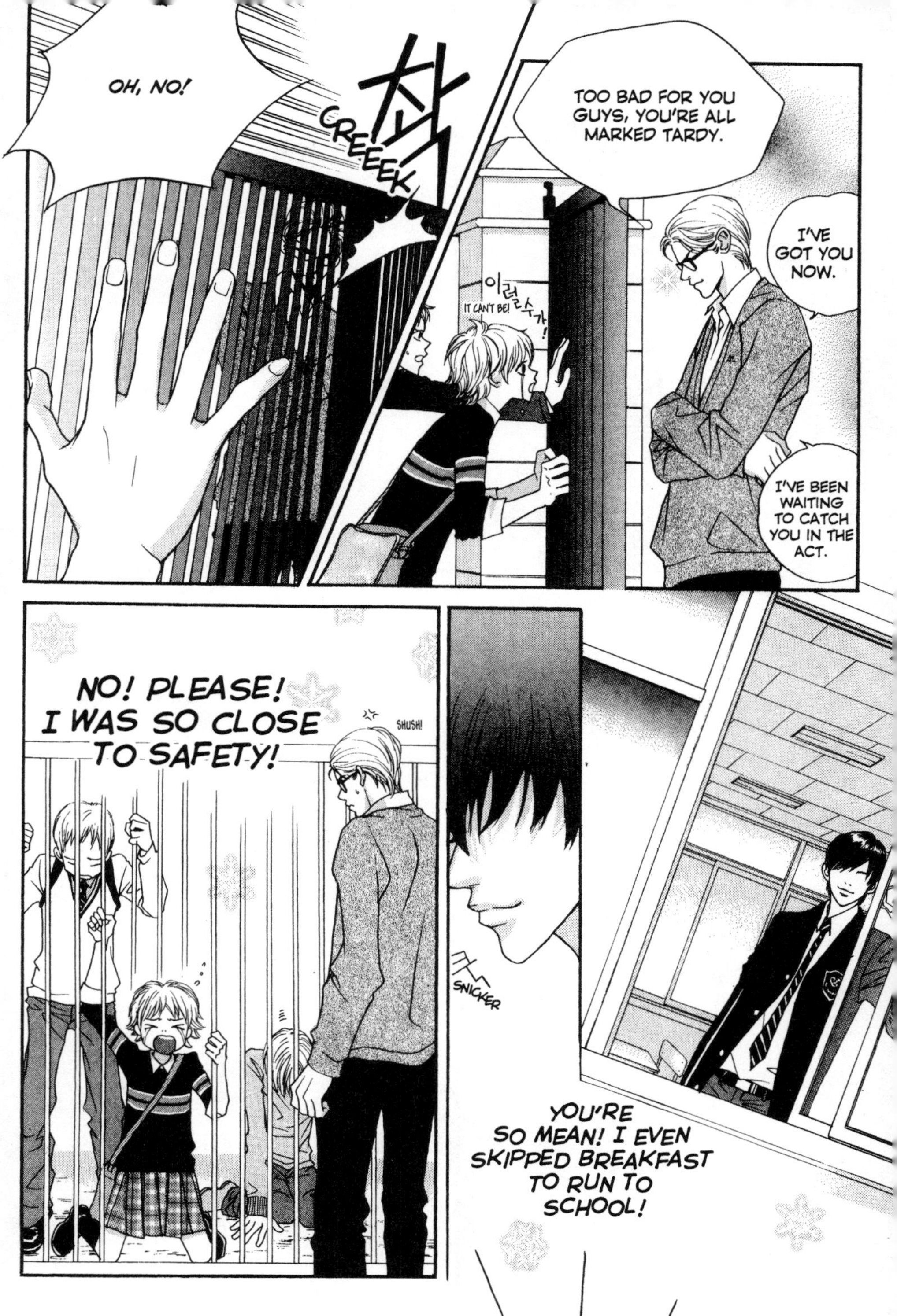
OH, NO!
착
CREEEEK
이럴수가!
IT CAN'T BE!
TOO BAD FOR YOU GUYS, YOU'RE ALL MARKED TARDY.
I'VE GOT YOU NOW.
I'VE BEEN WAITING TO CATCH YOU IN THE ACT.
NO! PLEASE! I WAS SO CLOSE TO SAFETY!
SHUSH!
SNICKER
YOU'RE SO MEAN! I EVEN SKIPPED BREAKFAST TO RUN TO SCHOOL!

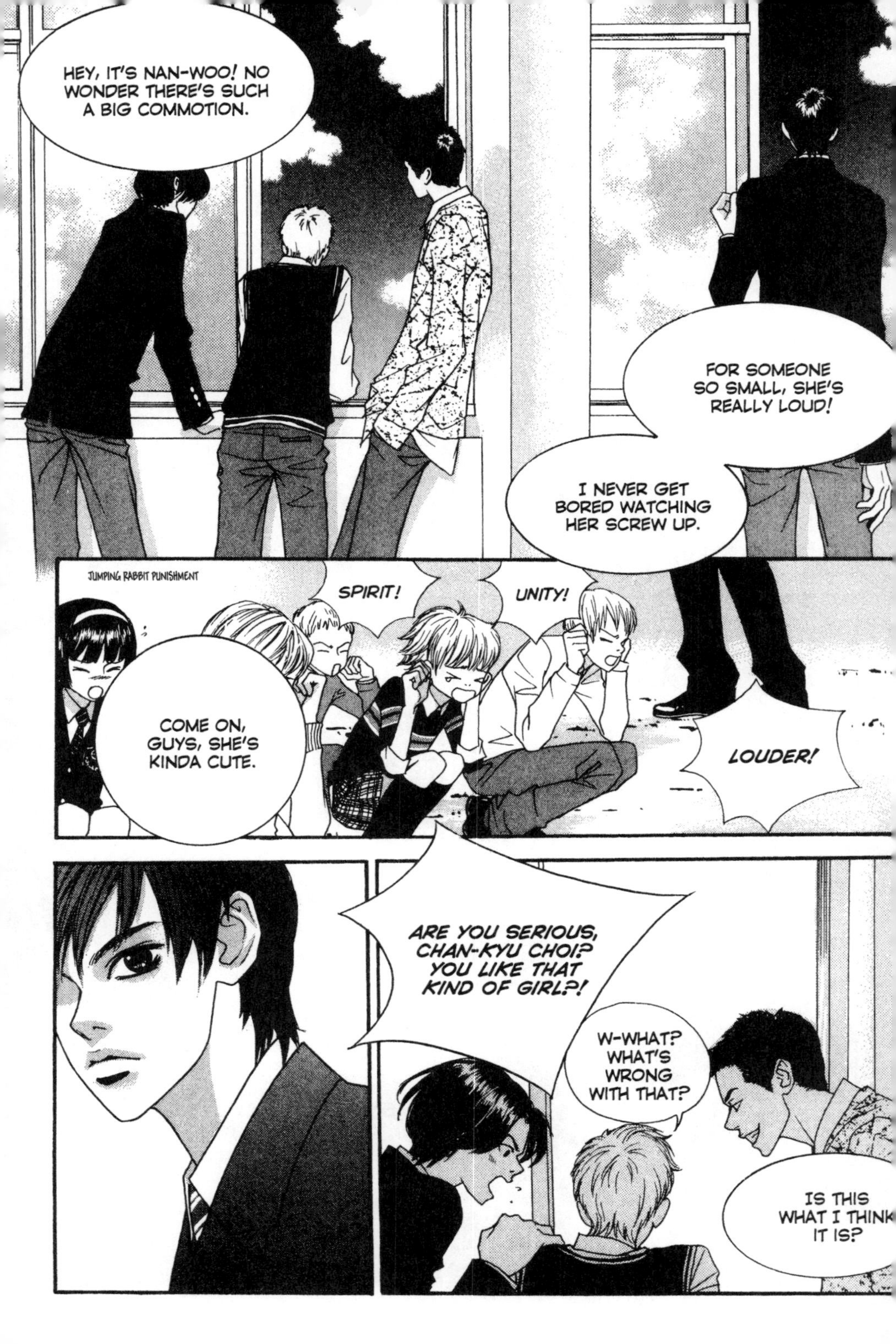
HEY, IT'S NAN-WOO! NO WONDER THERE'S SUCH A BIG COMMOTION.
FOR SOMEONE SO SMALL, SHE'S REALLY LOUD!
I NEVER GET BORED WATCHING HER SCREW UP.
JUMPING RABBIT PUNISHMENT
SPIRIT!
UNITY!
COME ON, GUYS, SHE'S KINDA CUTE.
LOUDER!
ARE YOU SERIOUS, CHAN-KYU CHOI? YOU LIKE THAT KIND OF GIRL?!
W-WHAT? WHAT'S WRONG WITH THAT?
IS THIS WHAT I THINK IT IS?

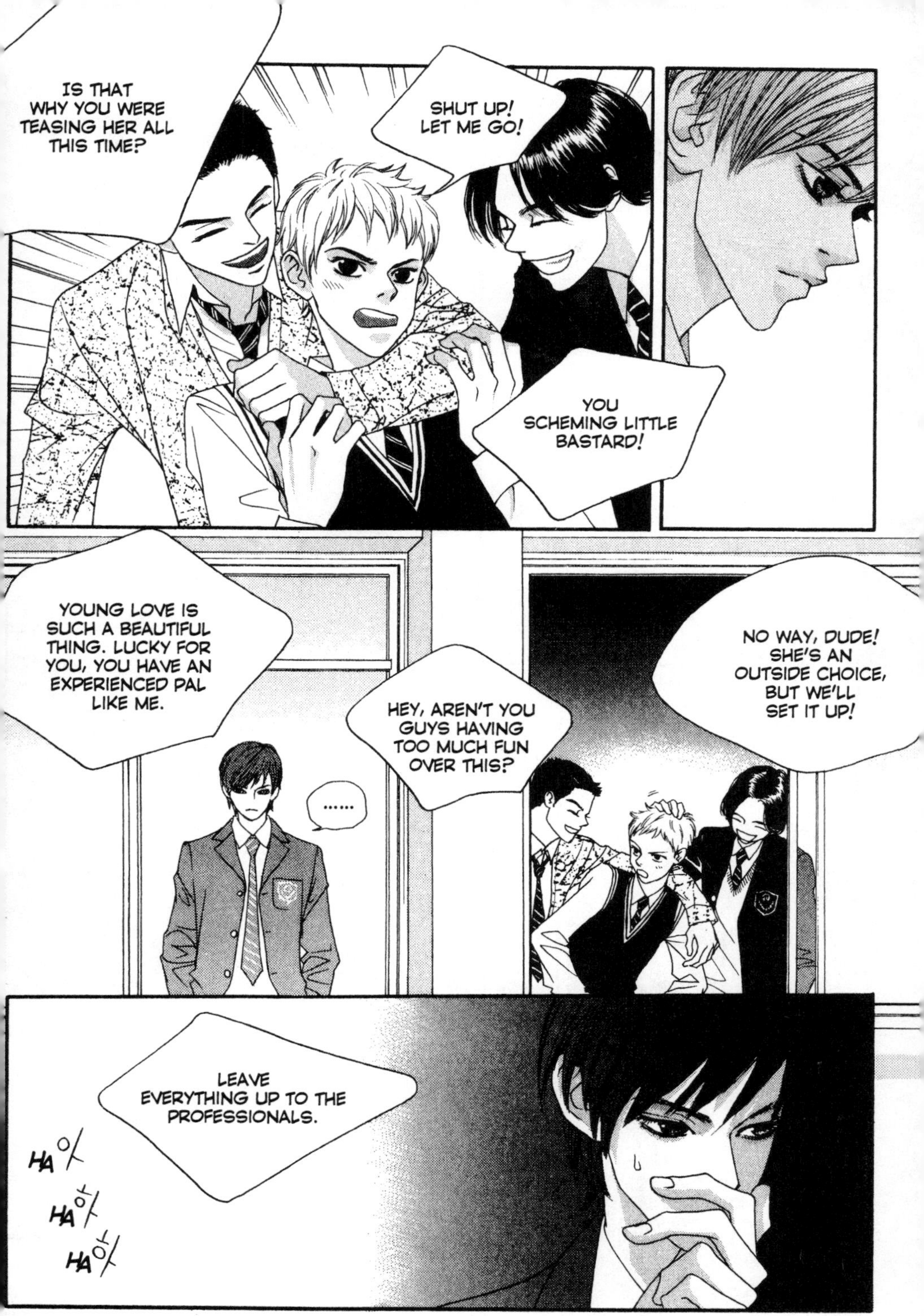
IS THAT WHY YOU WERE TEASING HER ALL THIS TIME?
SHUT UP! LET ME GO!
YOU SCHEMING LITTLE BASTARD!
YOUNG LOVE IS SUCH A BEAUTIFUL THING. LUCKY FOR YOU, YOU HAVE AN EXPERIENCED PAL LIKE ME.
......
HEY, AREN'T YOU GUYS HAVING TOO MUCH FUN OVER THIS?
NO WAY, DUDE! SHE'S AN OUTSIDE CHOICE, BUT WE'LL SET IT UP!
LEAVE EVERYTHING UP TO THE PROFESSIONALS.
HA
HA
HA

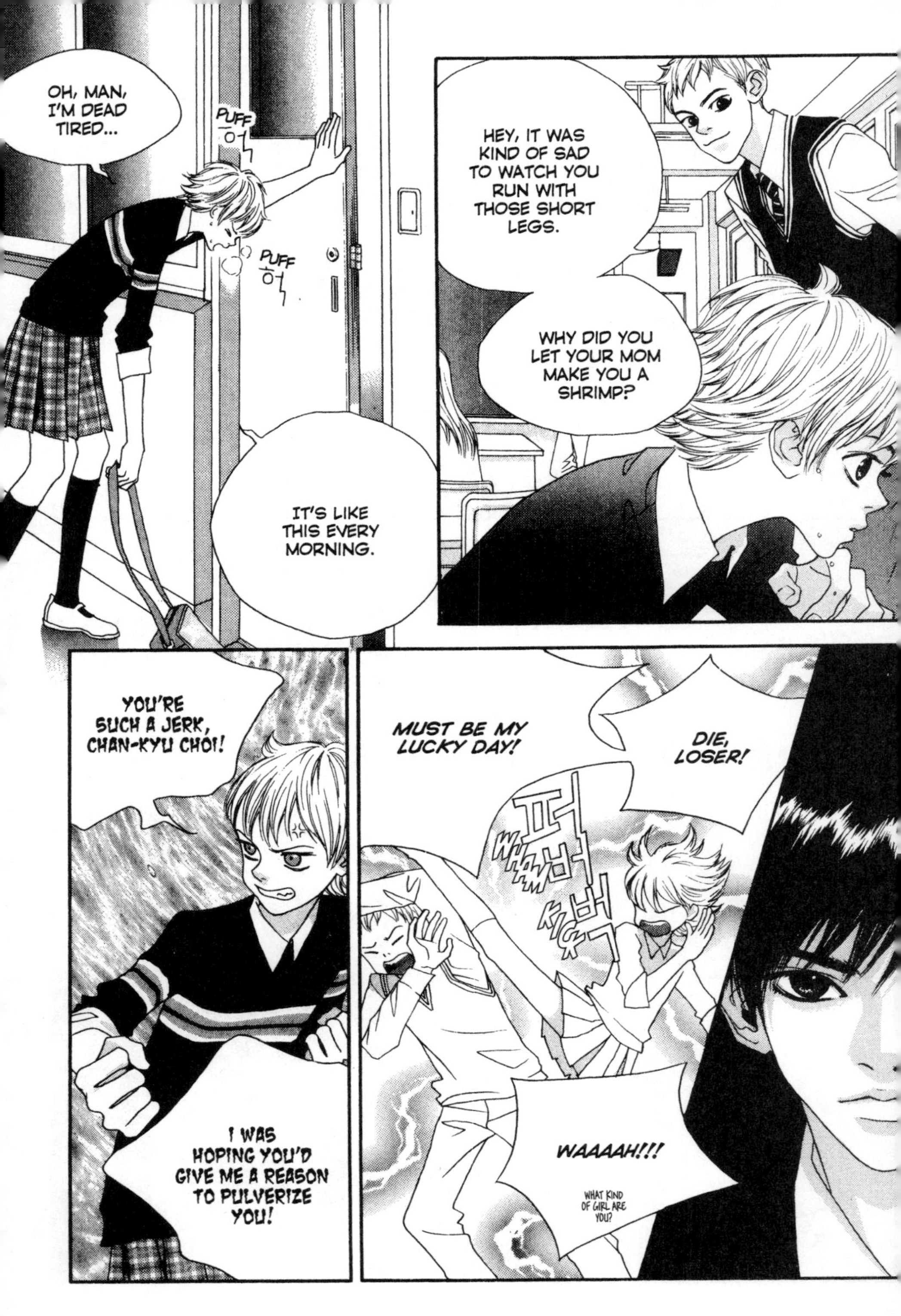
OH, MAN, I'M DEAD TIRED...
PUFF
PUFF
IT'S LIKE THIS EVERY MORNING.
HEY, IT WAS KIND OF SAD TO WATCH YOU RUN WITH THOSE SHORT LEGS.
WHY DID YOU LET YOUR MOM MAKE YOU A SHRIMP?
YOU'RE SUCH A JERK, CHAN-KYU CHOI!
I WAS HOPING YOU'D GIVE ME A REASON TO PULVERIZE YOU!
MUST BE MY LUCKY DAY!
DIE, LOSER!
WHAM
KICK
WAAAAH!!!
WHAT KIND OF GIRL ARE YOU?

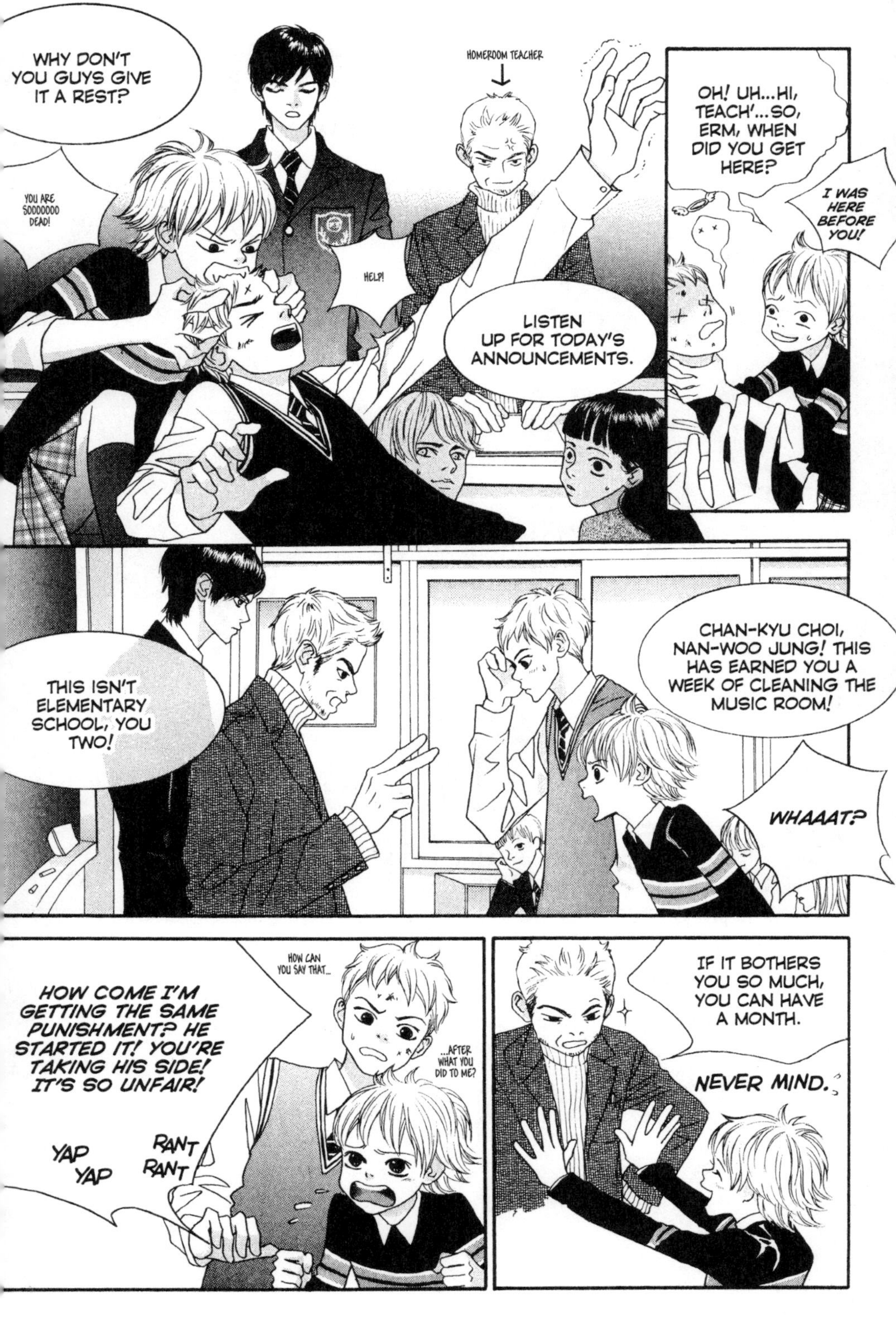
WHY DON'T YOU GUYS GIVE IT A REST?
YOU ARE SOOOOOOO DEAD!
HELP!
HOMEROOM TEACHER
LISTEN UP FOR TODAY'S ANNOUNCEMENTS.
OH! UH...HI, TEACH'...SO, ERM, WHEN DID YOU GET HERE?
I WAS HERE BEFORE YOU!
THIS ISN'T ELEMENTARY SCHOOL, YOU TWO!
CHAN-KYU CHOI, NAN-WOO JUNG! THIS HAS EARNED YOU A WEEK OF CLEANING THE MUSIC ROOM!
WHAAAT?
HOW COME I'M GETTING THE SAME PUNISHMENT? HE STARTED IT! YOU'RE TAKING HIS SIDE! IT'S SO UNFAIR!
YAP YAP
RANT RANT
HOW CAN YOU SAY THAT...
...AFTER WHAT YOU DID TO ME?
IF IT BOTHERS YOU SO MUCH, YOU CAN HAVE A MONTH.
NEVER MIND.

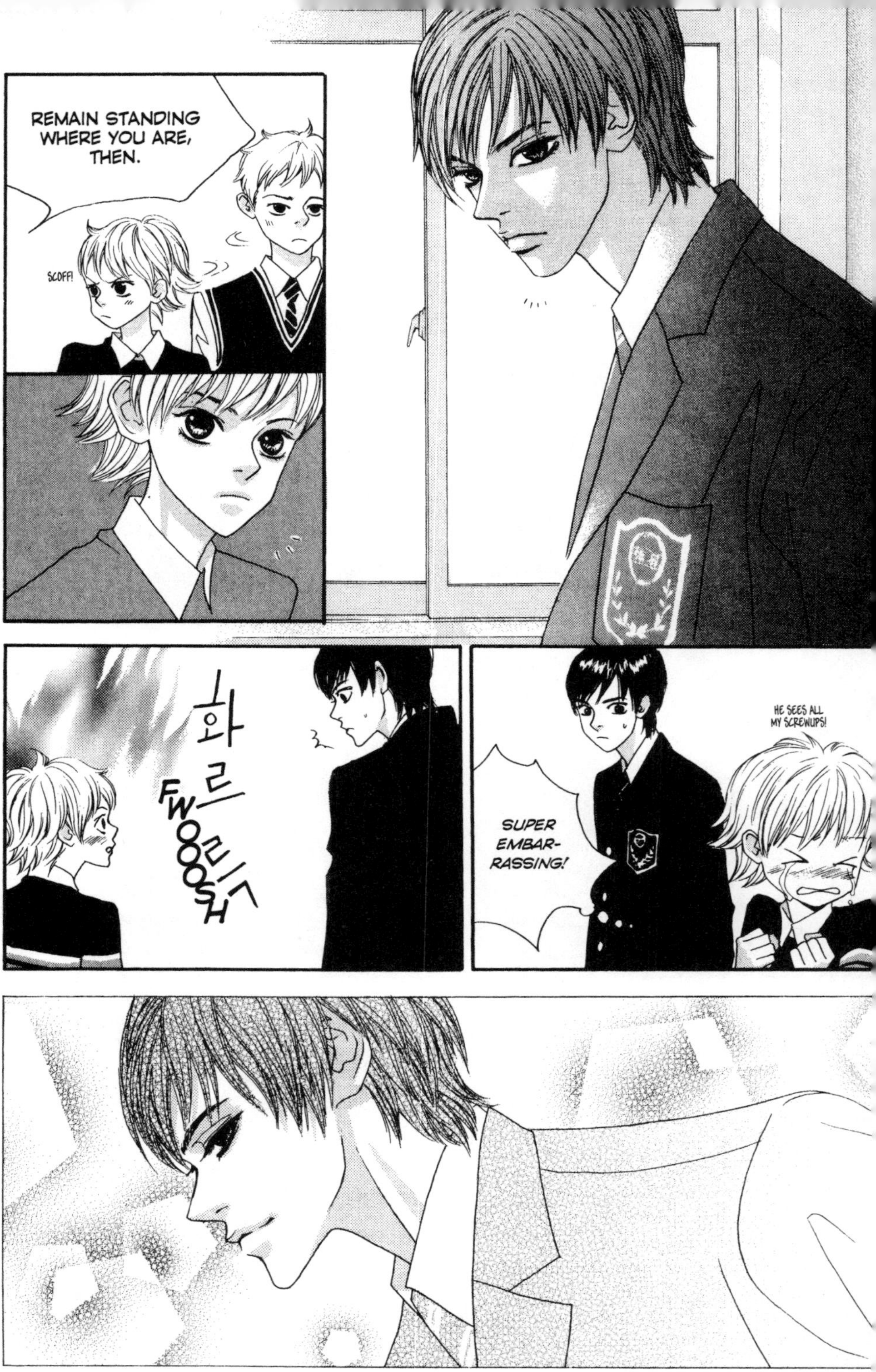
REMAIN STANDING WHERE YOU ARE, THEN.
SCOFF!
화르릇
FWOOOSH
SUPER EMBARRASSING!
HE SEES ALL MY SCREWUPS!

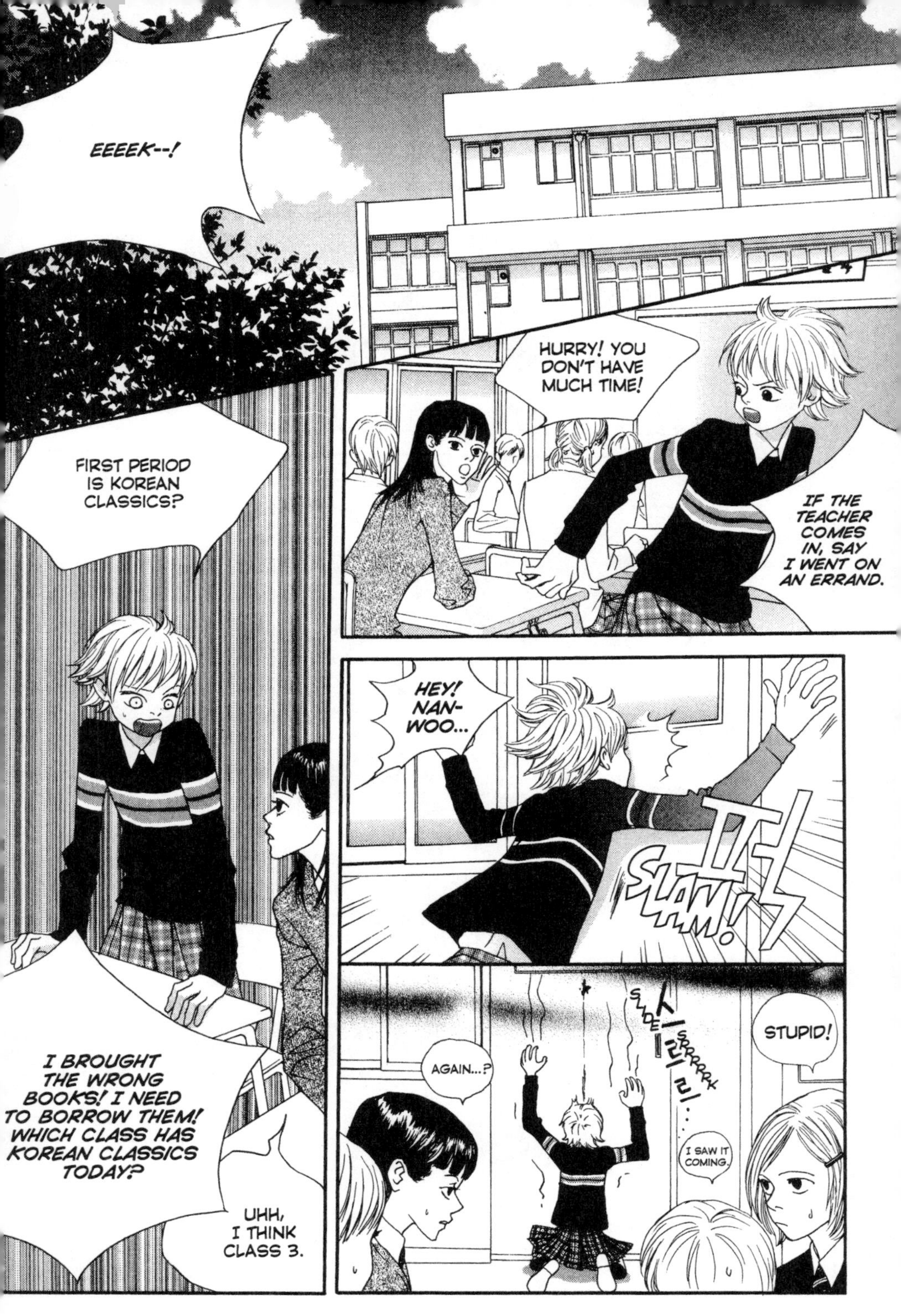
EEEEK--!
FIRST PERIOD IS KOREAN CLASSICS?
I BROUGHT THE WRONG BOOKS! I NEED TO BORROW THEM! WHICH CLASS HAS KOREAN CLASSICS TODAY?
UHH, I THINK CLASS 3.
HURRY! YOU DON'T HAVE MUCH TIME!
IF THE TEACHER COMES IN, SAY I WENT ON AN ERRAND.
HEY! NAN-WOO...
SLAM!
SLIDE
SRRRRRK
AGAIN...?
STUPID!
I SAW IT COMING.

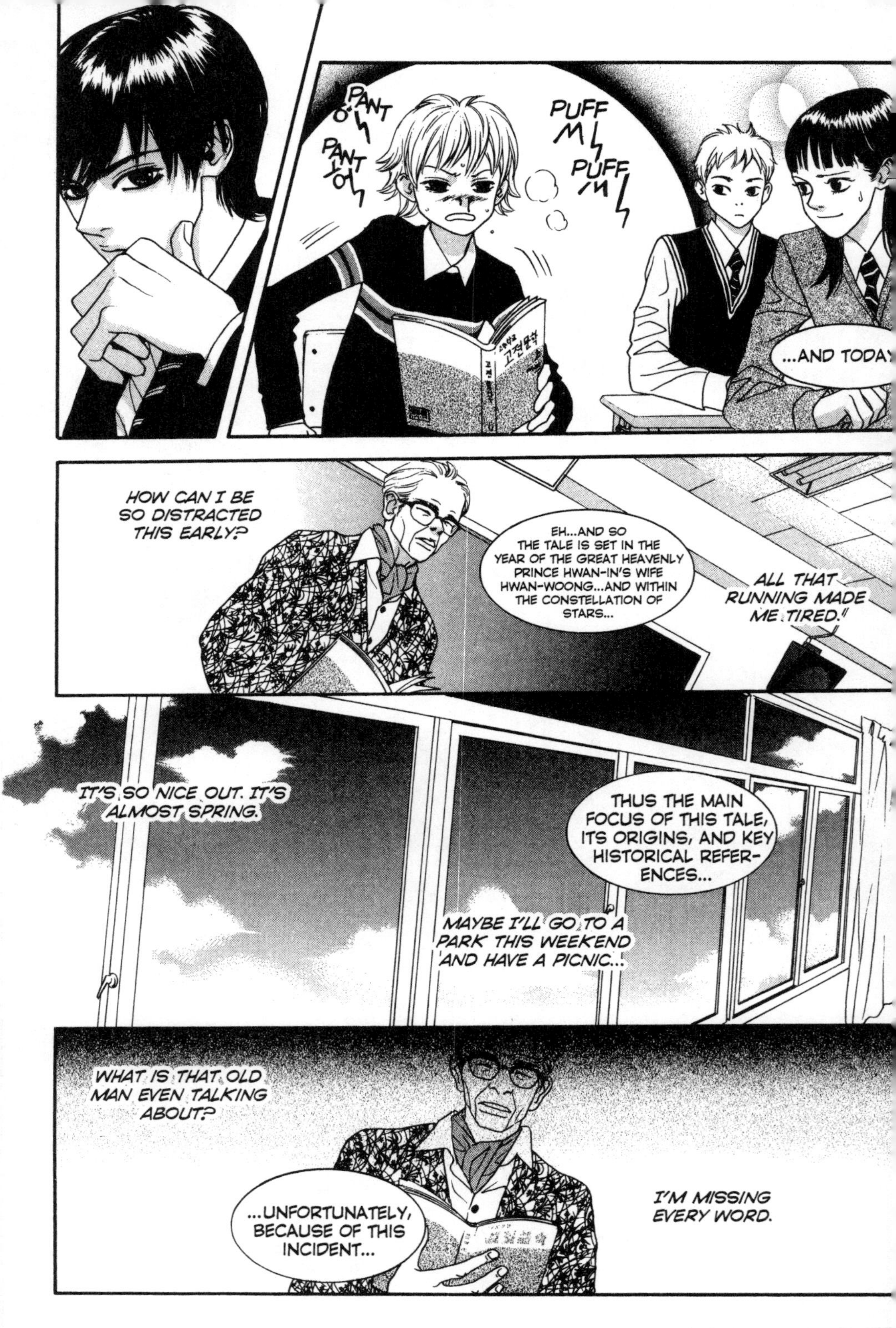

PANT
PANT
PUFF
PUFF
...AND TODAY
HOW CAN I BE SO DISTRACTED THIS EARLY?
EH...AND SO THE TALE IS SET IN THE YEAR OF THE GREAT HEAVENLY PRINCE HWAN-IN'S WIFE HWAN-WOONG...AND WITHIN THE CONSTELLATION OF STARS...
ALL THAT RUNNING MADE ME TIRED.
IT'S SO NICE OUT. IT'S ALMOST SPRING.
THUS THE MAIN FOCUS OF THIS TALE, ITS ORIGINS, AND KEY HISTORICAL REFERENCES...
MAYBE I'LL GO TO A PARK THIS WEEKEND AND HAVE A PICNIC...
WHAT IS THAT OLD MAN EVEN TALKING ABOUT?
...UNFORTUNATELY, BECAUSE OF THIS INCIDENT...
I'M MISSING EVERY WORD.

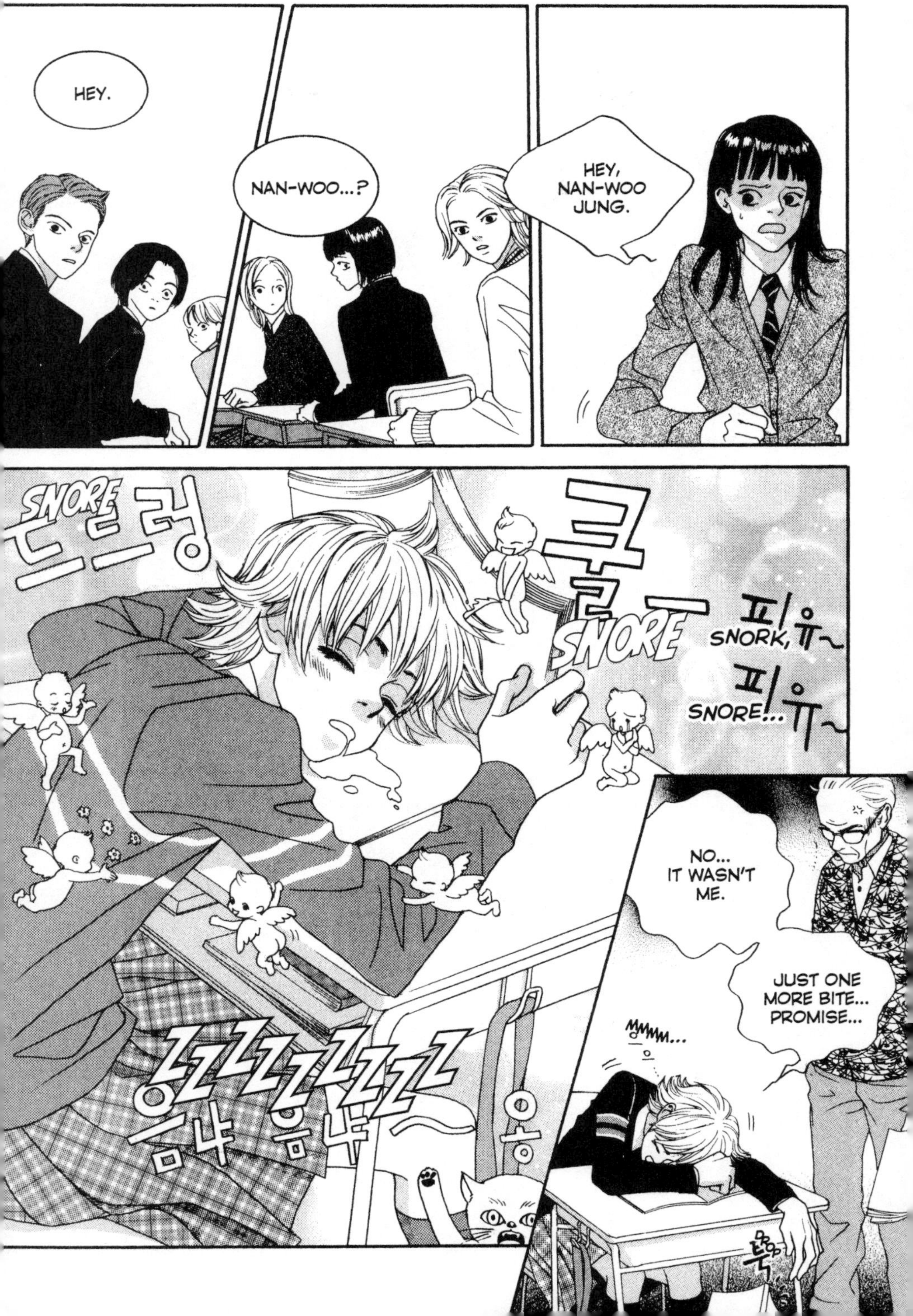
HEY.
NAN-WOO...?
HEY, NAN-WOO JUNG.
SNORE
SNORE
SNORK,
SNORE!...
NO... IT WASN'T ME.
JUST ONE MORE BITE... PROMISE...
MMMM...
DROP

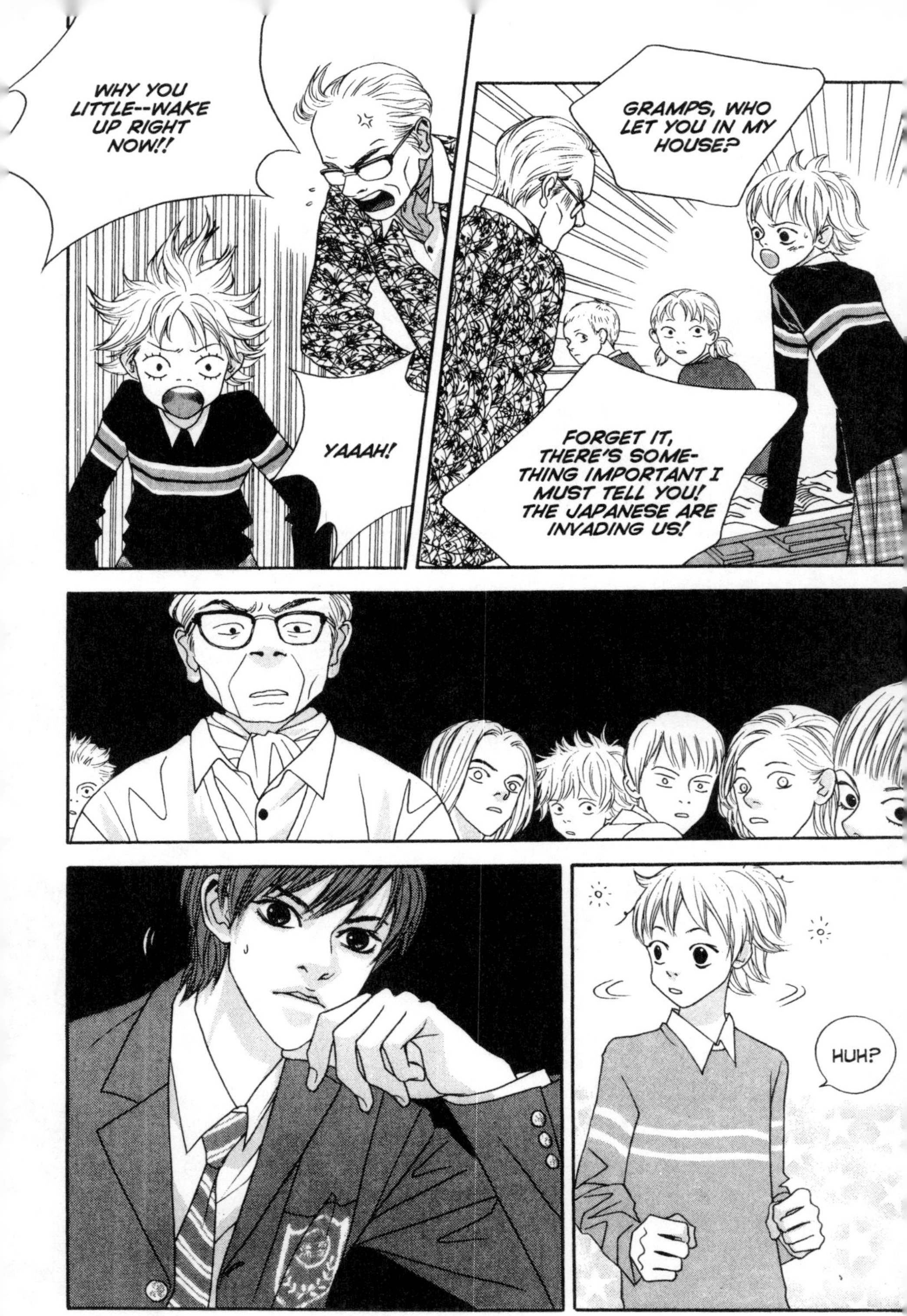
WHY YOU LITTLE--WAKE UP RIGHT NOW!!
YAAAH!
GRAMPS, WHO LET YOU IN MY HOUSE?
FORGET IT, THERE'S SOME-THING IMPORTANT I MUST TELL YOU! THE JAPANESE ARE INVADING US!
HUH?

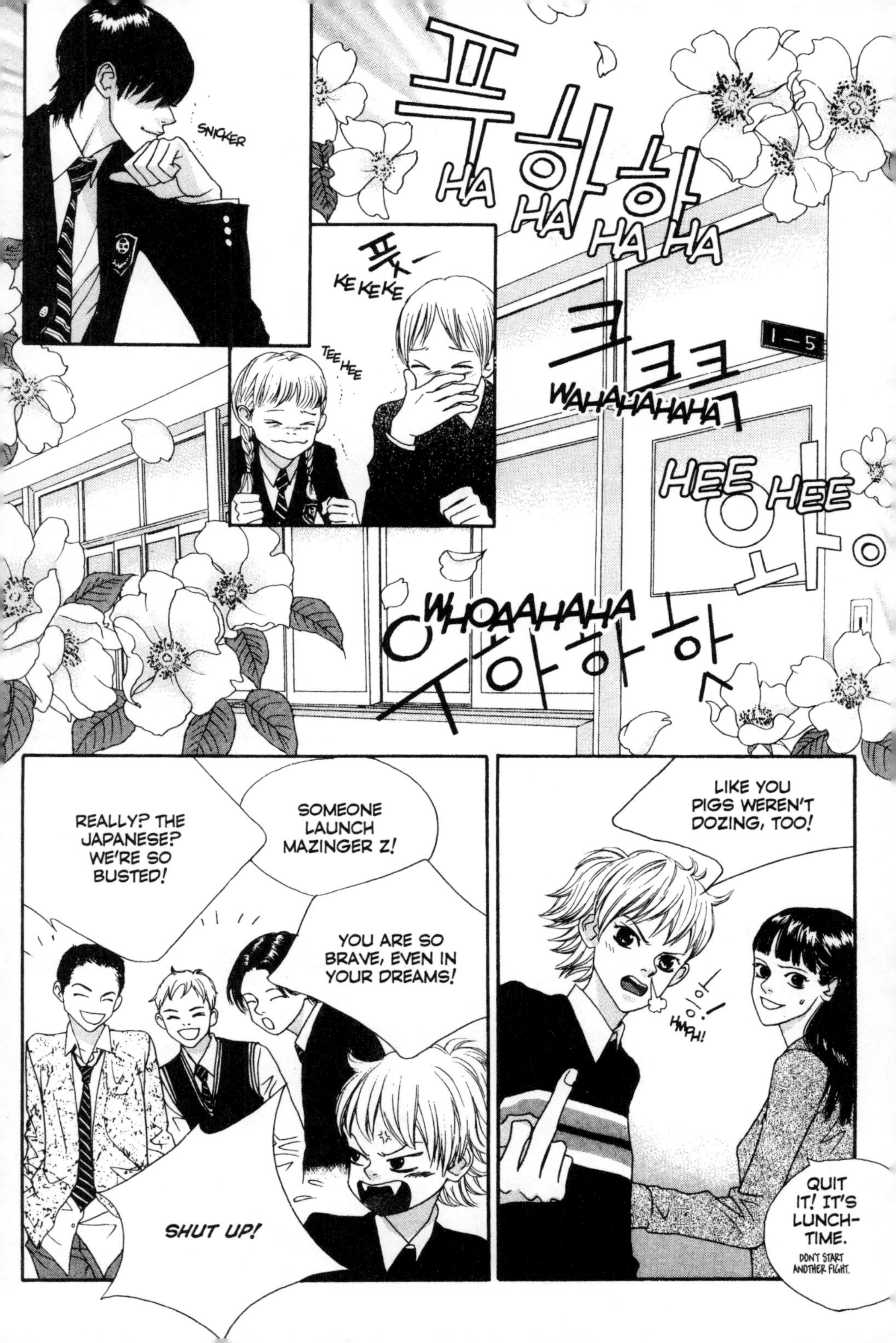
SNICKER
푸하핫
HA HA HA HA
픽—
KE KE KE
TEE HEE
1-5
크크크
WAHAHAHAHA
HEE HEE
WHOAAHAHA
REALLY? THE JAPANESE? WE'RE SO BUSTED!
SOMEONE LAUNCH MAZINGER Z!
YOU ARE SO BRAVE, EVEN IN YOUR DREAMS!
SHUT UP!
LIKE YOU PIGS WEREN'T DOZING, TOO!
HMPH!
QUIT IT! IT'S LUNCH-TIME.
DON'T START ANOTHER FIGHT.

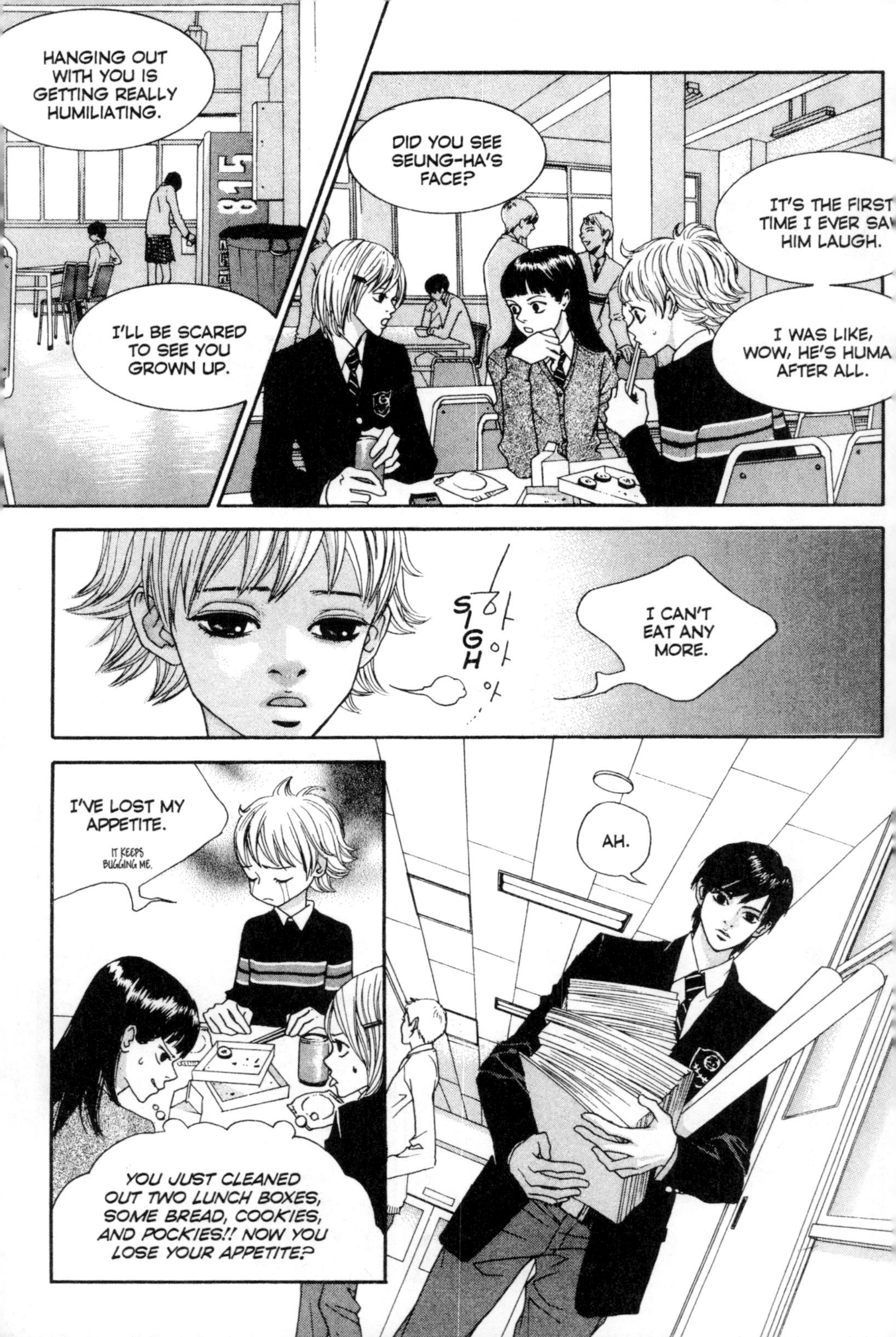
HANGING OUT WITH YOU IS GETTING REALLY HUMILIATING.
I'LL BE SCARED TO SEE YOU GROWN UP.
DID YOU SEE SEUNG-HA'S FACE?
IT'S THE FIRST TIME I EVER SA HIM LAUGH.
I WAS LIKE, WOW, HE'S HUMA AFTER ALL.
SIGH
하아아
I CAN'T EAT ANY MORE.
I'VE LOST MY APPETITE.
IT KEEPS BUGGING ME.
YOU JUST CLEANED OUT TWO LUNCH BOXES, SOME BREAD, COOKIES, AND POCKIES!! NOW YOU LOSE YOUR APPETITE?
AH.

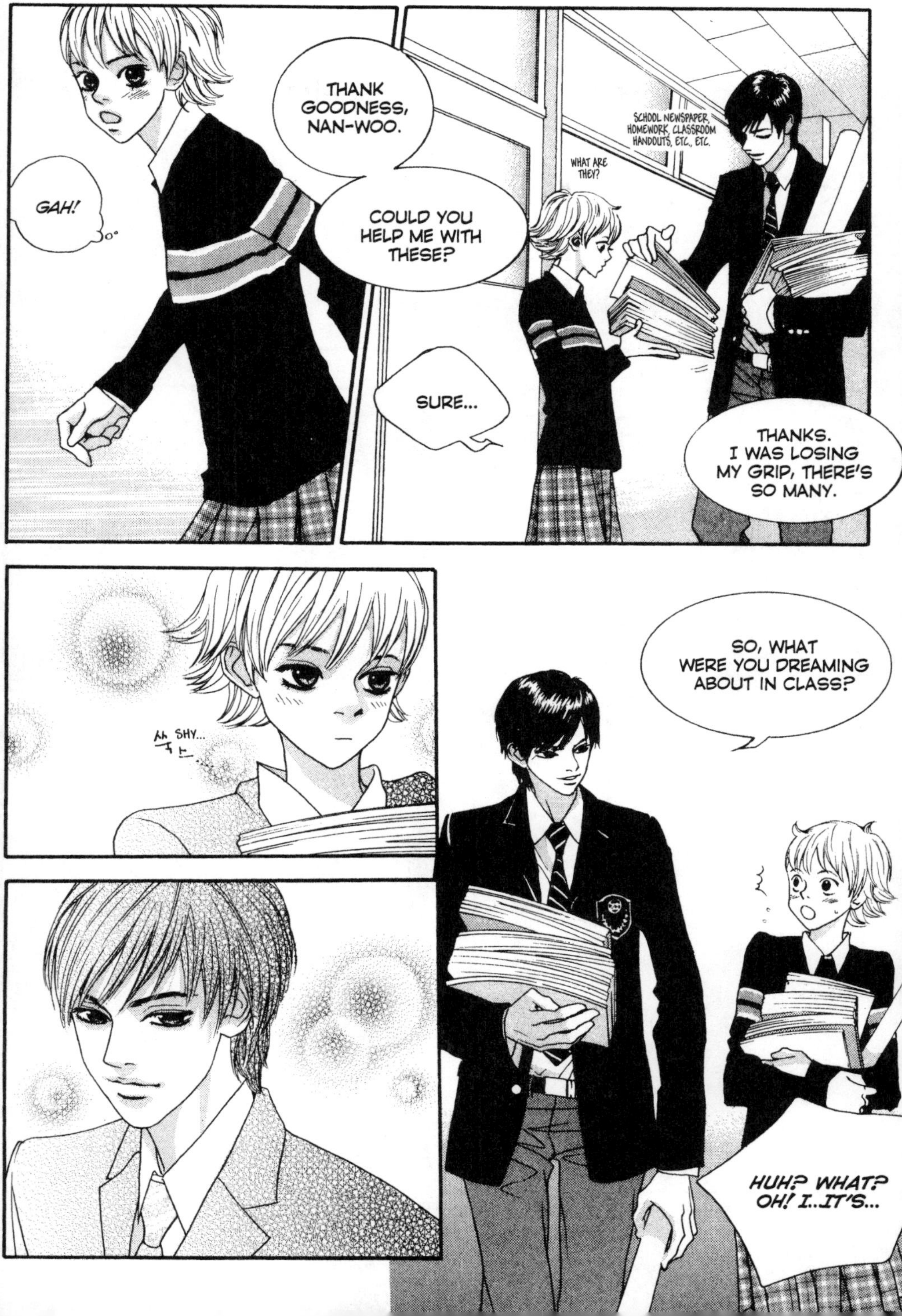
GAH!
THANK GOODNESS, NAN-WOO.
COULD YOU HELP ME WITH THESE?
WHAT ARE THEY?
SCHOOL NEWSPAPER, HOMEWORK, CLASSROOM HANDOUTS, ETC., ETC.
SURE...
THANKS. I WAS LOSING MY GRIP, THERE'S SO MANY.
SHY...
SO, WHAT WERE YOU DREAMING ABOUT IN CLASS?
HUH? WHAT? OH! I..IT'S...

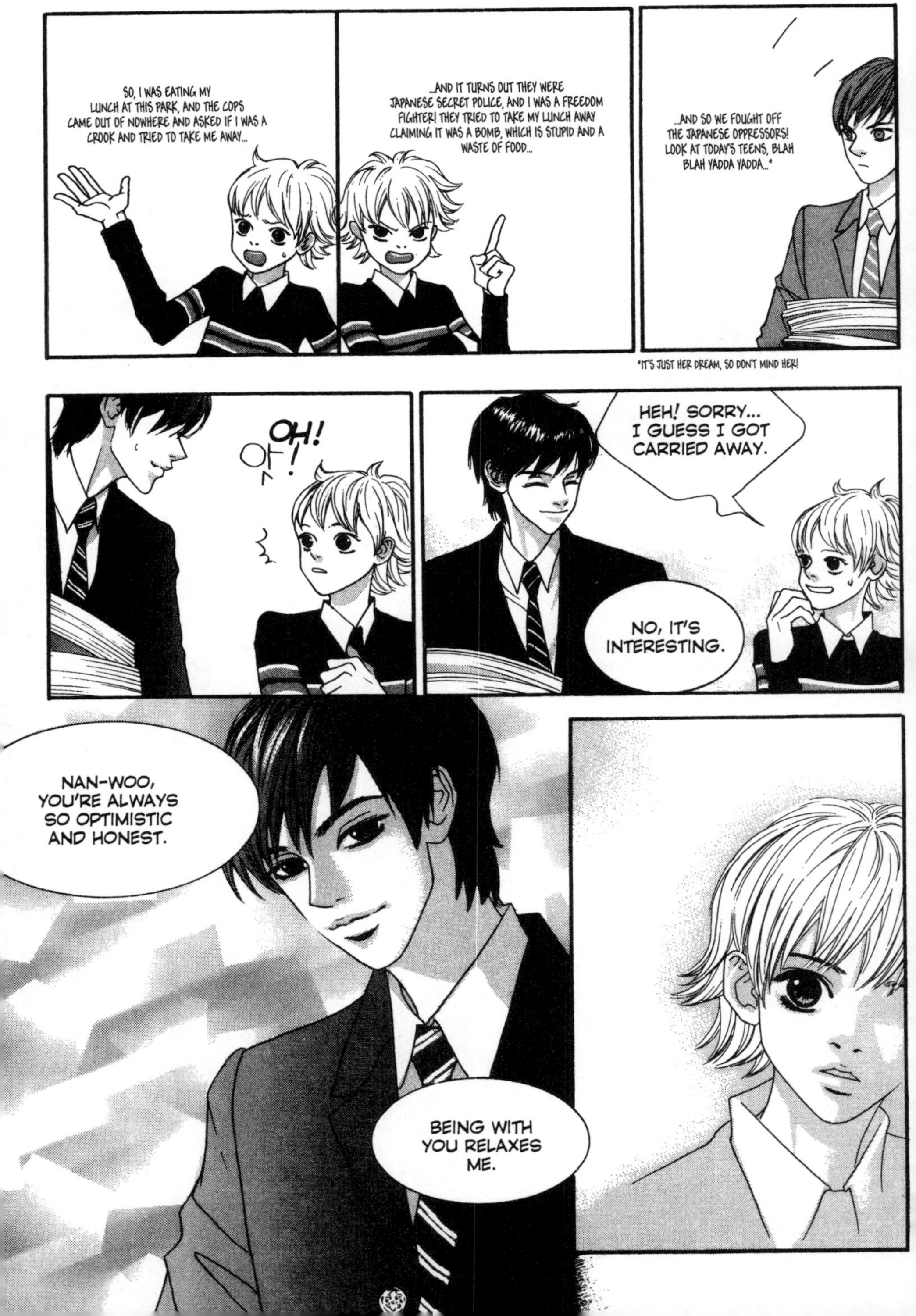
SO, I WAS EATING MY LUNCH AT THIS PARK, AND THE COPS CAME OUT OF NOWHERE AND ASKED IF I WAS A CROOK AND TRIED TO TAKE ME AWAY...
...AND IT TURNS OUT THEY WERE JAPANESE SECRET POLICE, AND I WAS A FREEDOM FIGHTER! THEY TRIED TO TAKE MY LUNCH AWAY CLAIMING IT WAS A BOMB, WHICH IS STUPID AND A WASTE OF FOOD...
...AND SO WE FOUGHT OFF THE JAPANESE OPPRESSORS! LOOK AT TODAY'S TEENS, BLAH BLAH YADDA YADDA...*
*IT'S JUST HER DREAM, SO DON'T MIND HER!
OH!
앗!
HEH! SORRY... I GUESS I GOT CARRIED AWAY.
NO, IT'S INTERESTING.
NAN-WOO, YOU'RE ALWAYS SO OPTIMISTIC AND HONEST.
BEING WITH YOU RELAXES ME.

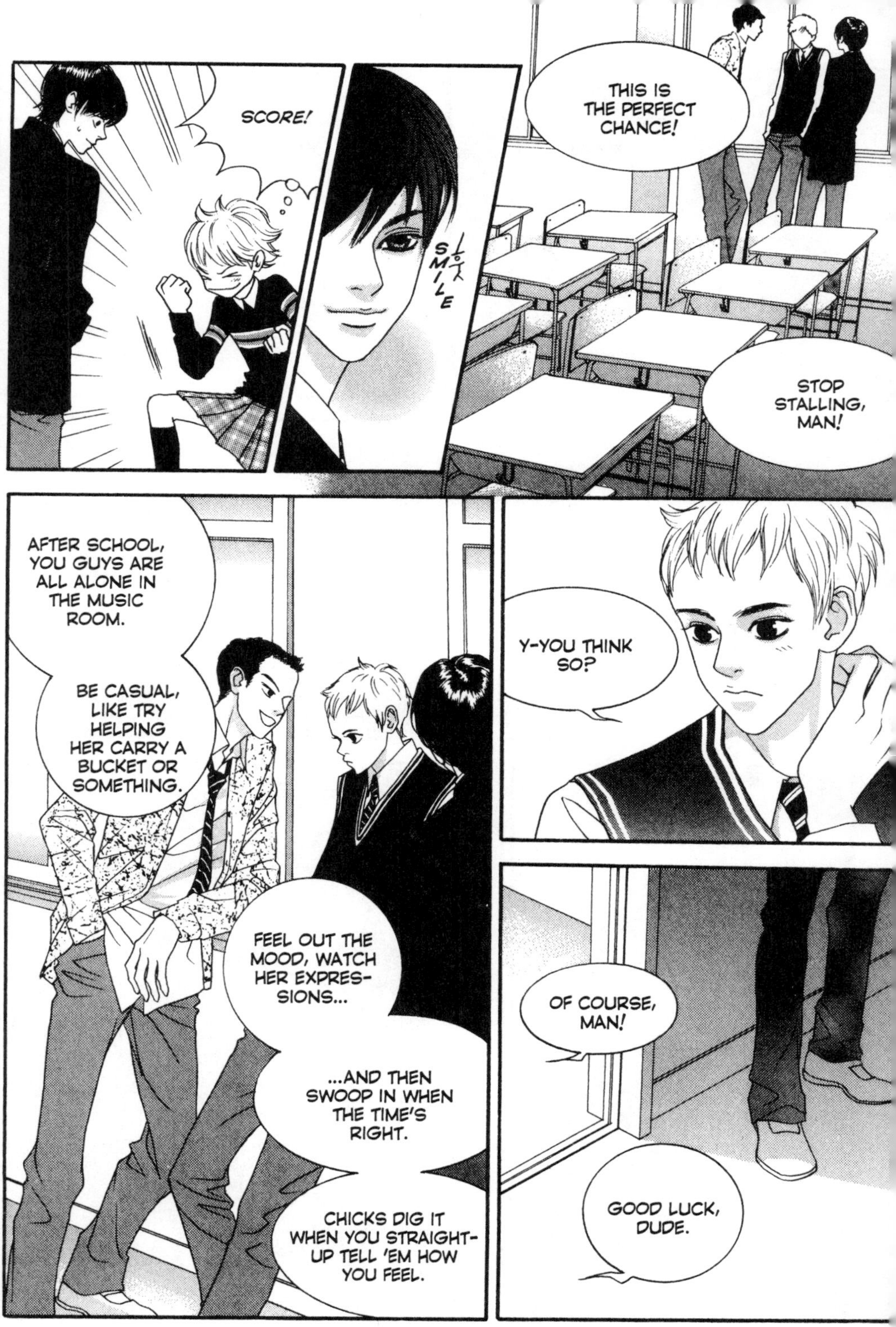
SCORE!
SMILE
THIS IS THE PERFECT CHANCE!
STOP STALLING, MAN!
AFTER SCHOOL, YOU GUYS ARE ALL ALONE IN THE MUSIC ROOM.
BE CASUAL, LIKE TRY HELPING HER CARRY A BUCKET OR SOMETHING.
FEEL OUT THE MOOD, WATCH HER EXPRES-SIONS...
...AND THEN SWOOP IN WHEN THE TIME'S RIGHT.
CHICKS DIG IT WHEN YOU STRAIGHT-UP TELL 'EM HOW YOU FEEL.
Y-YOU THINK SO?
OF COURSE, MAN!
GOOD LUCK, DUDE.

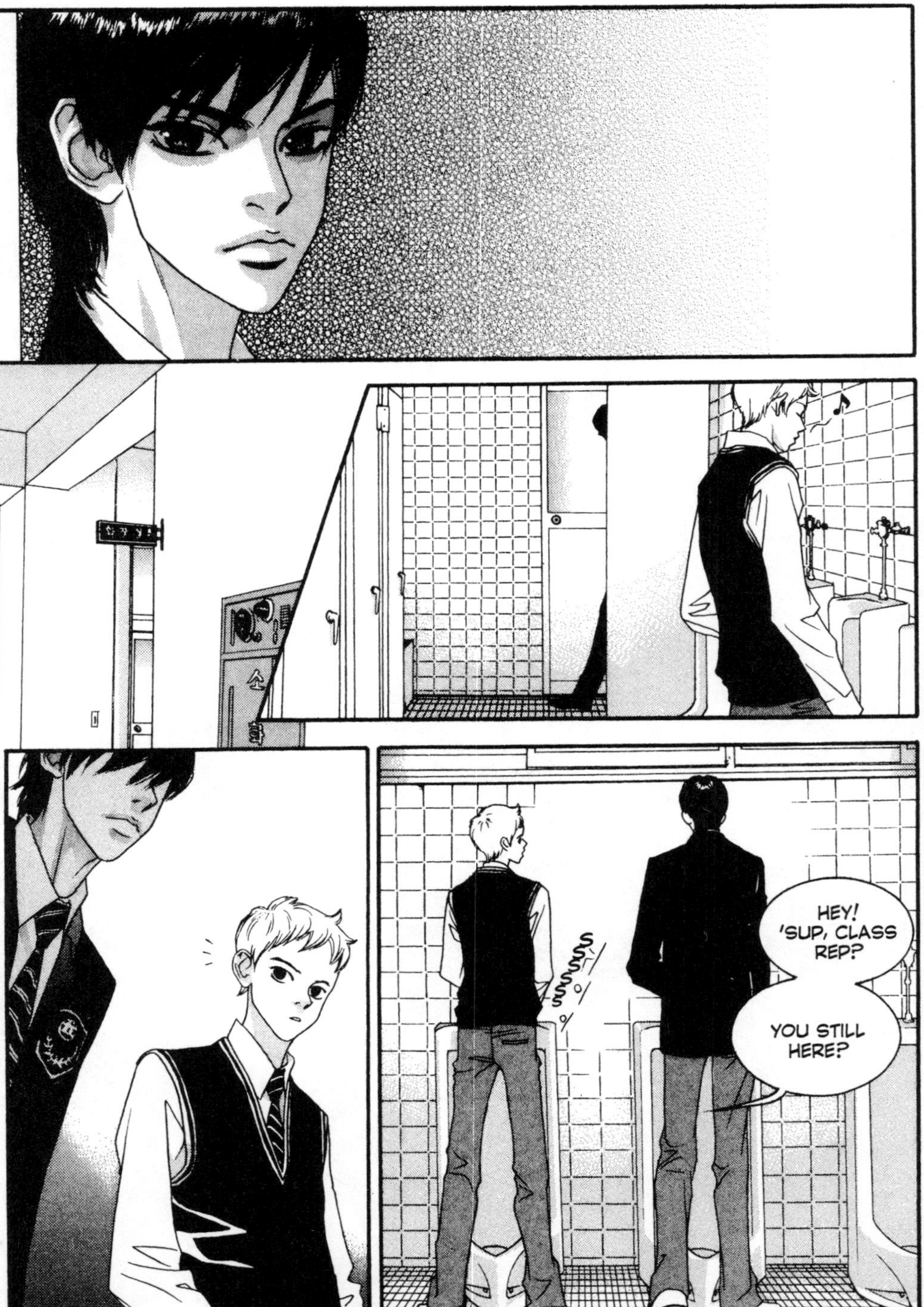
HEY! 'SUP, CLASS REP?
YOU STILL HERE?

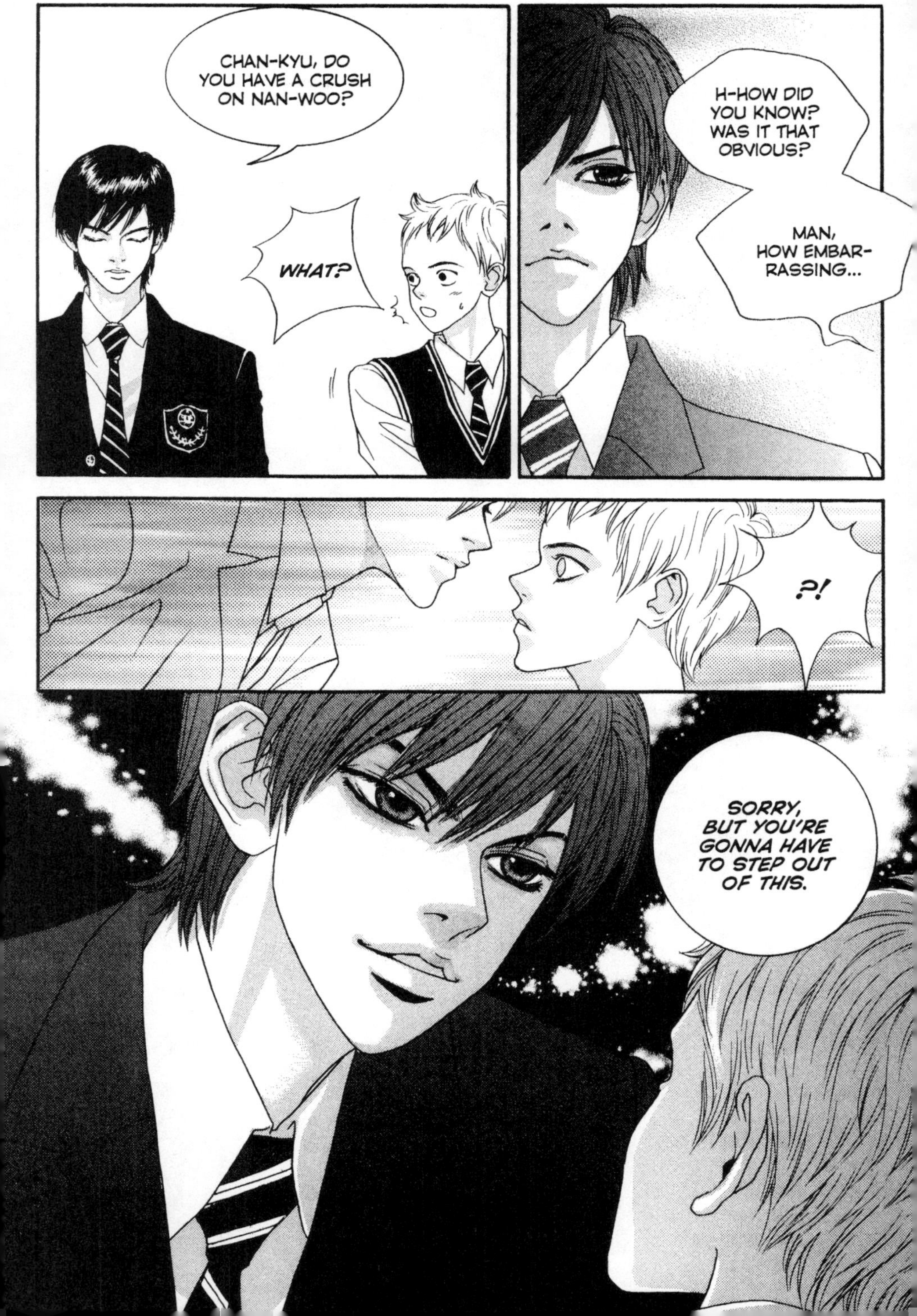
CHAN-KYU, DO YOU HAVE A CRUSH ON NAN-WOO?
WHAT?
H-HOW DID YOU KNOW? WAS IT THAT OBVIOUS?
MAN, HOW EMBAR-RASSING...
?!
SORRY, BUT YOU'RE GONNA HAVE TO STEP OUT OF THIS.

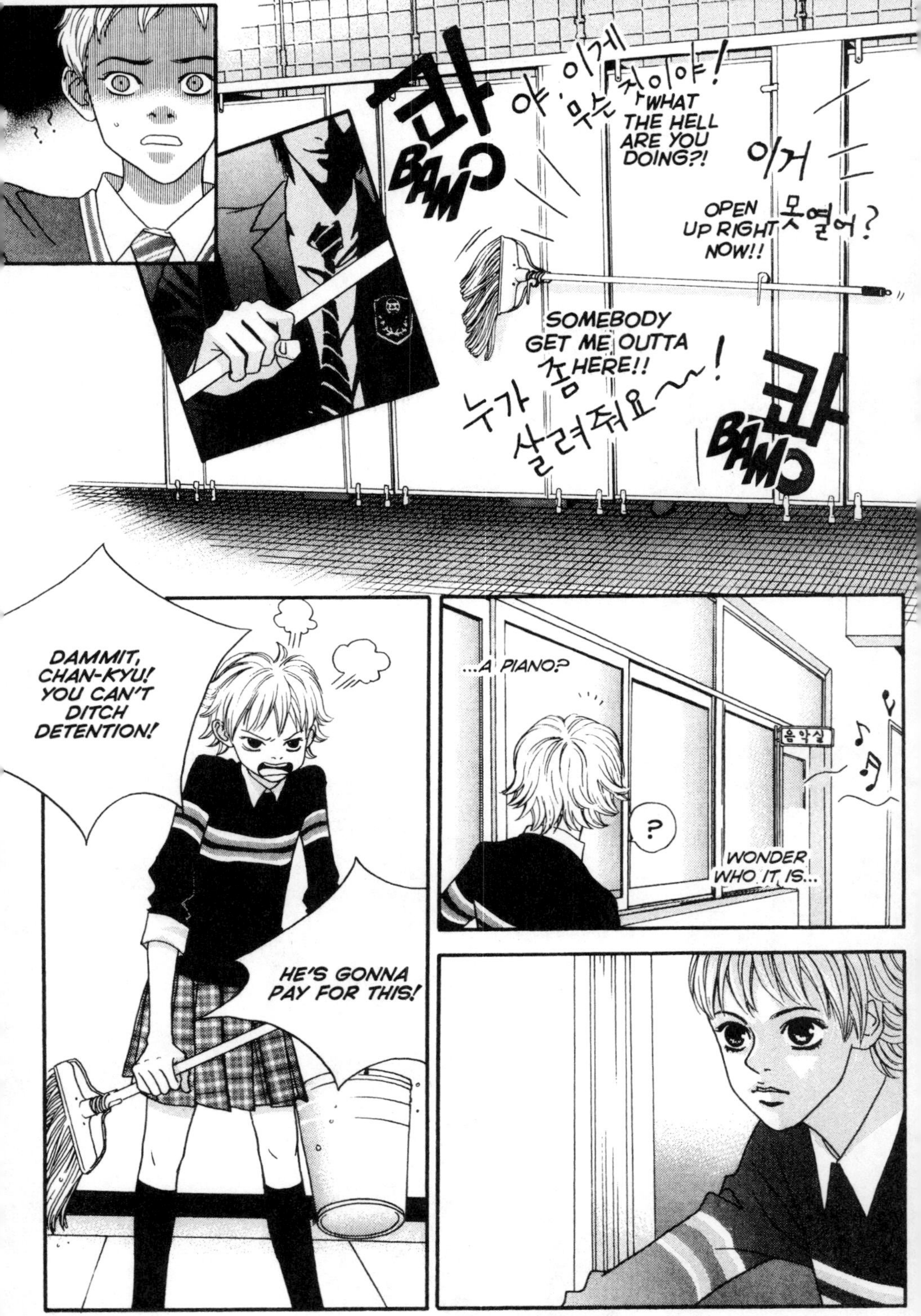
BAM
야, 이게 무슨 짓이야!
WHAT THE HELL ARE YOU DOING?!
이거 못열어?
OPEN UP RIGHT NOW!!
SOMEBODY GET ME OUTTA HERE!!
누가 좀 살려줘요~~!
BAM
DAMMIT, CHAN-KYU! YOU CAN'T DITCH DETENTION!
HE'S GONNA PAY FOR THIS!
...A PIANO?
?
음악실
WONDER WHO IT IS...

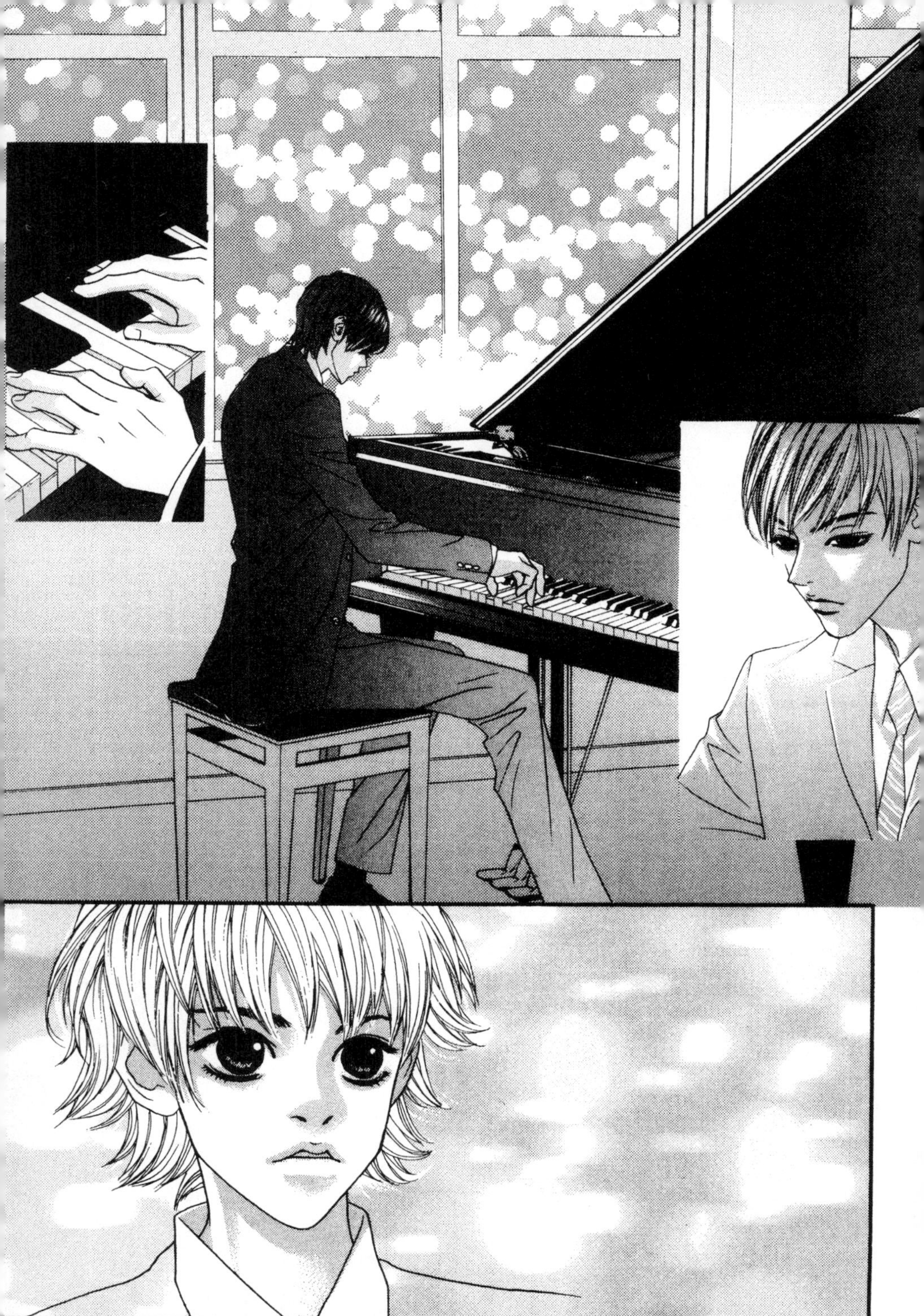

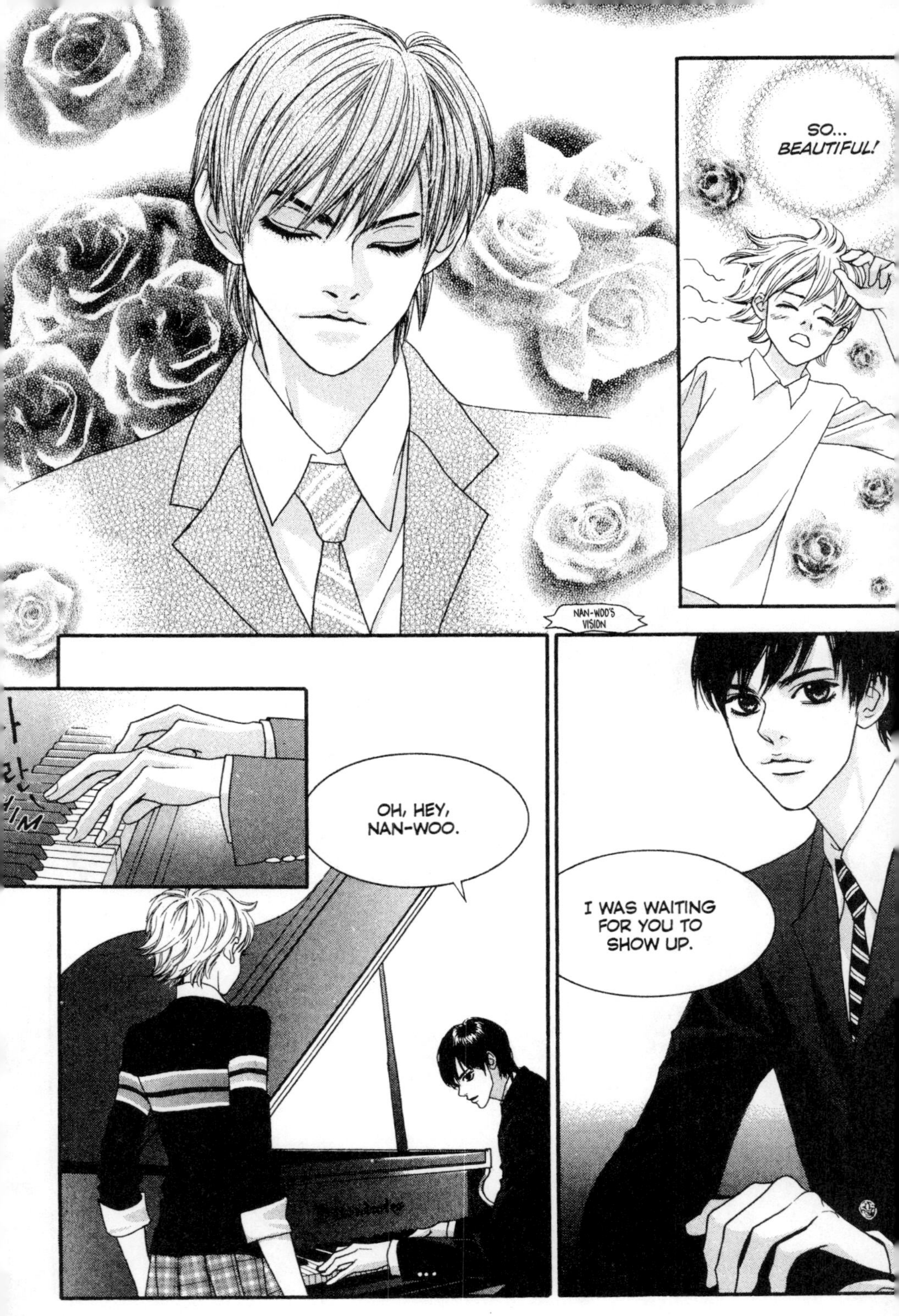
SO... BEAUTIFUL!
NAN-WOO'S VISION
OH, HEY, NAN-WOO.
I WAS WAITING FOR YOU TO SHOW UP.

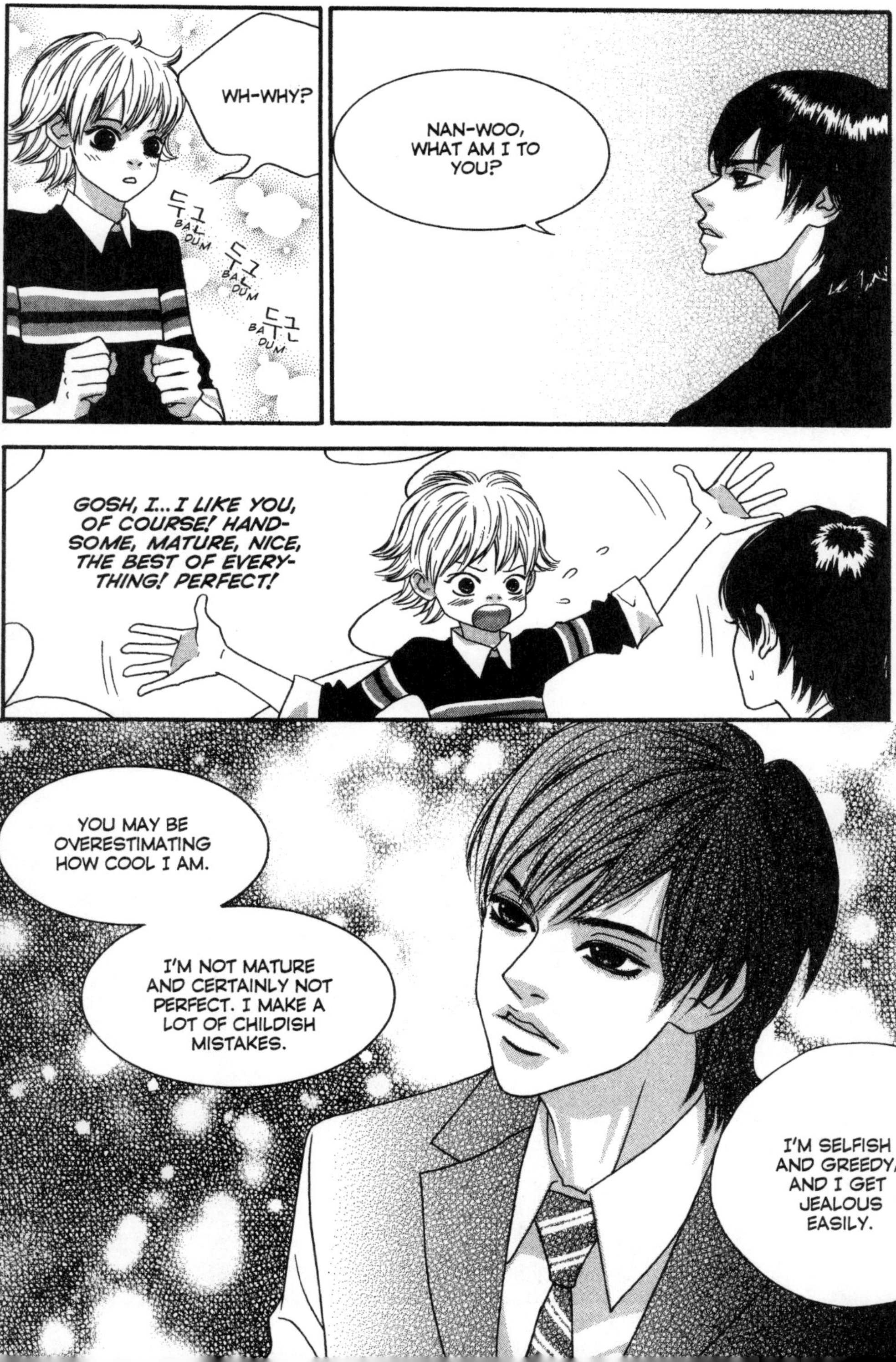
WH-WHY?
두근 BA DUM
두근 BA DUM
두근 BA DUM
NAN-WOO, WHAT AM I TO YOU?
GOSH, I...I LIKE YOU, OF COURSE! HAND-SOME, MATURE, NICE, THE BEST OF EVERY-THING! PERFECT!
YOU MAY BE OVERESTIMATING HOW COOL I AM.
I'M NOT MATURE AND CERTAINLY NOT PERFECT. I MAKE A LOT OF CHILDISH MISTAKES.
I'M SELFISH AND GREEDY, AND I GET JEALOUS EASILY.

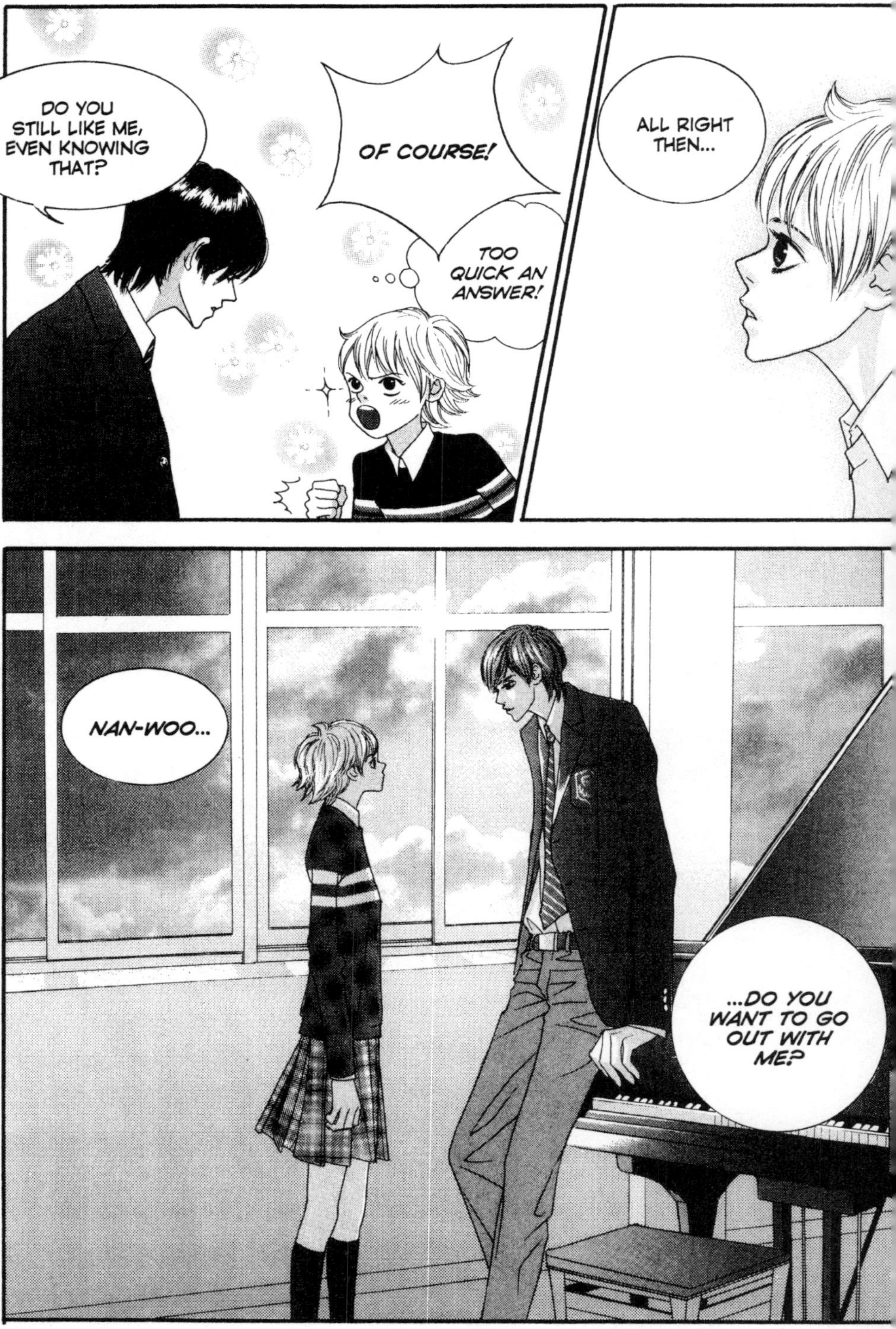
DO YOU STILL LIKE ME, EVEN KNOWING THAT?
OF COURSE!
TOO QUICK AN ANSWER!
ALL RIGHT THEN...
NAN-WOO...
...DO YOU WANT TO GO OUT WITH ME?

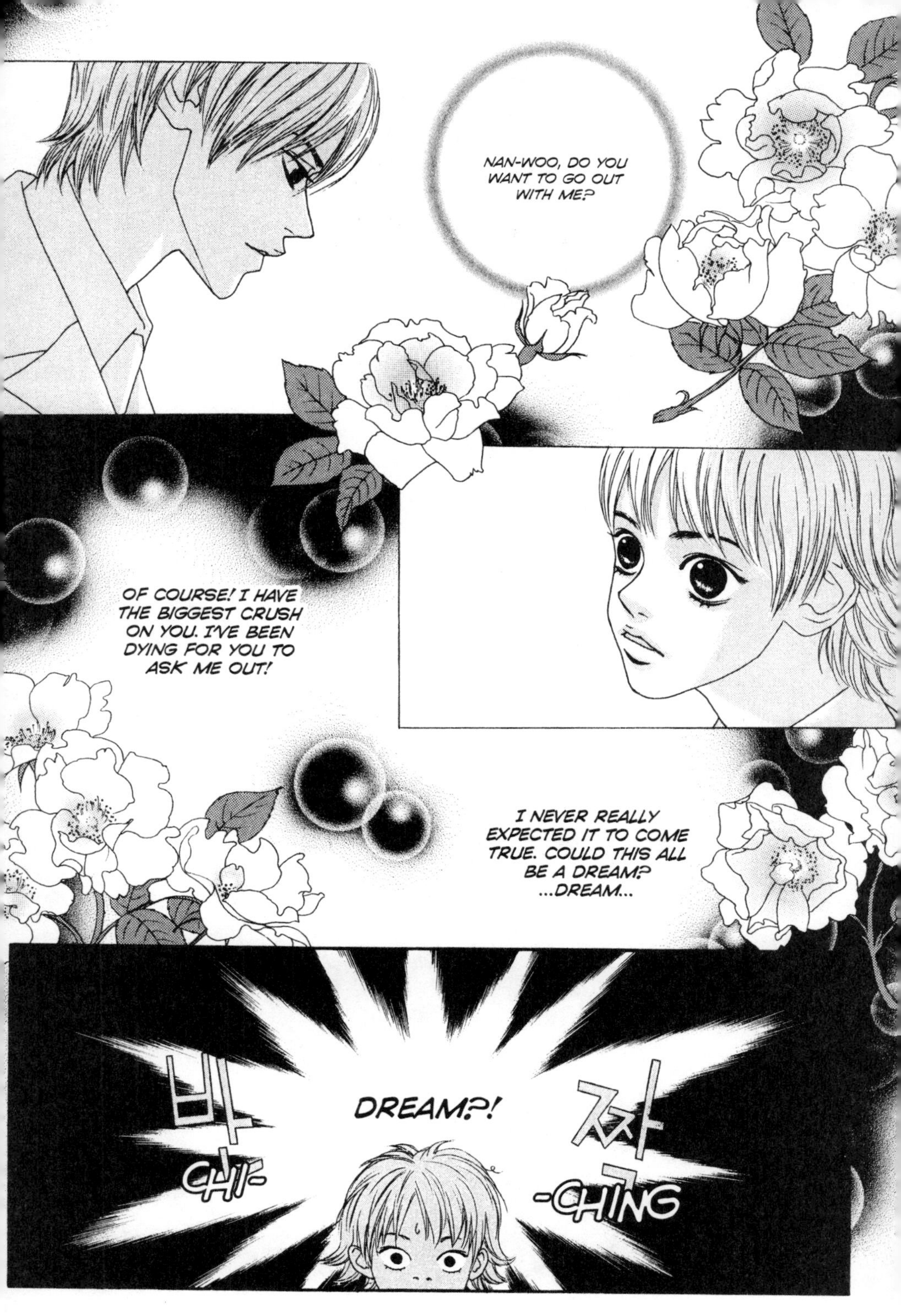
NAN-WOO, DO YOU WANT TO GO OUT WITH ME?
OF COURSE! I HAVE THE BIGGEST CRUSH ON YOU. I'VE BEEN DYING FOR YOU TO ASK ME OUT!
I NEVER REALLY EXPECTED IT TO COME TRUE. COULD THIS ALL BE A DREAM? ...DREAM...
DREAM?!
CHI-
-CHING

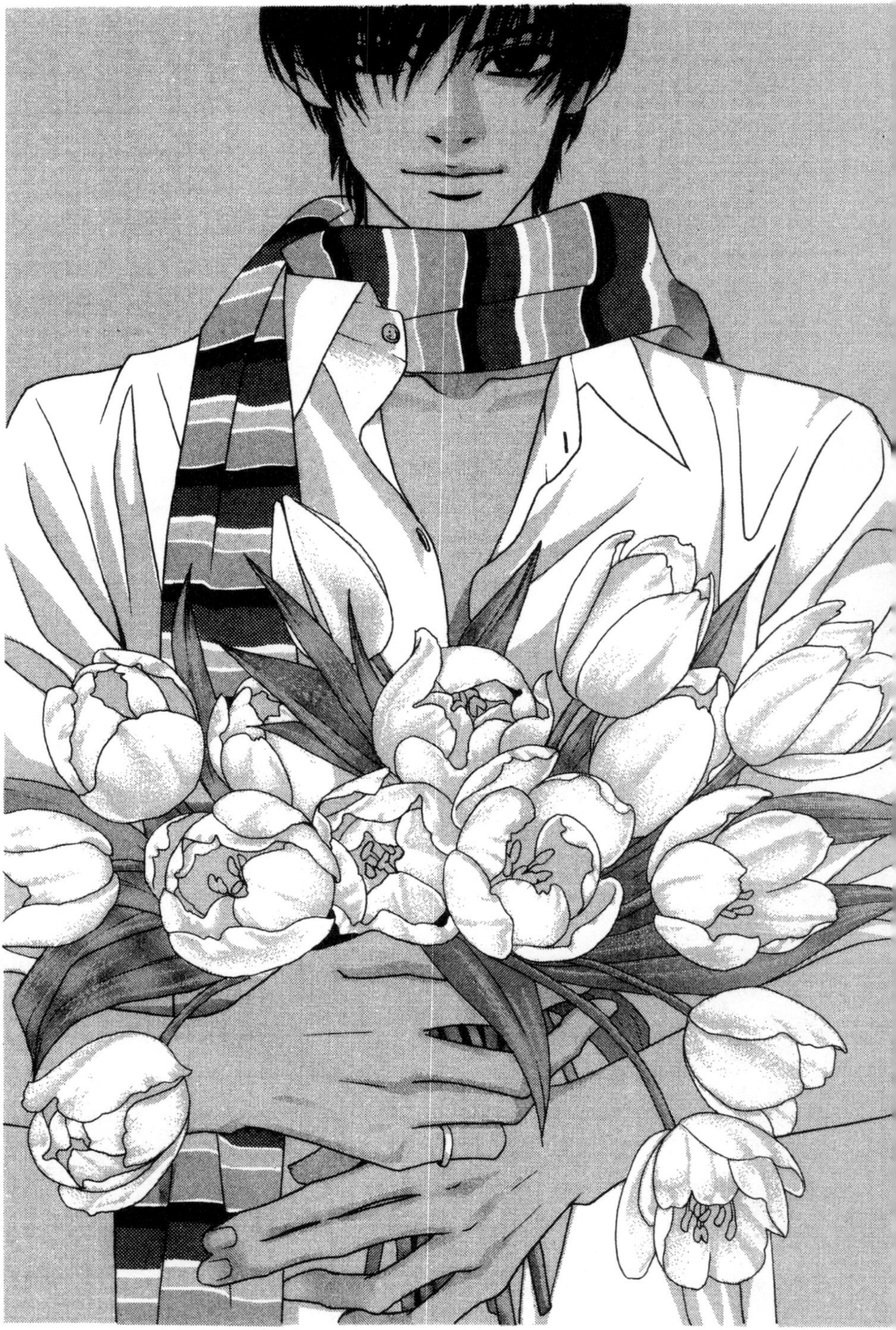

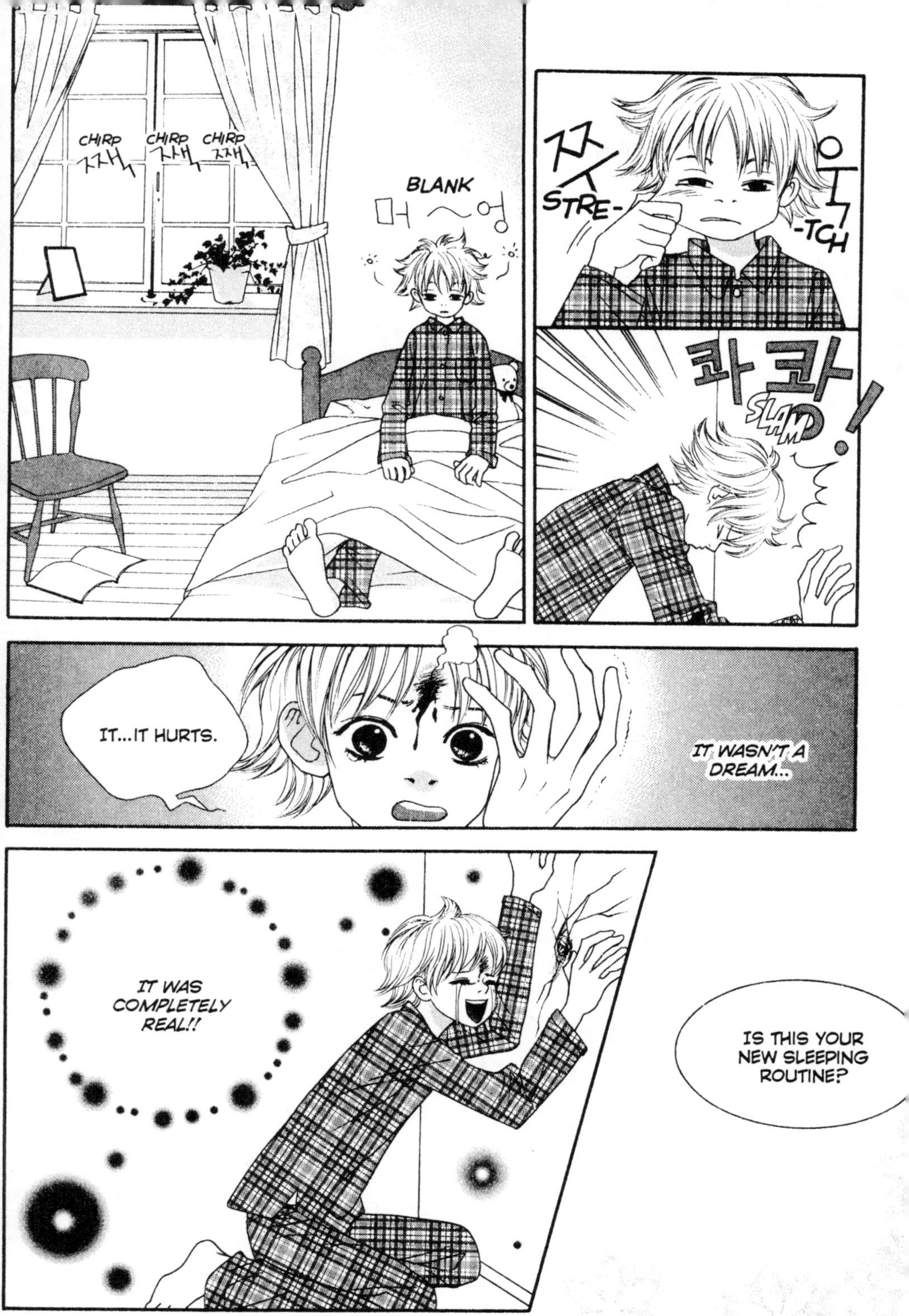
CHIRP
CHIRP
CHIRP
BLANK
STRE-
-TCH
콰콰
SLAM!
IT...IT HURTS.
IT WASN'T A DREAM...
IT WAS COMPLETELY REAL!!
IS THIS YOUR NEW SLEEPING ROUTINE?

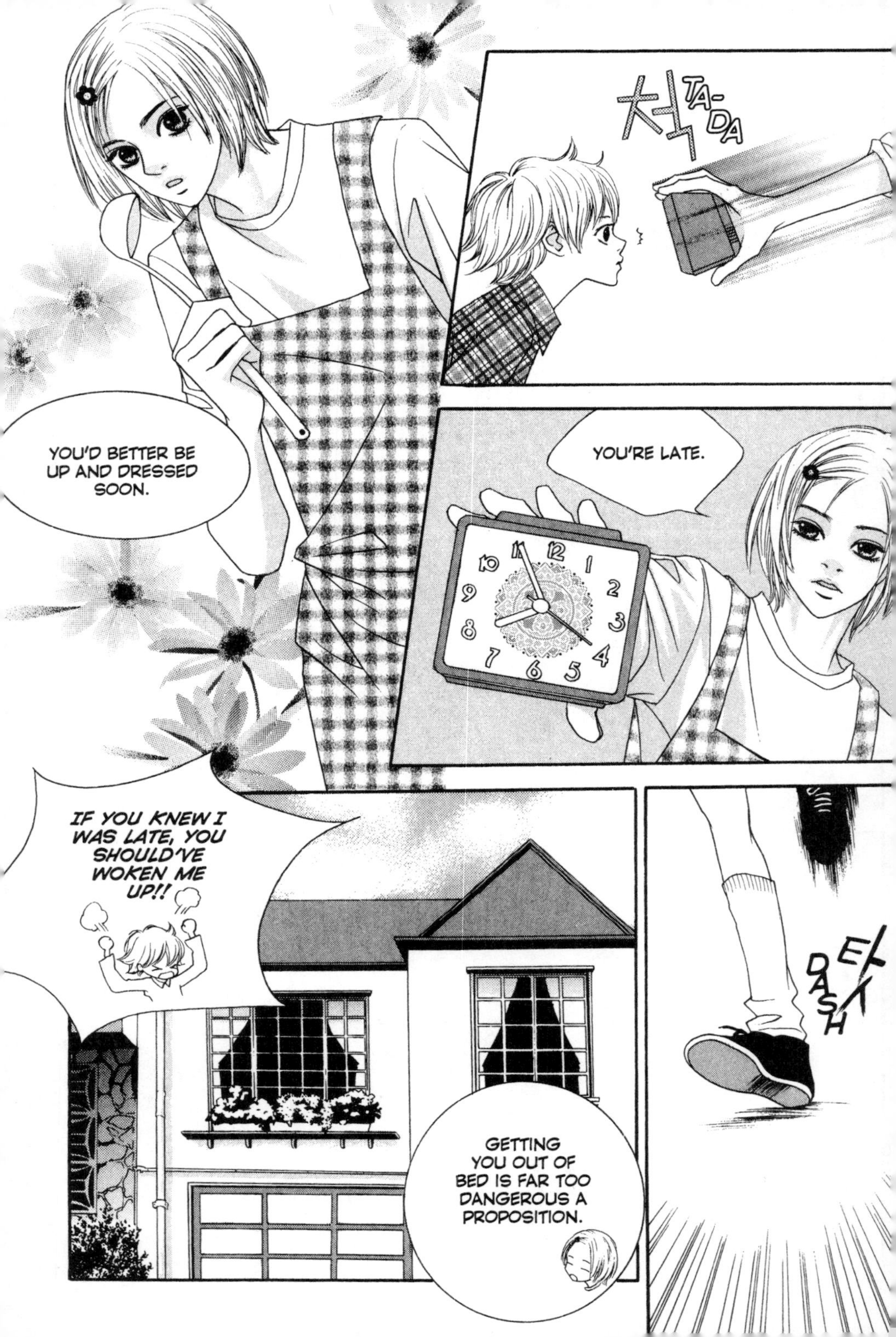

YOU'D BETTER BE UP AND DRESSED SOON.
TA-DA
YOU'RE LATE.
IF YOU KNEW I WAS LATE, YOU SHOULD'VE WOKEN ME UP!!
GETTING YOU OUT OF BED IS FAR TOO DANGEROUS A PROPOSITION.
DASH

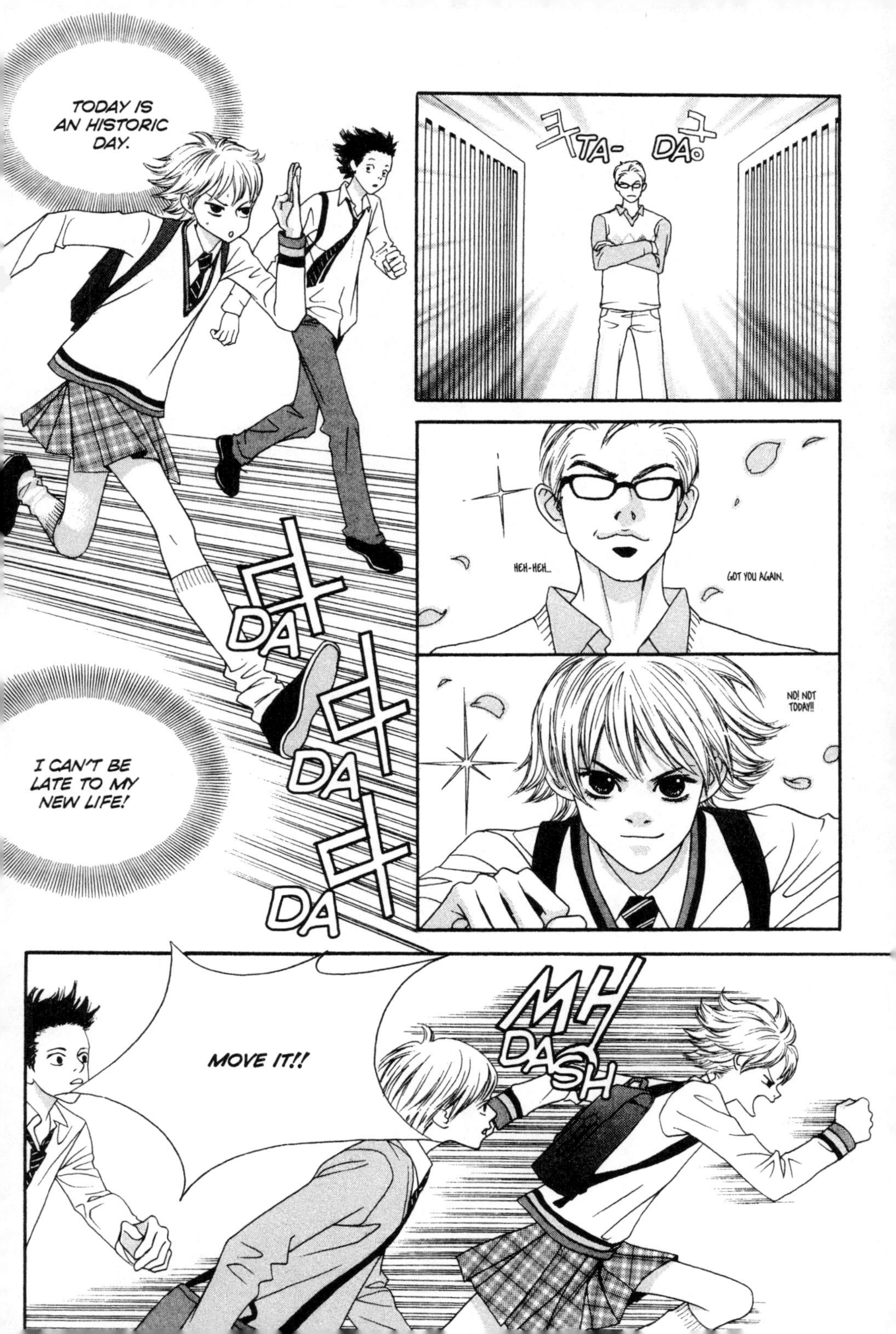
TODAY IS AN HISTORIC DAY.
DA
DA
DA
I CAN'T BE LATE TO MY NEW LIFE!
TA- DA
HEH-HEH...
GOT YOU AGAIN.
NO! NOT TODAY!!
MOVE IT!!
MH
DASH

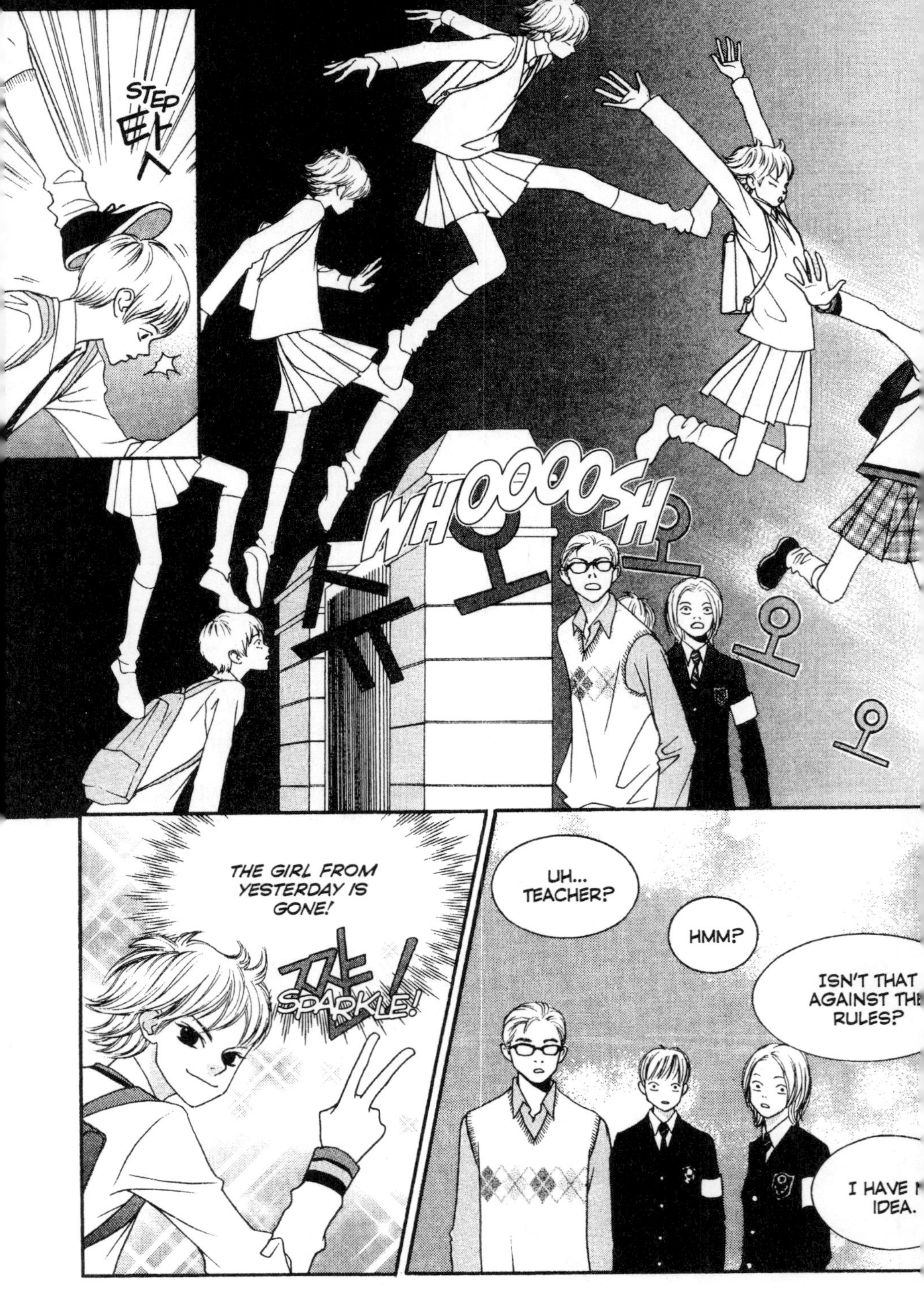
STEP
WHOOOOSH
THE GIRL FROM YESTERDAY IS GONE!
SPARKLE!
UH... TEACHER?
HMM?
ISN'T THAT AGAINST TH RULES?
I HAVE IDEA.

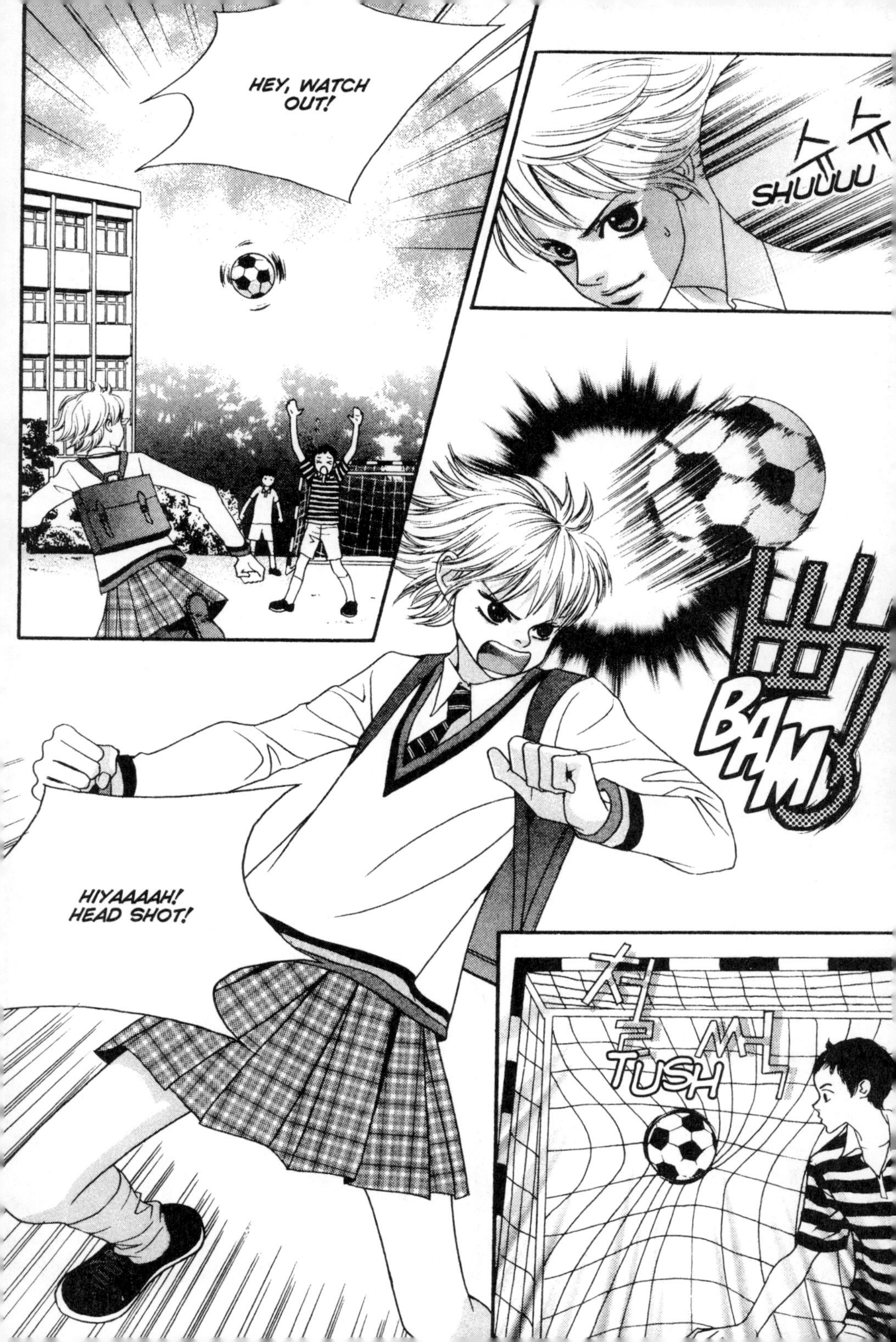
HEY, WATCH OUT!
슈슈
SHUUUU
BAM!
HIYAAAAH! HEAD SHOT!
TUSH

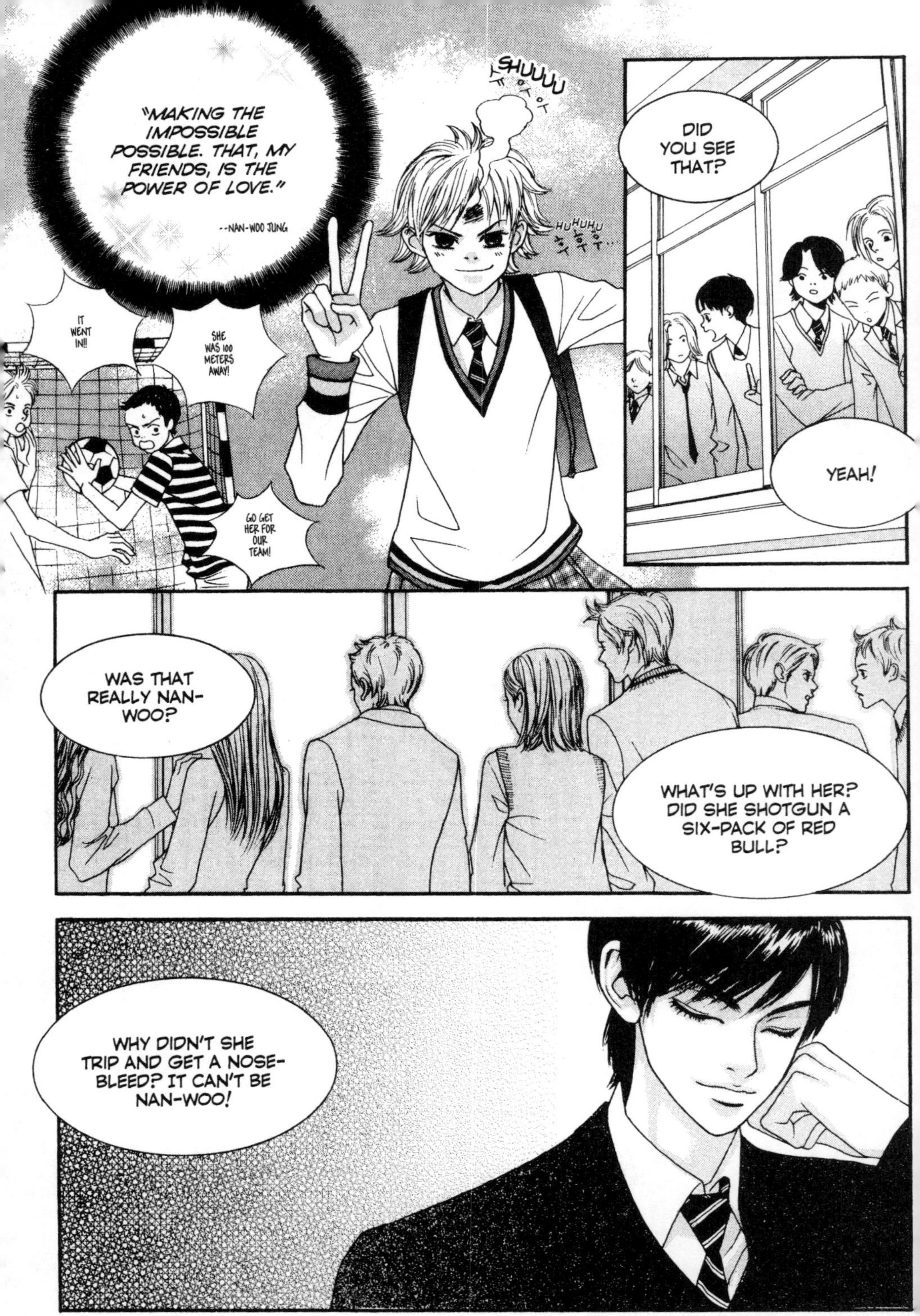
"MAKING THE IMPOSSIBLE POSSIBLE. THAT, MY FRIENDS, IS THE POWER OF LOVE."
--NAN-WOO JUNG
SHUUUU
HUHUHU
IT WENT IN!!
SHE WAS 100 METERS AWAY!
GO GET HER FOR OUR TEAM!
DID YOU SEE THAT?
YEAH!
WAS THAT REALLY NAN-WOO?
WHAT'S UP WITH HER? DID SHE SHOTGUN A SIX-PACK OF RED BULL?
WHY DIDN'T SHE TRIP AND GET A NOSE-BLEED? IT CAN'T BE NAN-WOO!

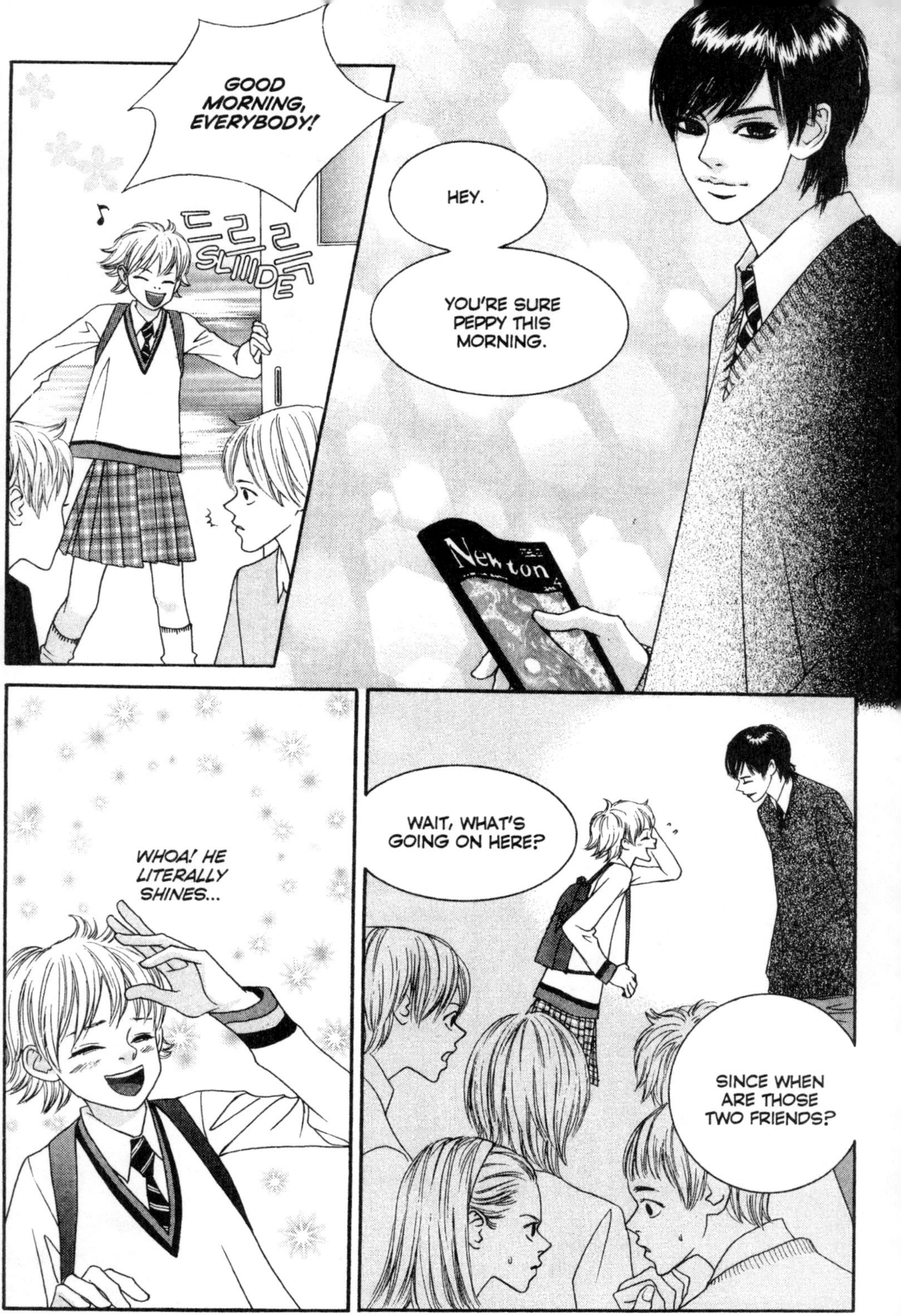
GOOD MORNING, EVERYBODY!
SLIIIDE
HEY.
YOU'RE SURE PEPPY THIS MORNING.
Newton
WHOA! HE LITERALLY SHINES...
WAIT, WHAT'S GOING ON HERE?
SINCE WHEN ARE THOSE TWO FRIENDS?

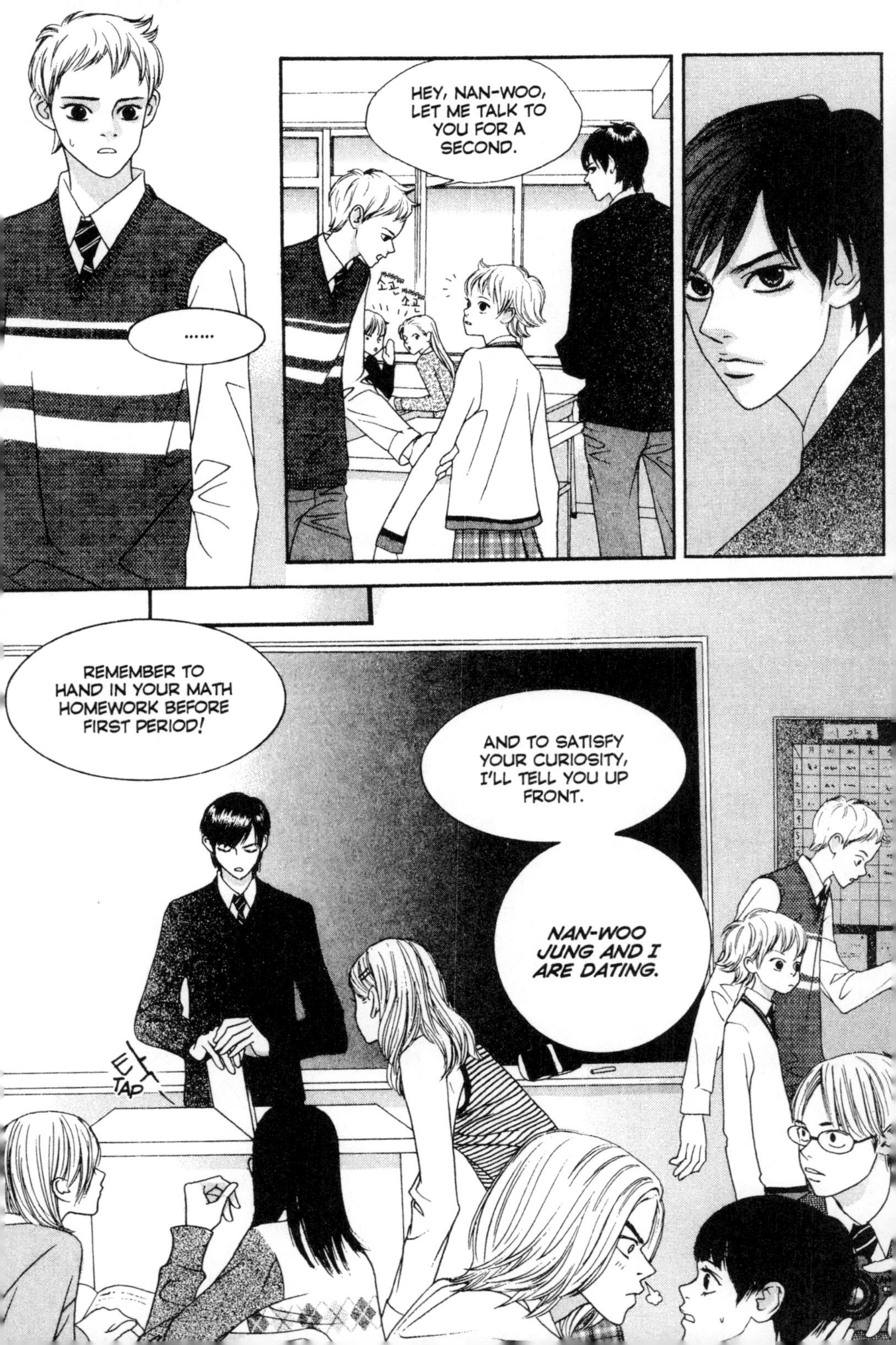
......
HEY, NAN-WOO, LET ME TALK TO YOU FOR A SECOND.
REMEMBER TO HAND IN YOUR MATH HOMEWORK BEFORE FIRST PERIOD!
AND TO SATISFY YOUR CURIOSITY, I'LL TELL YOU UP FRONT.
NAN-WOO JUNG AND I ARE DATING.
TAP

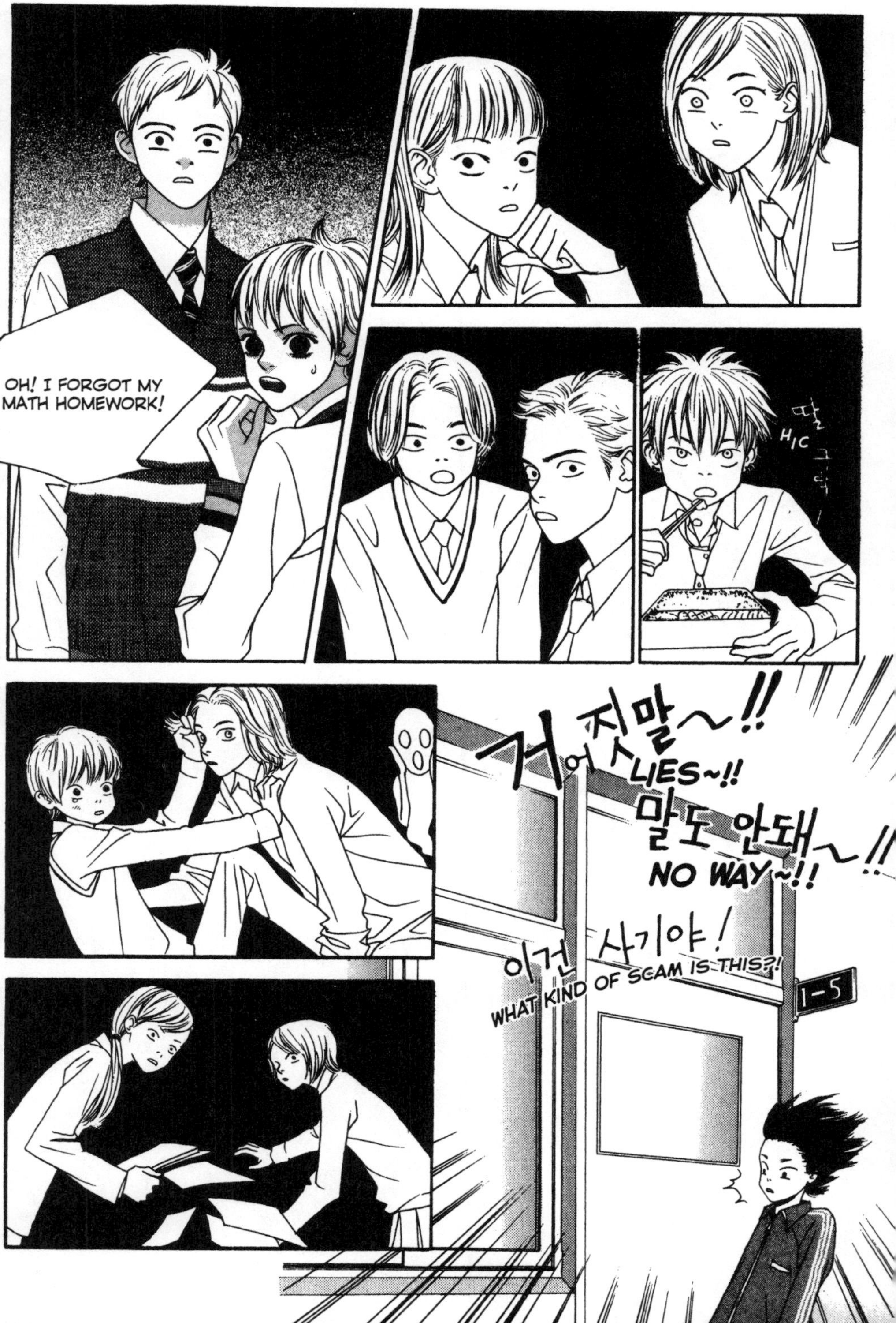
OH! I FORGOT MY MATH HOMEWORK!
HIC
거어짓말~!!
LIES~!!
말도 안돼~!!
NO WAY~!!
이건 사기야!
WHAT KIND OF SCAM IS THIS?!
1-5

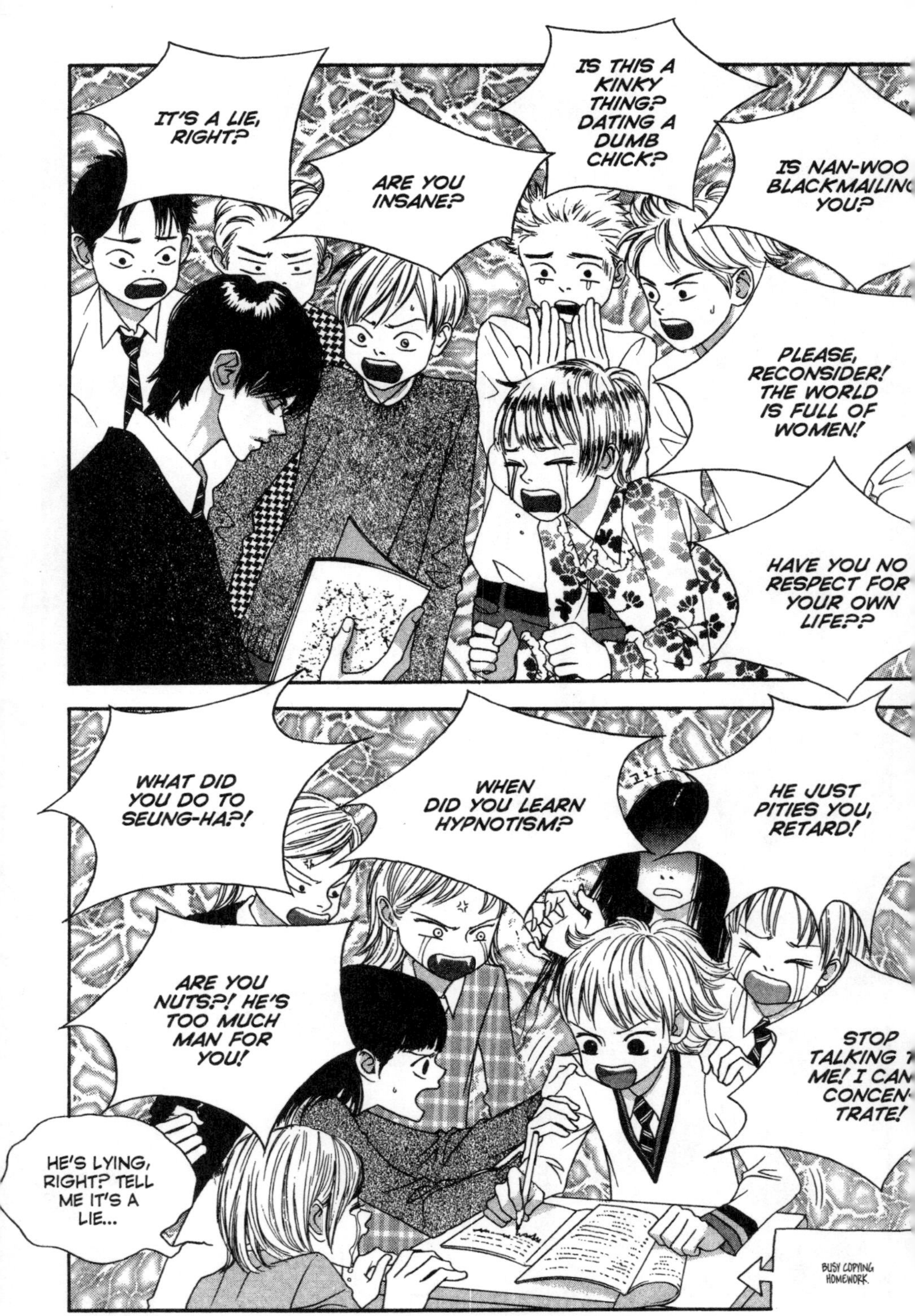
IT'S A LIE, RIGHT?
ARE YOU INSANE?
IS THIS A KINKY THING? DATING A DUMB CHICK?
IS NAN-WOO BLACKMAILIN YOU?
PLEASE, RECONSIDER! THE WORLD IS FULL OF WOMEN!
HAVE YOU NO RESPECT FOR YOUR OWN LIFE??
WHAT DID YOU DO TO SEUNG-HA?!
WHEN DID YOU LEARN HYPNOTISM?
HE JUST PITIES YOU, RETARD!
ARE YOU NUTS?! HE'S TOO MUCH MAN FOR YOU!
STOP TALKING T ME! I CAN CONCEN-TRATE!
HE'S LYING, RIGHT? TELL ME IT'S A LIE...
BUSY COPYING HOMEWORK.

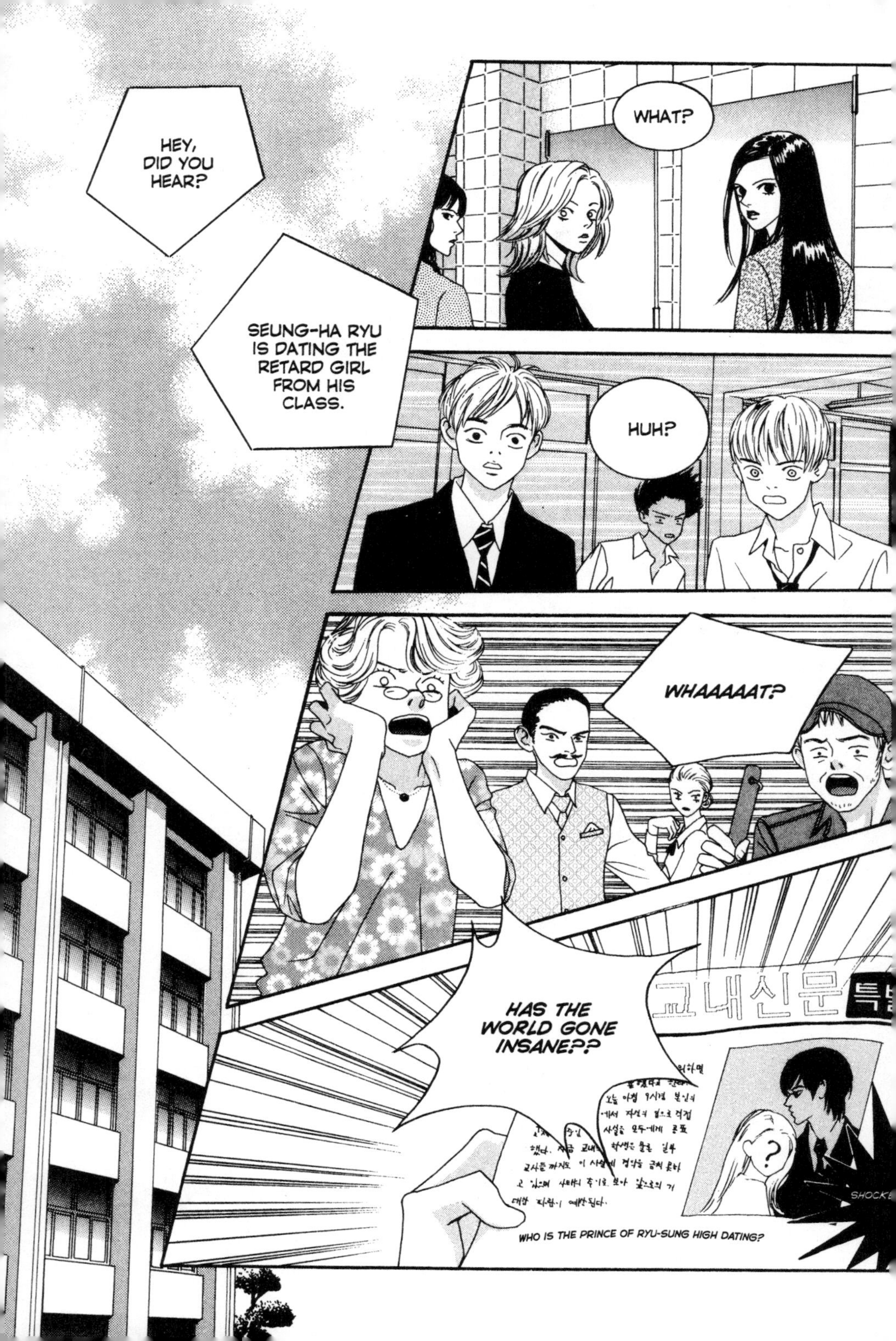
HEY, DID YOU HEAR?
SEUNG-HA RYU IS DATING THE RETARD GIRL FROM HIS CLASS.
WHAT?
HUH?
WHAAAAAT?
HAS THE WORLD GONE INSANE??
교내신문
WHO IS THE PRINCE OF RYU-SUNG HIGH DATING?

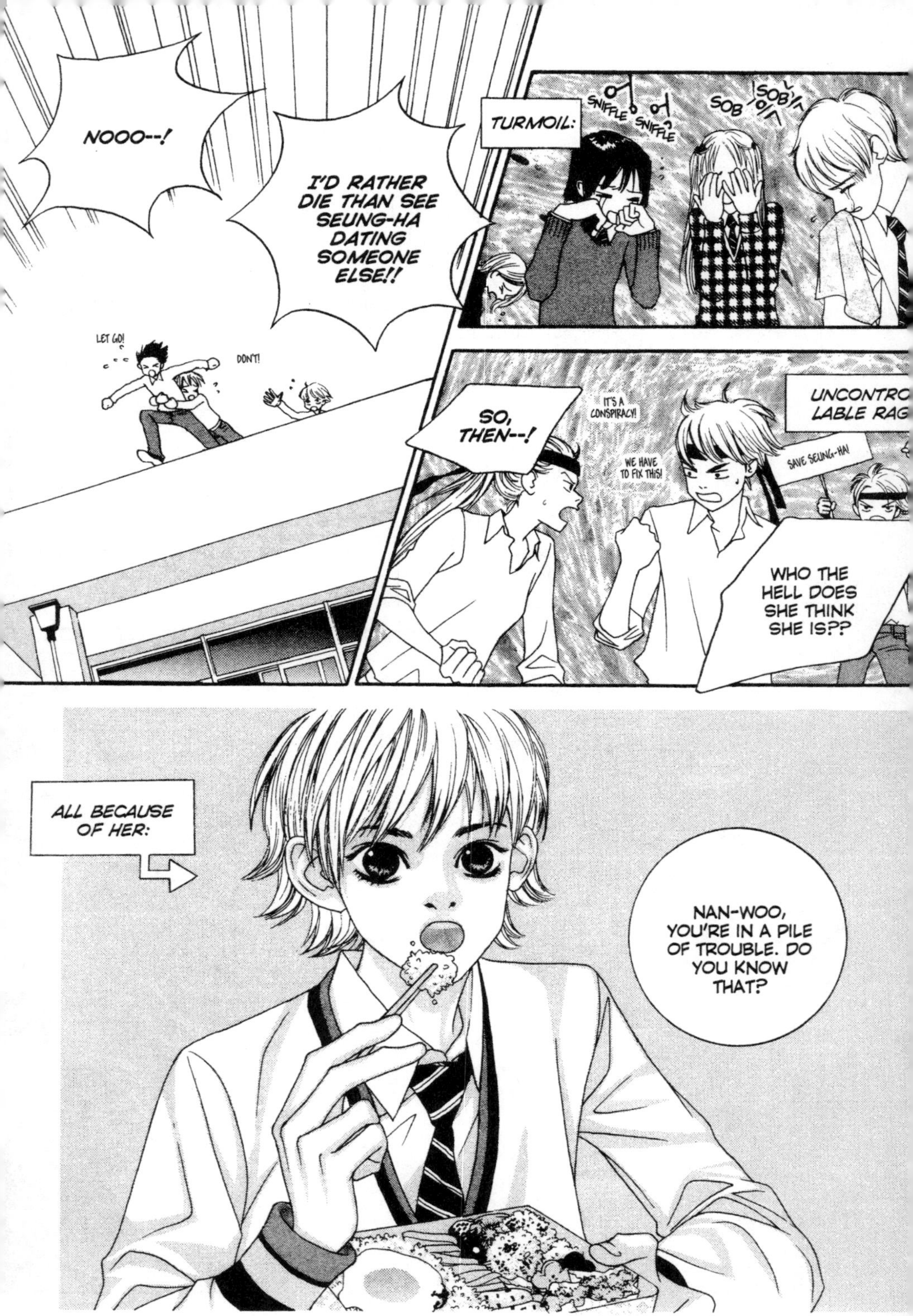
NOOO--!
I'D RATHER DIE THAN SEE SEUNG-HA DATING SOMEONE ELSE!!
LET GO!
DON'T!
TURMOIL:
SNIFFLE
SNIFFLE
SOB
SOB
SO, THEN--!
IT'S A CONSPIRACY!
WE HAVE TO FIX THIS!
UNCONTRO LABLE RAG
SAVE SEUNG-HA!
WHO THE HELL DOES SHE THINK SHE IS??
ALL BECAUSE OF HER:
NAN-WOO, YOU'RE IN A PILE OF TROUBLE. DO YOU KNOW THAT?

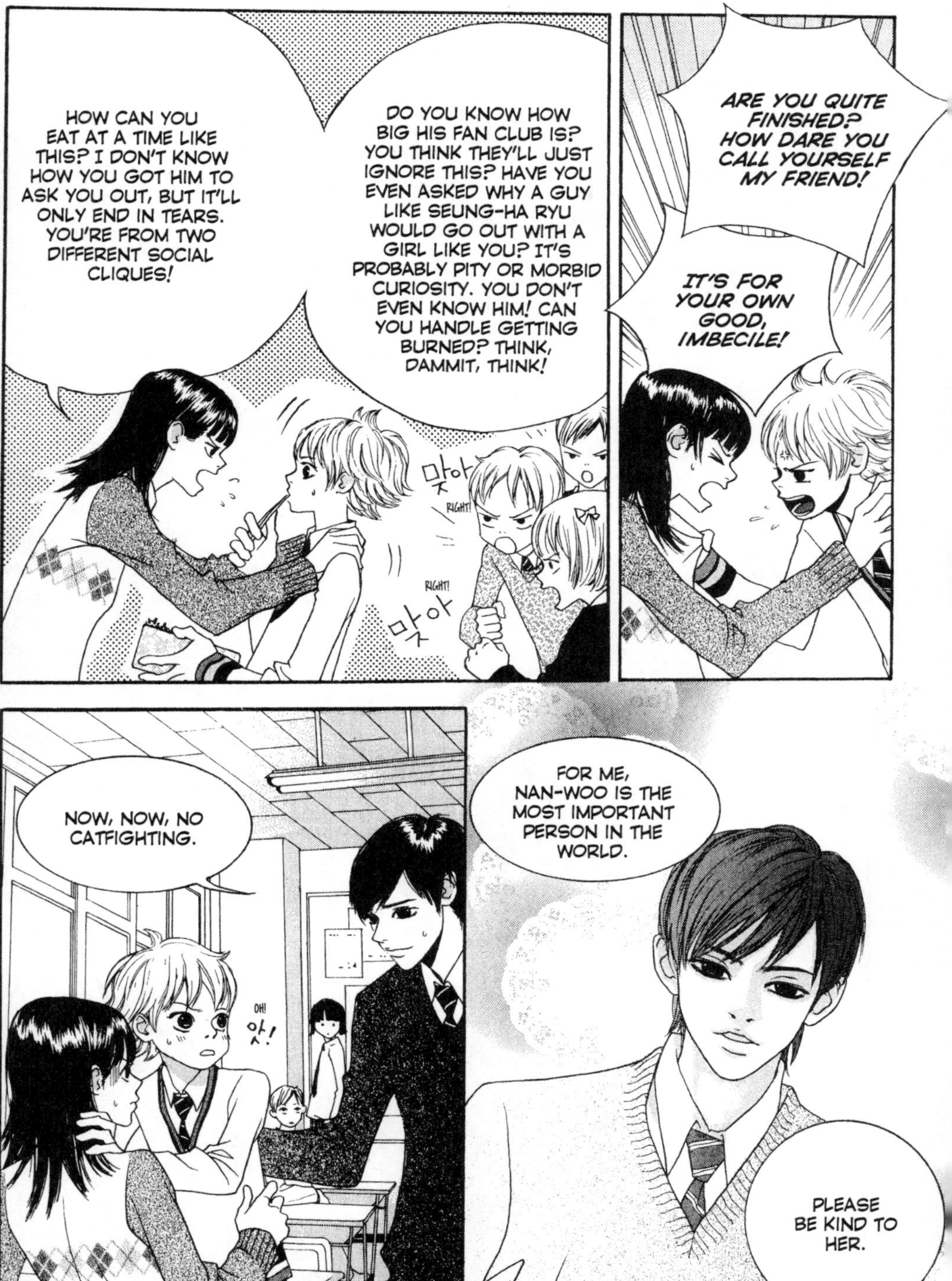
HOW CAN YOU EAT AT A TIME LIKE THIS? I DON'T KNOW HOW YOU GOT HIM TO ASK YOU OUT, BUT IT'LL ONLY END IN TEARS. YOU'RE FROM TWO DIFFERENT SOCIAL CLIQUES!
DO YOU KNOW HOW BIG HIS FAN CLUB IS? YOU THINK THEY'LL JUST IGNORE THIS? HAVE YOU EVEN ASKED WHY A GUY LIKE SEUNG-HA RYU WOULD GO OUT WITH A GIRL LIKE YOU? IT'S PROBABLY PITY OR MORBID CURIOSITY. YOU DON'T EVEN KNOW HIM! CAN YOU HANDLE GETTING BURNED? THINK, DAMMIT, THINK!
맞아 RIGHT!
맞아 RIGHT!
ARE YOU QUITE FINISHED? HOW DARE YOU CALL YOURSELF MY FRIEND!
IT'S FOR YOUR OWN GOOD, IMBECILE!
NOW, NOW, NO CATFIGHTING.
앗! OH!
FOR ME, NAN-WOO IS THE MOST IMPORTANT PERSON IN THE WORLD.
PLEASE BE KIND TO HER.

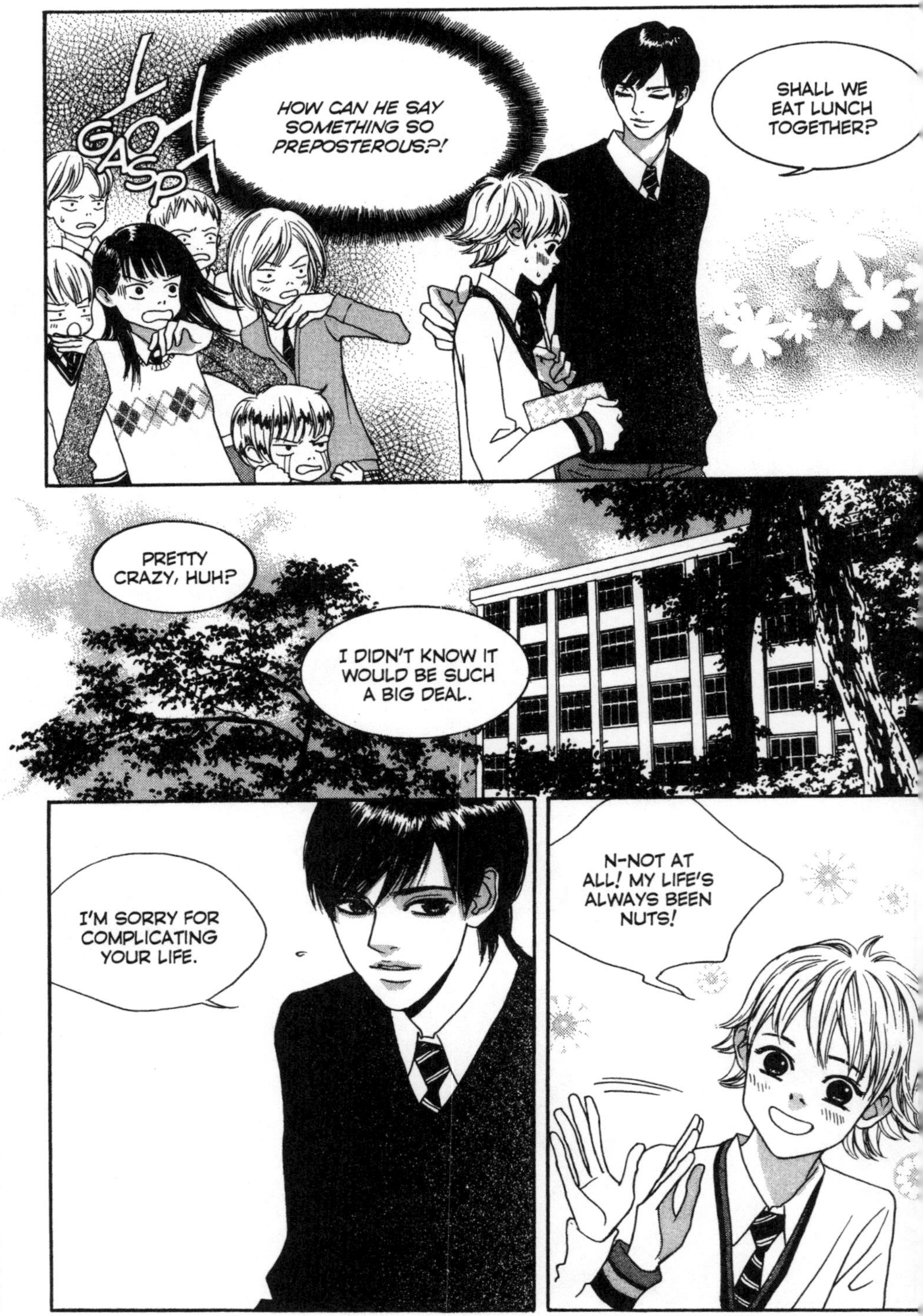
GO
GASP
HOW CAN HE SAY SOMETHING SO PREPOSTEROUS?!
SHALL WE EAT LUNCH TOGETHER?
PRETTY CRAZY, HUH?
I DIDN'T KNOW IT WOULD BE SUCH A BIG DEAL.
I'M SORRY FOR COMPLICATING YOUR LIFE.
N-NOT AT ALL! MY LIFE'S ALWAYS BEEN NUTS!

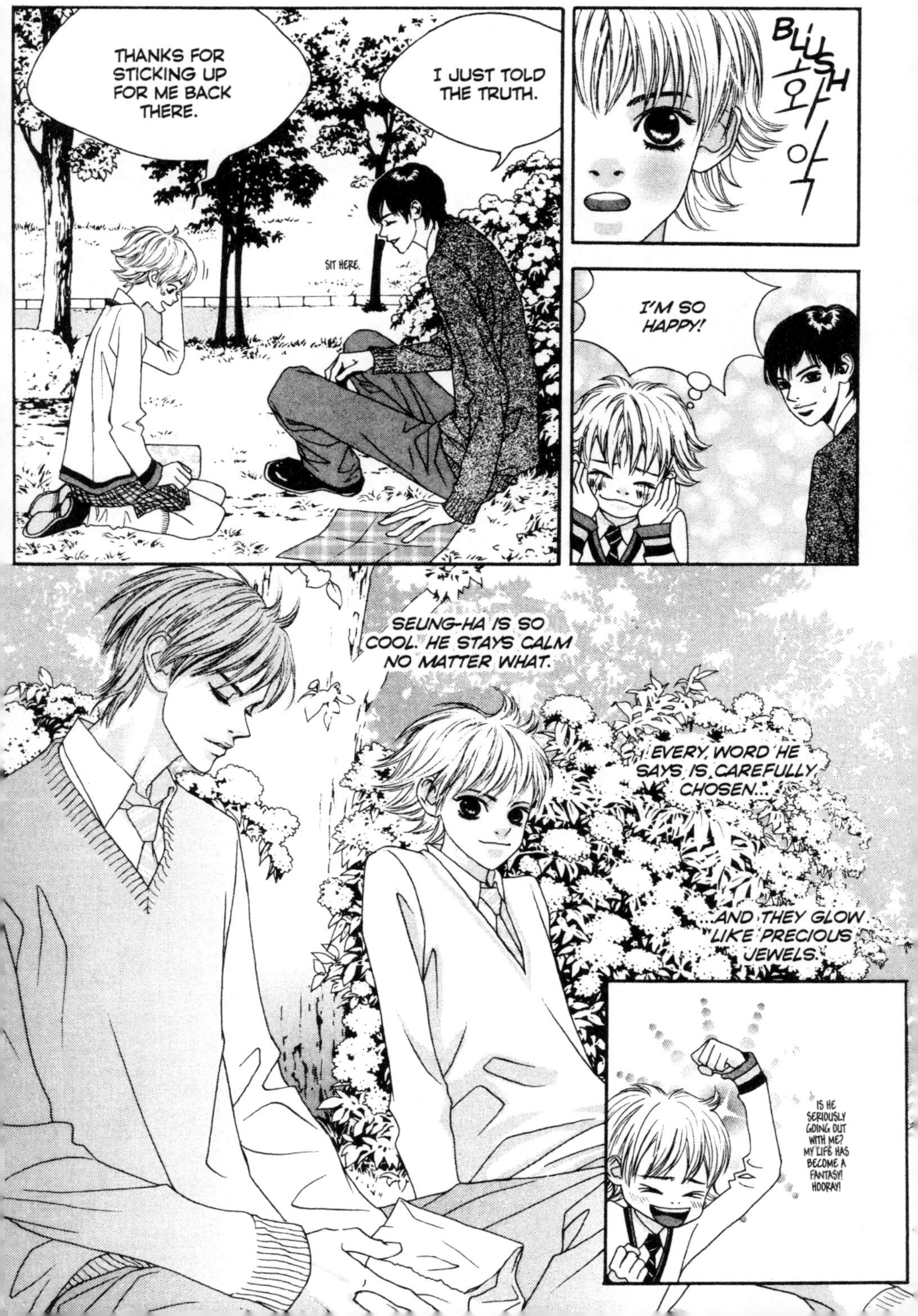
THANKS FOR STICKING UP FOR ME BACK THERE.
I JUST TOLD THE TRUTH.
SIT HERE.
BLUSH
화아악
I'M SO HAPPY!
SEUNG-HA IS SO COOL. HE STAYS CALM NO MATTER WHAT.
EVERY WORD HE SAYS IS CAREFULLY CHOSEN...
...AND THEY GLOW LIKE PRECIOUS JEWELS.
IS HE SERIOUSLY GOING OUT WITH ME? MY LIFE HAS BECOME A FANTASY! HOORAY!

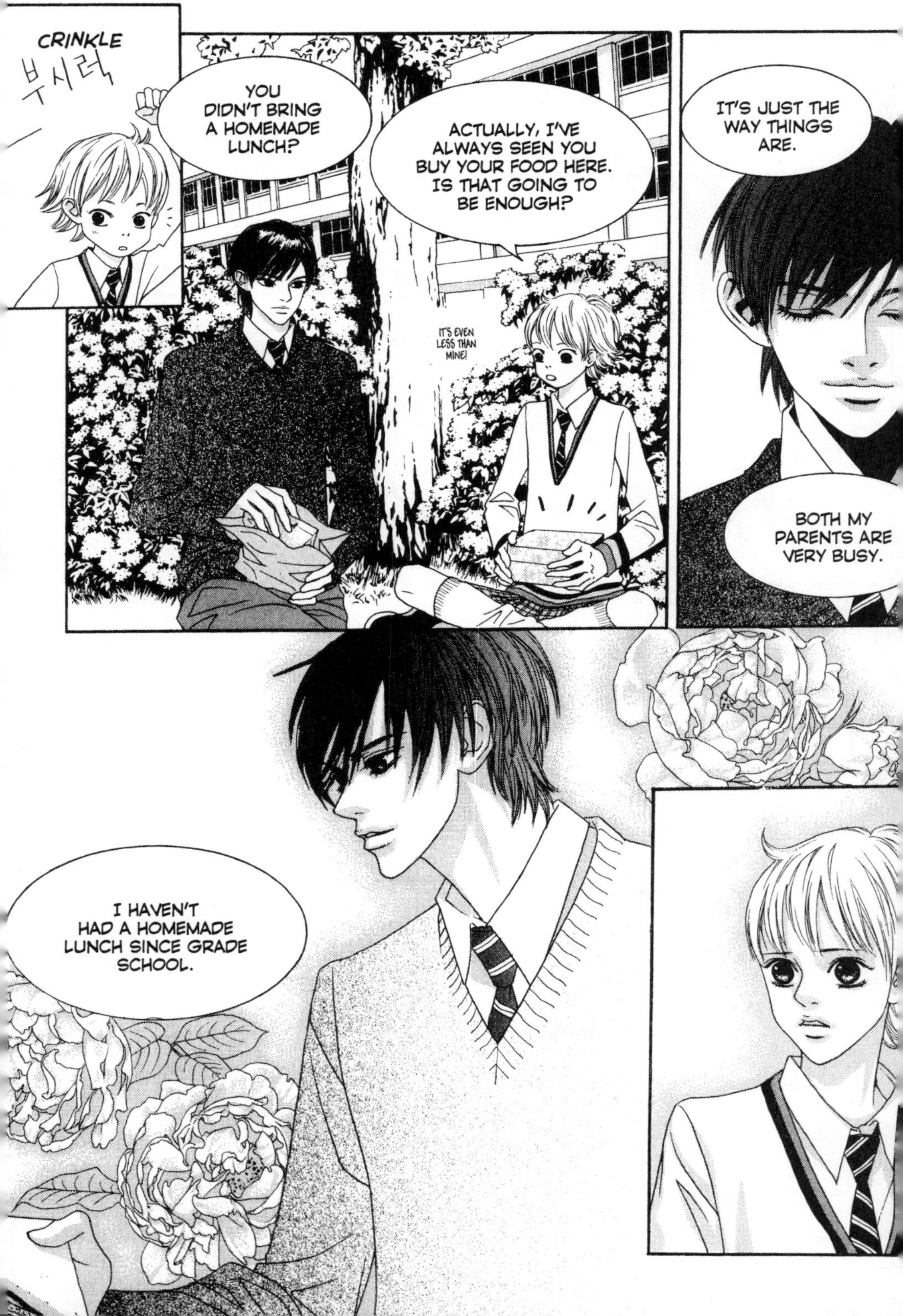
CRINKLE
부시럭
YOU DIDN'T BRING A HOMEMADE LUNCH?
ACTUALLY, I'VE ALWAYS SEEN YOU BUY YOUR FOOD HERE. IS THAT GOING TO BE ENOUGH?
IT'S EVEN LESS THAN MINE!
IT'S JUST THE WAY THINGS ARE.
BOTH MY PARENTS ARE VERY BUSY.
I HAVEN'T HAD A HOMEMADE LUNCH SINCE GRADE SCHOOL.

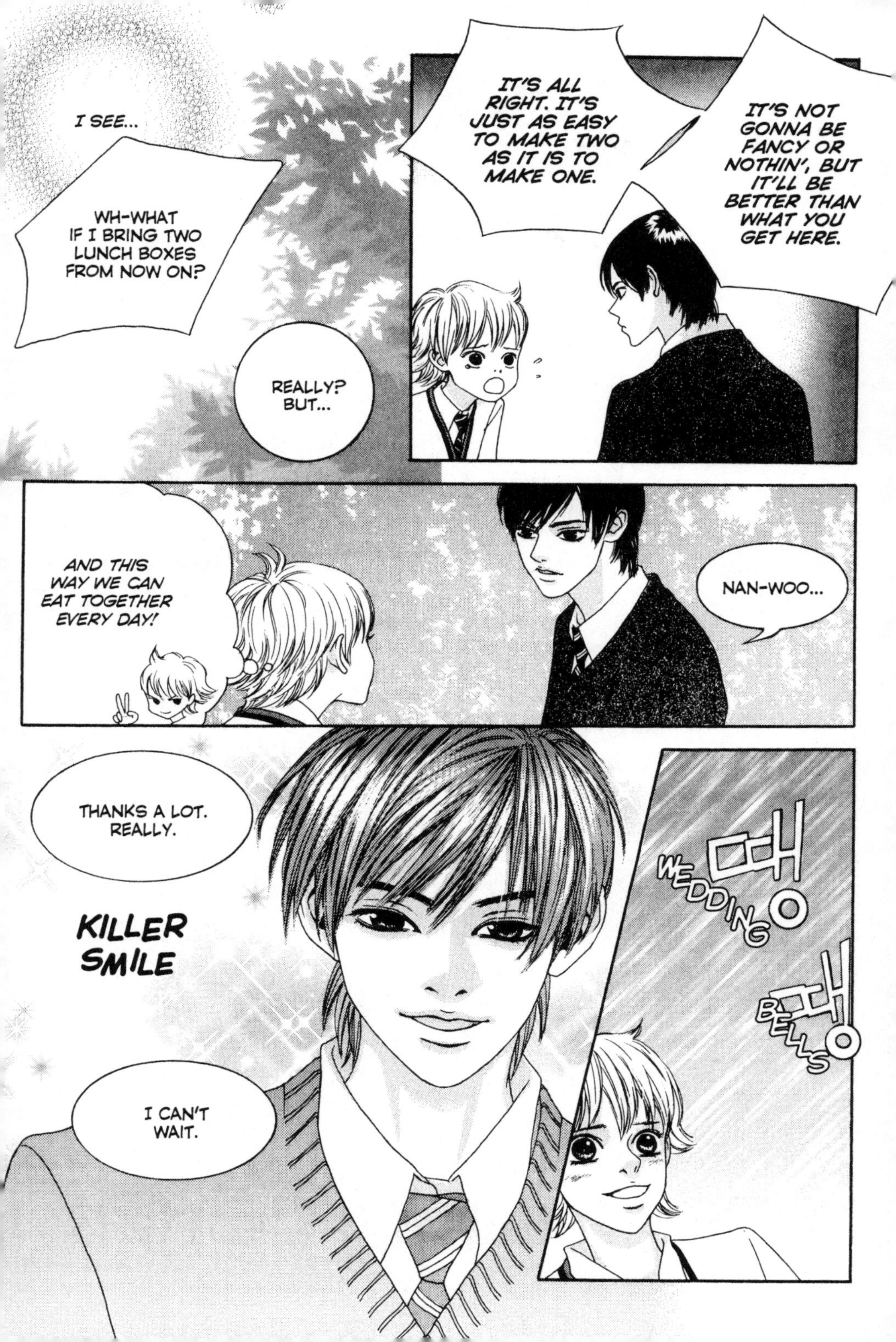
I SEE...
WH-WHAT IF I BRING TWO LUNCH BOXES FROM NOW ON?
REALLY? BUT...
IT'S ALL RIGHT. IT'S JUST AS EASY TO MAKE TWO AS IT IS TO MAKE ONE.
IT'S NOT GONNA BE FANCY OR NOTHIN', BUT IT'LL BE BETTER THAN WHAT YOU GET HERE.
AND THIS WAY WE CAN EAT TOGETHER EVERY DAY!
NAN-WOO...
THANKS A LOT. REALLY.
KILLER SMILE
I CAN'T WAIT.
OOOH WEDDING
BOOOH BELLS

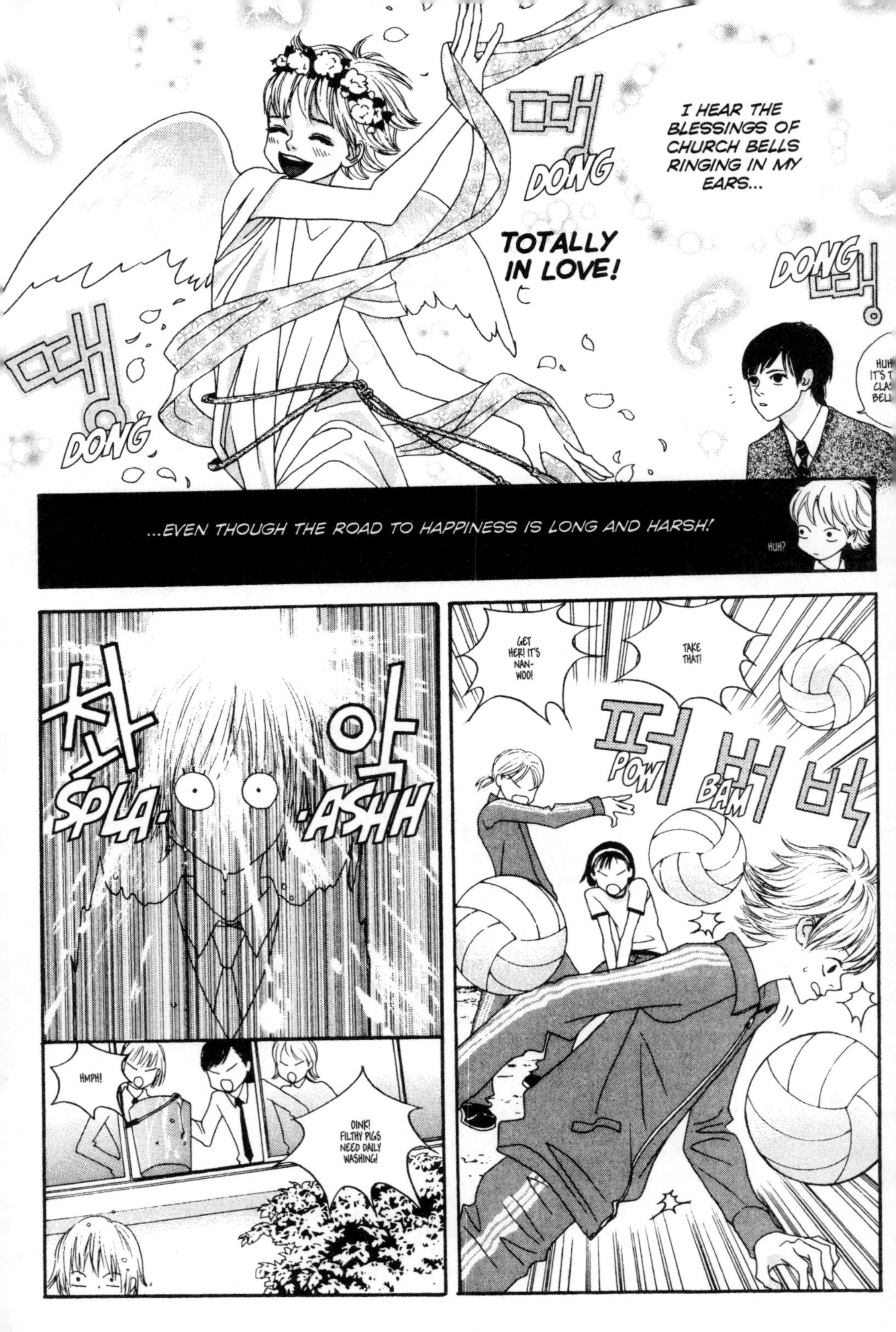

I HEAR THE BLESSINGS OF CHURCH BELLS RINGING IN MY EARS...
DONG
TOTALLY IN LOVE!
DONG
DONG
...EVEN THOUGH THE ROAD TO HAPPINESS IS LONG AND HARSH!
HUH?
SPLA- -ASHH
HMPH!
OINK! FILTHY PIGS NEED DAILY WASHING!
GET HER! IT'S NAN-WOO!
TAKE THAT!
POW
BAM

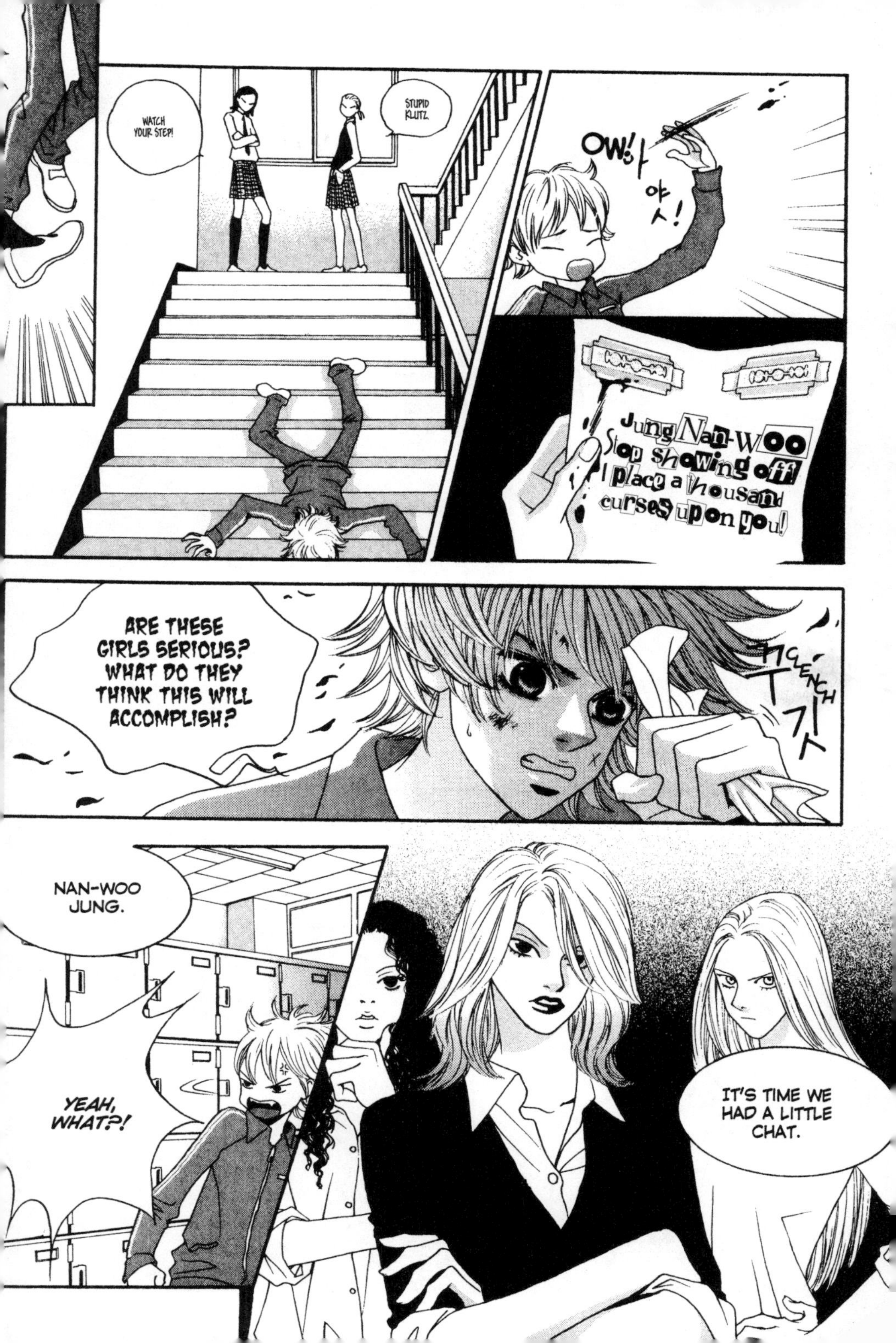
WATCH YOUR STEP!
STUPID KLUTZ.
OW!
Jung Nan-Woo
Stop showing off!
I place a thousand curses upon you!
ARE THESE GIRLS SERIOUS? WHAT DO THEY THINK THIS WILL ACCOMPLISH?
CLENCH
NAN-WOO JUNG.
YEAH, WHAT?!
IT'S TIME WE HAD A LITTLE CHAT.

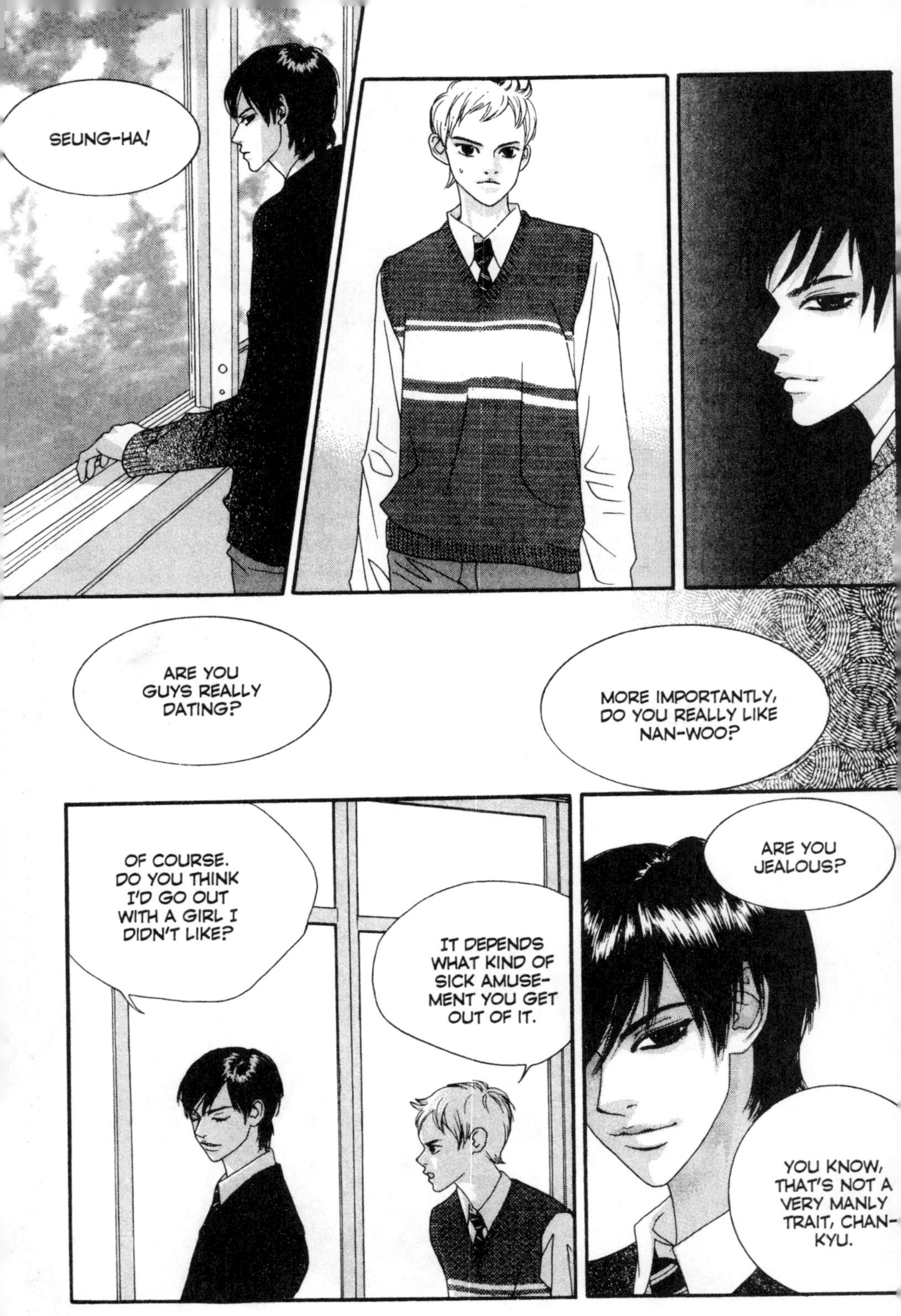
SEUNG-HA!
ARE YOU GUYS REALLY DATING?
MORE IMPORTANTLY, DO YOU REALLY LIKE NAN-WOO?
OF COURSE. DO YOU THINK I'D GO OUT WITH A GIRL I DIDN'T LIKE?
IT DEPENDS WHAT KIND OF SICK AMUSE-MENT YOU GET OUT OF IT.
ARE YOU JEALOUS?
YOU KNOW, THAT'S NOT A VERY MANLY TRAIT, CHAN-KYU.

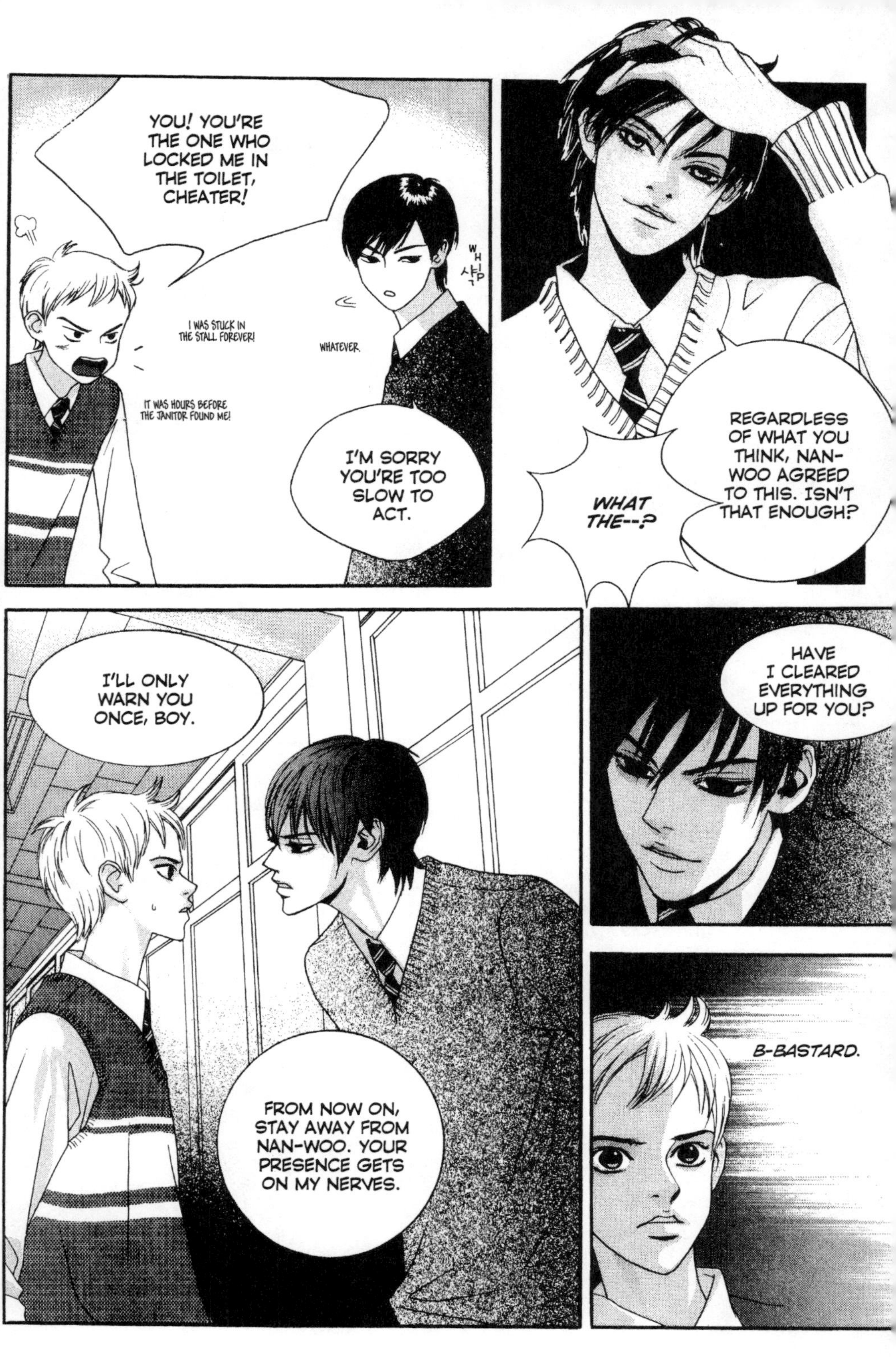
YOU! YOU'RE THE ONE WHO LOCKED ME IN THE TOILET, CHEATER!
I WAS STUCK IN THE STALL FOREVER!
IT WAS HOURS BEFORE THE JANITOR FOUND ME!
WHIP
WHATEVER.
I'M SORRY YOU'RE TOO SLOW TO ACT.
WHAT THE--?
REGARDLESS OF WHAT YOU THINK, NAN-WOO AGREED TO THIS. ISN'T THAT ENOUGH?
I'LL ONLY WARN YOU ONCE, BOY.
FROM NOW ON, STAY AWAY FROM NAN-WOO. YOUR PRESENCE GETS ON MY NERVES.
HAVE I CLEARED EVERYTHING UP FOR YOU?
B-BASTARD.

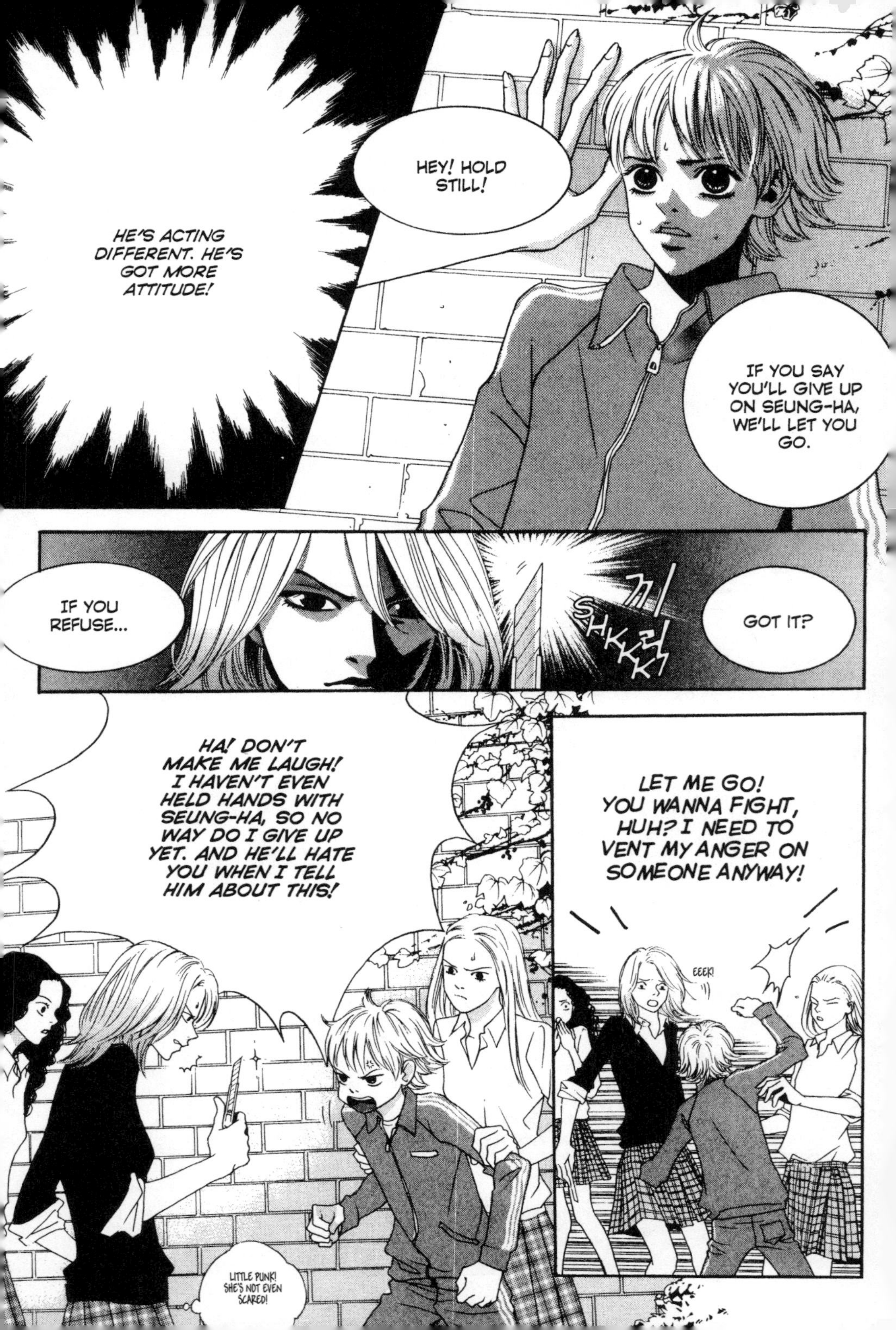
HE'S ACTING DIFFERENT. HE'S GOT MORE ATTITUDE!
HEY! HOLD STILL!
IF YOU SAY YOU'LL GIVE UP ON SEUNG-HA, WE'LL LET YOU GO.
IF YOU REFUSE...
SHKKKK
GOT IT?
HA! DON'T MAKE ME LAUGH! I HAVEN'T EVEN HELD HANDS WITH SEUNG-HA, SO NO WAY DO I GIVE UP YET. AND HE'LL HATE YOU WHEN I TELL HIM ABOUT THIS!
LITTLE PUNK! SHE'S NOT EVEN SCARED!
LET ME GO! YOU WANNA FIGHT, HUH? I NEED TO VENT MY ANGER ON SOMEONE ANYWAY!
EEEK!

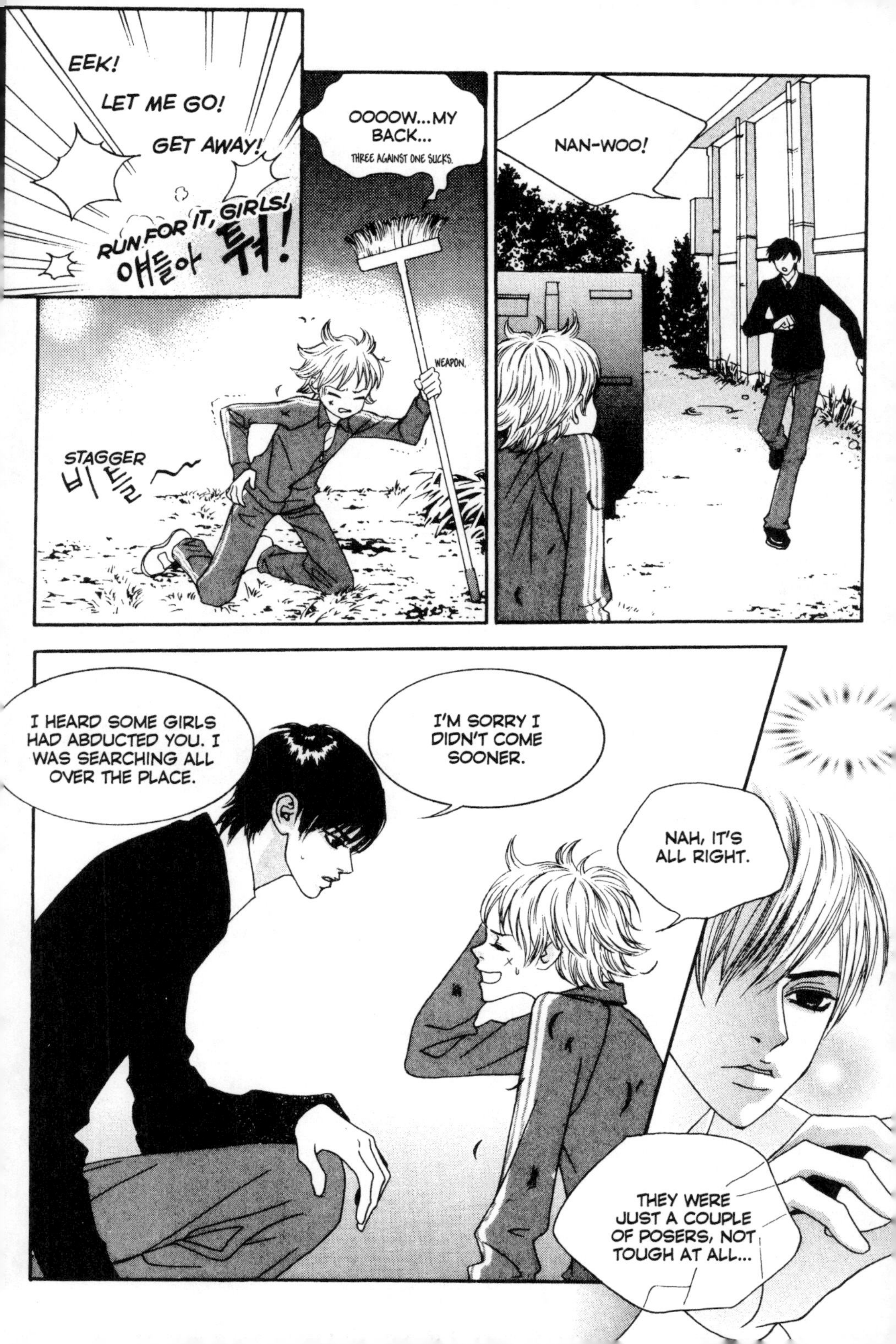
EEK!
LET ME GO!
GET AWAY!
RUN FOR IT, GIRLS!
얘들아 튀어!
OOOOW...MY BACK...
THREE AGAINST ONE SUCKS.
WEAPON.
STAGGER
비틀
NAN-WOO!
I HEARD SOME GIRLS HAD ABDUCTED YOU. I WAS SEARCHING ALL OVER THE PLACE.
I'M SORRY I DIDN'T COME SOONER.
NAH, IT'S ALL RIGHT.
THEY WERE JUST A COUPLE OF POSERS, NOT TOUGH AT ALL...

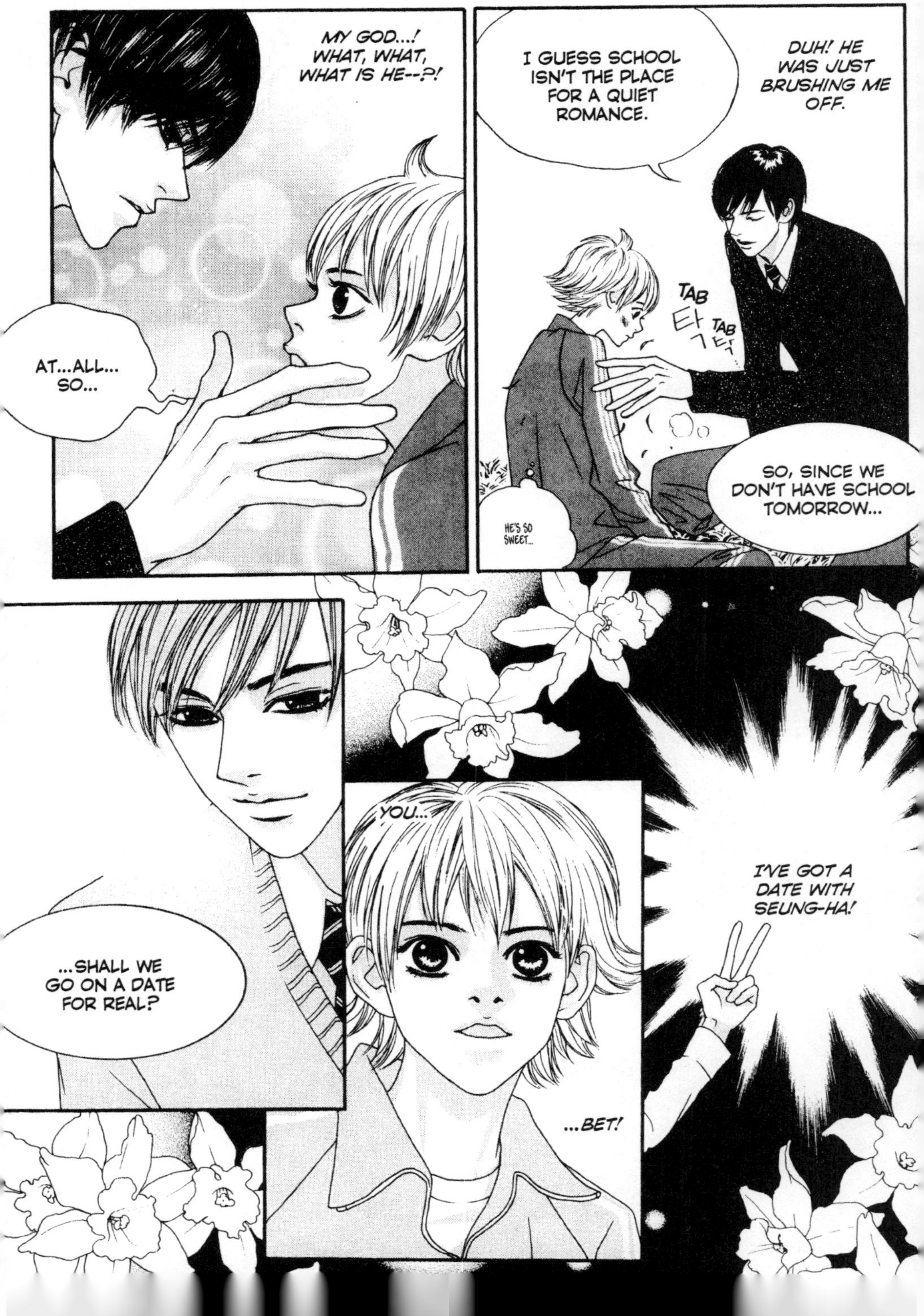
MY GOD...! WHAT, WHAT, WHAT IS HE--?!
AT...ALL... SO...
I GUESS SCHOOL ISN'T THE PLACE FOR A QUIET ROMANCE.
DUH! HE WAS JUST BRUSHING ME OFF.
TAB
타
TAB
닥
HE'S SO SWEET...
SO, SINCE WE DON'T HAVE SCHOOL TOMORROW...
...SHALL WE GO ON A DATE FOR REAL?
YOU...
...BET!
I'VE GOT A DATE WITH SEUNG-HA!

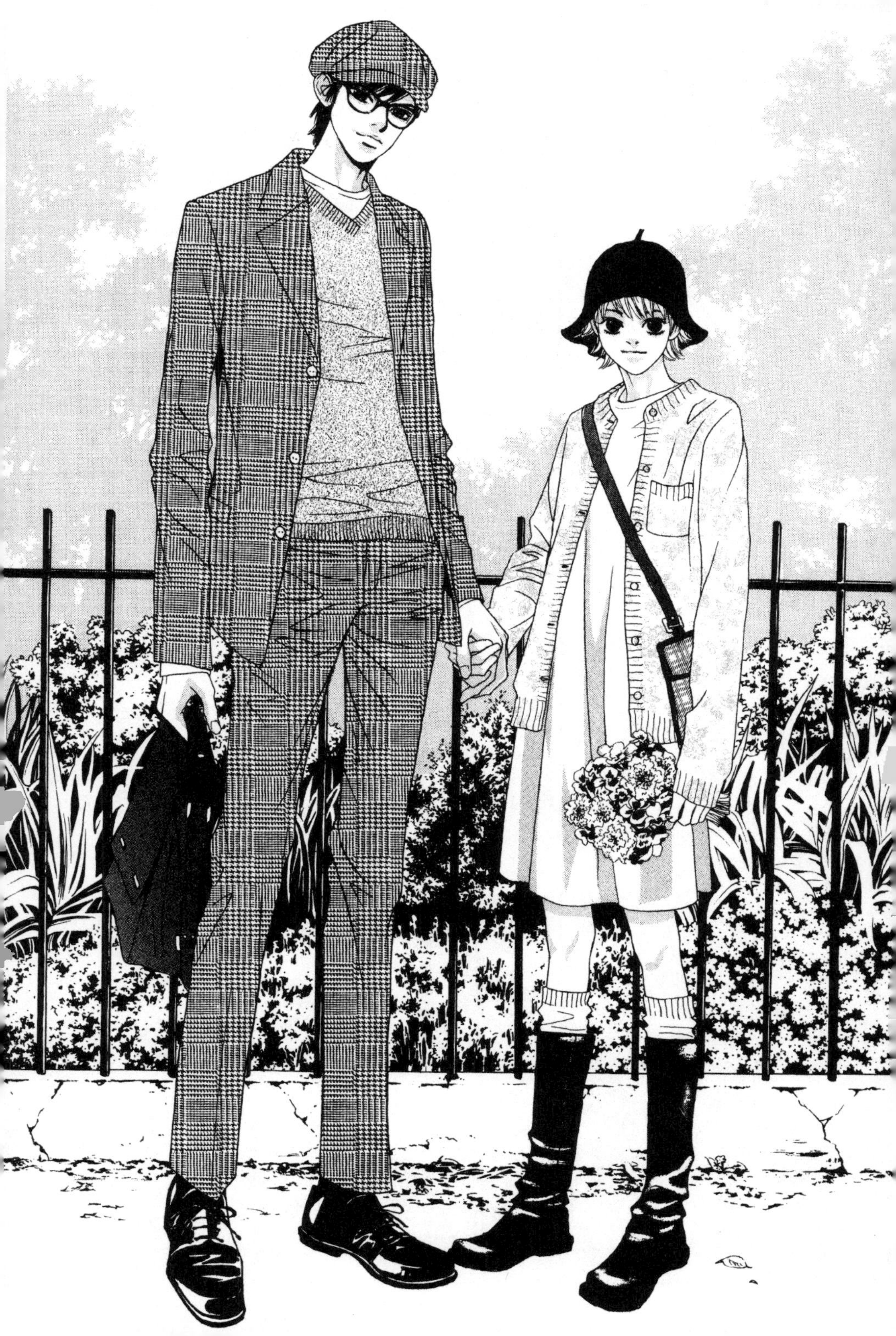

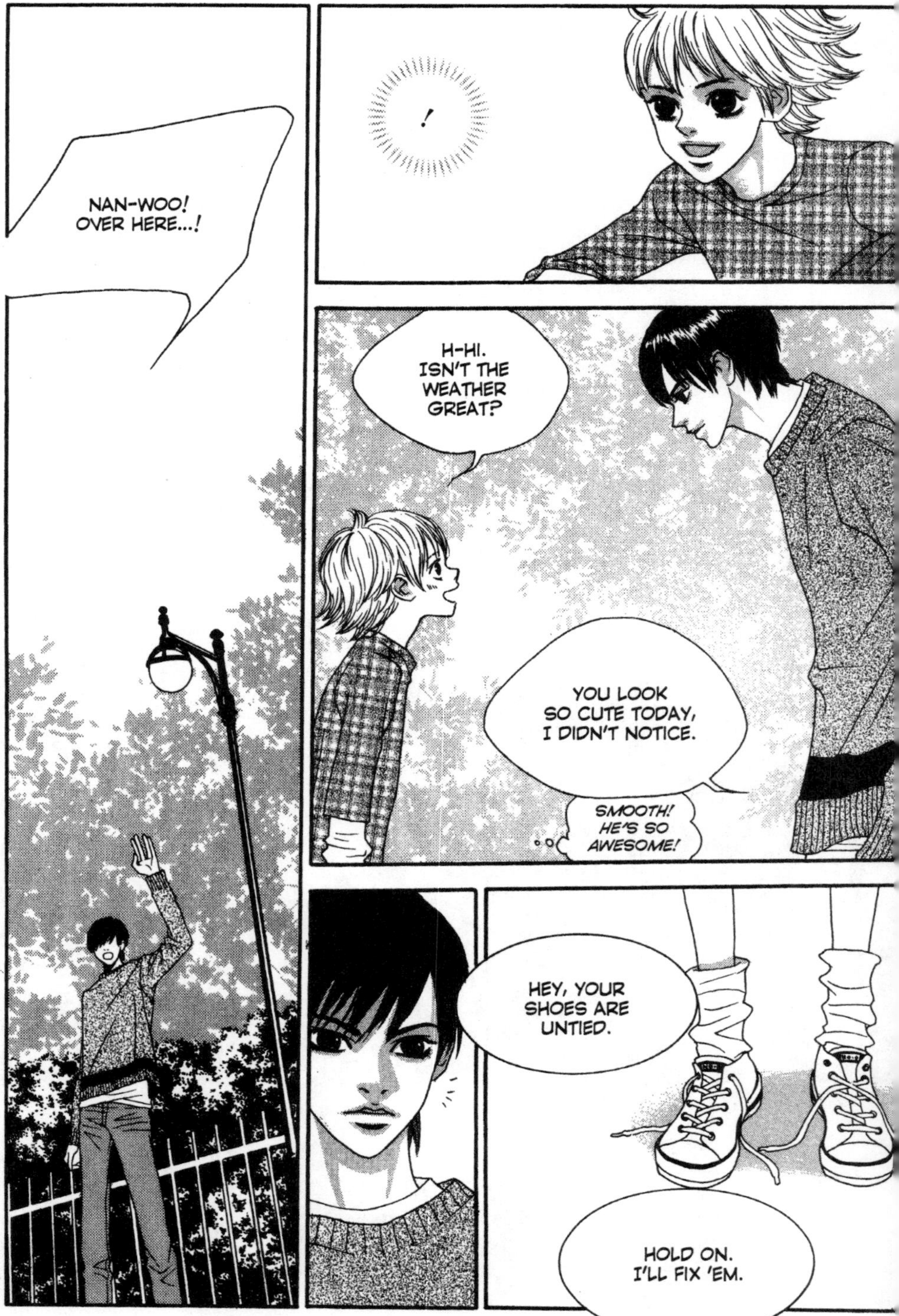
NAN-WOO! OVER HERE...!
!
H-HI. ISN'T THE WEATHER GREAT?
YOU LOOK SO CUTE TODAY, I DIDN'T NOTICE.
SMOOTH! HE'S SO AWESOME!
HEY, YOUR SHOES ARE UNTIED.
HOLD ON. I'LL FIX 'EM.

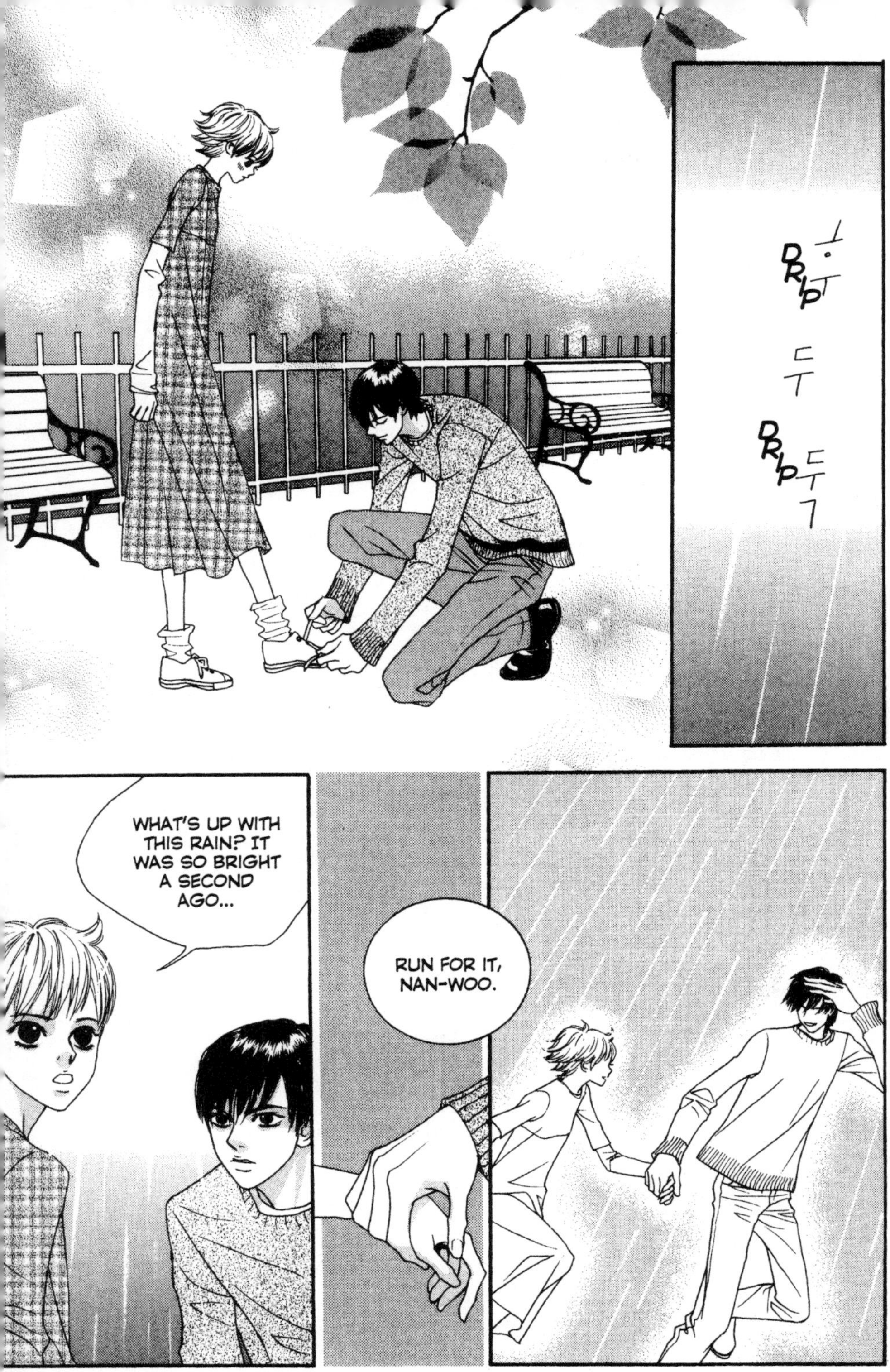
DRIP
DRIP
WHAT'S UP WITH THIS RAIN? IT WAS SO BRIGHT A SECOND AGO...
RUN FOR IT, NAN-WOO.

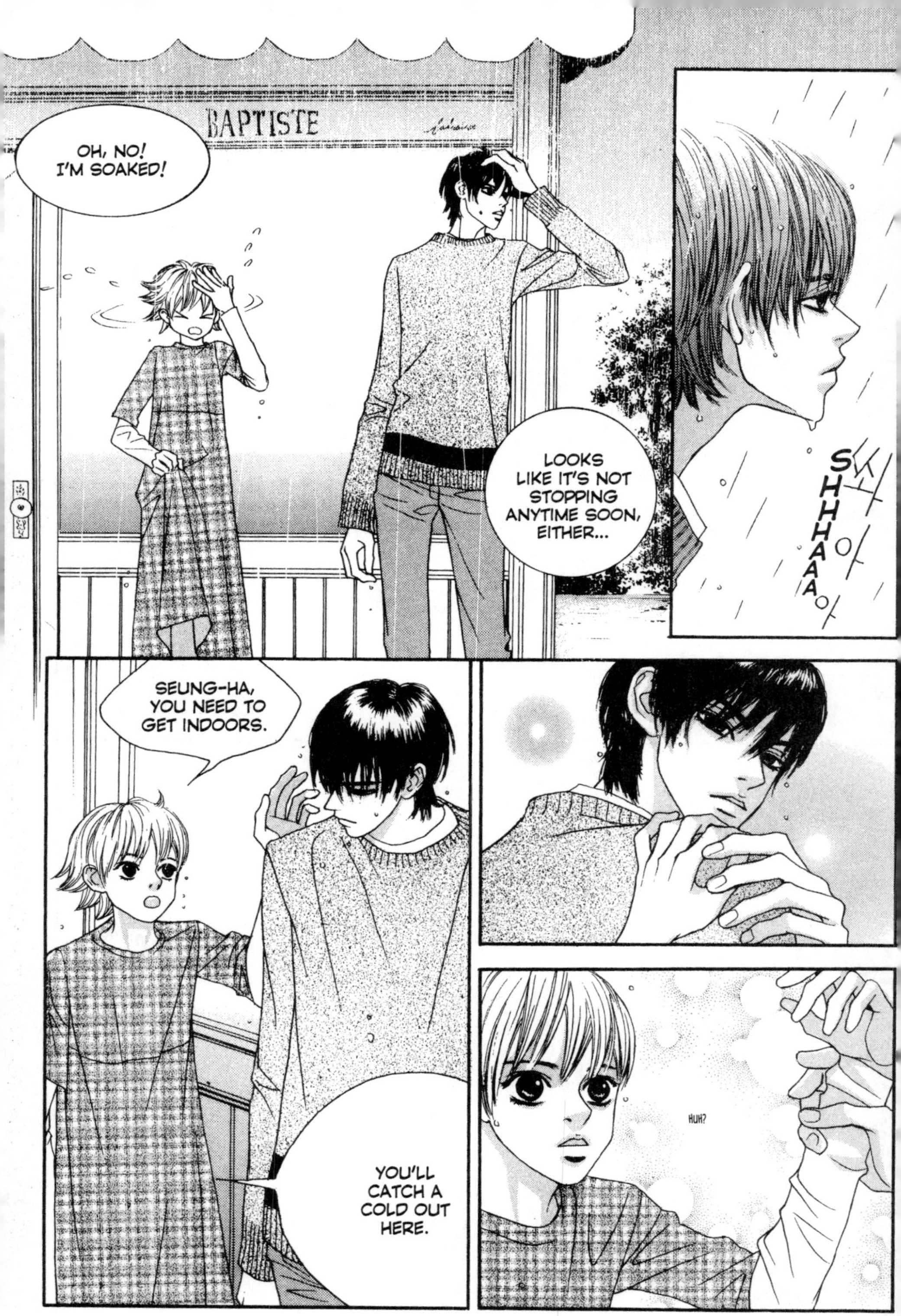
BAPTISTE
OH, NO! I'M SOAKED!
LOOKS LIKE IT'S NOT STOPPING ANYTIME SOON, EITHER...
SHHHAAA
SEUNG-HA, YOU NEED TO GET INDOORS.
YOU'LL CATCH A COLD OUT HERE.
HUH?

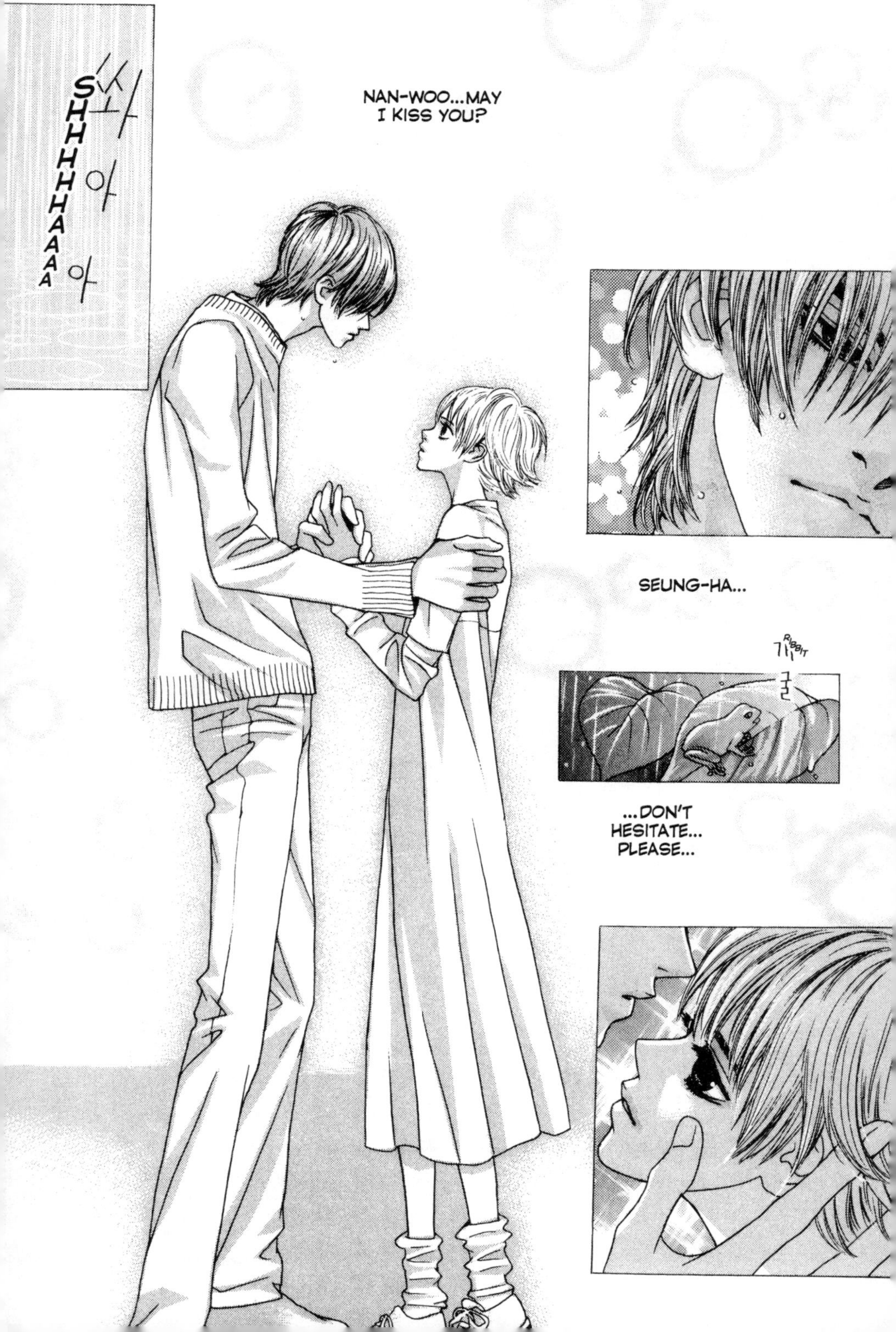
쏴아아
SHHHHHAAAA
NAN-WOO...MAY I KISS YOU?
SEUNG-HA...
개굴
RIBBIT
...DON'T HESITATE... PLEASE...

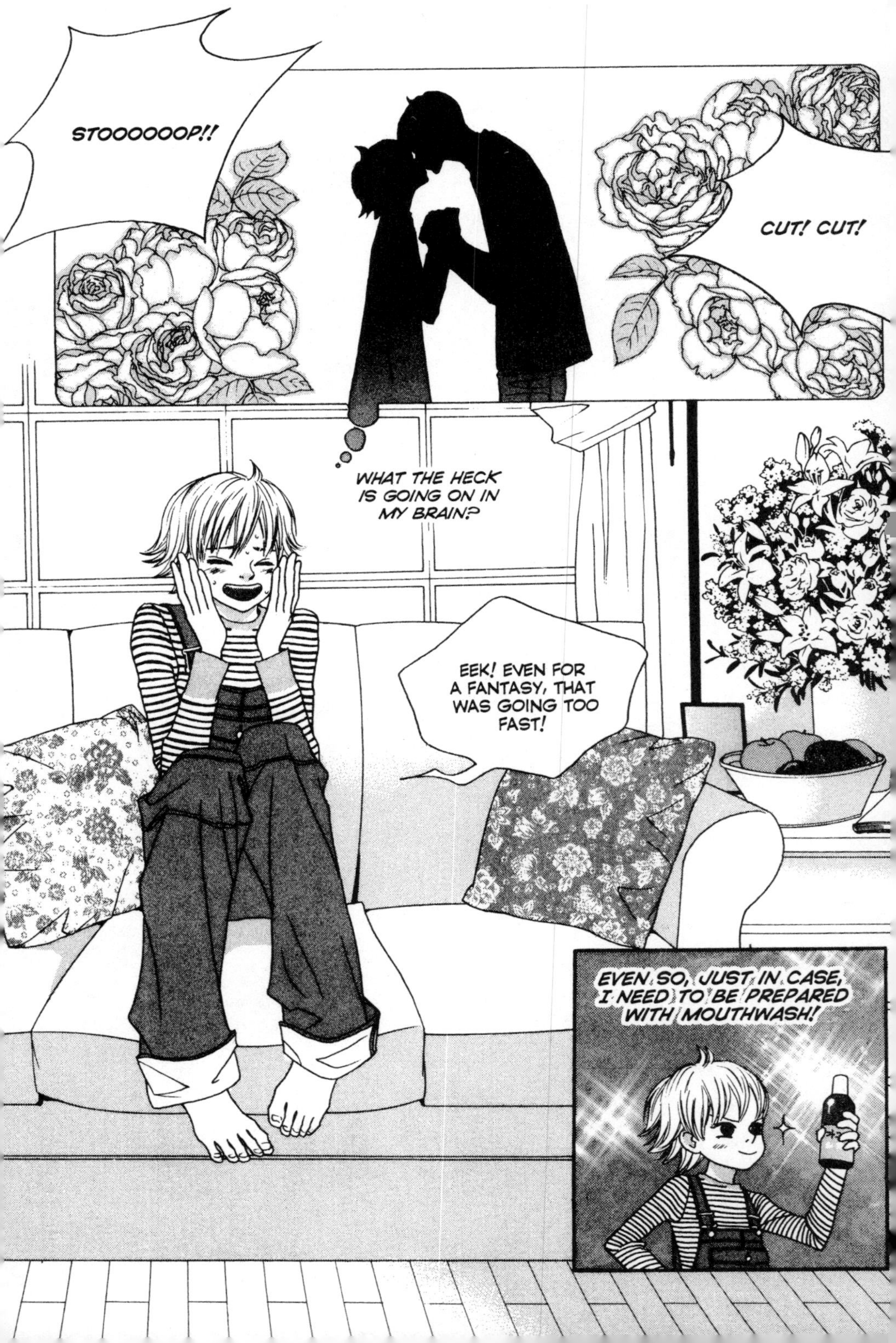
STOOOOOOP!!
CUT! CUT!
WHAT THE HECK IS GOING ON IN MY BRAIN?
EEK! EVEN FOR A FANTASY, THAT WAS GOING TOO FAST!
EVEN SO, JUST IN CASE, I NEED TO BE PREPARED WITH MOUTHWASH!

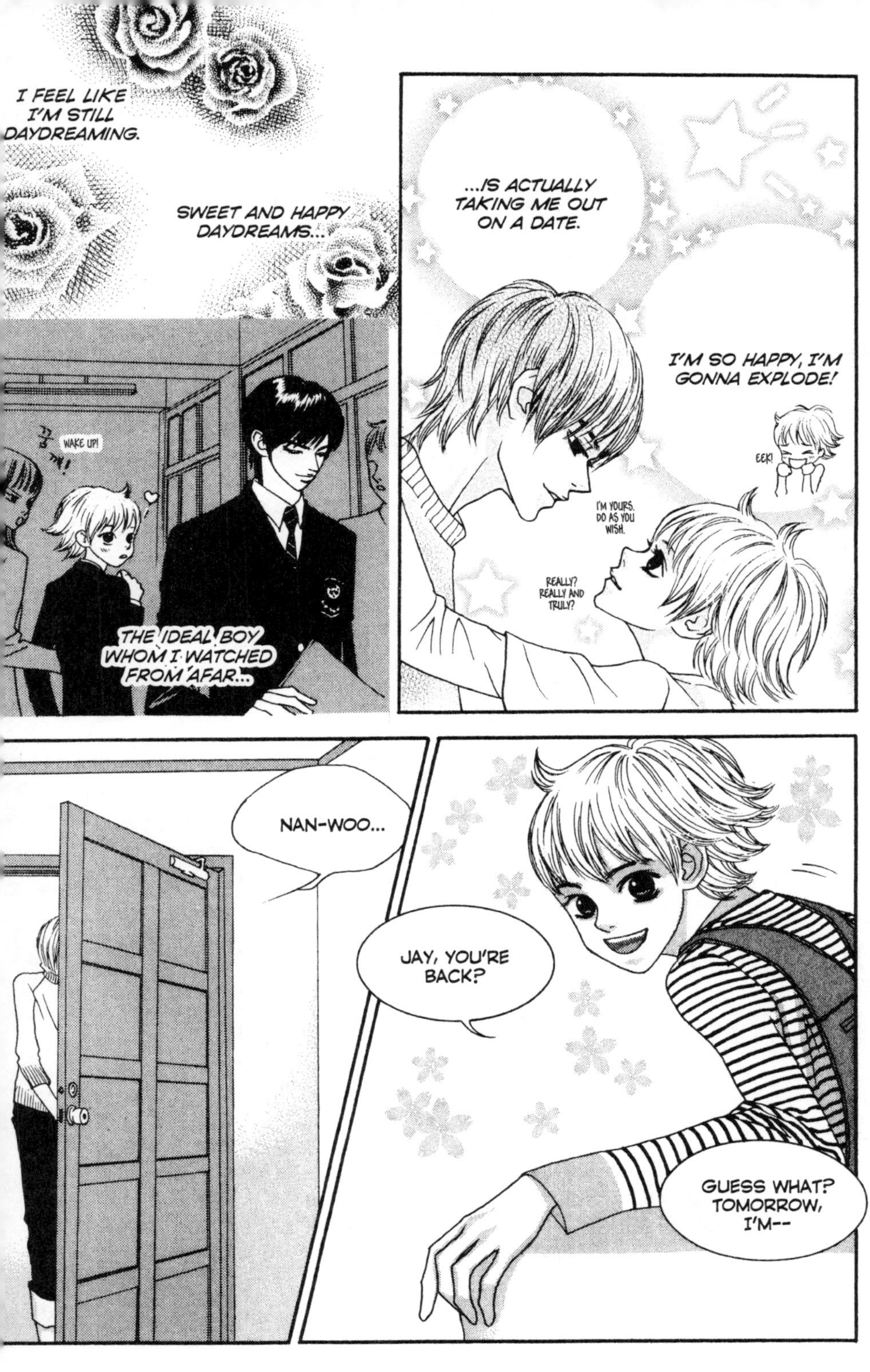

I FEEL LIKE I'M STILL DAYDREAMING.
SWEET AND HAPPY DAYDREAMS...
WAKE UP!
THE IDEAL BOY WHOM I WATCHED FROM AFAR...
...IS ACTUALLY TAKING ME OUT ON A DATE.
I'M SO HAPPY, I'M GONNA EXPLODE!
EEK!
I'M YOURS. DO AS YOU WISH.
REALLY? REALLY AND TRULY?
NAN-WOO...
JAY, YOU'RE BACK?
GUESS WHAT? TOMORROW, I'M--

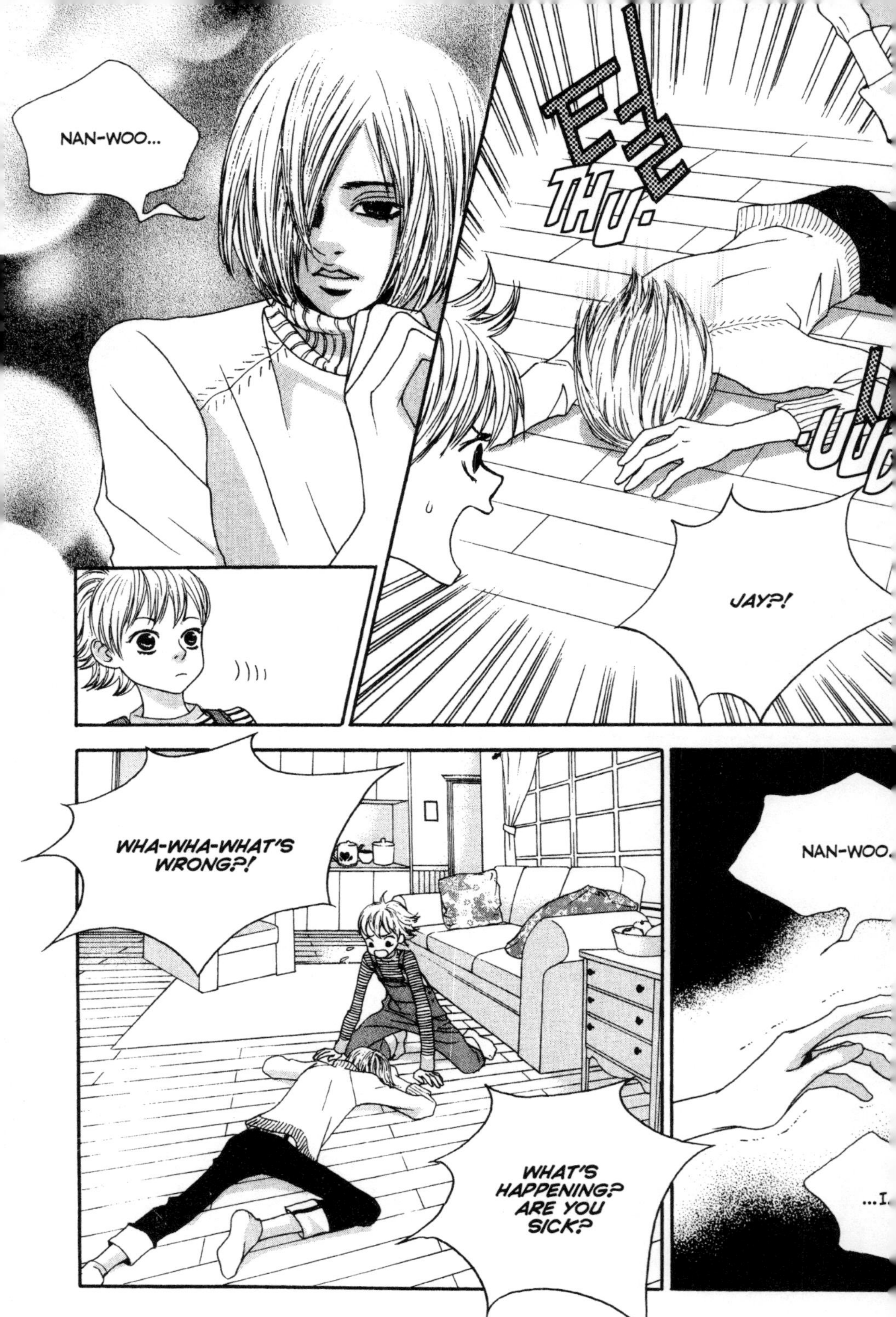
NAN-WOO...
털썩
THU.
.UUD
JAY?!
WHA-WHA-WHAT'S WRONG?!
WHAT'S HAPPENING? ARE YOU SICK?
NAN-WOO.
...I.

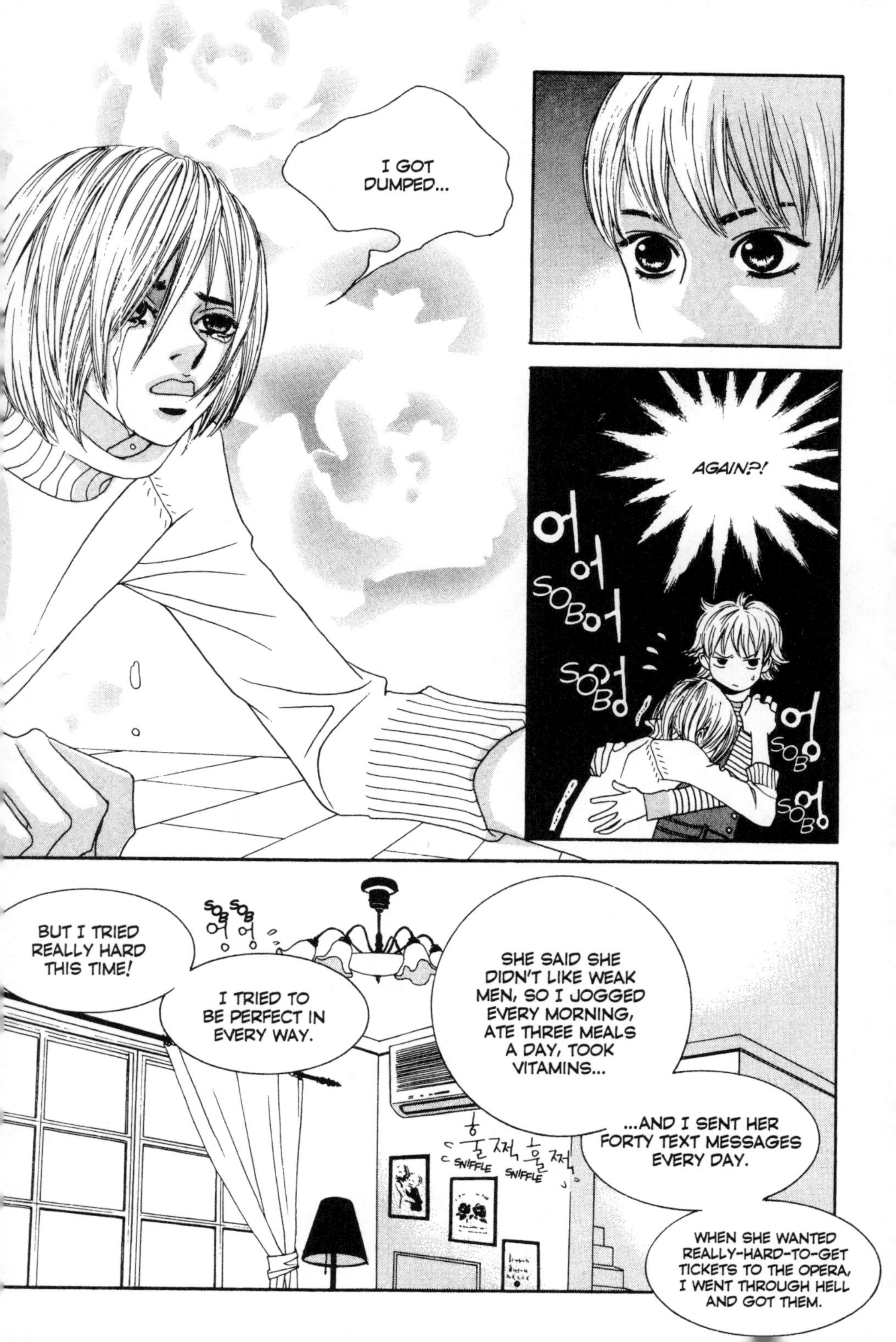

I GOT DUMPED...
AGAIN?!
어어어엉 SOB SOB
엉엉 SOB SOB
BUT I TRIED REALLY HARD THIS TIME!
SOB SOB 어엉
I TRIED TO BE PERFECT IN EVERY WAY.
SHE SAID SHE DIDN'T LIKE WEAK MEN, SO I JOGGED EVERY MORNING, ATE THREE MEALS A DAY, TOOK VITAMINS...
훌쩍 훌쩍 SNIFFLE SNIFFLE
...AND I SENT HER FORTY TEXT MESSAGES EVERY DAY.
WHEN SHE WANTED REALLY-HARD-TO-GET TICKETS TO THE OPERA, I WENT THROUGH HELL AND GOT THEM.

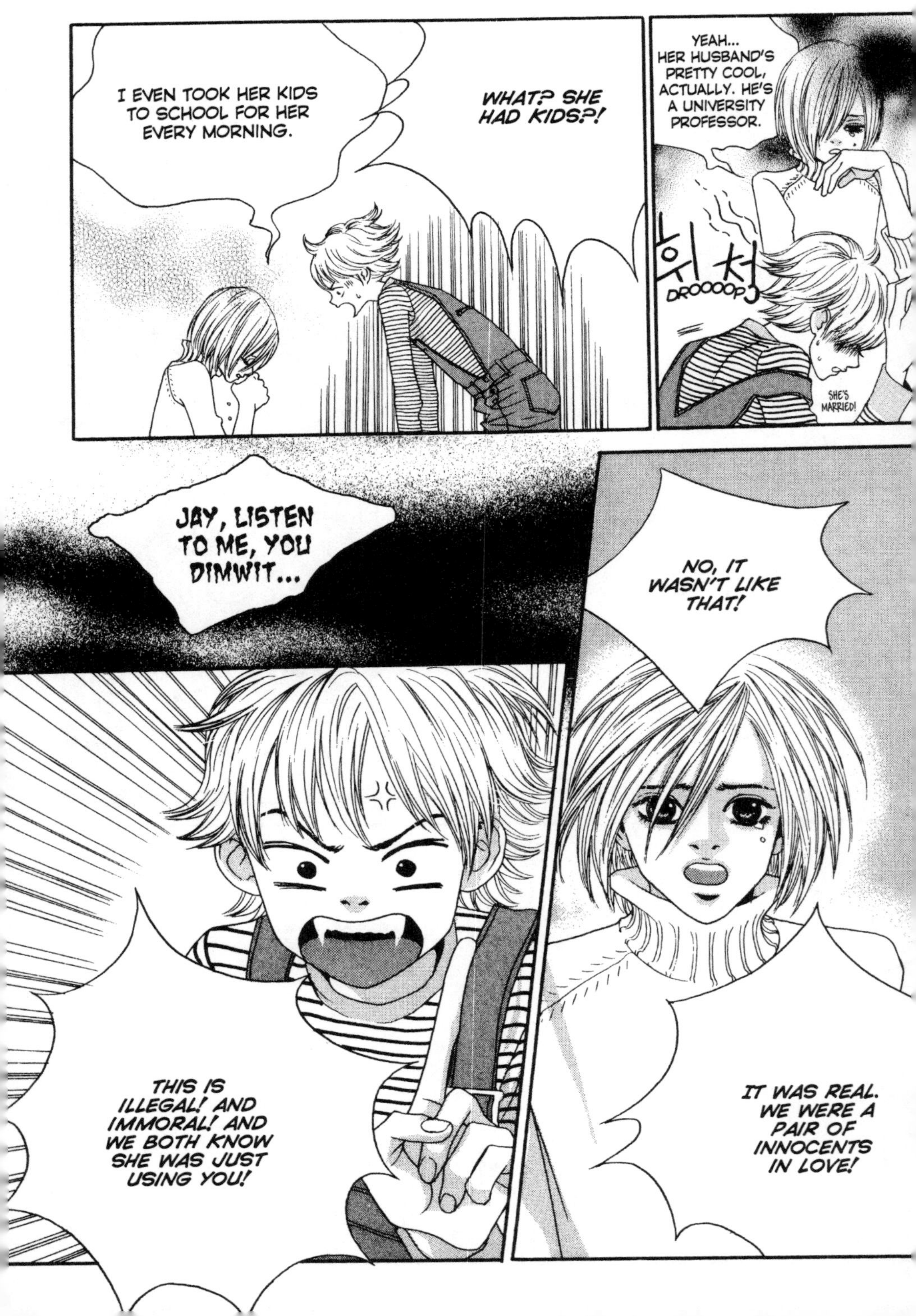

I EVEN TOOK HER KIDS TO SCHOOL FOR HER EVERY MORNING.
WHAT? SHE HAD KIDS?!
YEAH... HER HUSBAND'S PRETTY COOL, ACTUALLY. HE'S A UNIVERSITY PROFESSOR.
휘청
DROOOOP
SHE'S MARRIED!
JAY, LISTEN TO ME, YOU DIMWIT...
NO, IT WASN'T LIKE THAT!
THIS IS ILLEGAL! AND IMMORAL! AND WE BOTH KNOW SHE WAS JUST USING YOU!
IT WAS REAL. WE WERE A PAIR OF INNOCENTS IN LOVE!

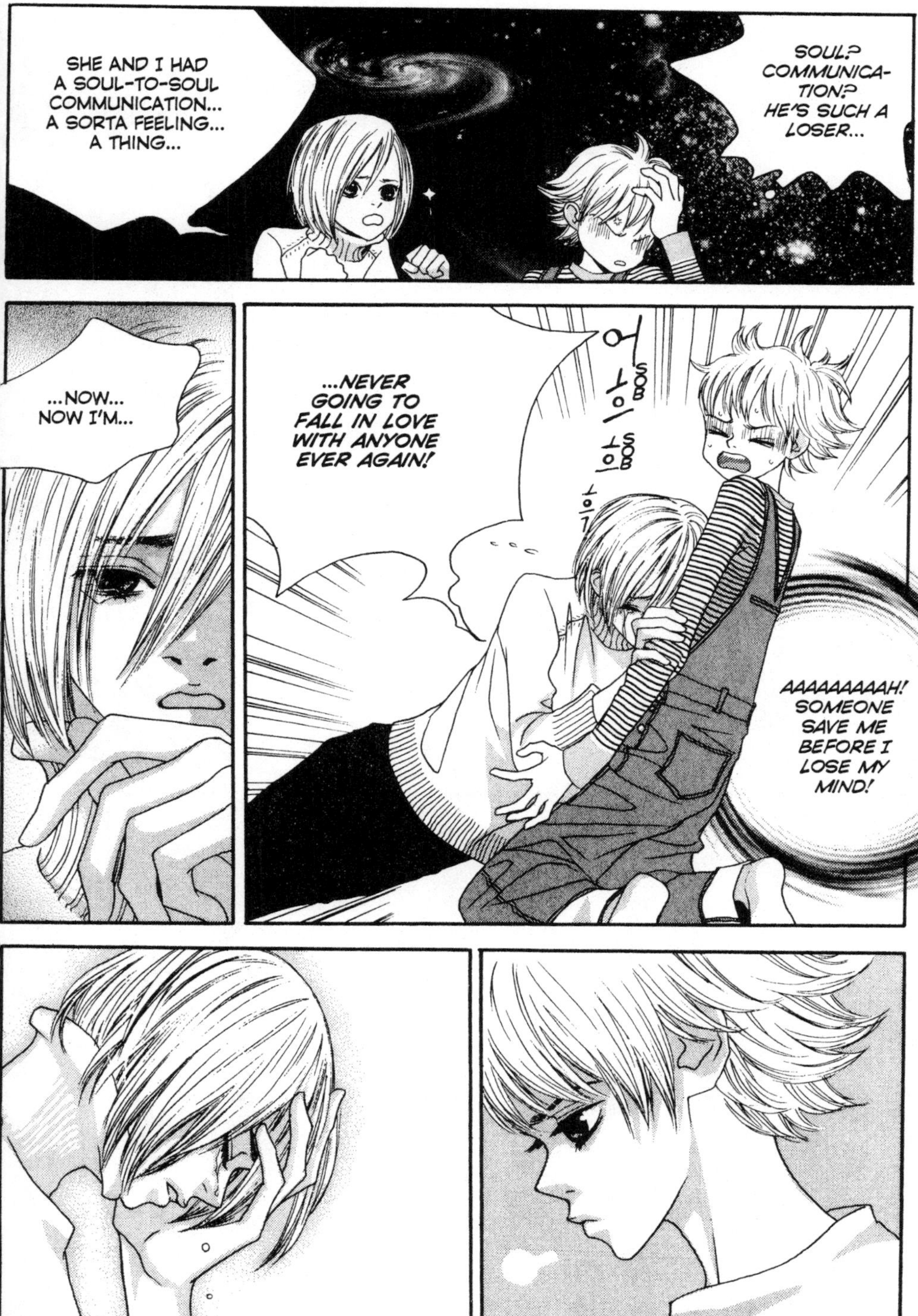
SHE AND I HAD A SOUL-TO-SOUL COMMUNICATION... A SORTA FEELING... A THING...
SOUL? COMMUNICATION? HE'S SUCH A LOSER...
...NOW... NOW I'M...
...NEVER GOING TO FALL IN LOVE WITH ANYONE EVER AGAIN!
SOB
SOB
AAAAAAAAAH! SOMEONE SAVE ME BEFORE I LOSE MY MIND!

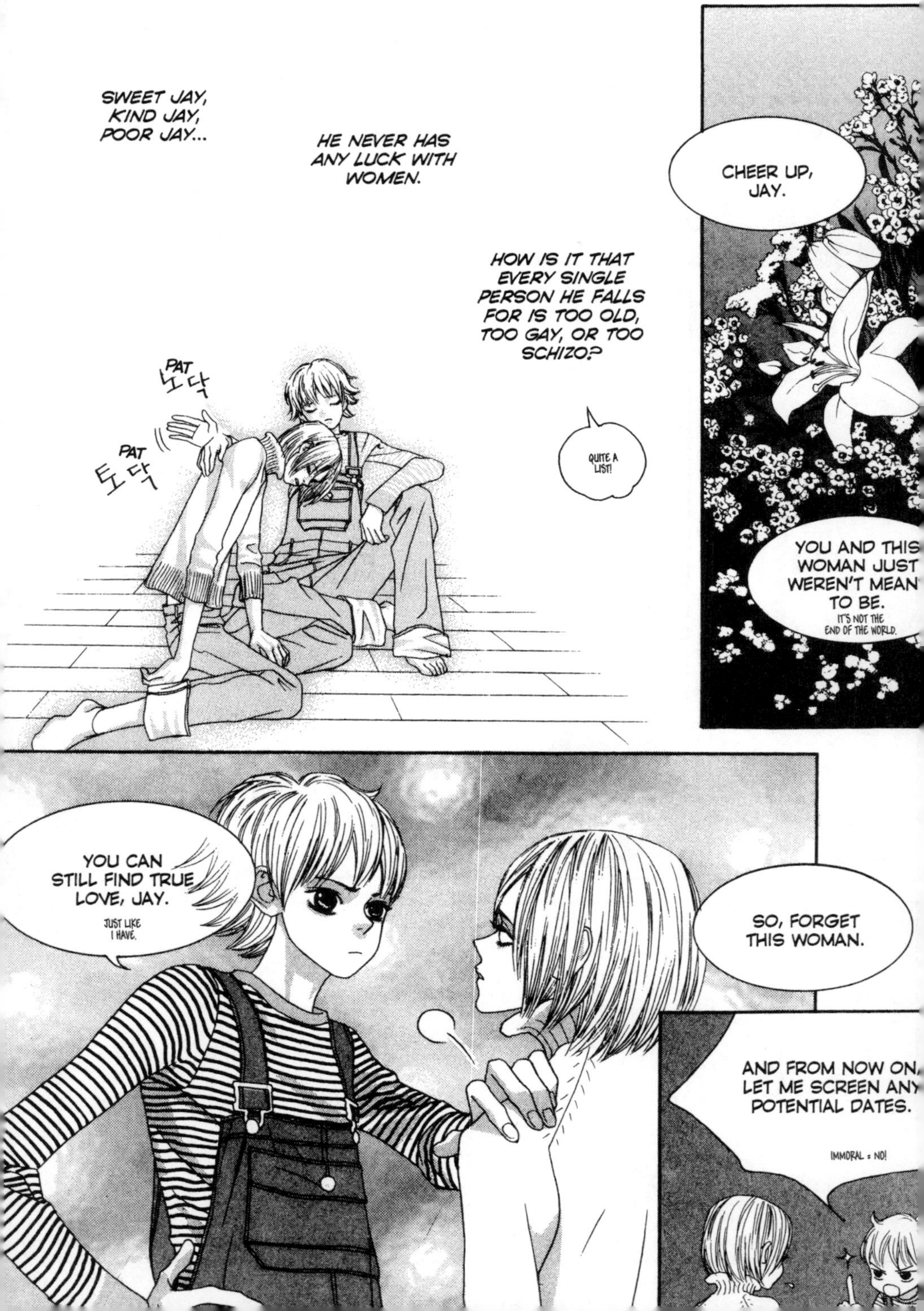
SWEET JAY, KIND JAY, POOR JAY...
HE NEVER HAS ANY LUCK WITH WOMEN.
HOW IS IT THAT EVERY SINGLE PERSON HE FALLS FOR IS TOO OLD, TOO GAY, OR TOO SCHIZO?
PAT
PAT
토닥
QUITE A LIST!
CHEER UP, JAY.
YOU AND THIS WOMAN JUST WEREN'T MEANT TO BE.
IT'S NOT THE END OF THE WORLD.
YOU CAN STILL FIND TRUE LOVE, JAY.
JUST LIKE I HAVE.
SO, FORGET THIS WOMAN.
AND FROM NOW ON, LET ME SCREEN ANY POTENTIAL DATES.
IMMORAL = NO!

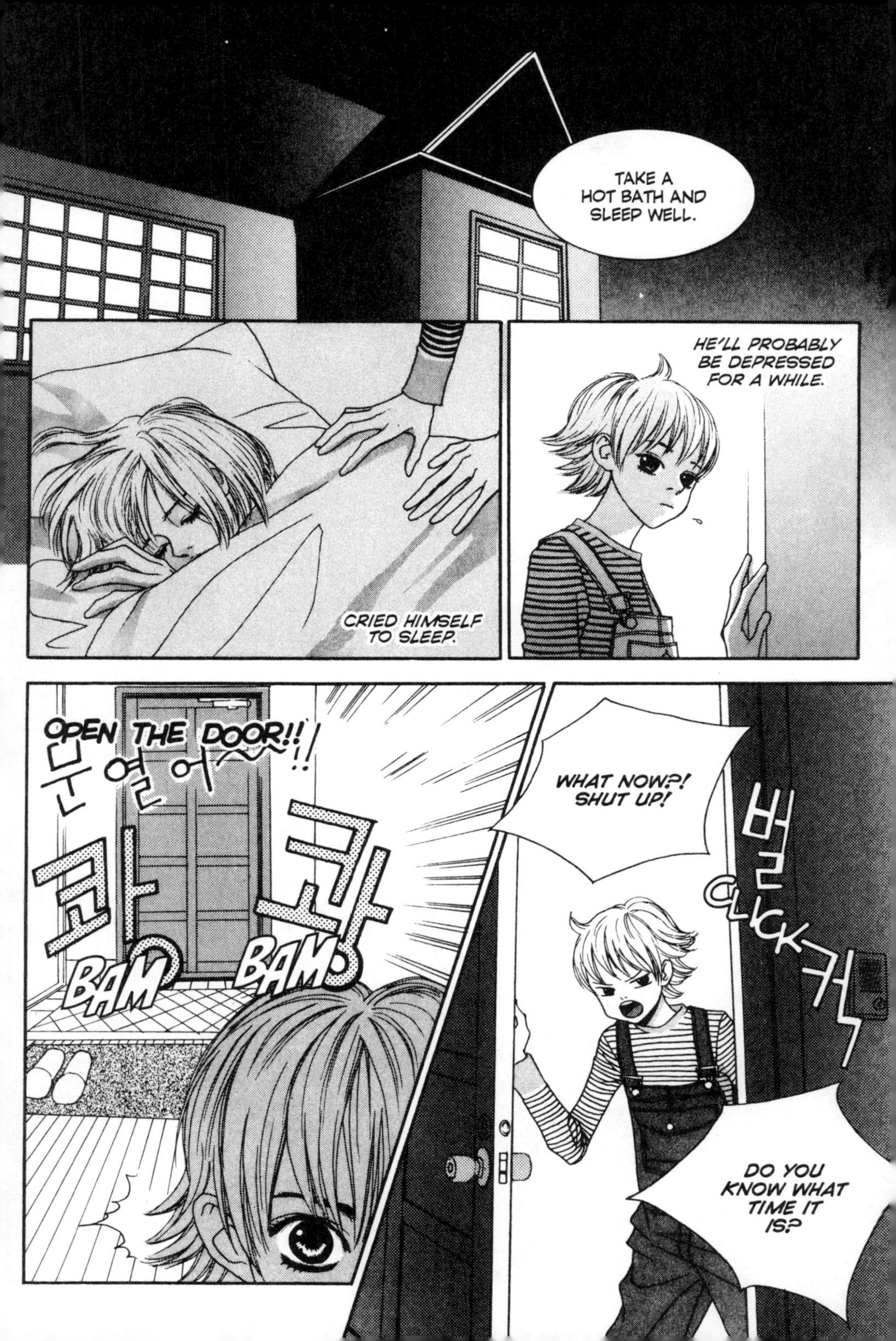
TAKE A HOT BATH AND SLEEP WELL.
CRIED HIMSELF TO SLEEP.
HE'LL PROBABLY BE DEPRESSED FOR A WHILE.
OPEN THE DOOR!!
문 열어~!!
쾅 쾅
BAM BAM
WHAT NOW?! SHUT UP!
벌컥
CLICK
DO YOU KNOW WHAT TIME IT IS?

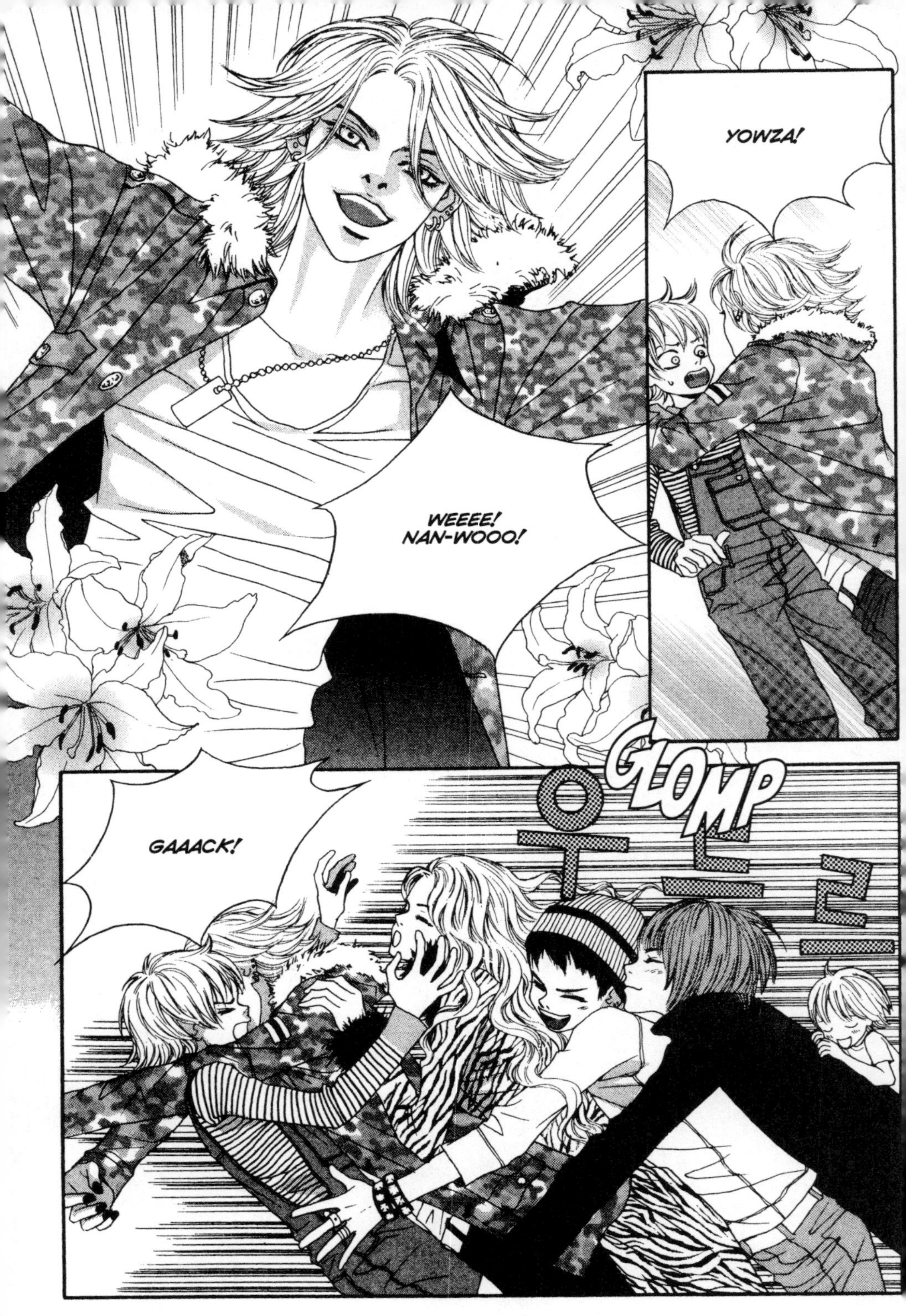
WEEEE! NAN-WOOO!
YOWZA!
GAAACK!
GLOMP

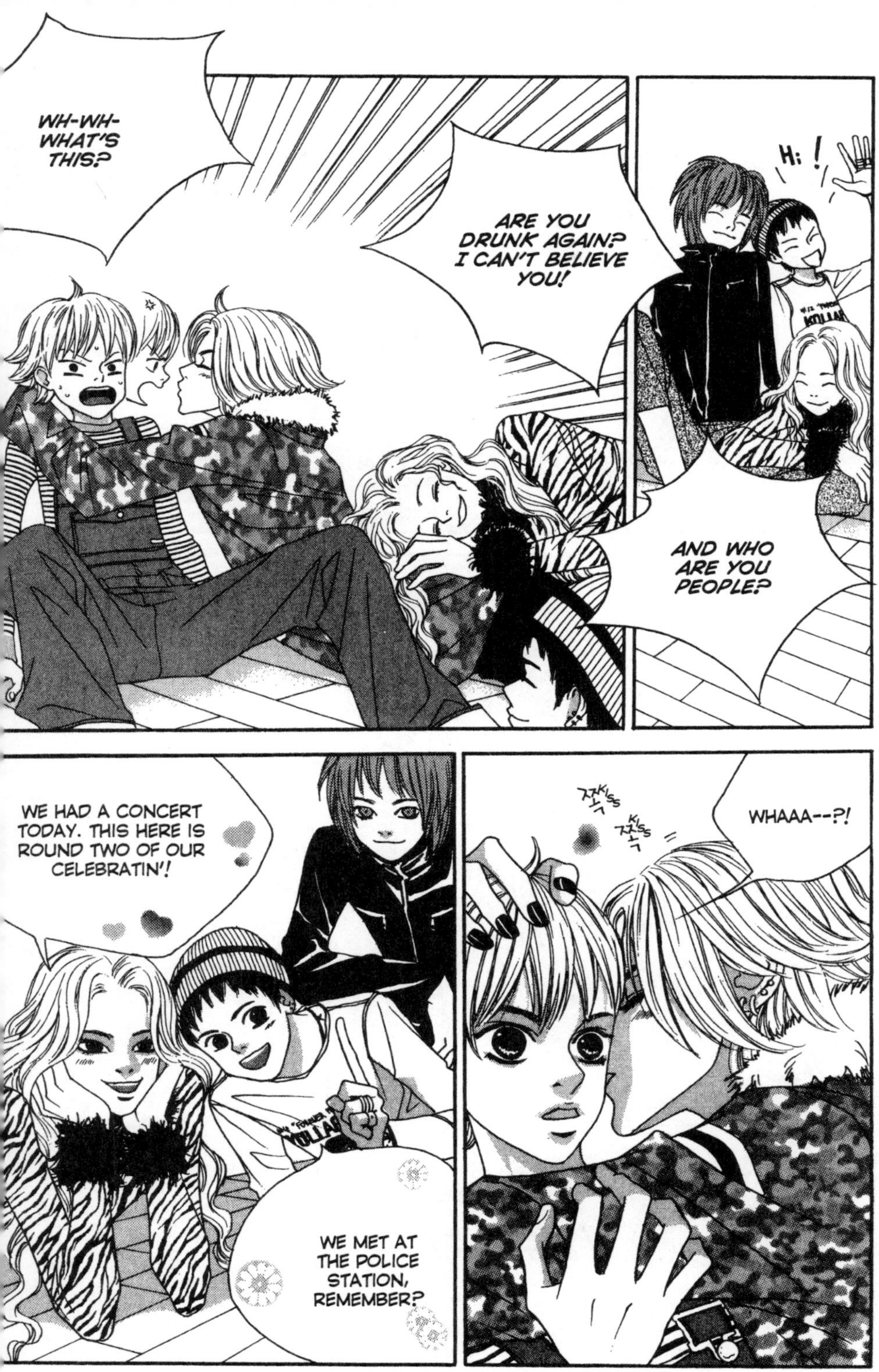
WH-WH-WHAT'S THIS?
ARE YOU DRUNK AGAIN? I CAN'T BELIEVE YOU!
Hi!
AND WHO ARE YOU PEOPLE?
WE HAD A CONCERT TODAY. THIS HERE IS ROUND TWO OF OUR CELEBRATIN'!
WE MET AT THE POLICE STATION, REMEMBER?
KISS
KISS
WHAAA--?!

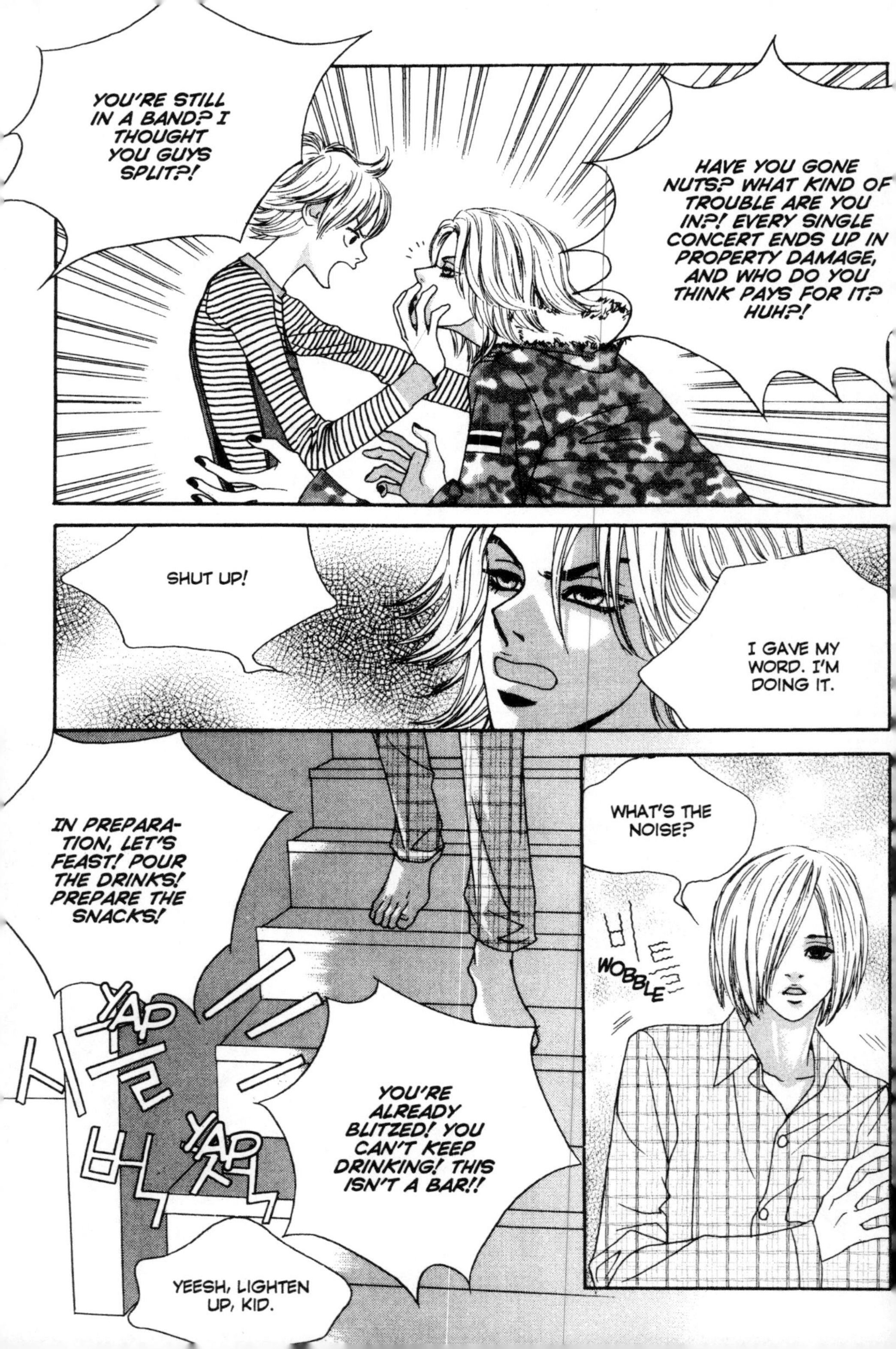
YOU'RE STILL IN A BAND? I THOUGHT YOU GUYS SPLIT?!
HAVE YOU GONE NUTS? WHAT KIND OF TROUBLE ARE YOU IN?! EVERY SINGLE CONCERT ENDS UP IN PROPERTY DAMAGE, AND WHO DO YOU THINK PAYS FOR IT? HUH?!
SHUT UP!
I GAVE MY WORD. I'M DOING IT.
IN PREPARA-TION, LET'S FEAST! POUR THE DRINKS! PREPARE THE SNACKS!
YAP
YAP
YOU'RE ALREADY BLITZED! YOU CAN'T KEEP DRINKING! THIS ISN'T A BAR!!
YEESH, LIGHTEN UP, KID.
WHAT'S THE NOISE?
WOBBLE

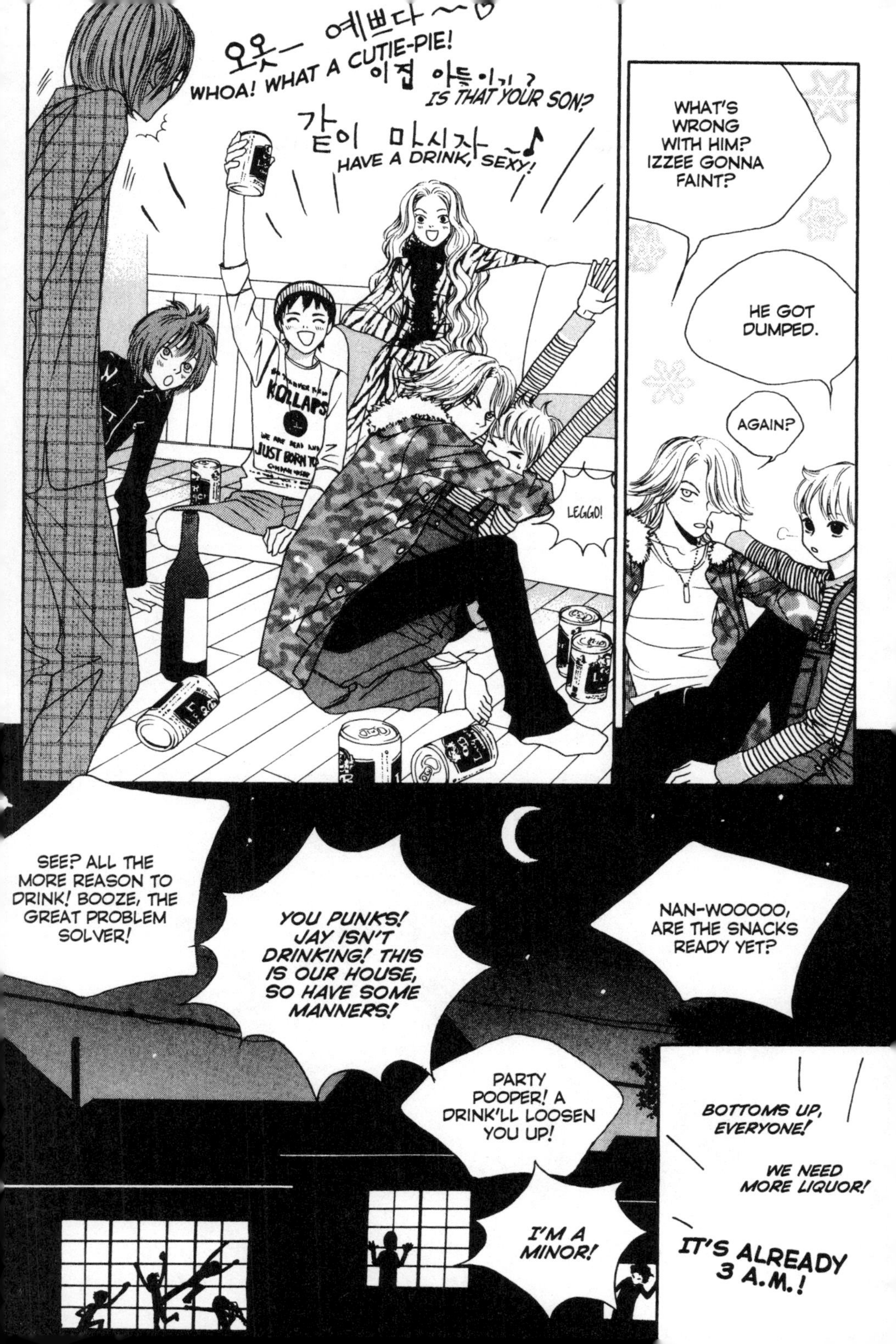
오옷— 예쁘다~~♡
WHOA! WHAT A CUTIE-PIE!
이집 아들이가?
IS THAT YOUR SON?
같이 마시자~♪
HAVE A DRINK, SEXY!
LEGGO!
WHAT'S WRONG WITH HIM? IZZEE GONNA FAINT?
HE GOT DUMPED.
AGAIN?
SEE? ALL THE MORE REASON TO DRINK! BOOZE, THE GREAT PROBLEM SOLVER!
YOU PUNKS! JAY ISN'T DRINKING! THIS IS OUR HOUSE, SO HAVE SOME MANNERS!
NAN-WOOOOO, ARE THE SNACKS READY YET?
PARTY POOPER! A DRINK'LL LOOSEN YOU UP!
I'M A MINOR!
BOTTOMS UP, EVERYONE!
WE NEED MORE LIQUOR!
IT'S ALREADY 3 A.M.!

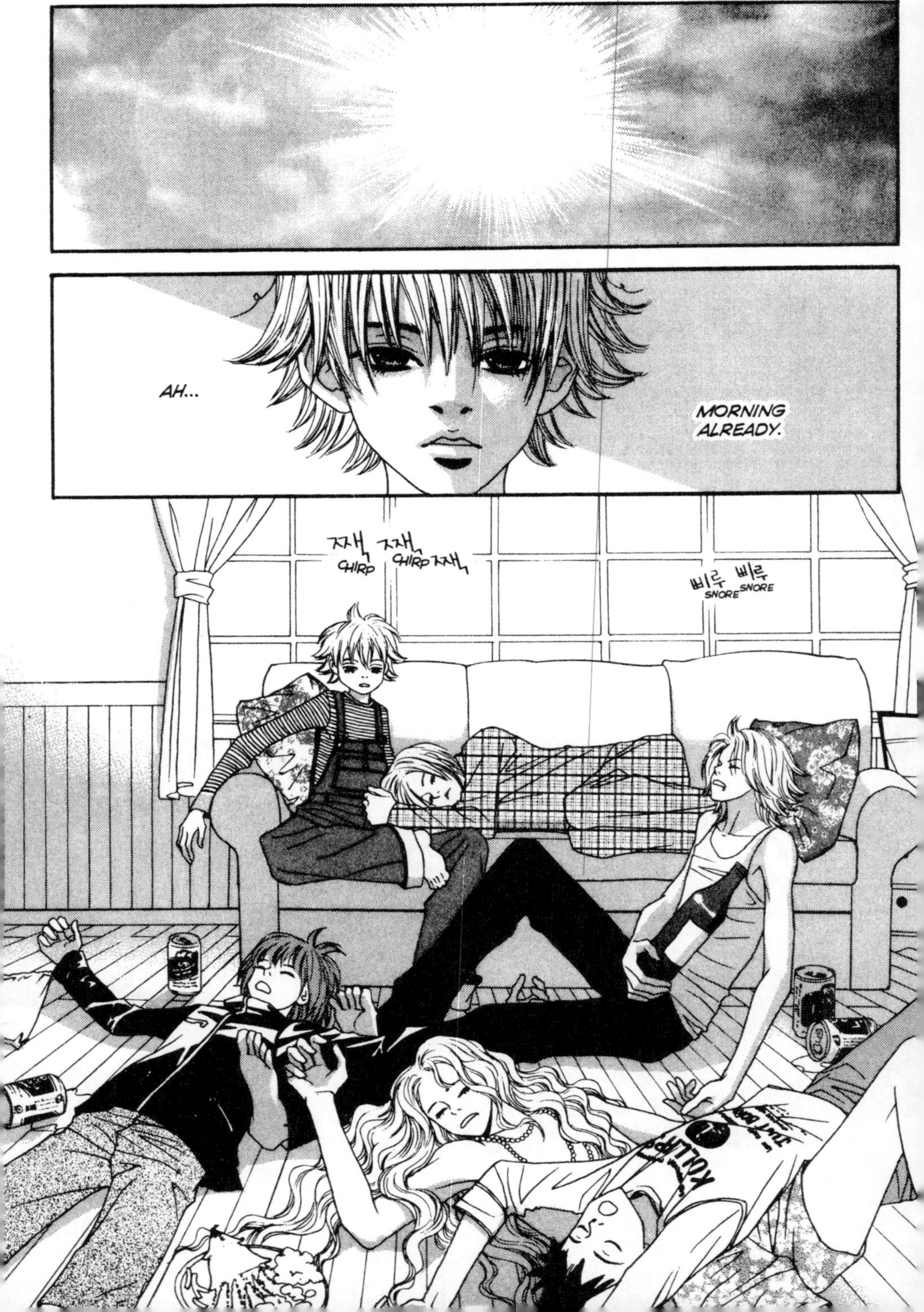
AH...
MORNING ALREADY.
짹 짹
CHIRP CHIRP 짹
삐루 삐루
SNORE SNORE

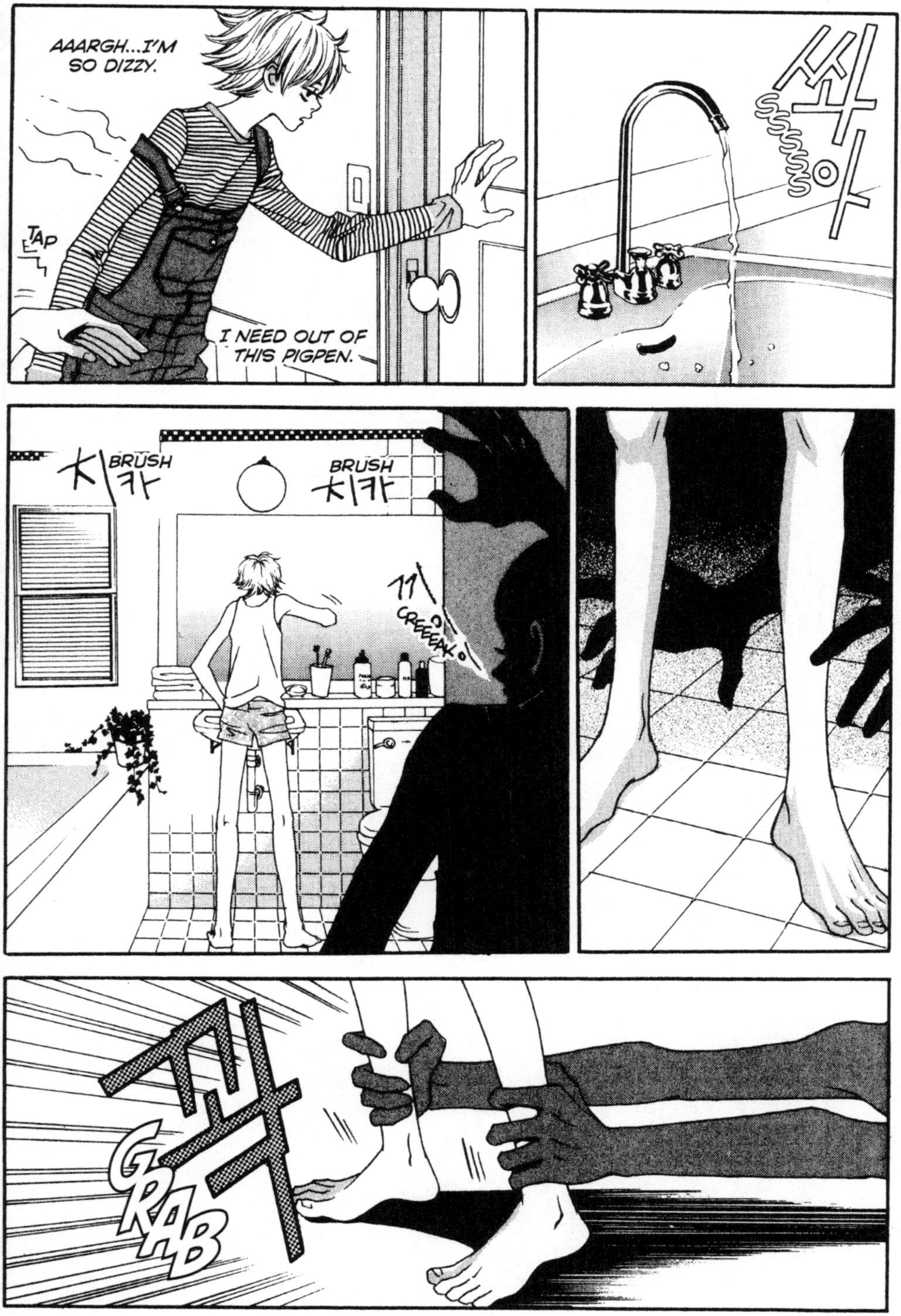
AAARGH...I'M SO DIZZY.
TAP
I NEED OUT OF THIS PIGPEN.
쏴아
SSSSS
치카 BRUSH
BRUSH 치카
CREEEAK
GRAB

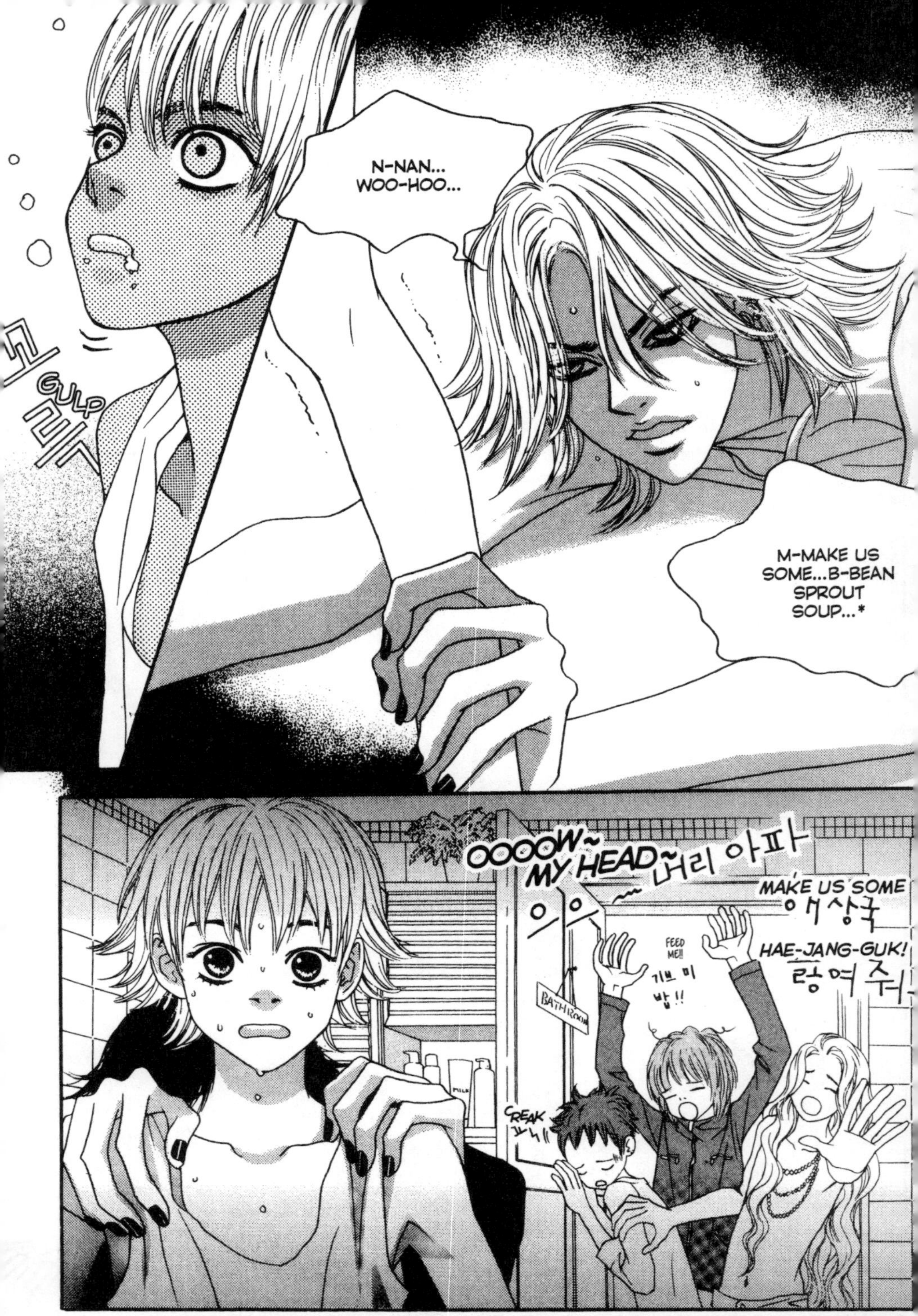
GULP
N-NAN... WOO-HOO...
M-MAKE US SOME...B-BEAN SPROUT SOUP...*
OOOOW~ MY HEAD~
MAKE US SOME
HAE-JANG-GUK!
FEED ME!!
기브 미 밥!!
BATHROOM
CREAK
MILK

* EDITOR'S NOTE: IT HAS BEEN SCIENTIFICALLY PROVEN THAT OF ALL THE TRADITIONAL KOREAN FOOD, BEAN SPROUT STEW AND HAE-JANG-GUK (STEW MADE FROM RARE BEEF AND COOKED BLOOD) ARE THE BEST FOR CURING HANGOVERS.

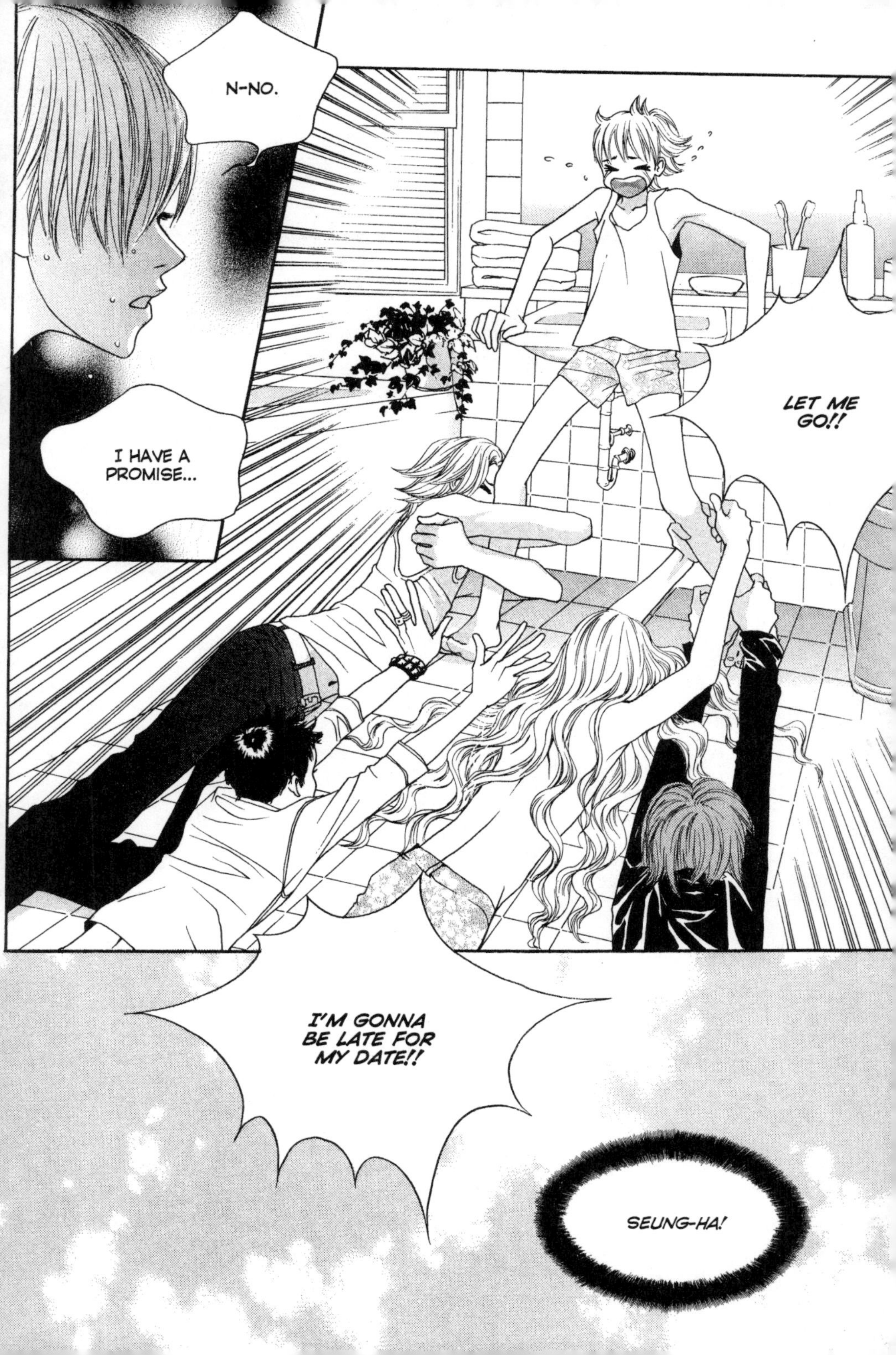
N-NO.
I HAVE A PROMISE...
LET ME GO!!
I'M GONNA BE LATE FOR MY DATE!!
SEUNG-HA!

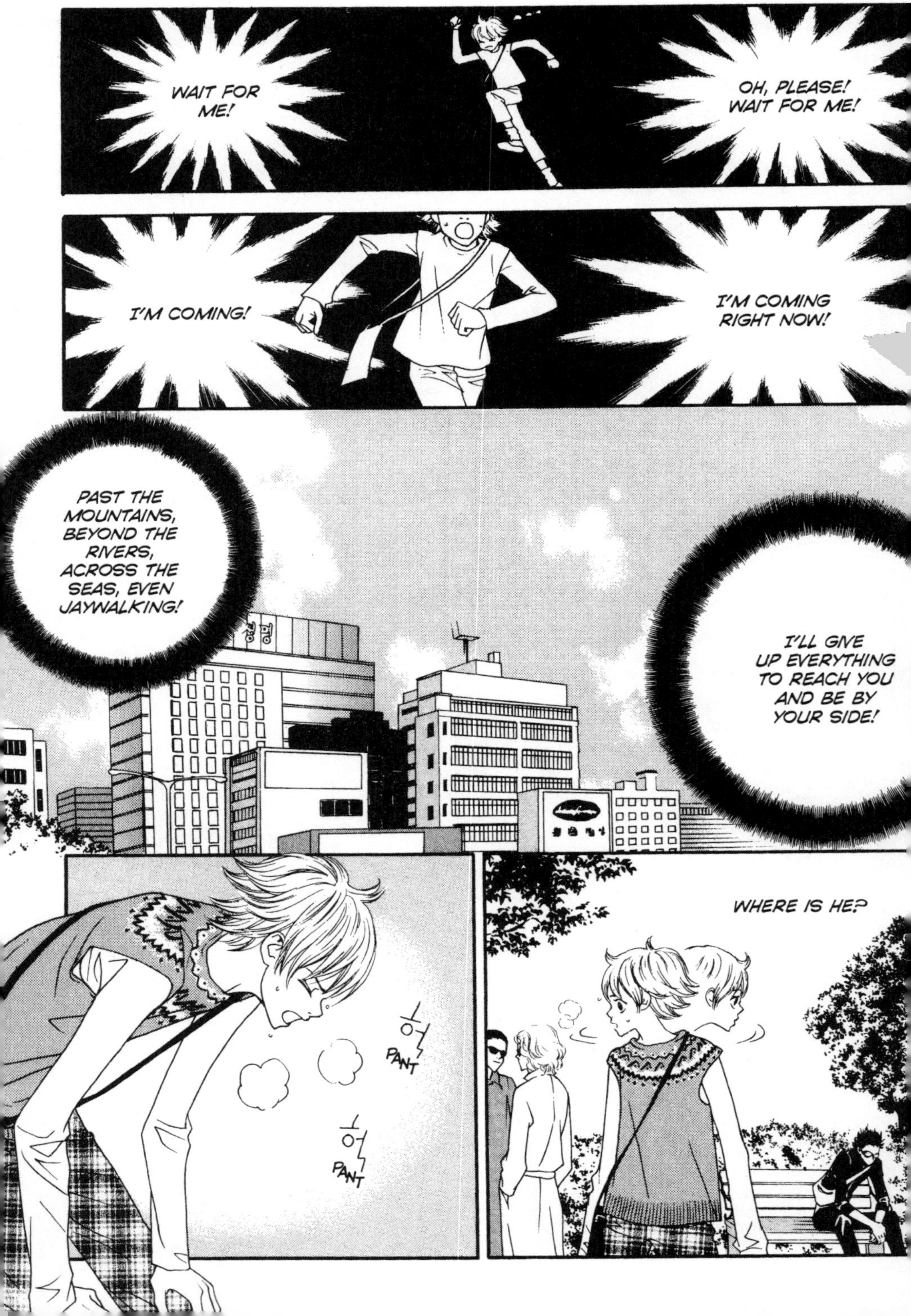
WAIT FOR ME!
OH, PLEASE! WAIT FOR ME!
I'M COMING!
I'M COMING RIGHT NOW!
PAST THE MOUNTAINS, BEYOND THE RIVERS, ACROSS THE SEAS, EVEN JAYWALKING!
I'LL GIVE UP EVERYTHING TO REACH YOU AND BE BY YOUR SIDE!
PANT
PANT
WHERE IS HE?

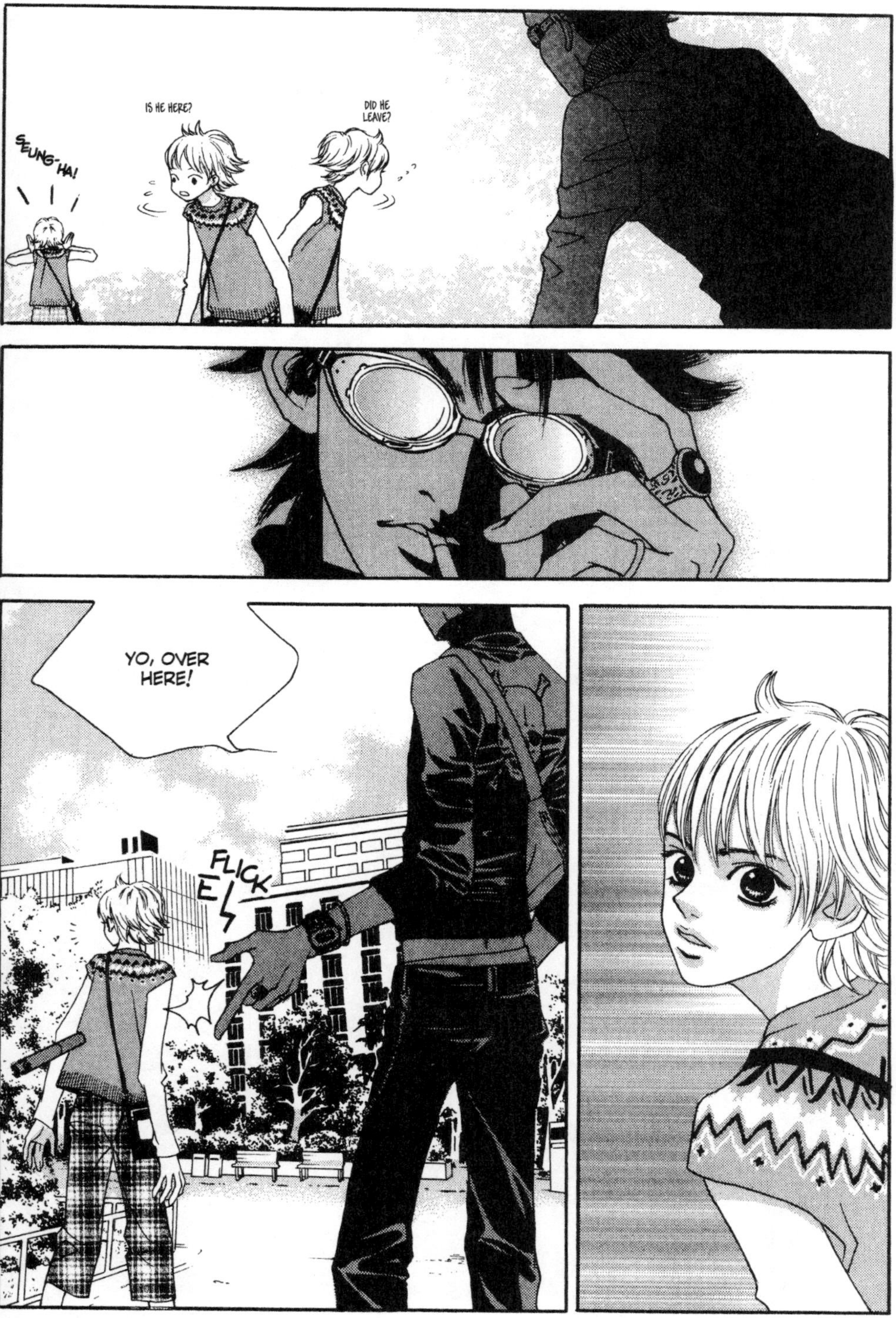
SEUNG-HA!
IS HE HERE?
DID HE LEAVE?
YO, OVER HERE!
FLICK

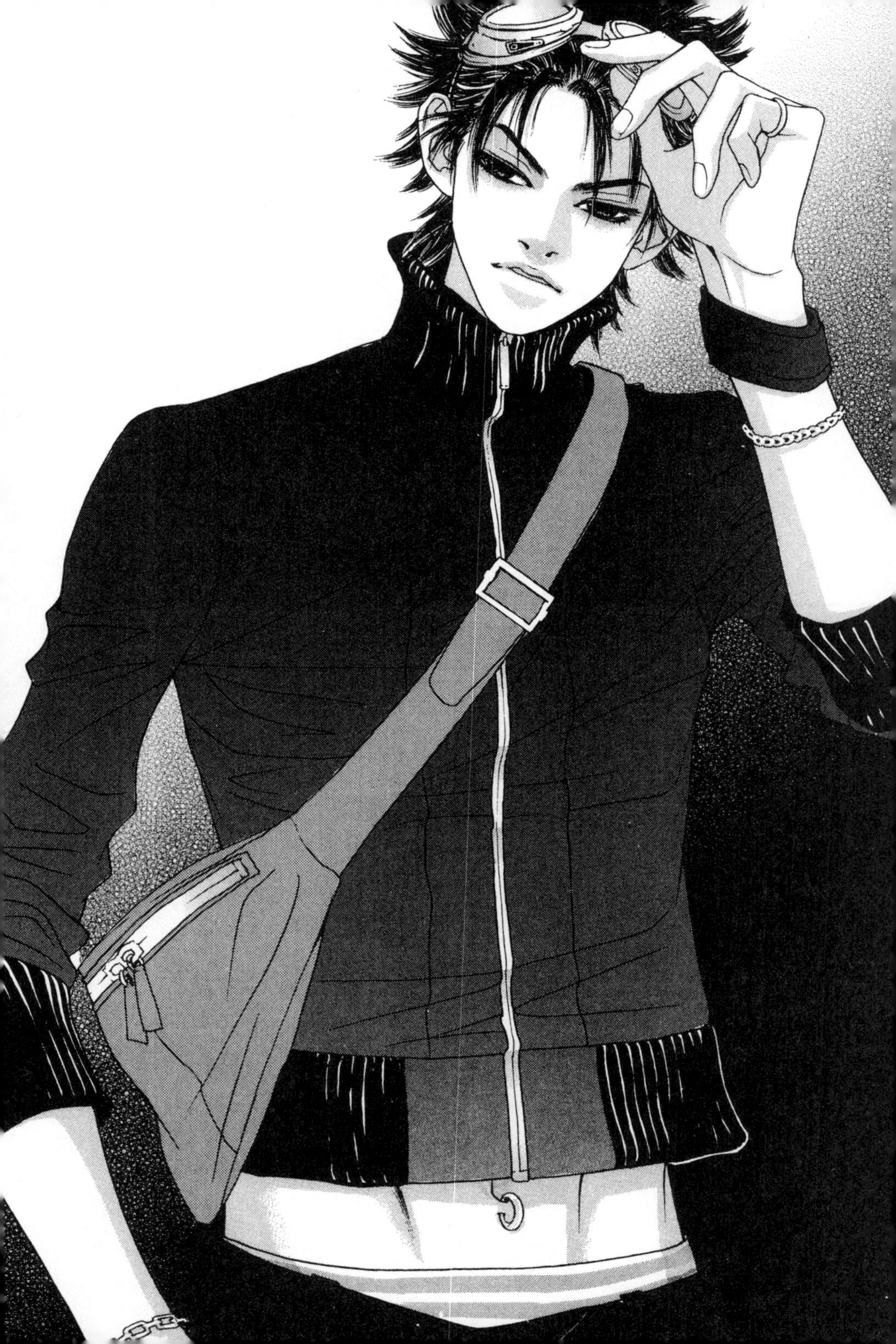

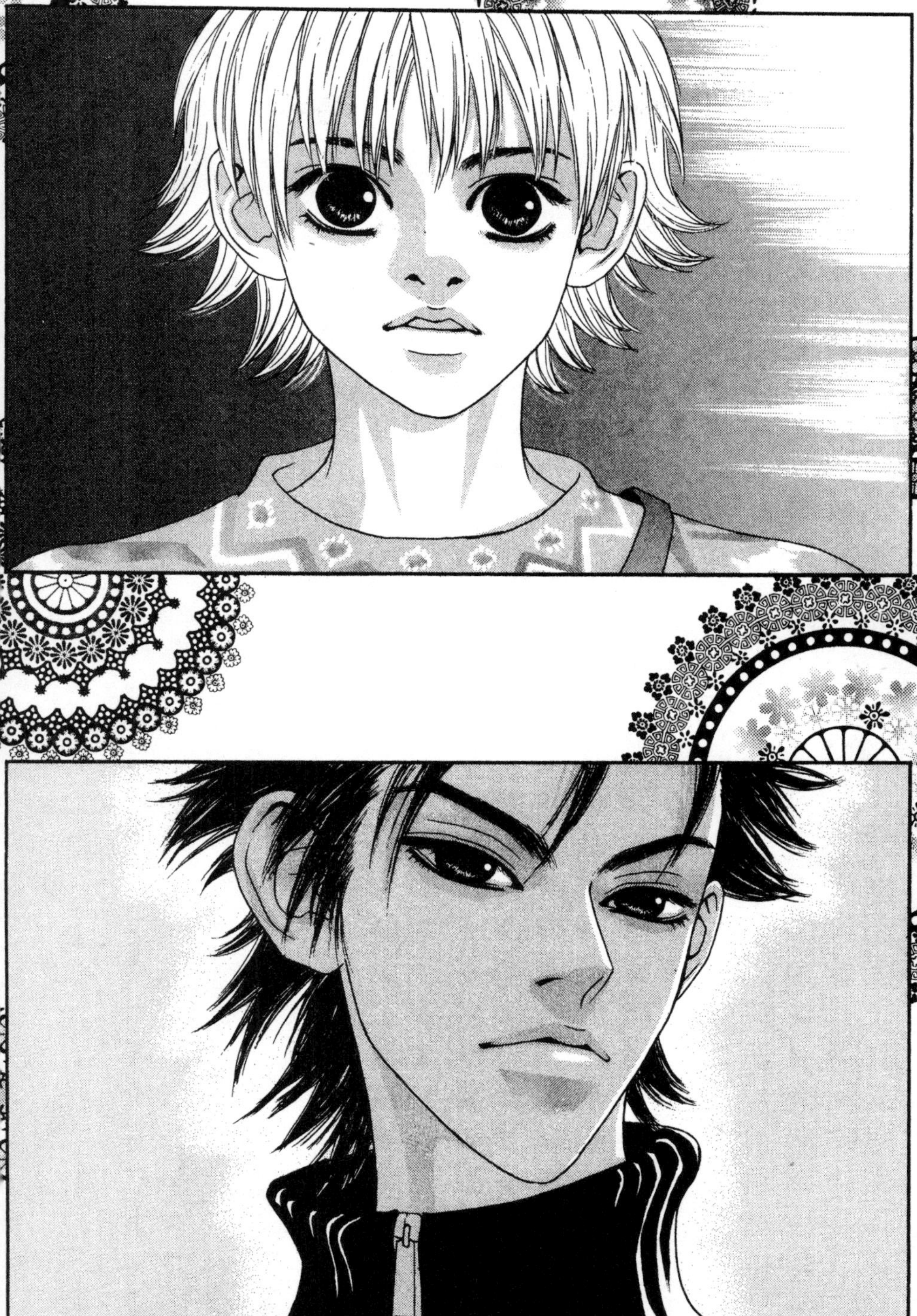

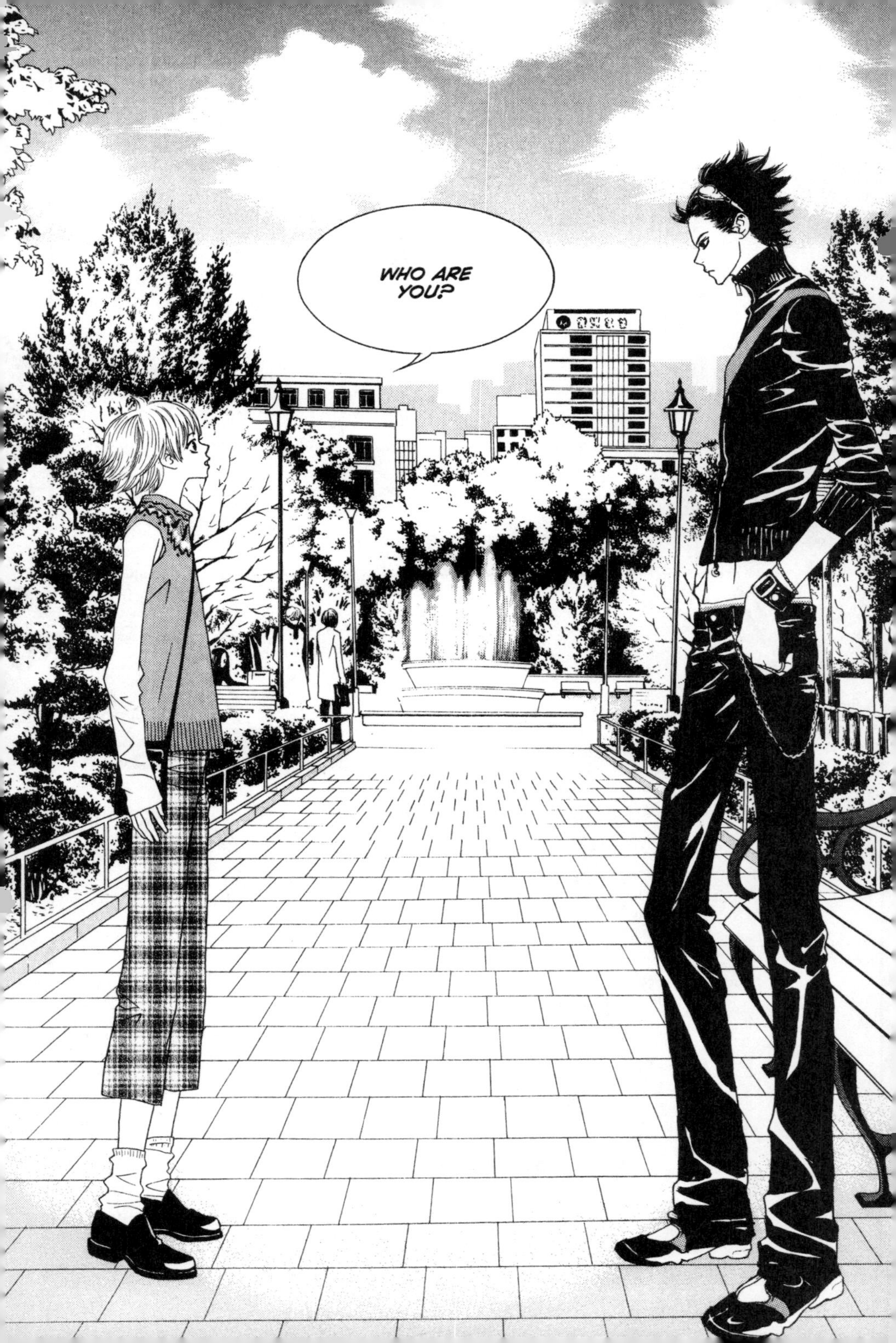
WHO ARE YOU?

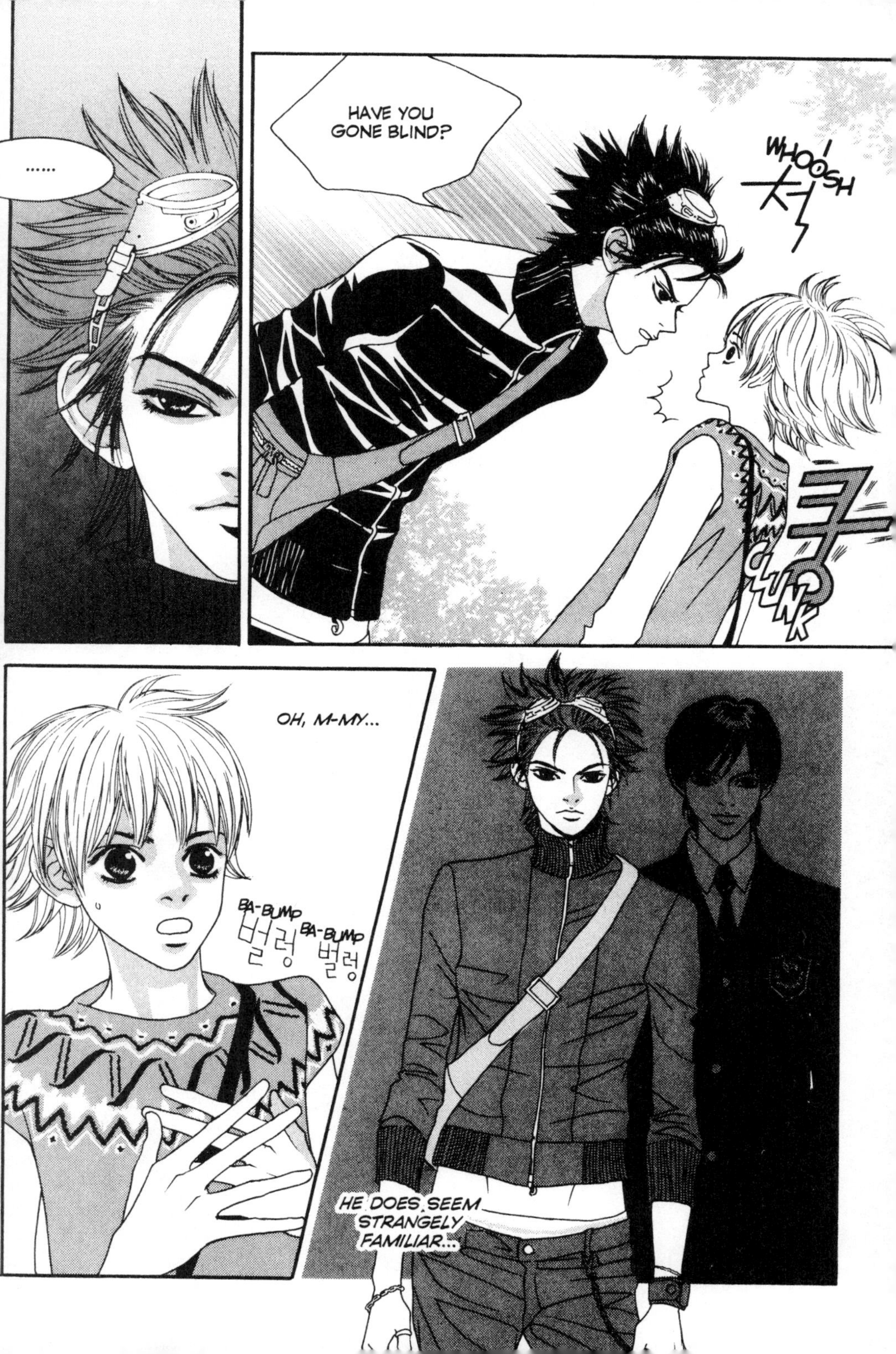
......
HAVE YOU GONE BLIND?
WHOOSH
척
쿵
CLUNK
OH, M-MY...
BA-BUMP
벌렁
BA-BUMP
벌렁
HE DOES SEEM STRANGELY FAMILIAR...

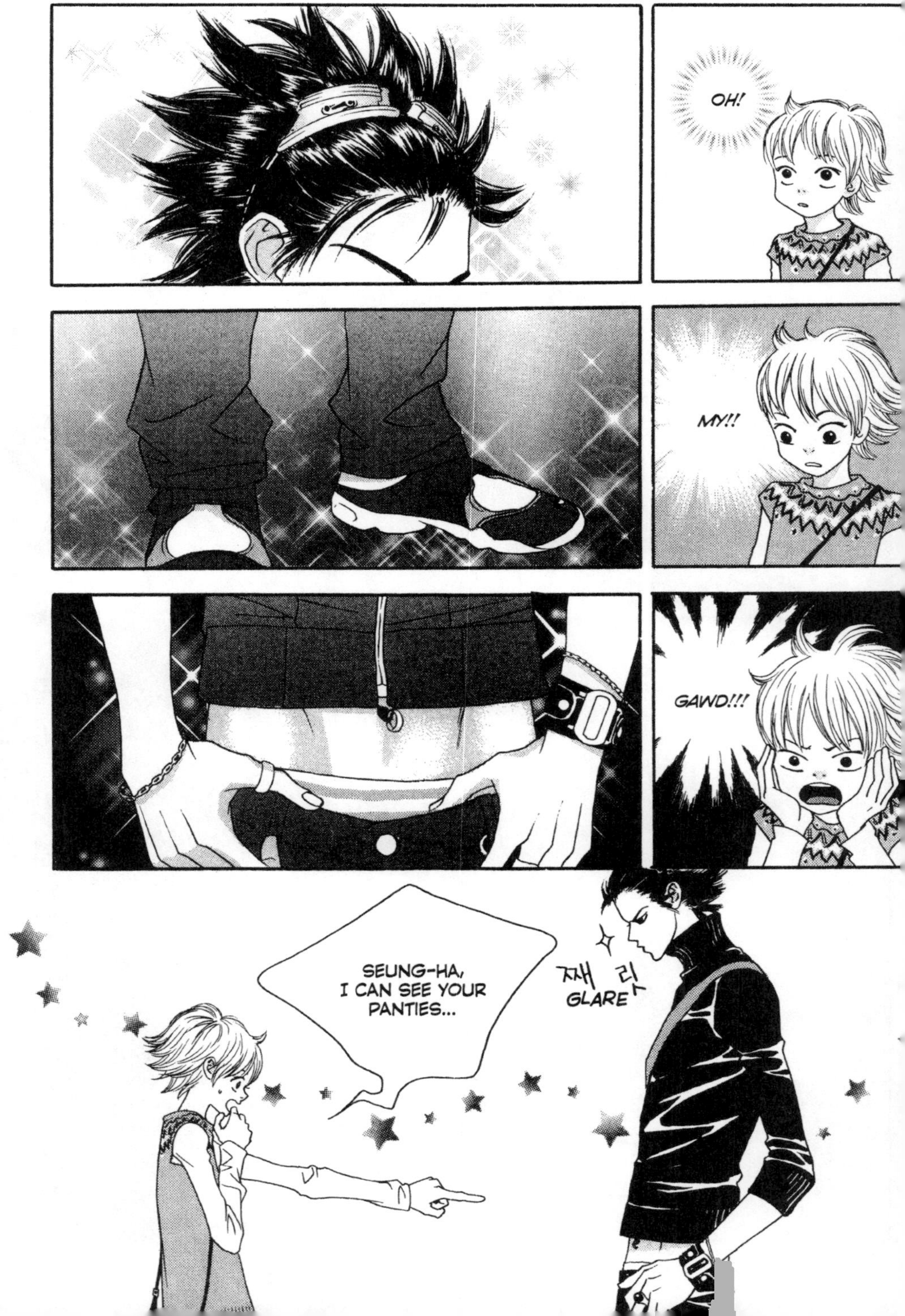
OH!
MY!!
GAWD!!!
SEUNG-HA, I CAN SEE YOUR PANTIES...
재 리 락
GLARE

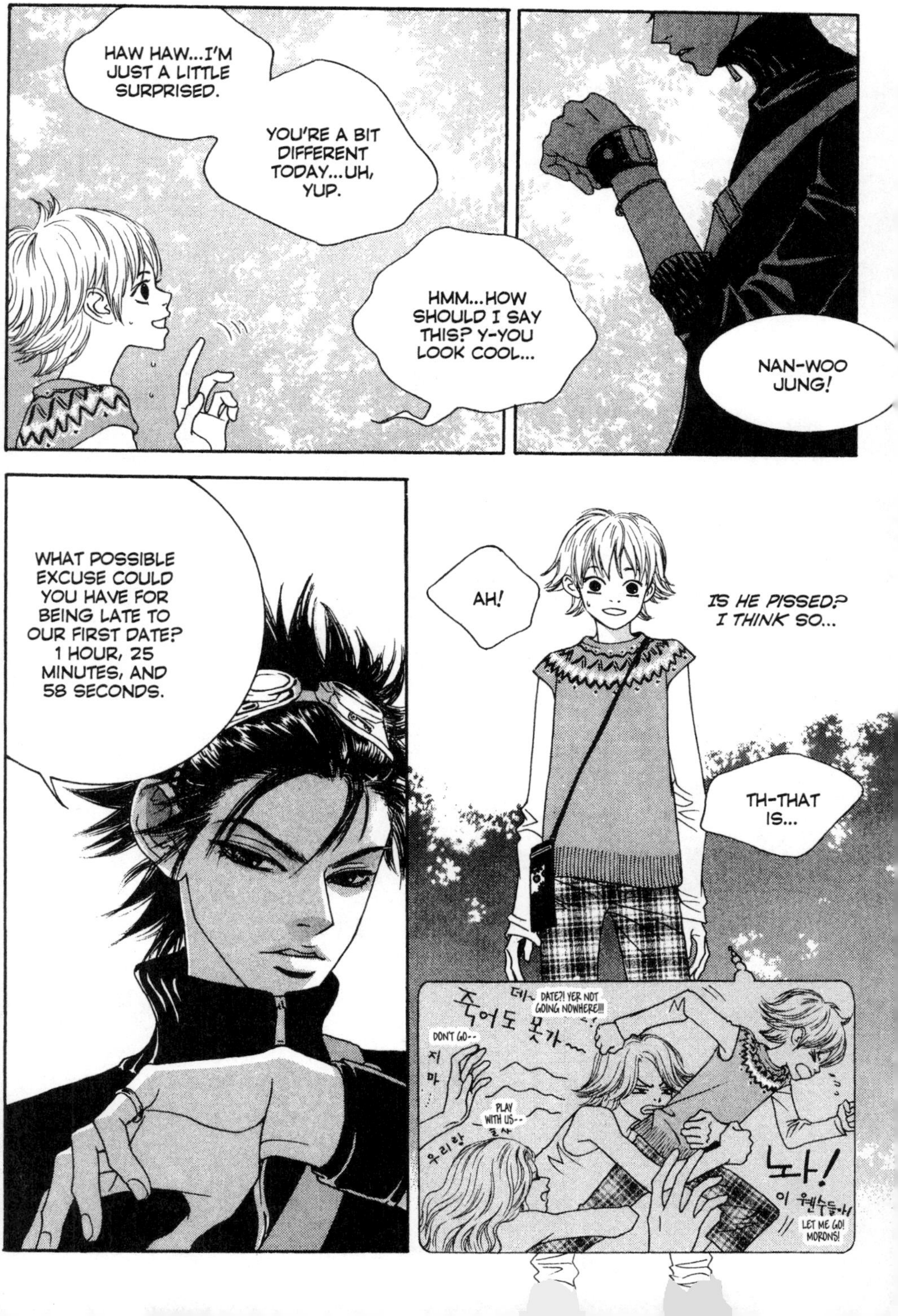
HAW HAW...I'M JUST A LITTLE SURPRISED.
YOU'RE A BIT DIFFERENT TODAY...UH, YUP.
HMM...HOW SHOULD I SAY THIS? Y-YOU LOOK COOL...
NAN-WOO JUNG!
WHAT POSSIBLE EXCUSE COULD YOU HAVE FOR BEING LATE TO OUR FIRST DATE? 1 HOUR, 25 MINUTES, AND 58 SECONDS.
AH!
IS HE PISSED? I THINK SO...
TH-THAT IS...
데~
DATE?! YER NOT GOING NOWHERE!!!
죽어도 못가~
DON'T GO--
지마
PLAY WITH US--
우리랑 놀자
놔!
이 웬수들아
LET ME GO! MORONS!

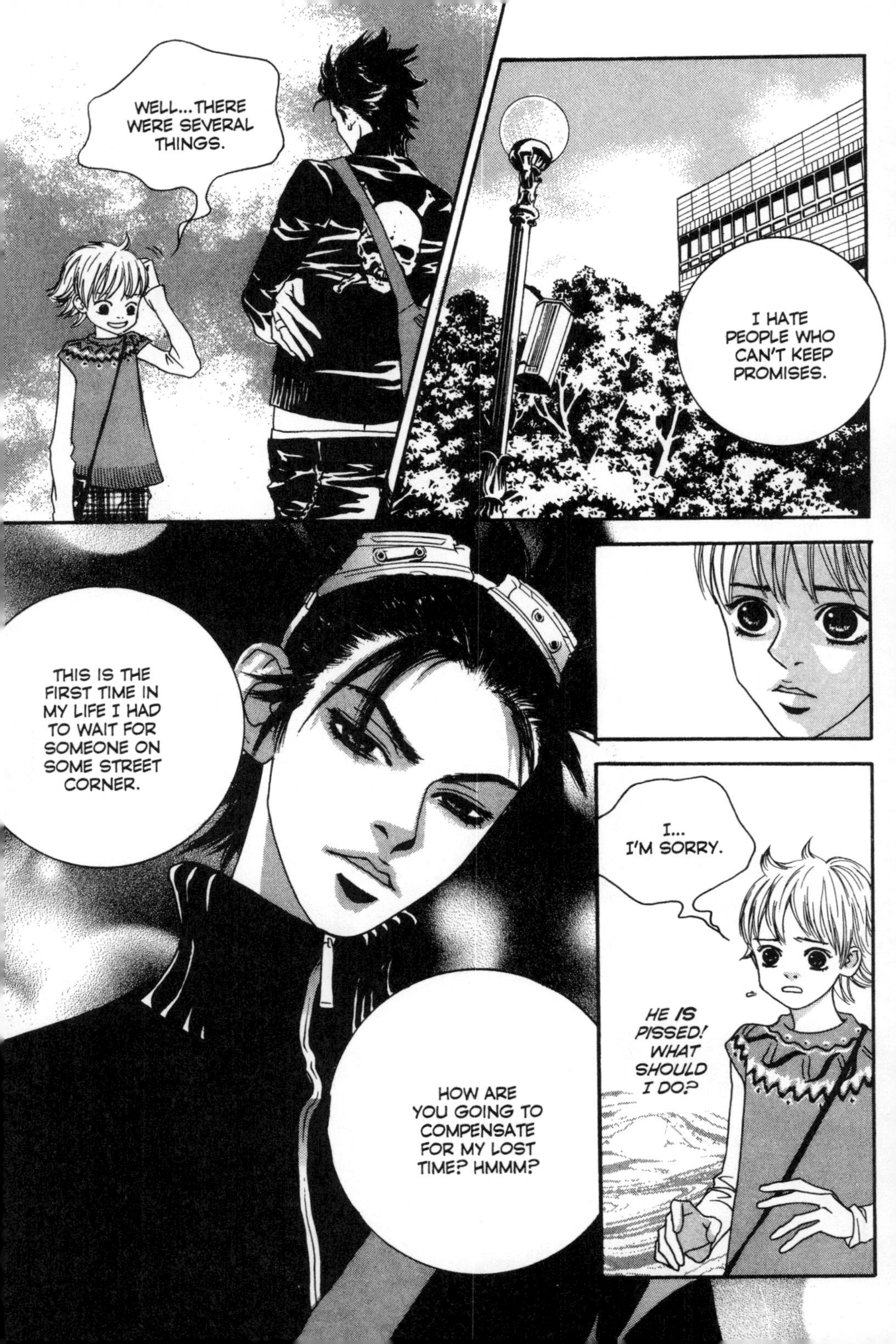
WELL...THERE WERE SEVERAL THINGS.
I HATE PEOPLE WHO CAN'T KEEP PROMISES.
THIS IS THE FIRST TIME IN MY LIFE I HAD TO WAIT FOR SOMEONE ON SOME STREET CORNER.
HOW ARE YOU GOING TO COMPENSATE FOR MY LOST TIME? HMMM?
I... I'M SORRY.
HE IS PISSED! WHAT SHOULD I DO?

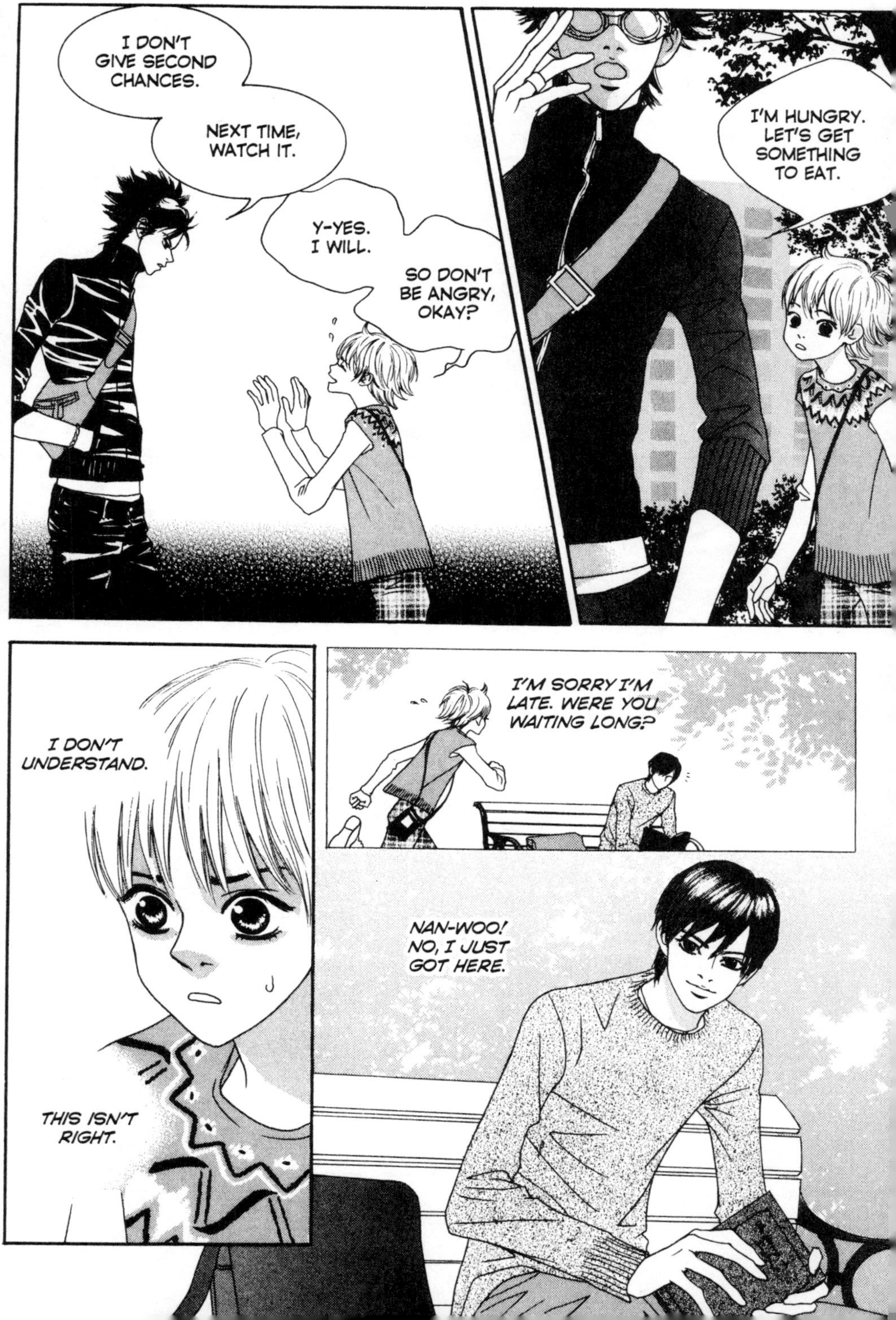
I DON'T GIVE SECOND CHANCES.
NEXT TIME, WATCH IT.
Y-YES. I WILL.
SO DON'T BE ANGRY, OKAY?
I'M HUNGRY. LET'S GET SOMETHING TO EAT.
I DON'T UNDERSTAND.
THIS ISN'T RIGHT.
I'M SORRY I'M LATE. WERE YOU WAITING LONG?
NAN-WOO! NO, I JUST GOT HERE.

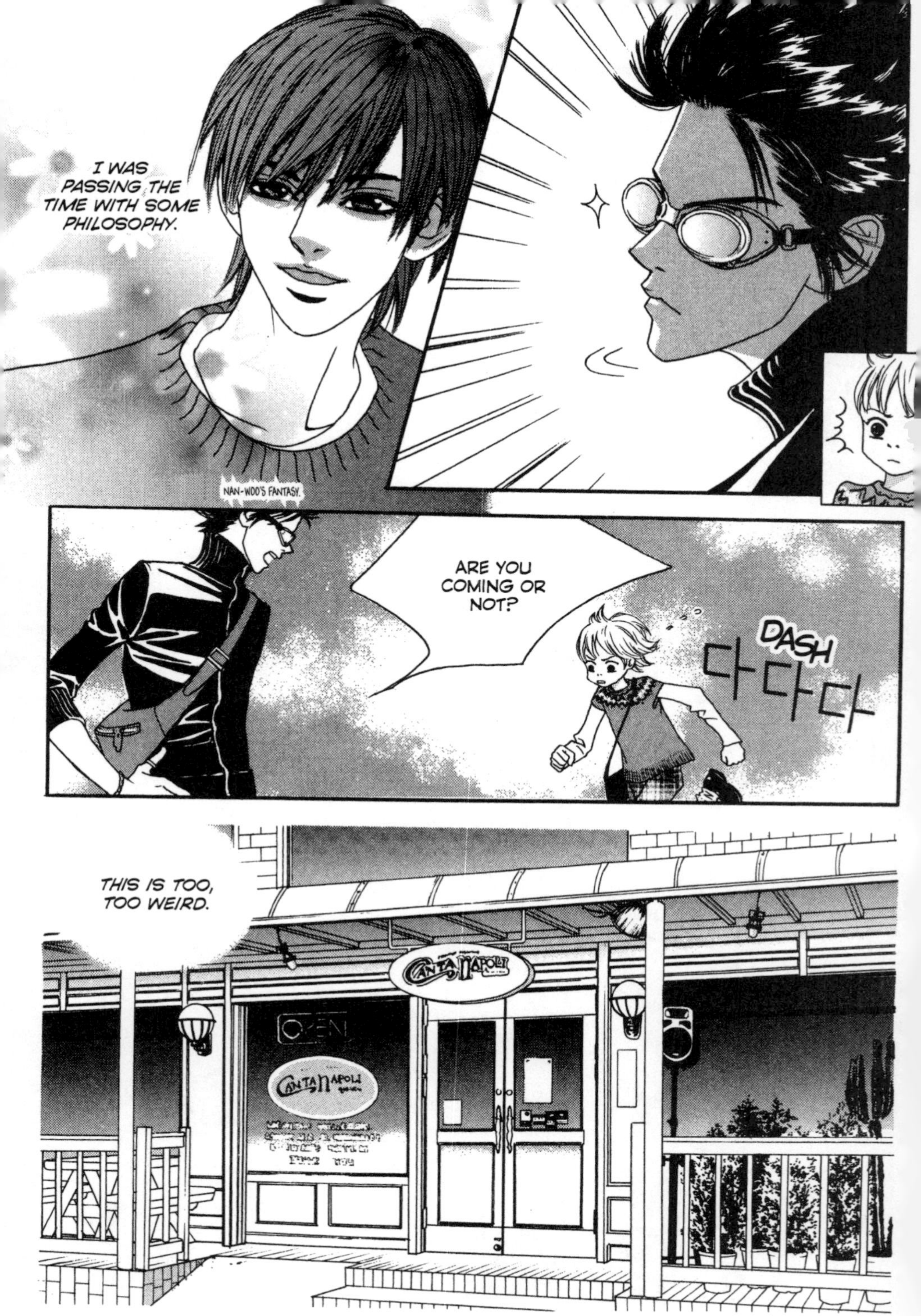
I WAS PASSING THE TIME WITH SOME PHILOSOPHY.
NAN-WOO'S FANTASY.
ARE YOU COMING OR NOT?
DASH
다다다
THIS IS TOO, TOO WEIRD.
CANTA NAPOLI
OPEN
CANTA NAPOLI

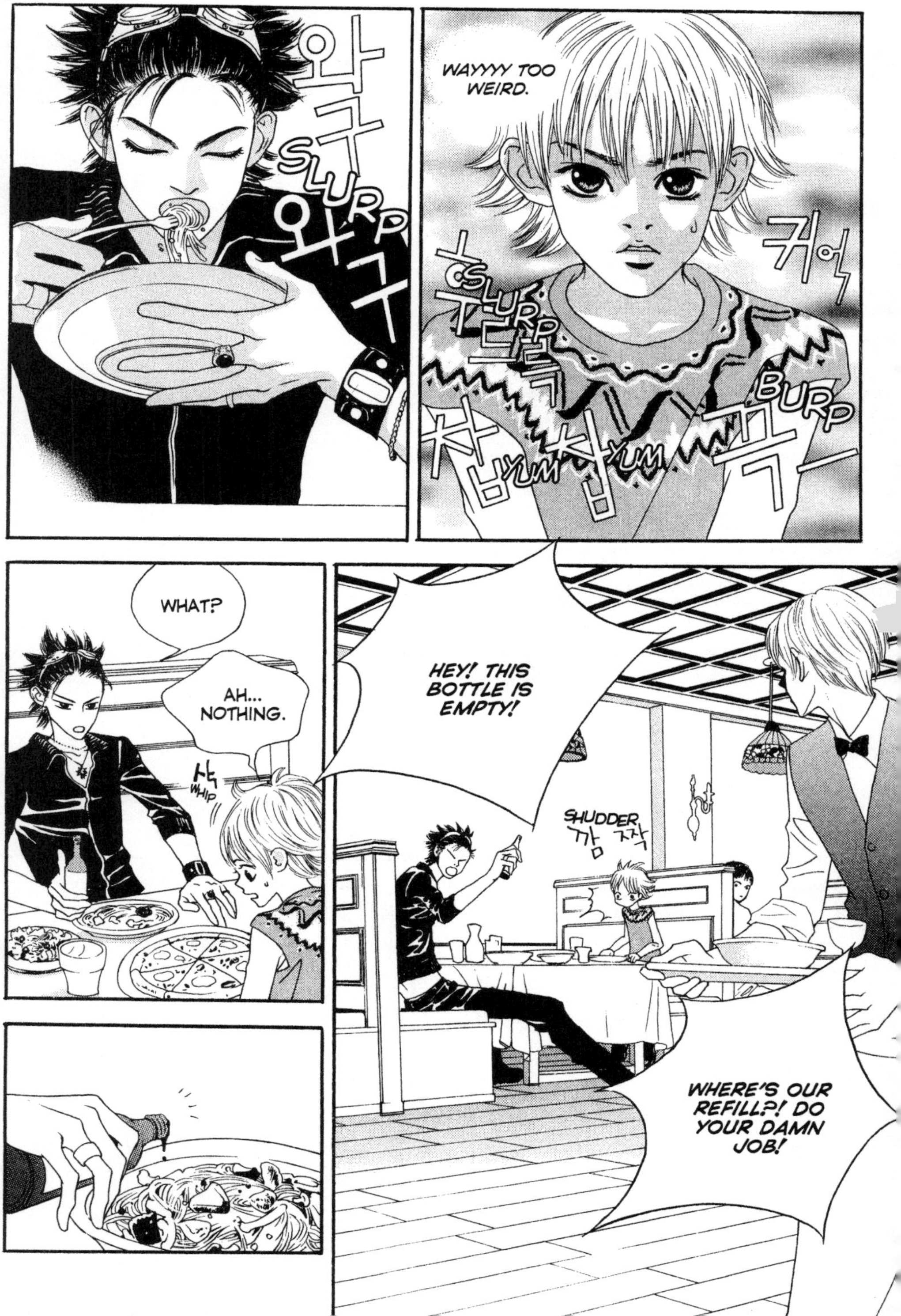
SLURP
WAYYYY TOO WEIRD.
SLURP
BURP
YUM YUM
WHAT?
AH... NOTHING.
WHIP
HEY! THIS BOTTLE IS EMPTY!
SHUDDER
깜짝
WHERE'S OUR REFILL?! DO YOUR DAMN JOB!

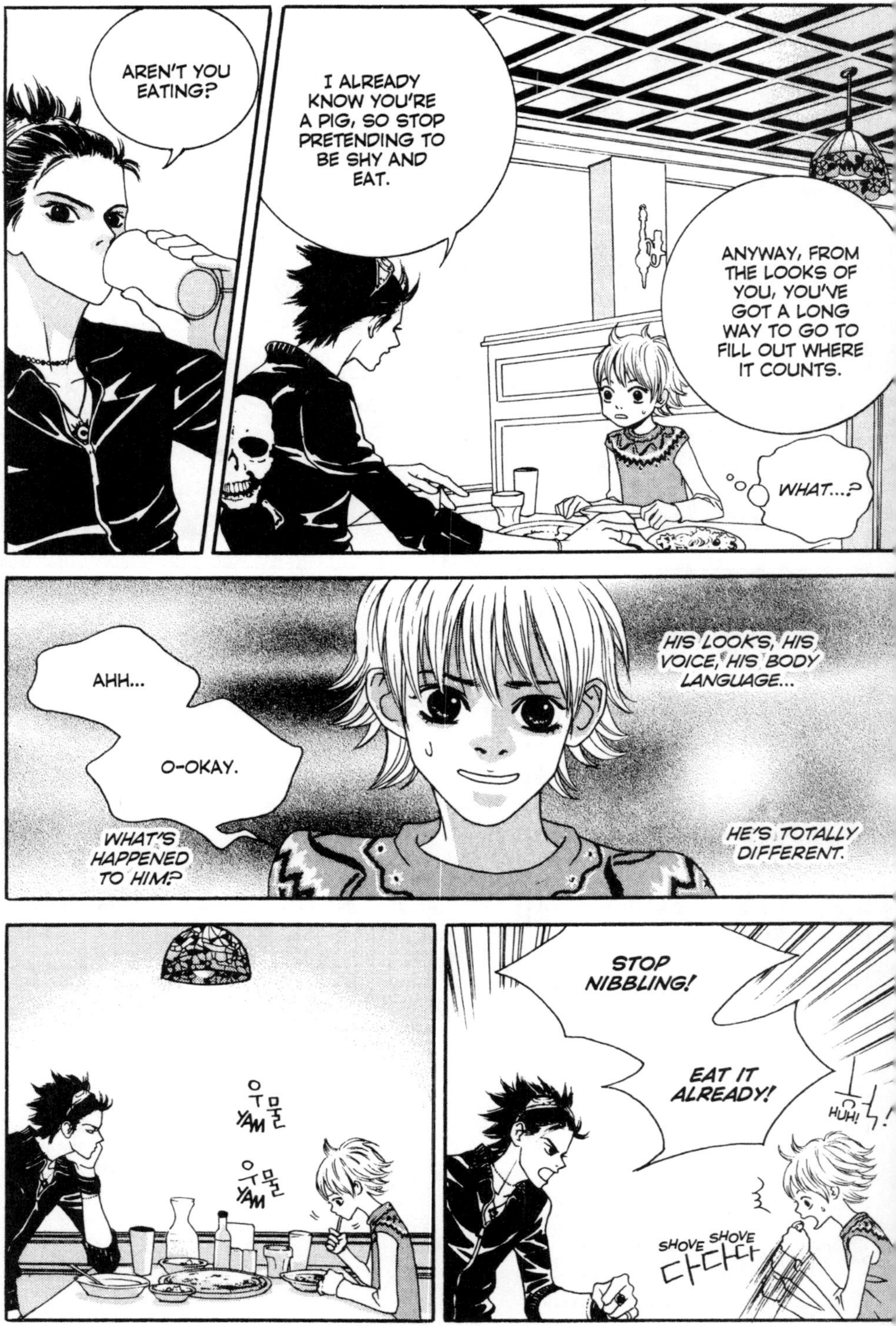
AREN'T YOU EATING?
I ALREADY KNOW YOU'RE A PIG, SO STOP PRETENDING TO BE SHY AND EAT.
ANYWAY, FROM THE LOOKS OF YOU, YOU'VE GOT A LONG WAY TO GO TO FILL OUT WHERE IT COUNTS.
WHAT...?
AHH...
O-OKAY.
WHAT'S HAPPENED TO HIM?
HIS LOOKS, HIS VOICE, HIS BODY LANGUAGE...
HE'S TOTALLY DIFFERENT.
우물 YAM
우물 YAM
STOP NIBBLING!
EAT IT ALREADY!
HUH!
SHOVE SHOVE 다다다

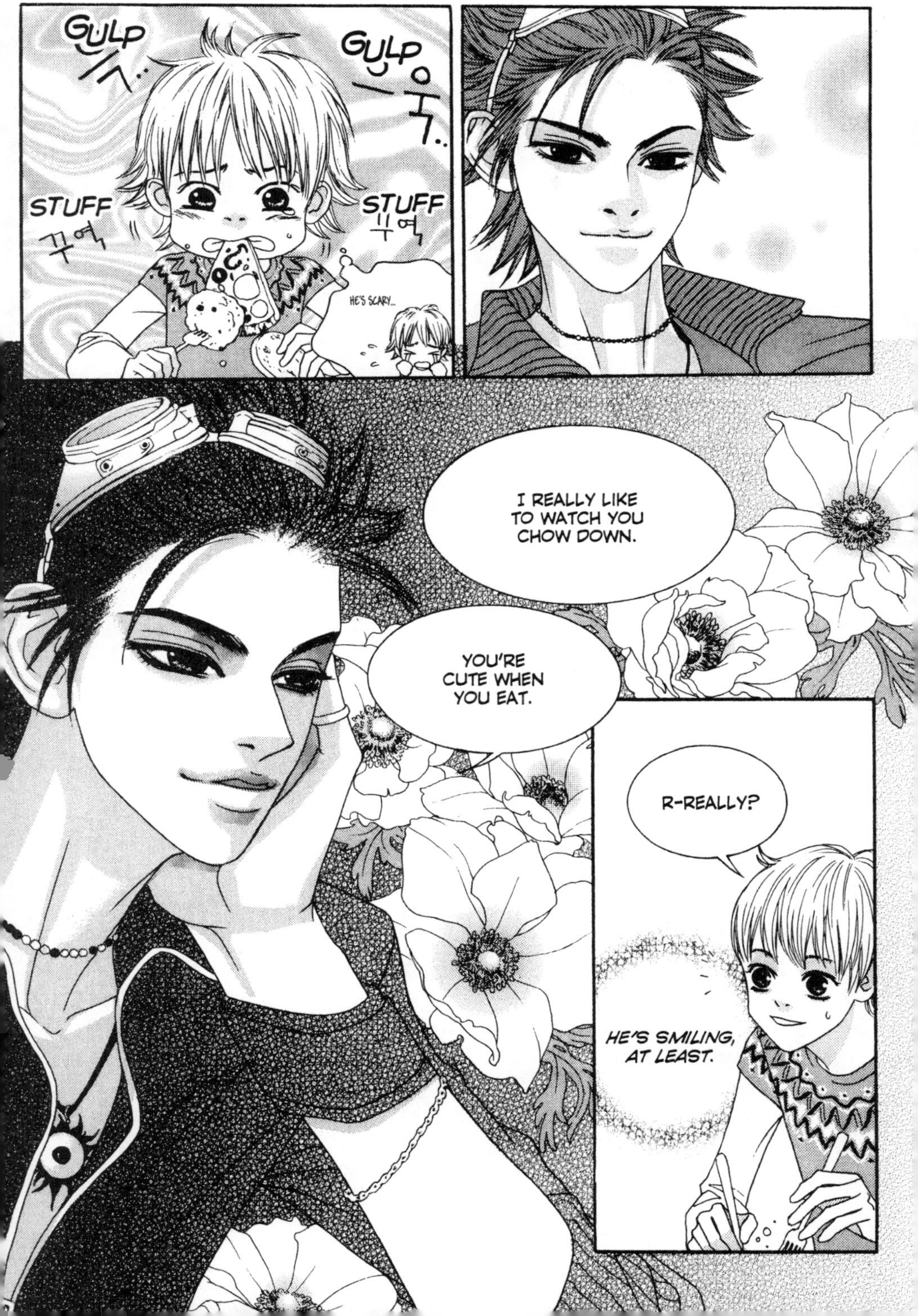
GULP
GULP
STUFF
STUFF
HE'S SCARY...
I REALLY LIKE TO WATCH YOU CHOW DOWN.
YOU'RE CUTE WHEN YOU EAT.
R-REALLY?
HE'S SMILING, AT LEAST.

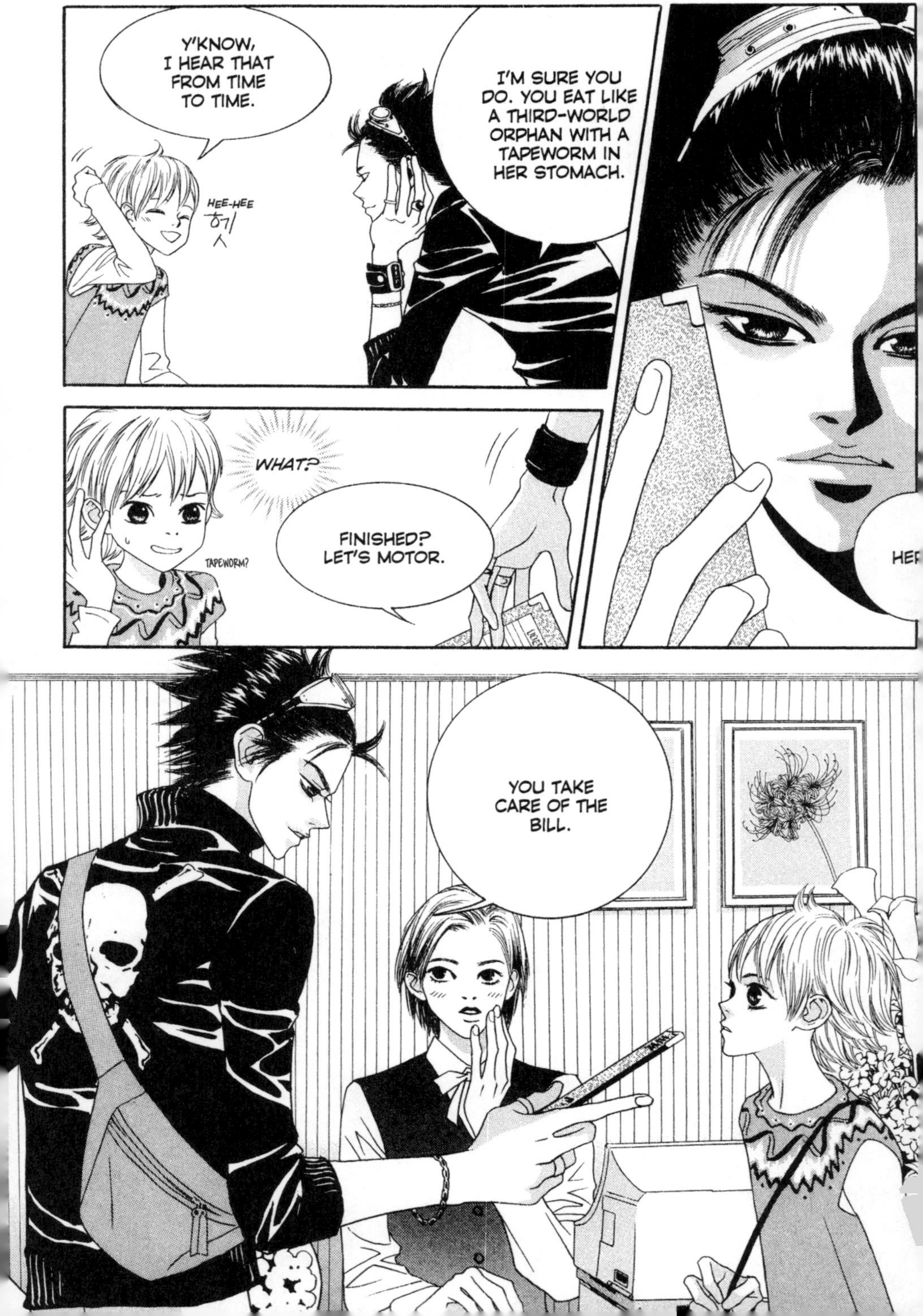
Y'KNOW, I HEAR THAT FROM TIME TO TIME.
HEE-HEE
I'M SURE YOU DO. YOU EAT LIKE A THIRD-WORLD ORPHAN WITH A TAPEWORM IN HER STOMACH.
WHAT?
TAPEWORM?
FINISHED? LET'S MOTOR.
YOU TAKE CARE OF THE BILL.

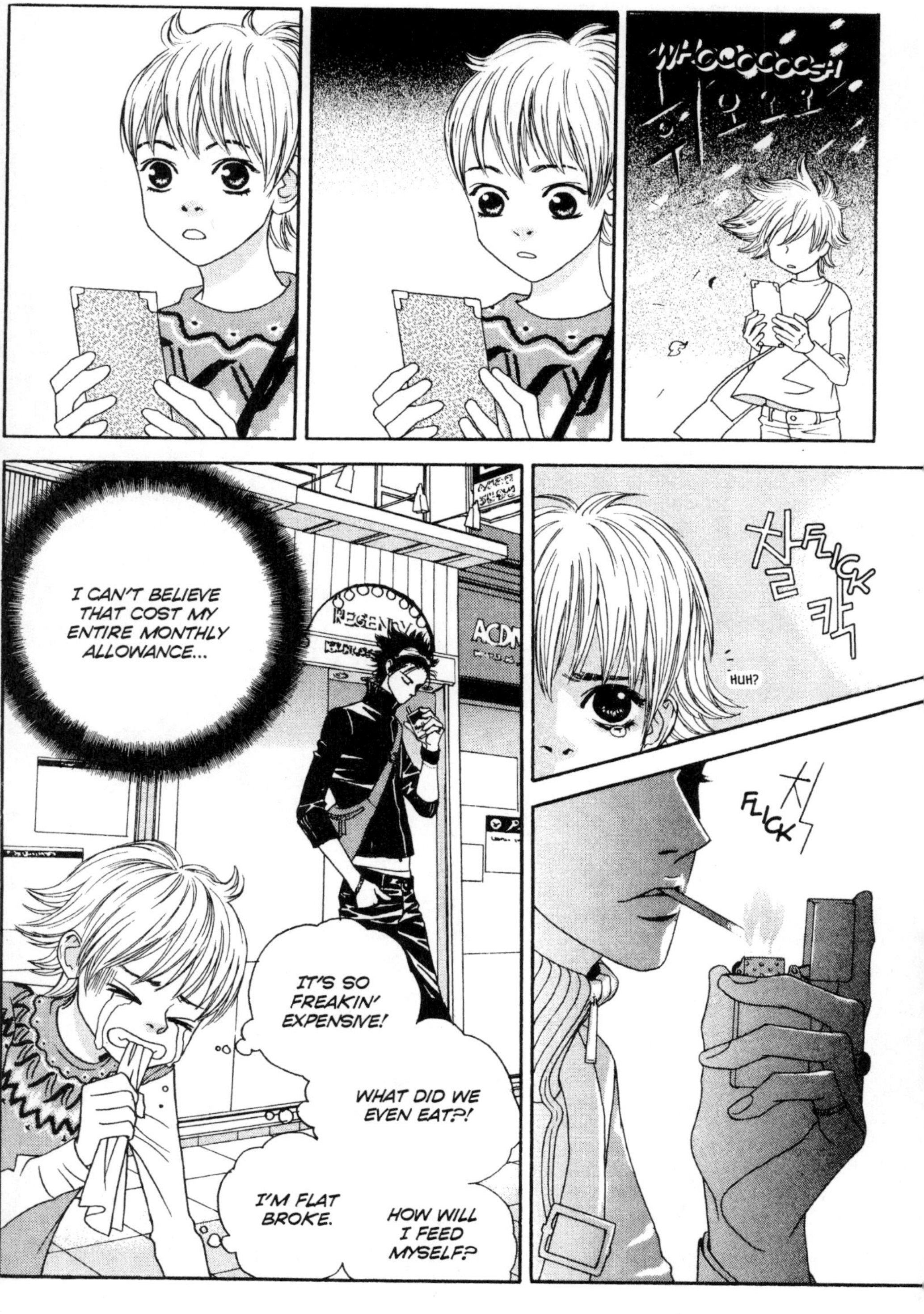
WHOOOOOOSH
I CAN'T BELIEVE THAT COST MY ENTIRE MONTHLY ALLOWANCE...
IT'S SO FREAKIN' EXPENSIVE!
WHAT DID WE EVEN EAT?!
I'M FLAT BROKE.
HOW WILL I FEED MYSELF?
FLICK
HUH?
FLICK

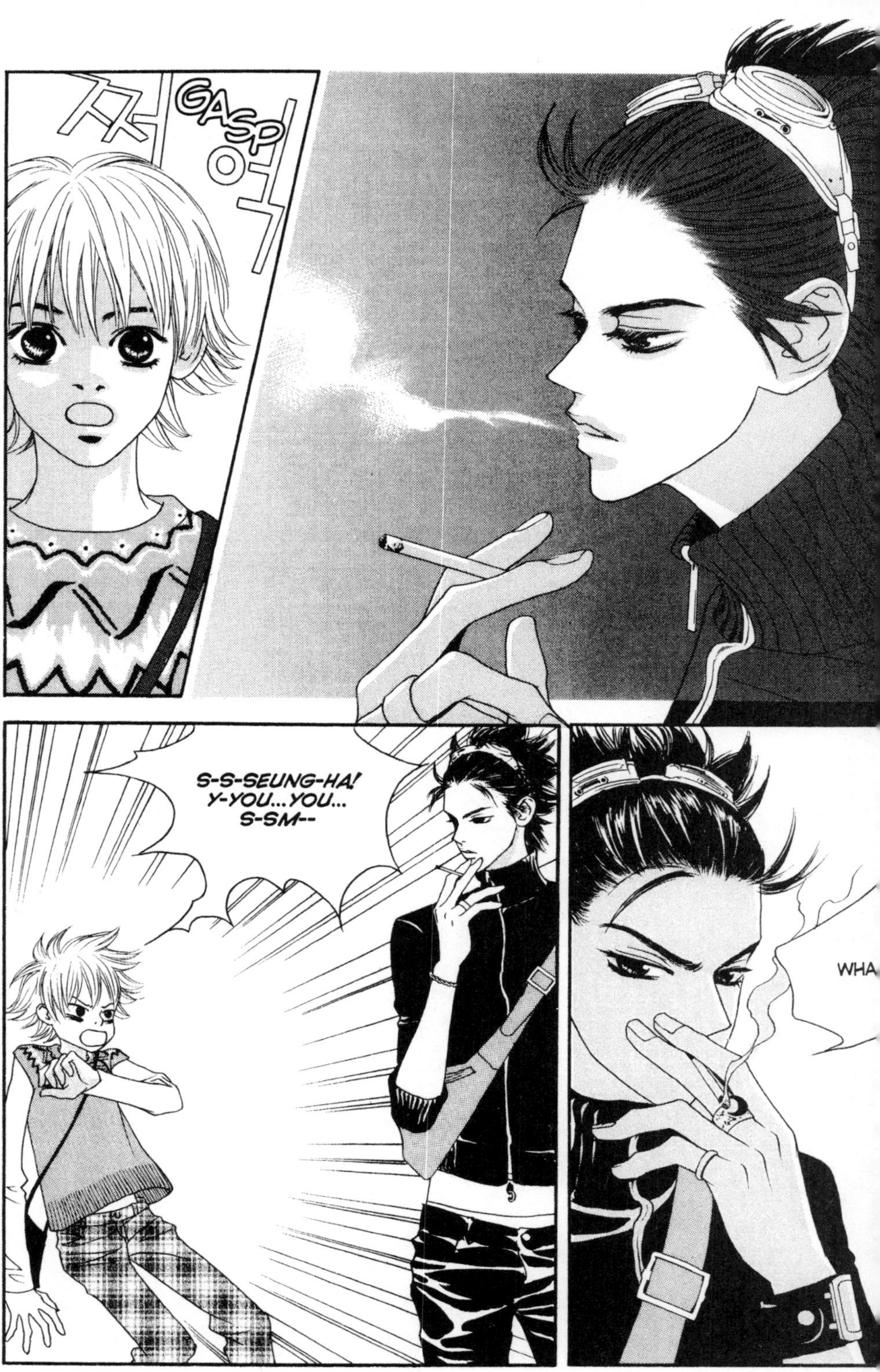

짜
GASP
엇
S-S-SEUNG-HA!
Y-YOU...YOU...
S-SM--
WHA

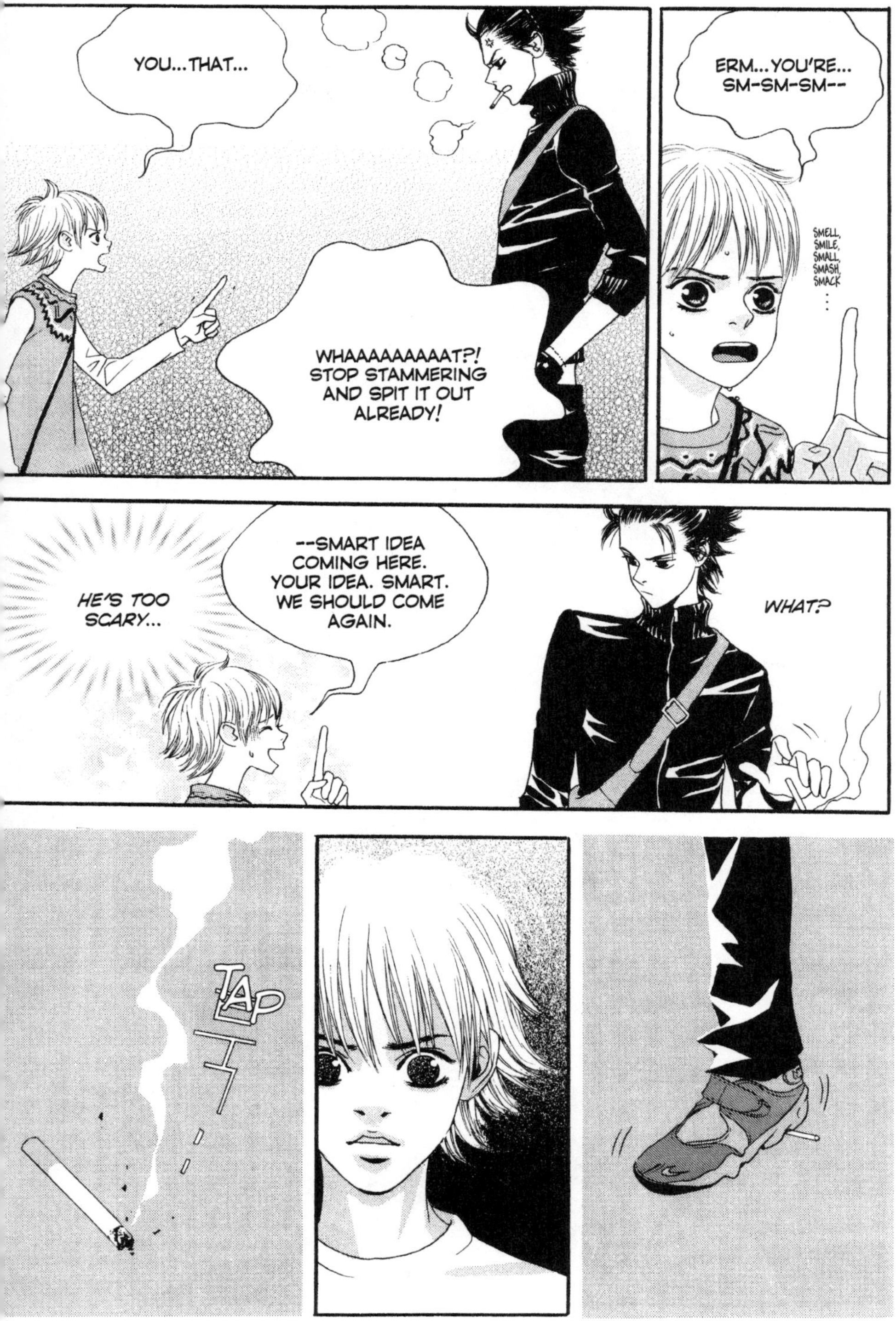
YOU...THAT...
WHAAAAAAAAAT?! STOP STAMMERING AND SPIT IT OUT ALREADY!
ERM...YOU'RE... SM-SM-SM--
SMELL, SMILE, SMALL, SMASH, SMACK ...
HE'S TOO SCARY...
--SMART IDEA COMING HERE. YOUR IDEA. SMART. WE SHOULD COME AGAIN.
WHAT?
TAP

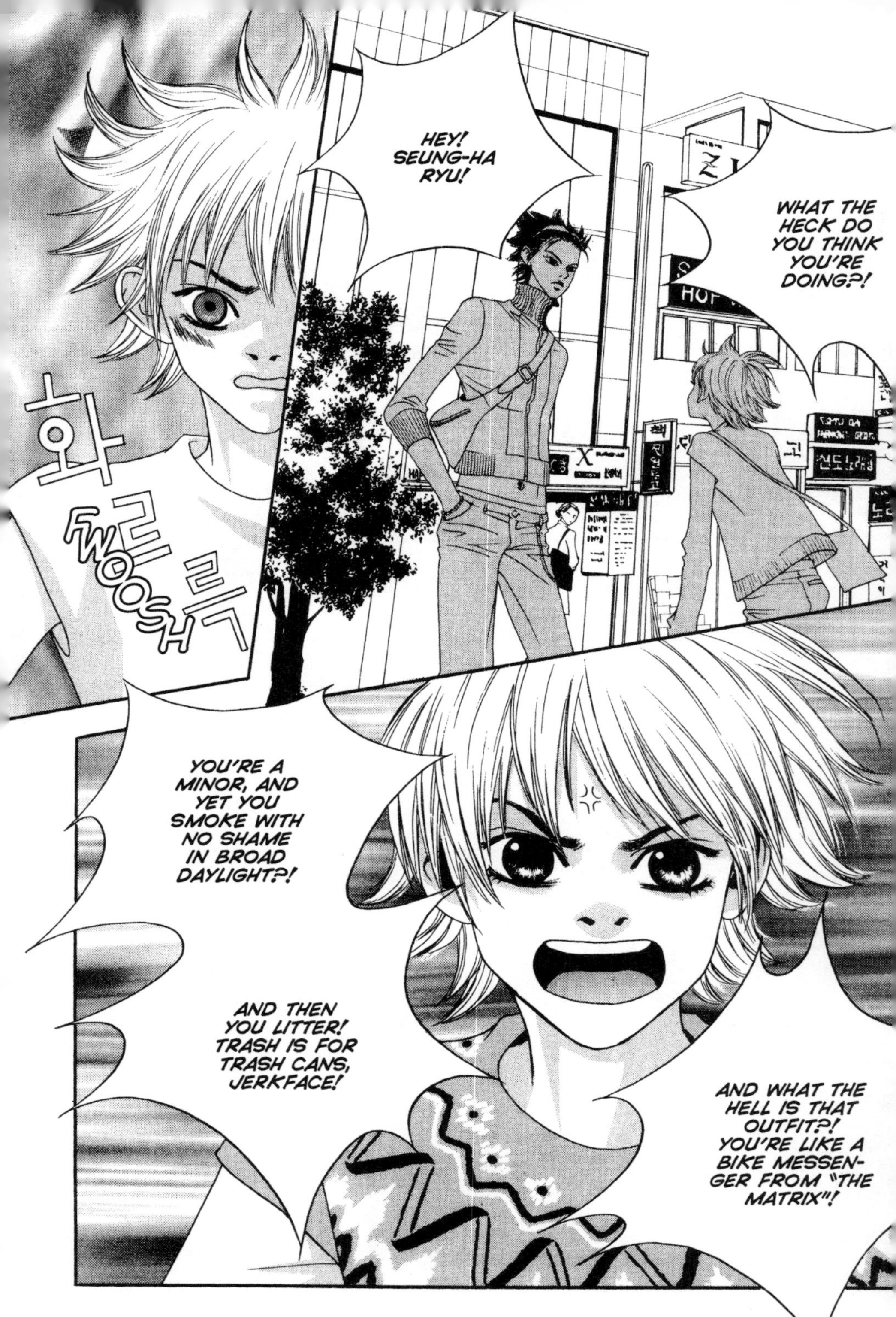
화르륵
FWOOSH
HEY! SEUNG-HA RYU!
WHAT THE HECK DO YOU THINK YOU'RE DOING?!
YOU'RE A MINOR, AND YET YOU SMOKE WITH NO SHAME IN BROAD DAYLIGHT?!
AND THEN YOU LITTER! TRASH IS FOR TRASH CANS, JERKFACE!
AND WHAT THE HELL IS THAT OUTFIT?! YOU'RE LIKE A BIKE MESSEN-GER FROM "THE MATRIX"!

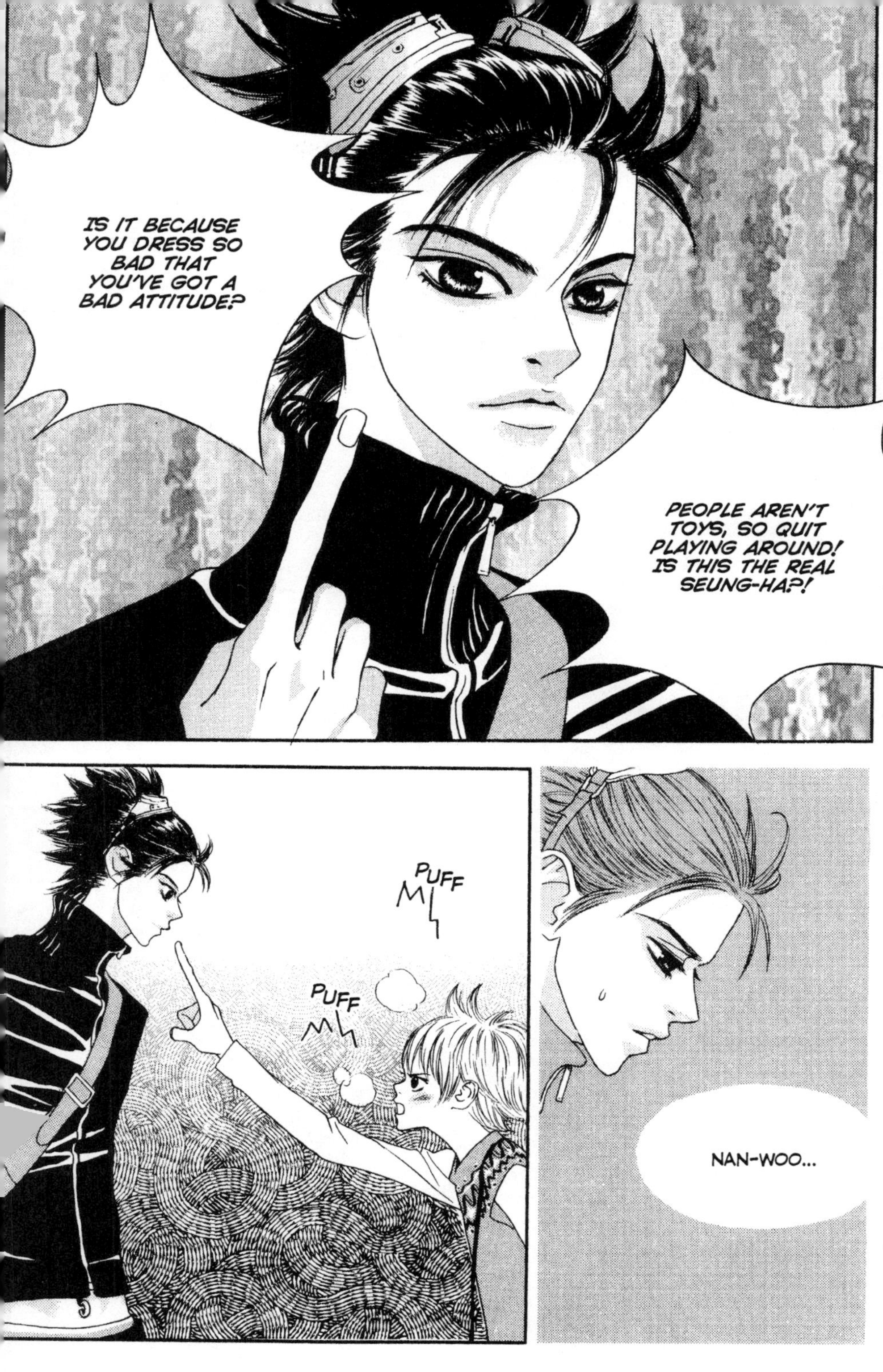
IS IT BECAUSE YOU DRESS SO BAD THAT YOU'VE GOT A BAD ATTITUDE?
PEOPLE AREN'T TOYS, SO QUIT PLAYING AROUND! IS THIS THE REAL SEUNG-HA?!
PUFF
PUFF
NAN-WOO...

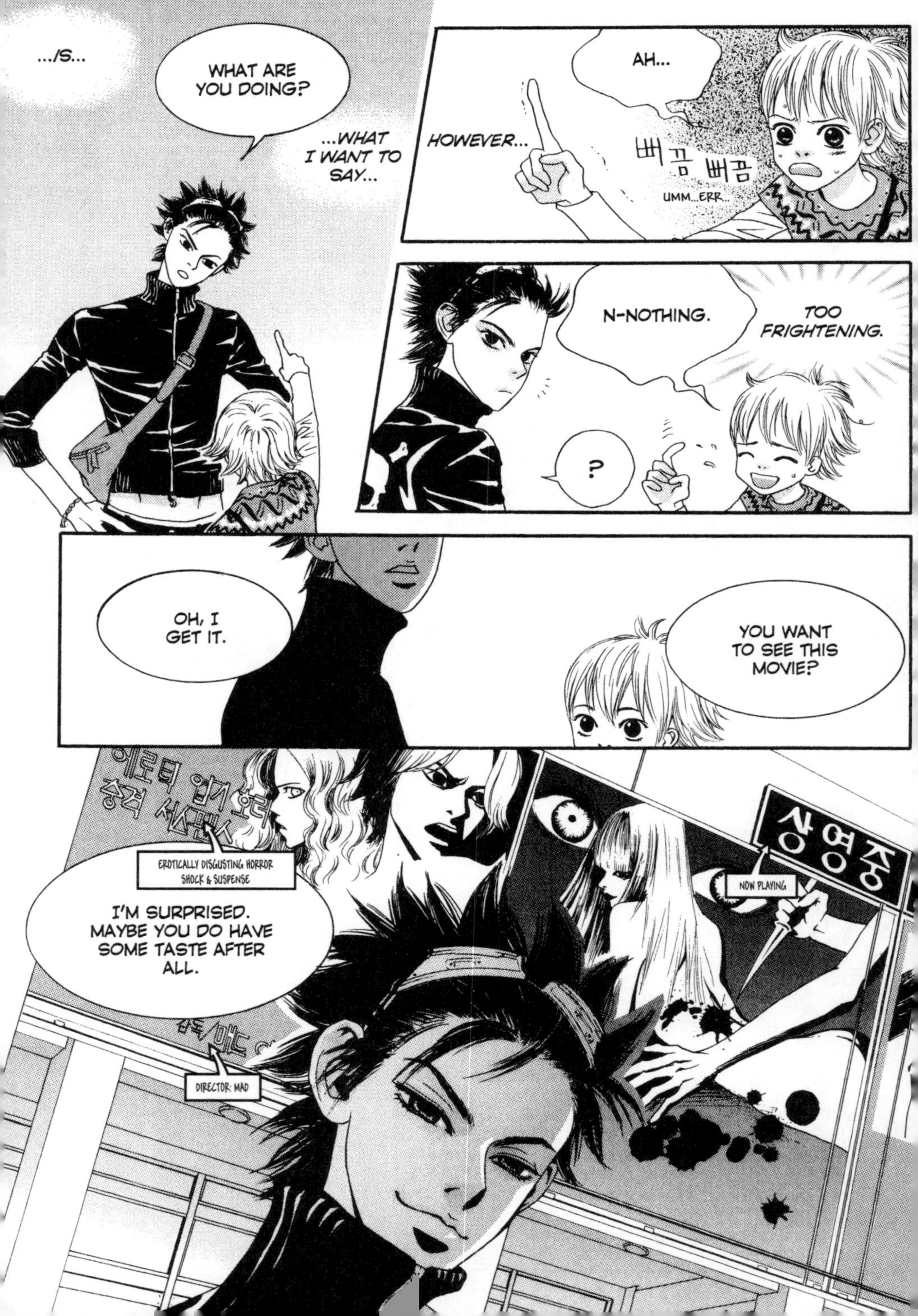
...IS...
WHAT ARE YOU DOING?
...WHAT I WANT TO SAY...
HOWEVER...
AH...
빼끔 빼끔
UMM...ERR..
N-NOTHING.
TOO FRIGHTENING.
?
OH, I GET IT.
YOU WANT TO SEE THIS MOVIE?
EROTICALLY DISGUSTING HORROR SHOCK & SUSPENSE
I'M SURPRISED. MAYBE YOU DO HAVE SOME TASTE AFTER ALL.
상영중
NOW PLAYING
DIRECTOR: MAD

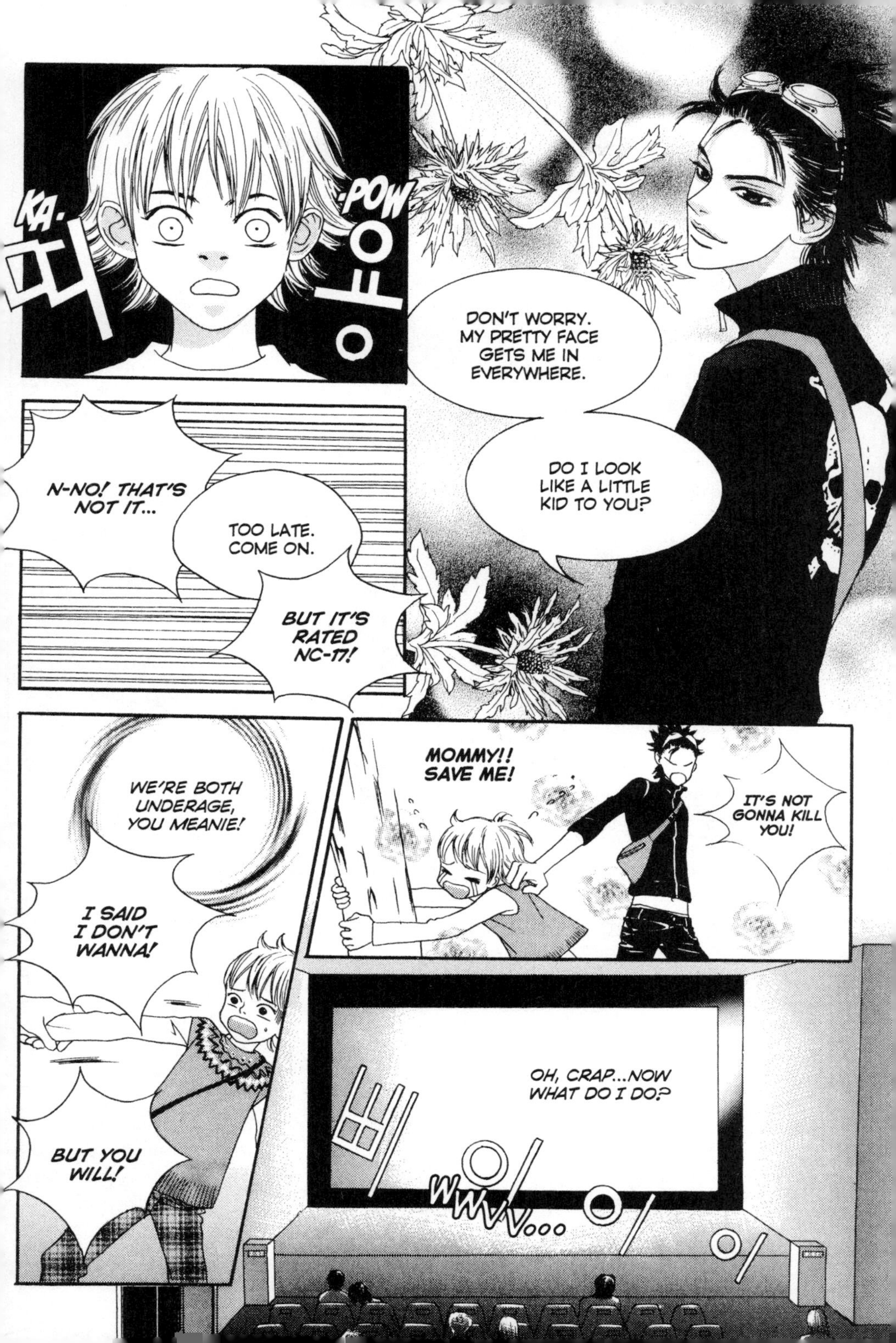
KA-
-POW
N-NO! THAT'S NOT IT...
TOO LATE. COME ON.
BUT IT'S RATED NC-17!
DON'T WORRY. MY PRETTY FACE GETS ME IN EVERYWHERE.
DO I LOOK LIKE A LITTLE KID TO YOU?
WE'RE BOTH UNDERAGE, YOU MEANIE!
I SAID I DON'T WANNA!
BUT YOU WILL!
MOMMY!! SAVE ME!
IT'S NOT GONNA KILL YOU!
OH, CRAP...NOW WHAT DO I DO?
WWVVooo

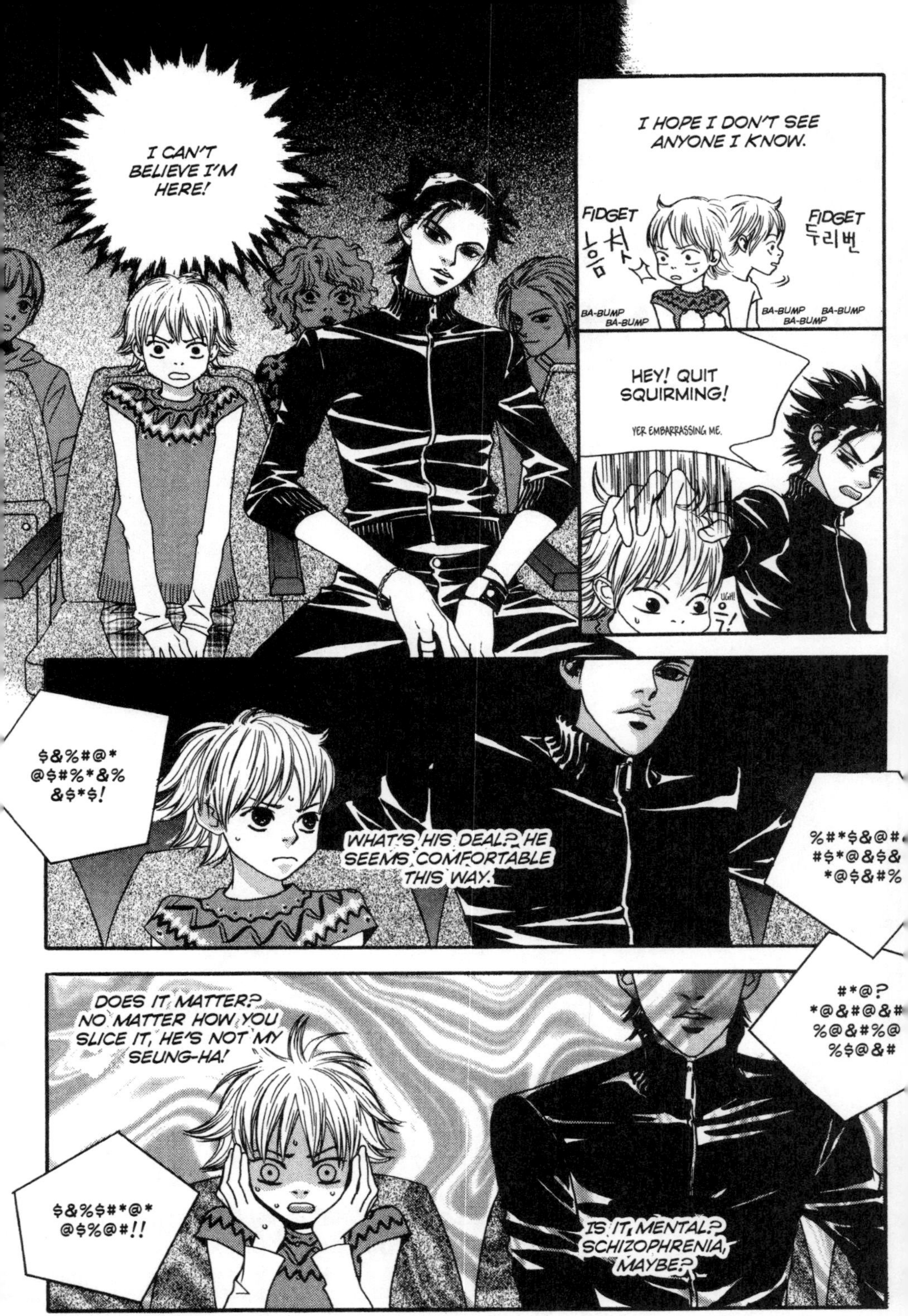

I CAN'T BELIEVE I'M HERE!
I HOPE I DON'T SEE ANYONE I KNOW.
FIDGET
흠칫
FIDGET
두리번
BA-BUMP BA-BUMP
BA-BUMP BA-BUMP BA-BUMP
HEY! QUIT SQUIRMING!
YER EMBARRASSING ME.
UGH!
윽!
$&%#@* @$#%*&% &$*$!
WHAT'S HIS DEAL? HE SEEMS COMFORTABLE THIS WAY.
%#*$&@# #$*@&$& *@$&#%
DOES IT MATTER? NO MATTER HOW YOU SLICE IT, HE'S NOT MY SEUNG-HA!
#*@? *@&#@&# %@&#%@ %$@&#
$&%$#*@* @$%@#!!
IS IT MENTAL? SCHIZOPHRENIA, MAYBE?

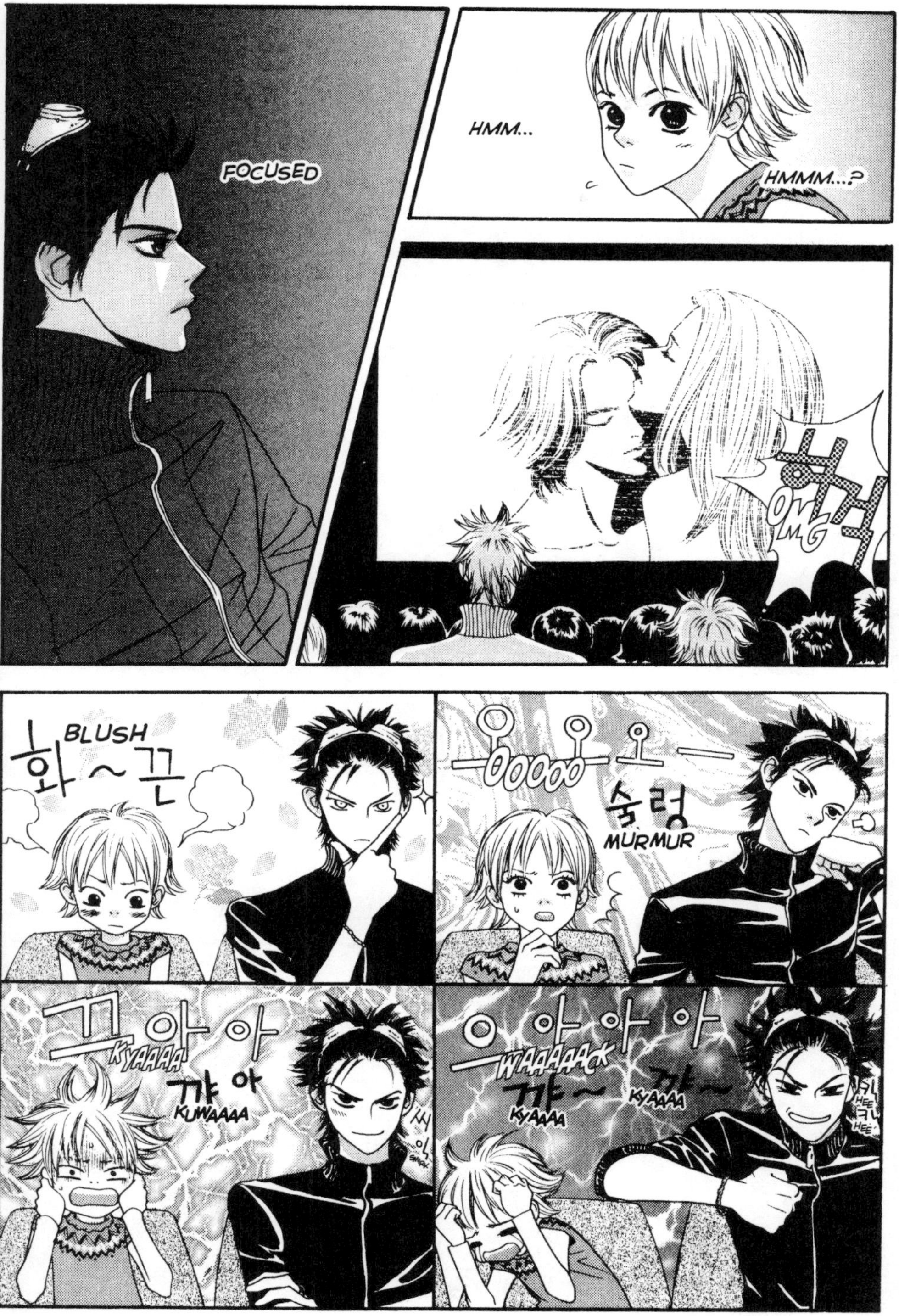
FOCUSED
HMM...
HMMM...?
헉
OMG
화~끈
BLUSH
오오오 오—
OOOOO
술렁
MURMUR
끄아아
KYAAAA
꺄아
KUWAAAA
씨익
SMIRK
으아아아
WAAAAACK
꺄~
KYAAAA
꺄~
KYAAAA
키
HEE
키
HEE

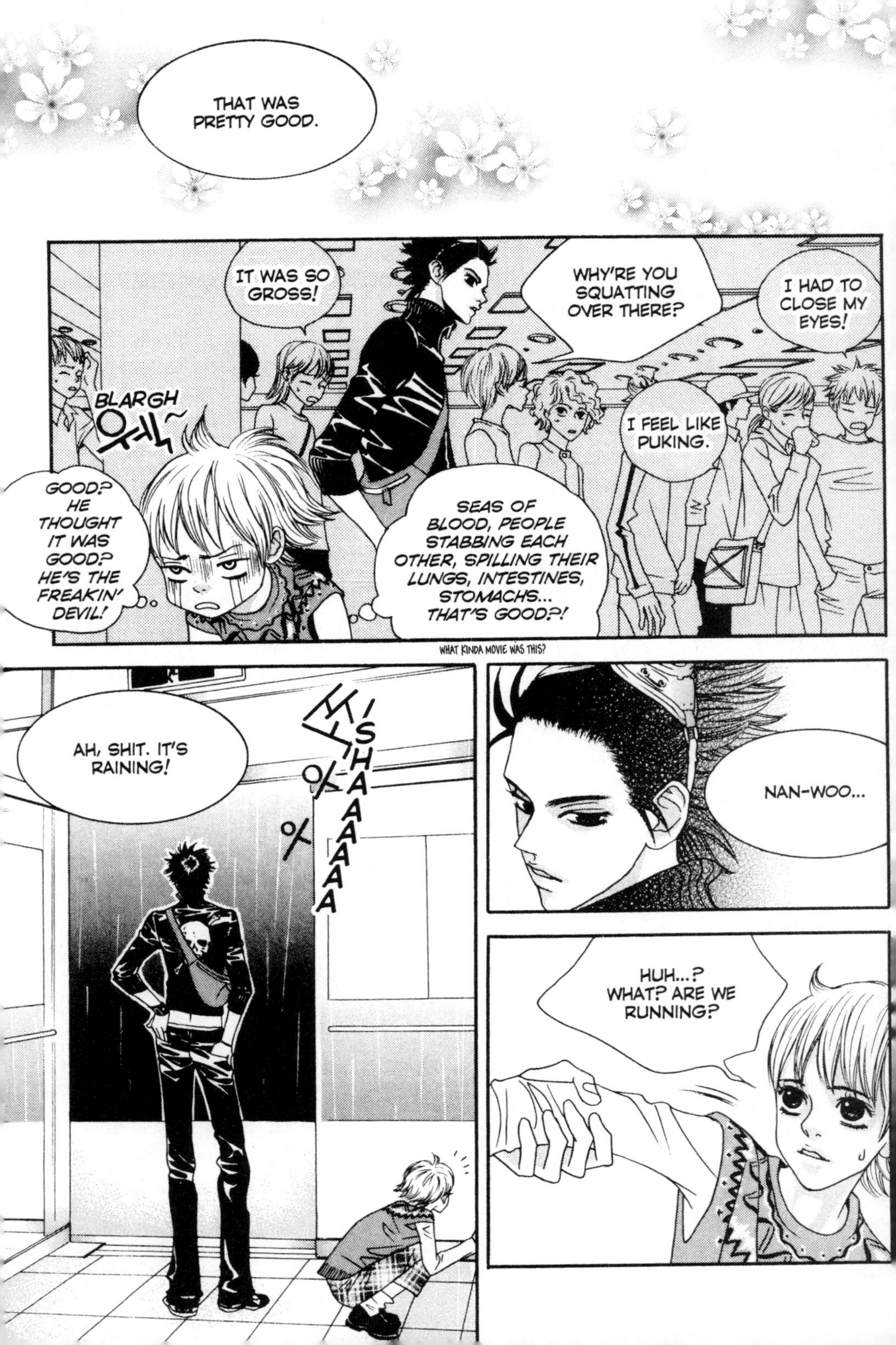

THAT WAS PRETTY GOOD.
IT WAS SO GROSS!
WHY'RE YOU SQUATTING OVER THERE?
I HAD TO CLOSE MY EYES!
BLARGH
I FEEL LIKE PUKING.
GOOD? HE THOUGHT IT WAS GOOD? HE'S THE FREAKIN' DEVIL!
SEAS OF BLOOD, PEOPLE STABBING EACH OTHER, SPILLING THEIR LUNGS, INTESTINES, STOMACHS... THAT'S GOOD?!
WHAT KINDA MOVIE WAS THIS?
AH, SHIT. IT'S RAINING!
SHAAAAAAA
NAN-WOO...
HUH...? WHAT? ARE WE RUNNING?

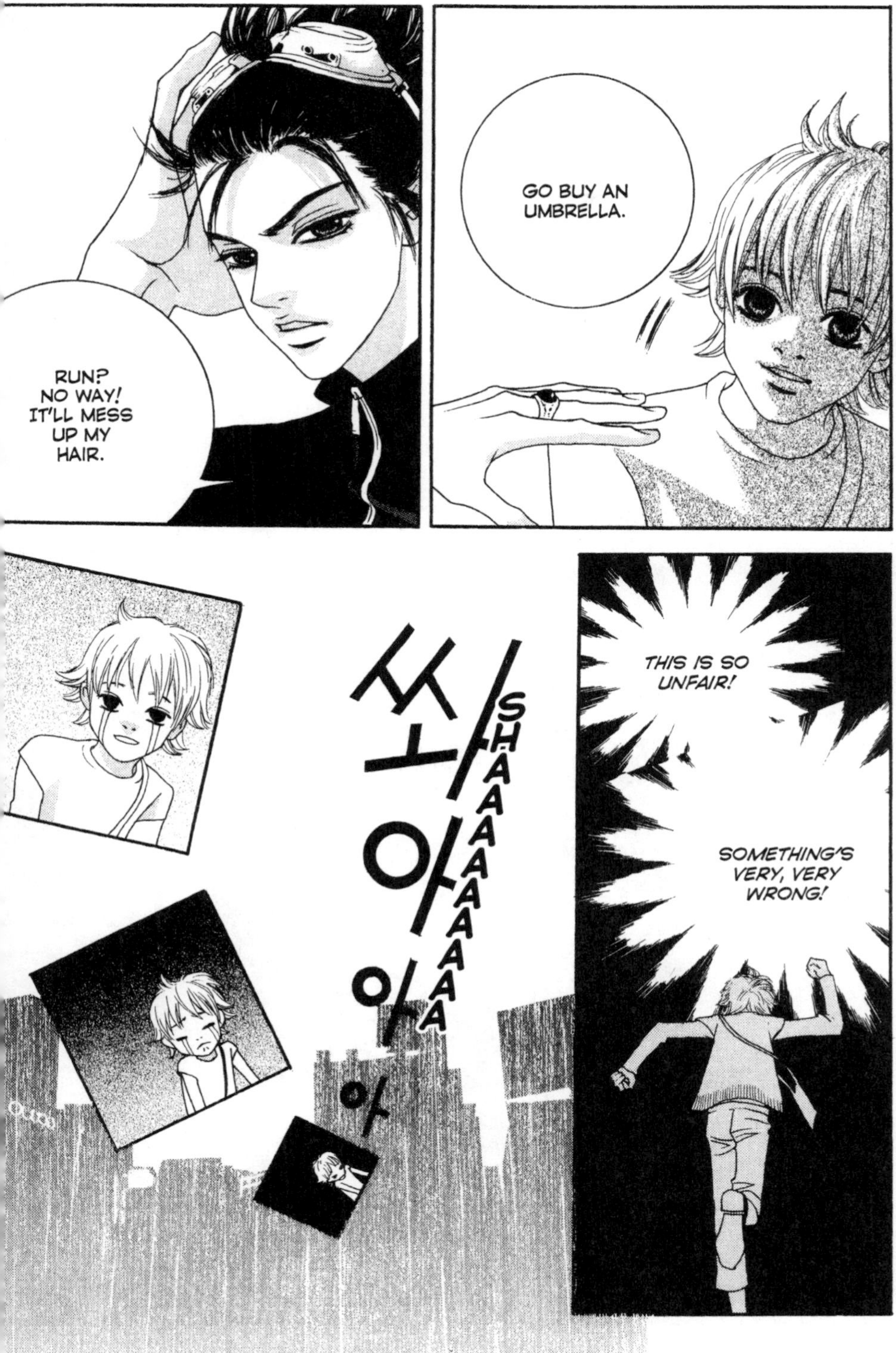
RUN? NO WAY! IT'LL MESS UP MY HAIR.
GO BUY AN UMBRELLA.
쏴아아아
SHAAAAAAAAA
THIS IS SO UNFAIR!
SOMETHING'S VERY, VERY WRONG!

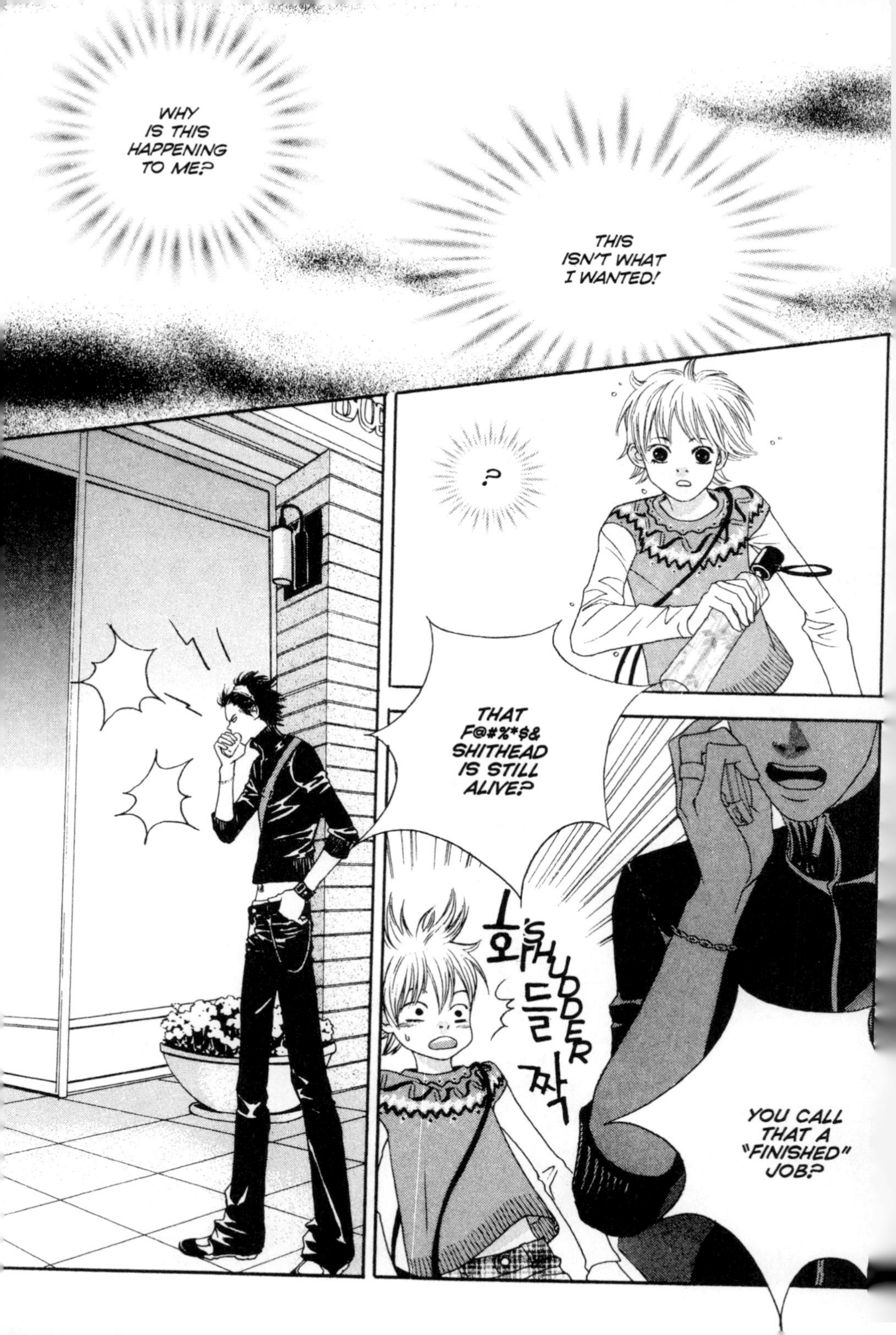

WHY IS THIS HAPPENING TO ME?
THIS ISN'T WHAT I WANTED!
THAT F@#%*$& SHITHEAD IS STILL ALIVE?
?
SHUDDER
YOU CALL THAT A "FINISHED" JOB?

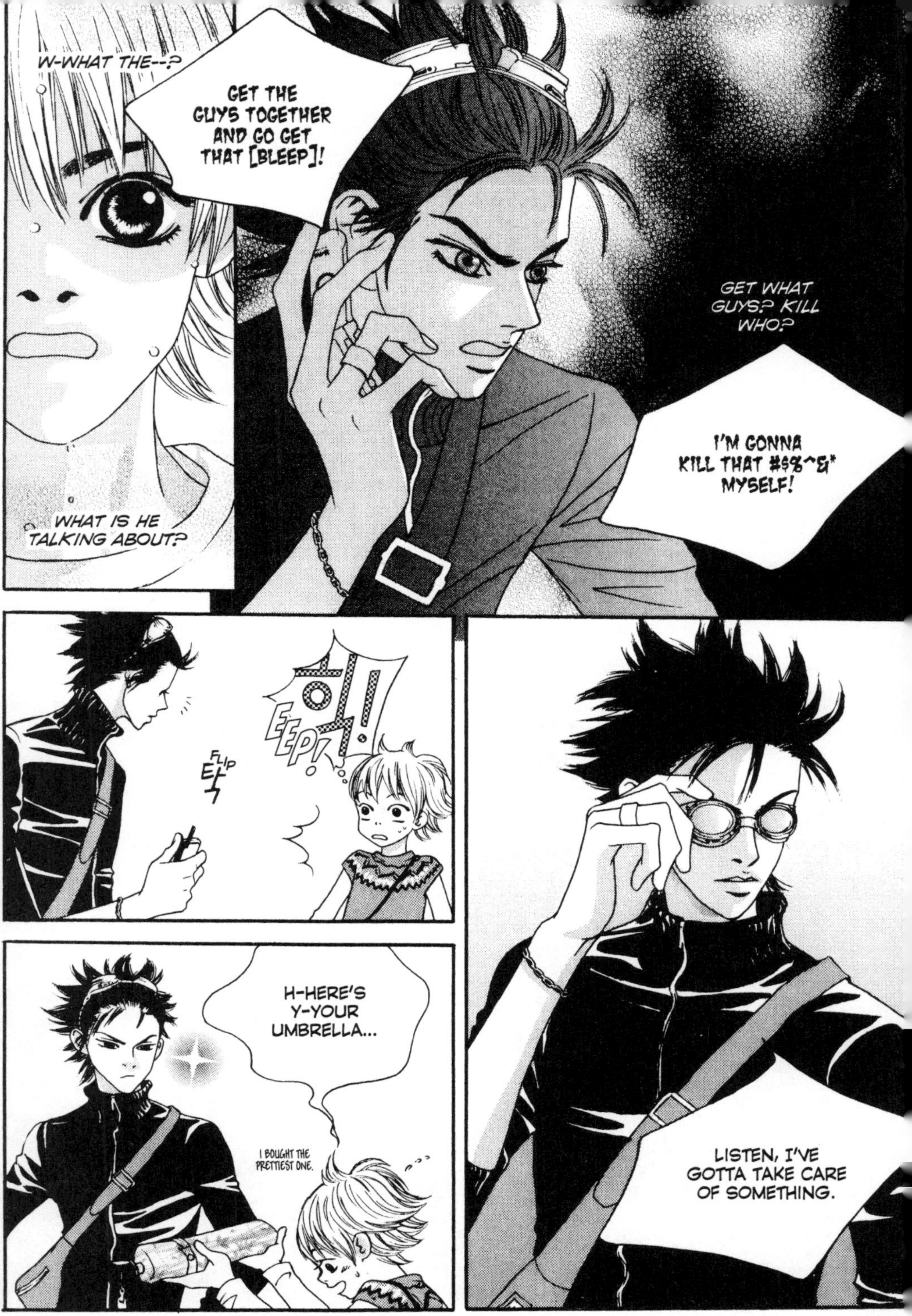
W-WHAT THE--?
WHAT IS HE TALKING ABOUT?
GET THE GUYS TOGETHER AND GO GET THAT [BLEEP]!
GET WHAT GUYS? KILL WHO?
I'M GONNA KILL THAT #$%^&* MYSELF!
FLIP 탁
헉 EEP!
H-HERE'S Y-YOUR UMBRELLA...
I BOUGHT THE PRETTIEST ONE.
LISTEN, I'VE GOTTA TAKE CARE OF SOMETHING.

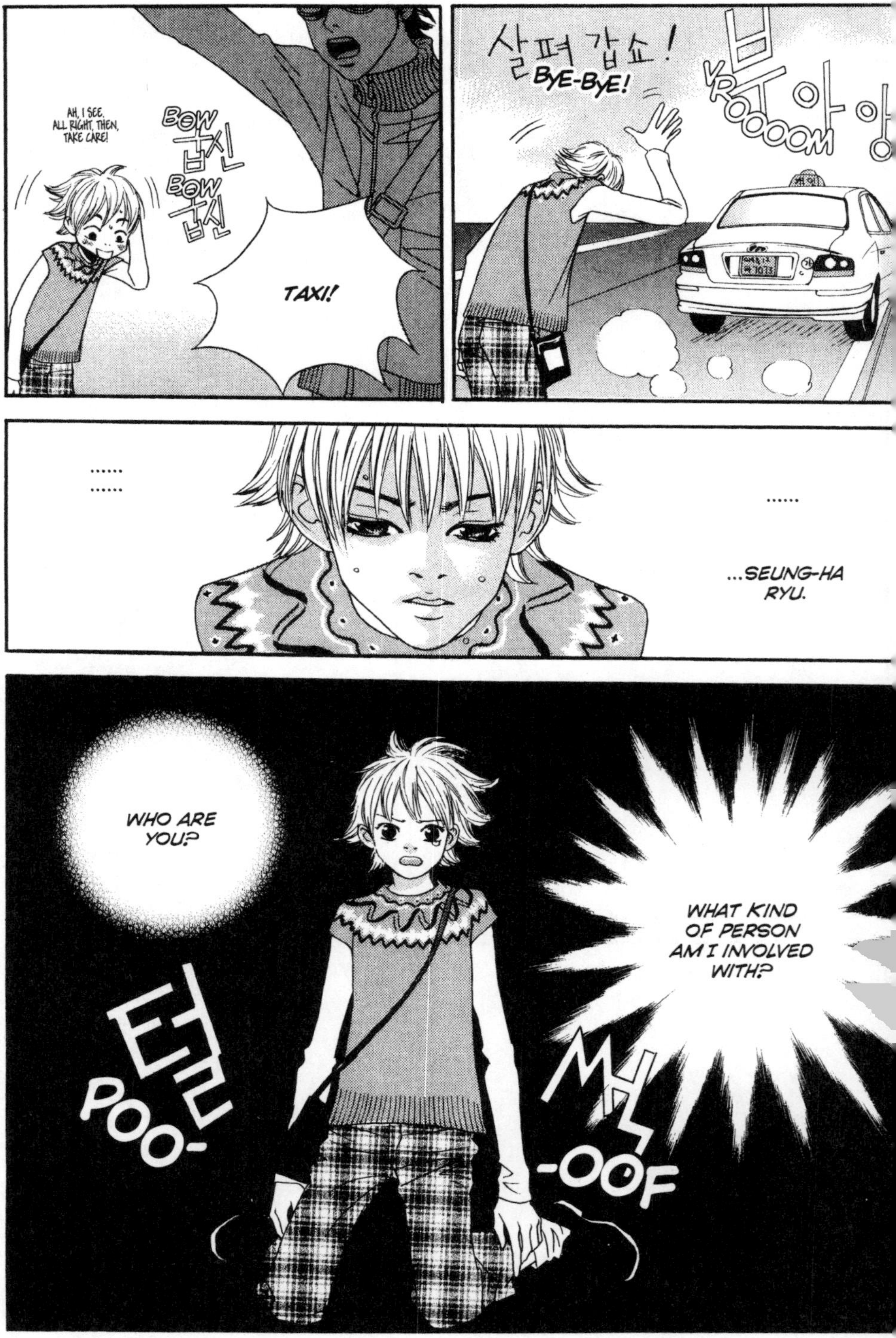
AH, I SEE. ALL RIGHT, THEN, TAKE CARE!
BOW 굽신
BOW 굽신
TAXI!
살펴 갑쇼!
BYE-BYE!
부아앙
VROOOOOM
......
......
......
...SEUNG-HA RYU.
WHO ARE YOU?
WHAT KIND OF PERSON AM I INVOLVED WITH?
털
POO-
썩
-OOF

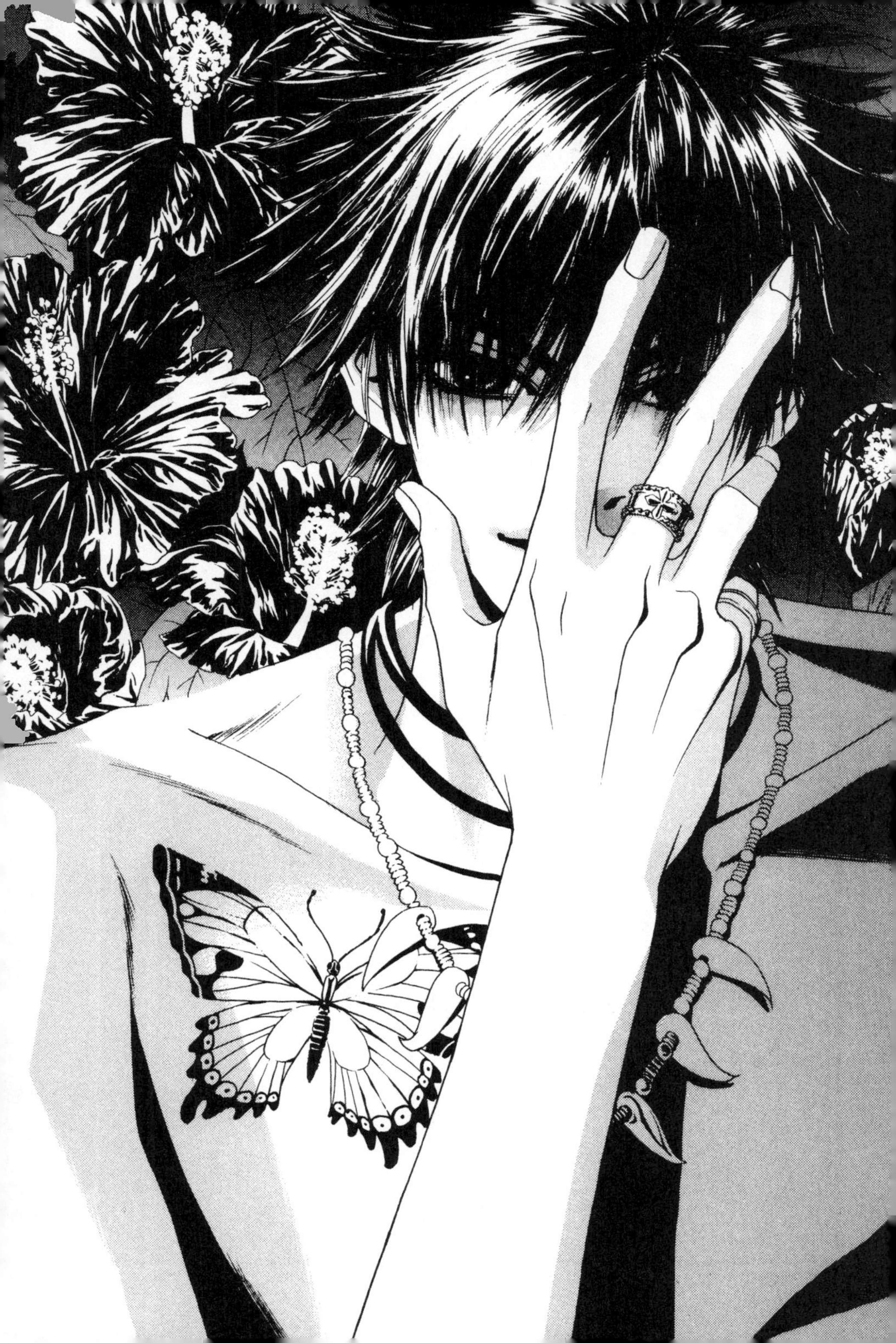

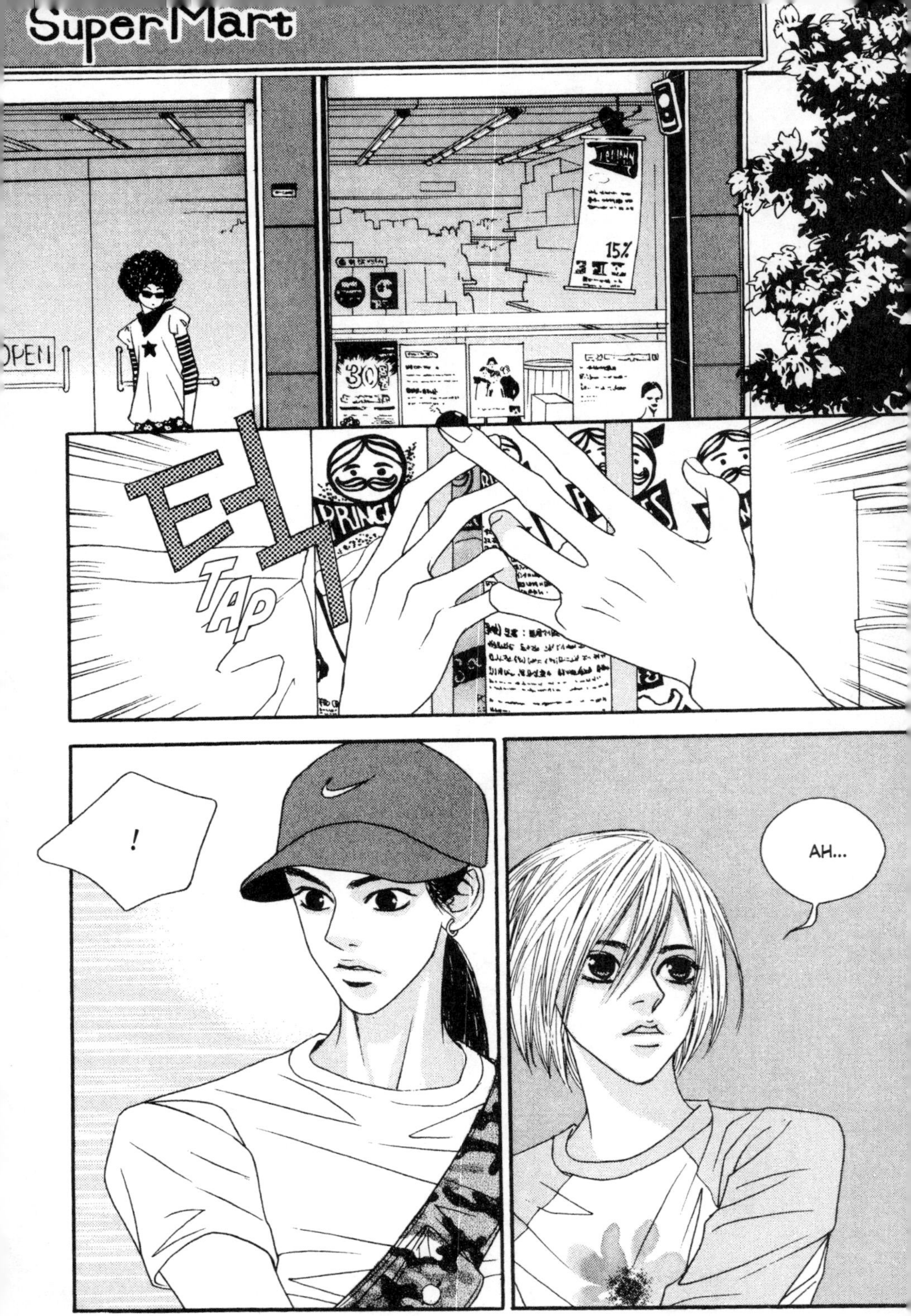
Super Mart
15%
TAP
!
AH...

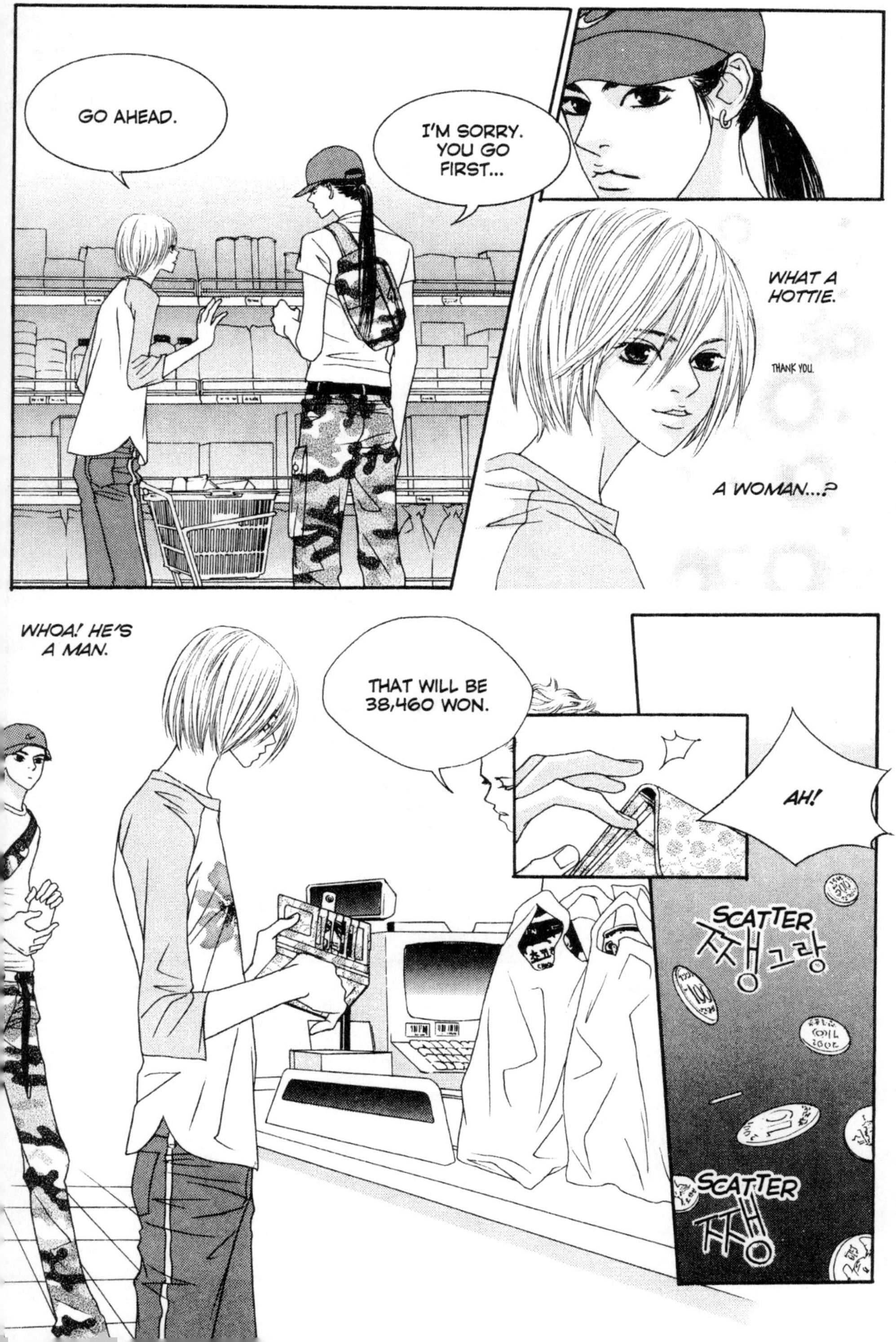
GO AHEAD.
I'M SORRY. YOU GO FIRST...
WHAT A HOTTIE.
THANK YOU.
A WOMAN...?
WHOA! HE'S A MAN.
THAT WILL BE 38,460 WON.
AH!
SCATTER
쨍그랑
SCATTER

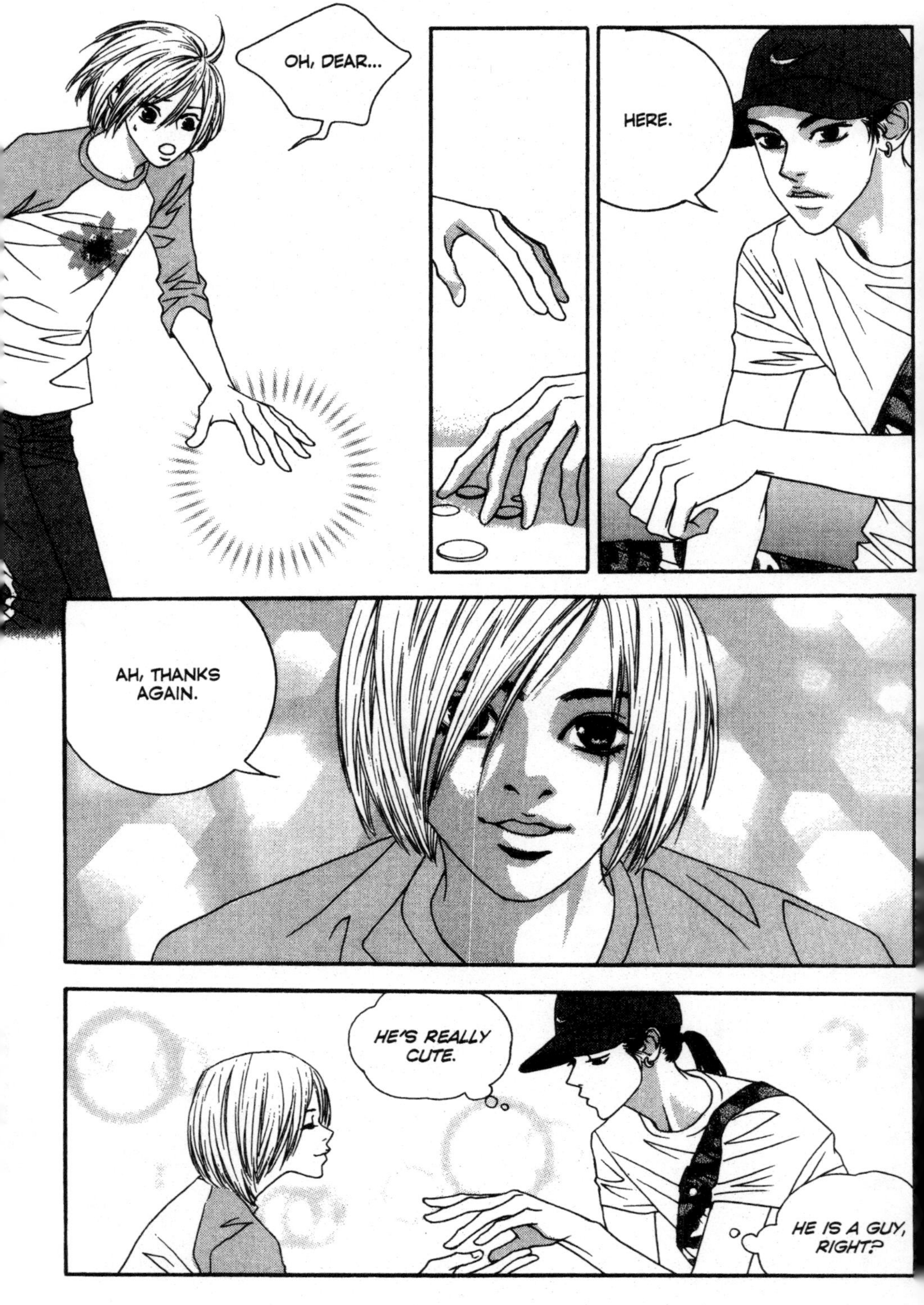
OH, DEAR...
HERE.
AH, THANKS AGAIN.
HE'S REALLY CUTE.
HE IS A GUY, RIGHT?

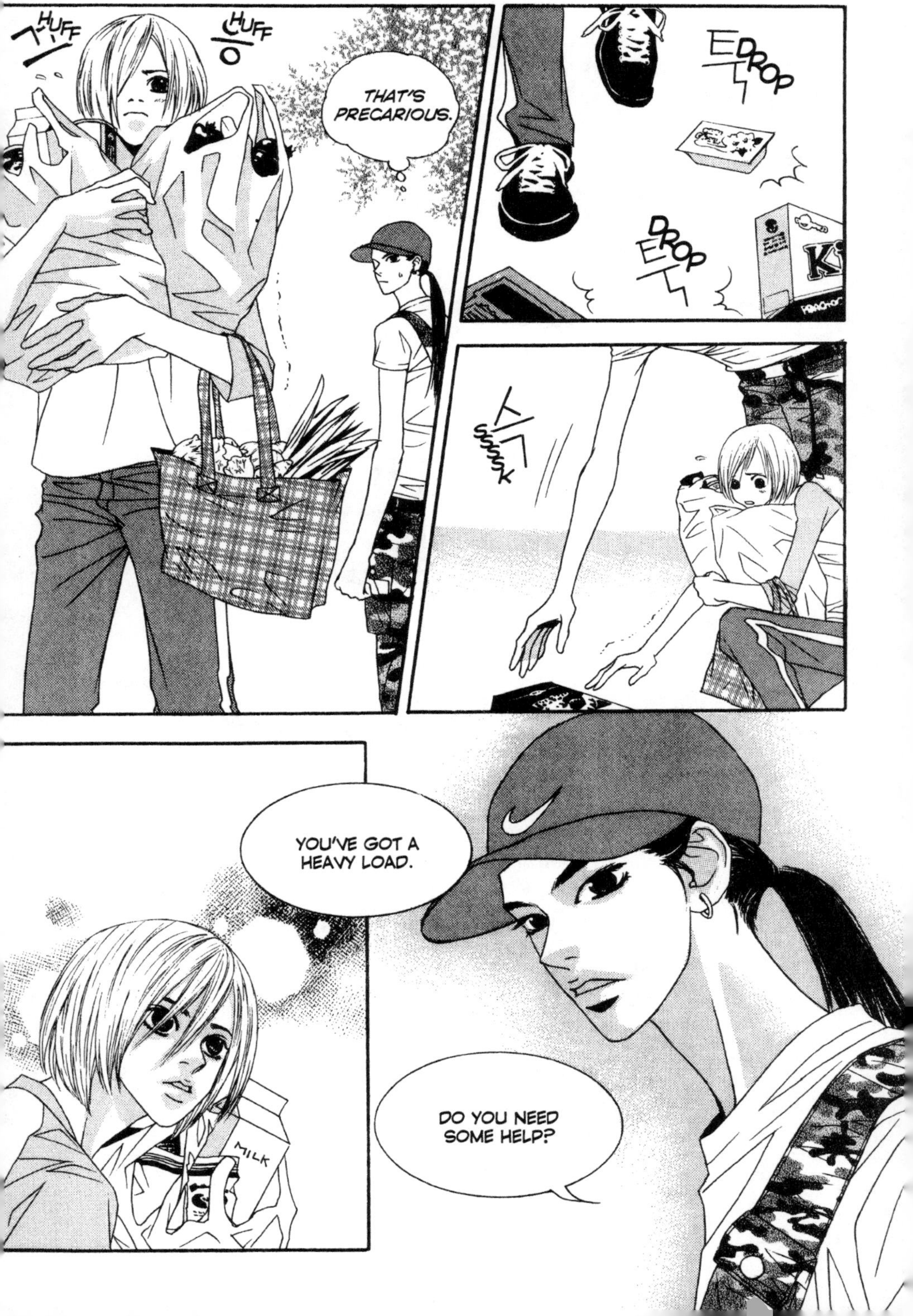
HUFF
HUFF
THAT'S PRECARIOUS.
DROP
DROP
SSSSK
YOU'VE GOT A HEAVY LOAD.
MILK
DO YOU NEED SOME HELP?

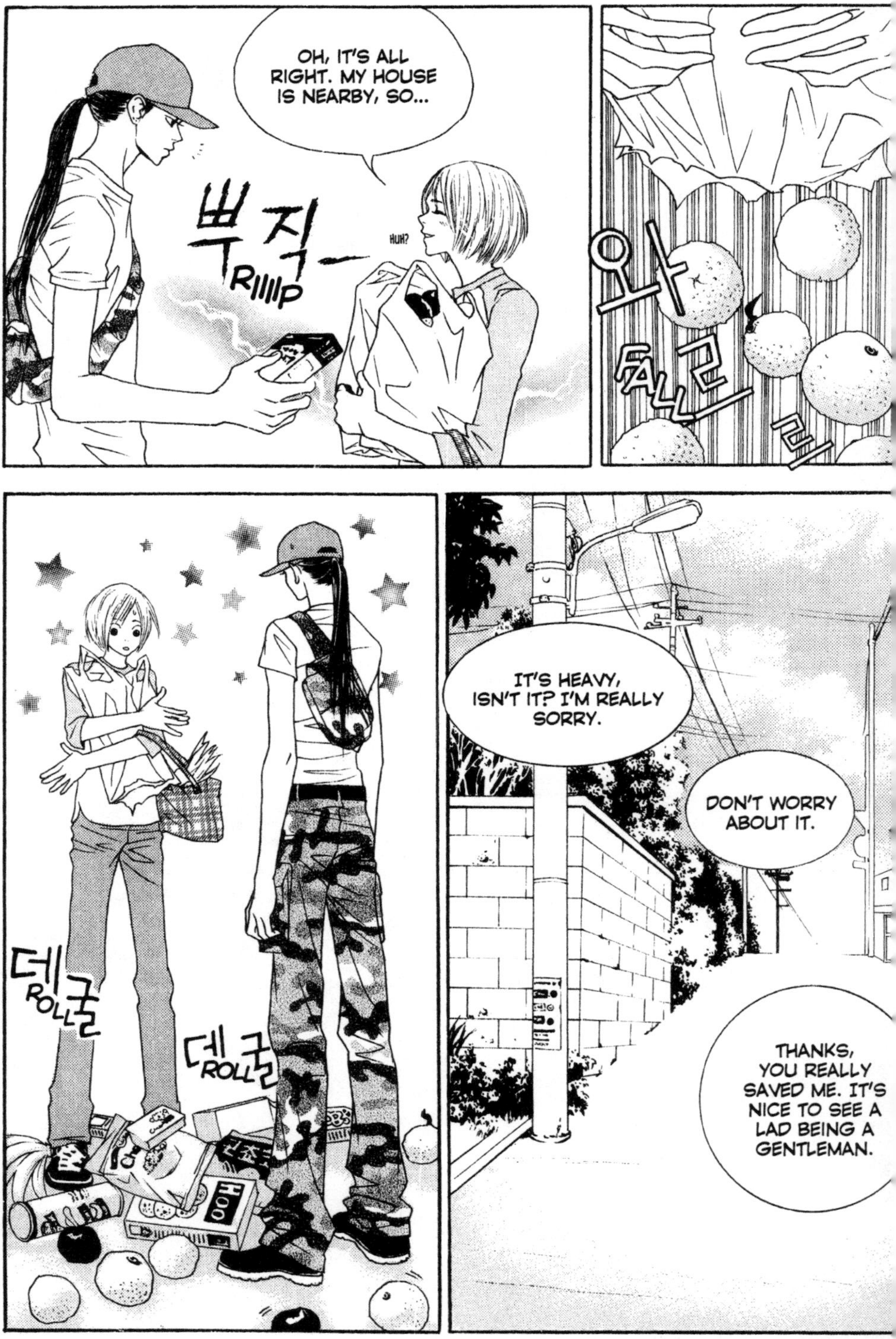
OH, IT'S ALL RIGHT. MY HOUSE IS NEARBY, SO...
HUH?
뿌직-
RIIIIP
FALL
데굴
ROLL
데굴
ROLL
IT'S HEAVY, ISN'T IT? I'M REALLY SORRY.
DON'T WORRY ABOUT IT.
THANKS, YOU REALLY SAVED ME. IT'S NICE TO SEE A LAD BEING A GENTLEMAN.

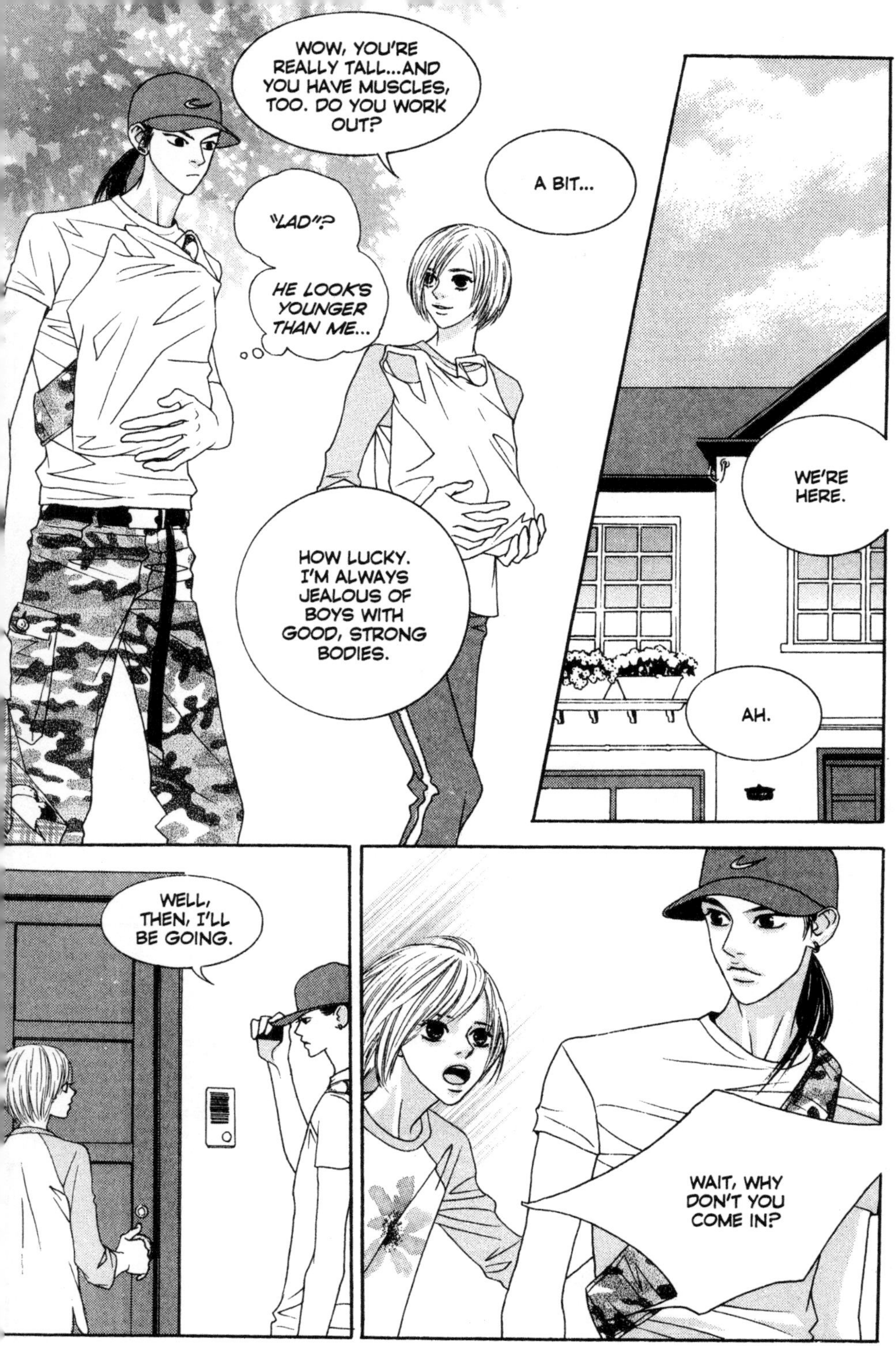
WOW, YOU'RE REALLY TALL...AND YOU HAVE MUSCLES, TOO. DO YOU WORK OUT?
A BIT...
"LAD"?
HE LOOKS YOUNGER THAN ME...
HOW LUCKY. I'M ALWAYS JEALOUS OF BOYS WITH GOOD, STRONG BODIES.
WE'RE HERE.
AH.
WELL, THEN, I'LL BE GOING.
WAIT, WHY DON'T YOU COME IN?

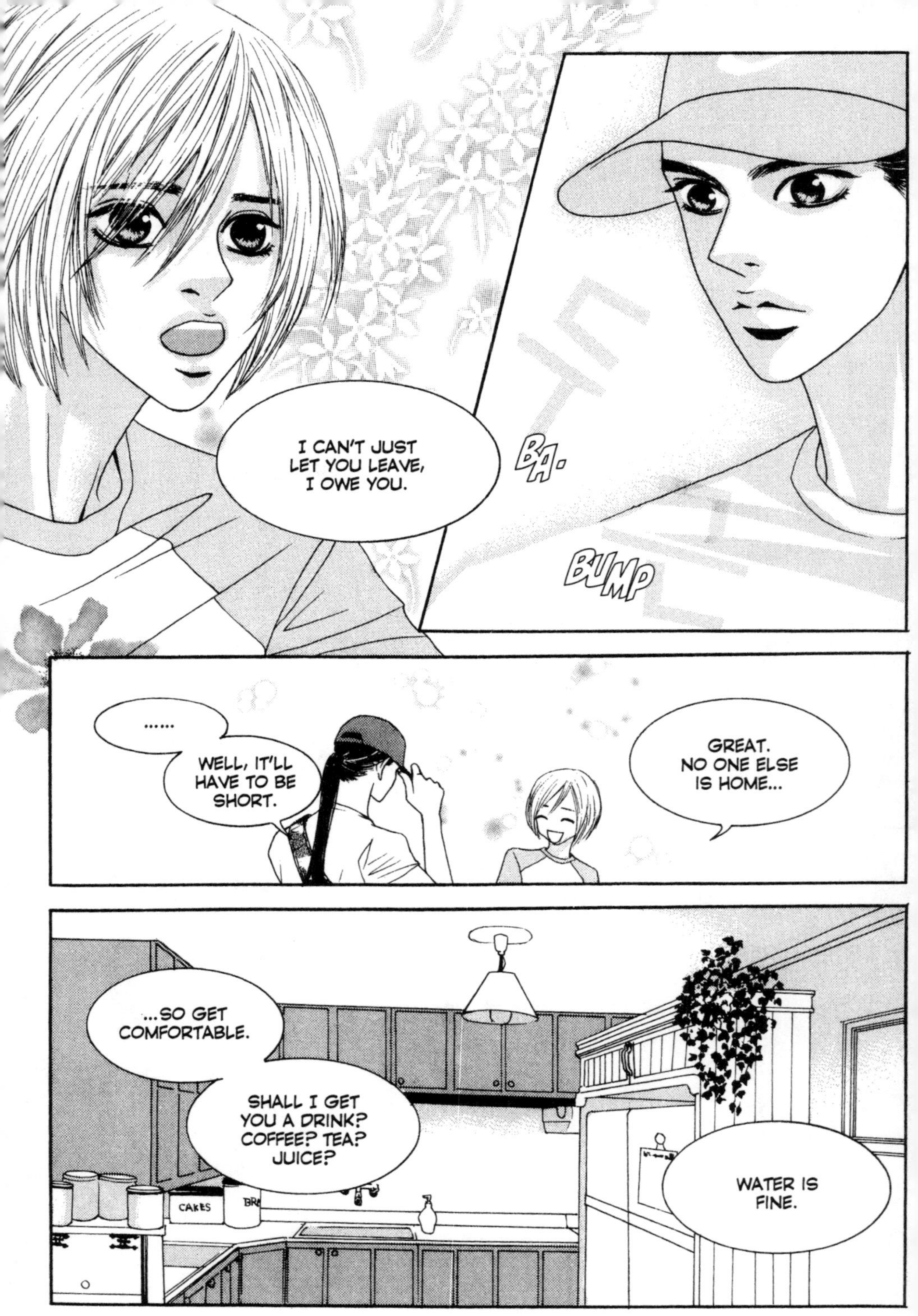
I CAN'T JUST LET YOU LEAVE, I OWE YOU.
BA-
BUMP
......
WELL, IT'LL HAVE TO BE SHORT.
GREAT. NO ONE ELSE IS HOME...
...SO GET COMFORTABLE.
SHALL I GET YOU A DRINK? COFFEE? TEA? JUICE?
CAKES
WATER IS FINE.

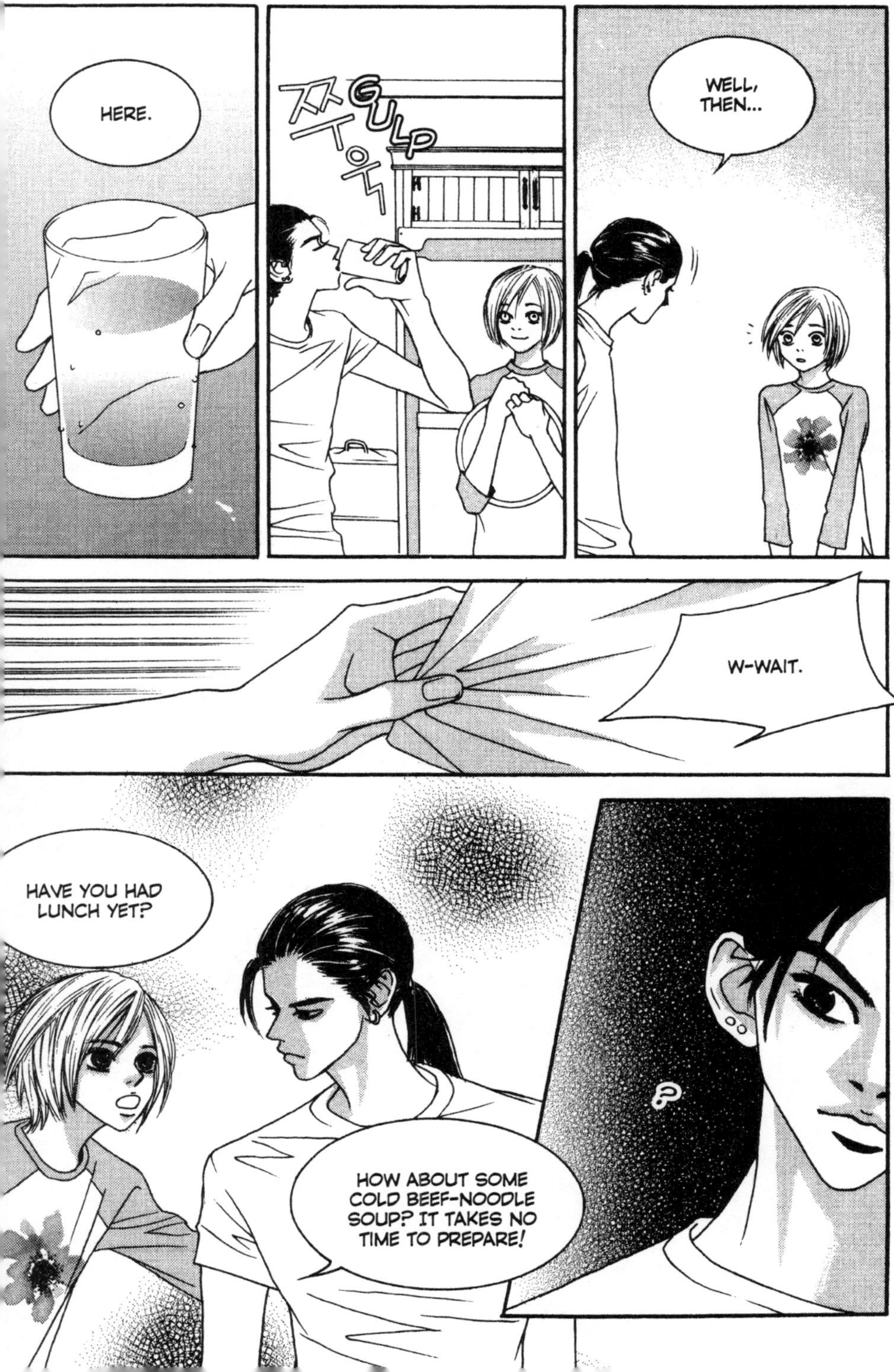
HERE.
GULP
WELL, THEN...
W-WAIT.
HAVE YOU HAD LUNCH YET?
HOW ABOUT SOME COLD BEEF-NOODLE SOUP? IT TAKES NO TIME TO PREPARE!

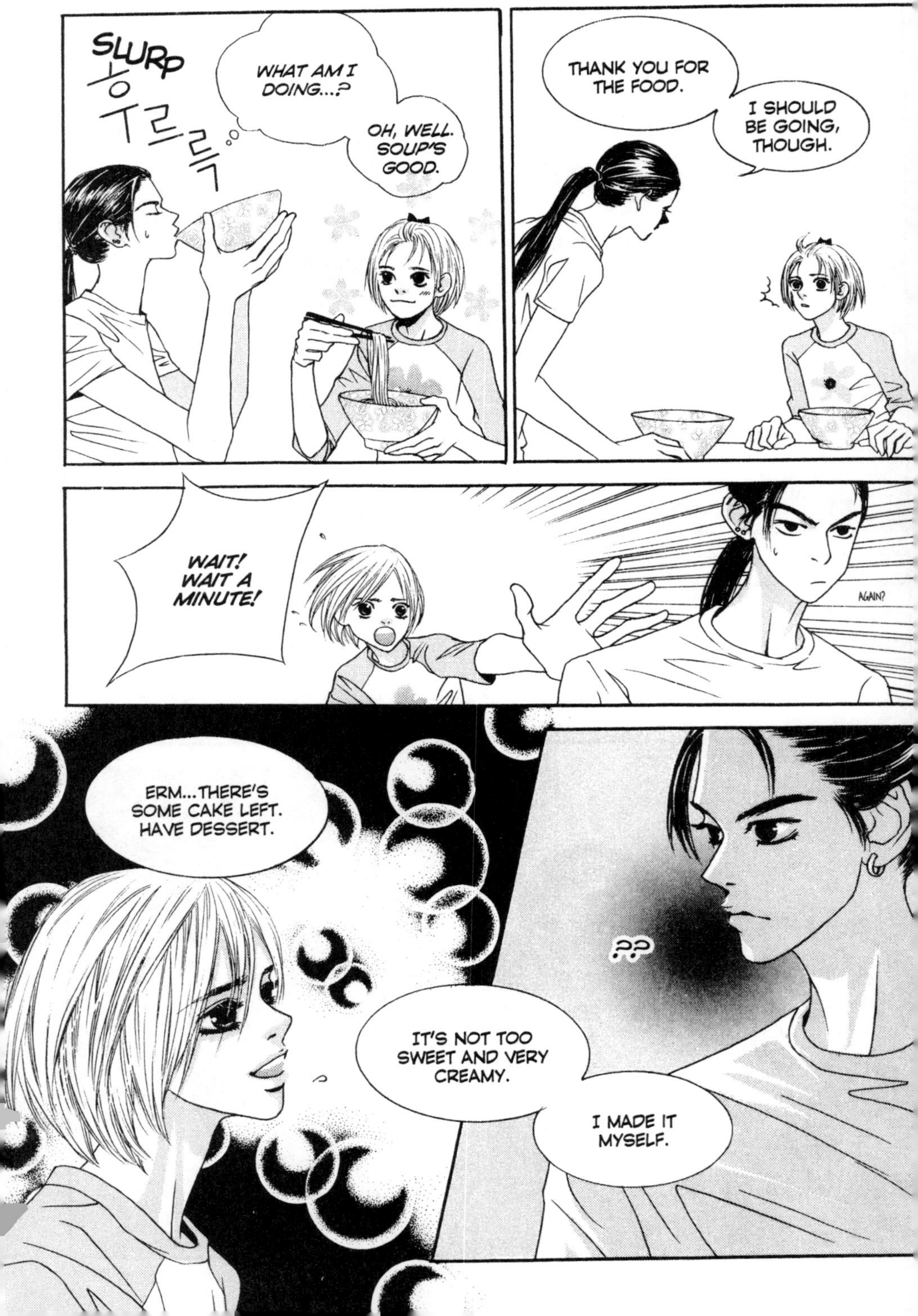
SLURP
WHAT AM I DOING...?
OH, WELL. SOUP'S GOOD.
THANK YOU FOR THE FOOD.
I SHOULD BE GOING, THOUGH.
WAIT! WAIT A MINUTE!
AGAIN?
ERM...THERE'S SOME CAKE LEFT. HAVE DESSERT.
??
IT'S NOT TOO SWEET AND VERY CREAMY.
I MADE IT MYSELF.

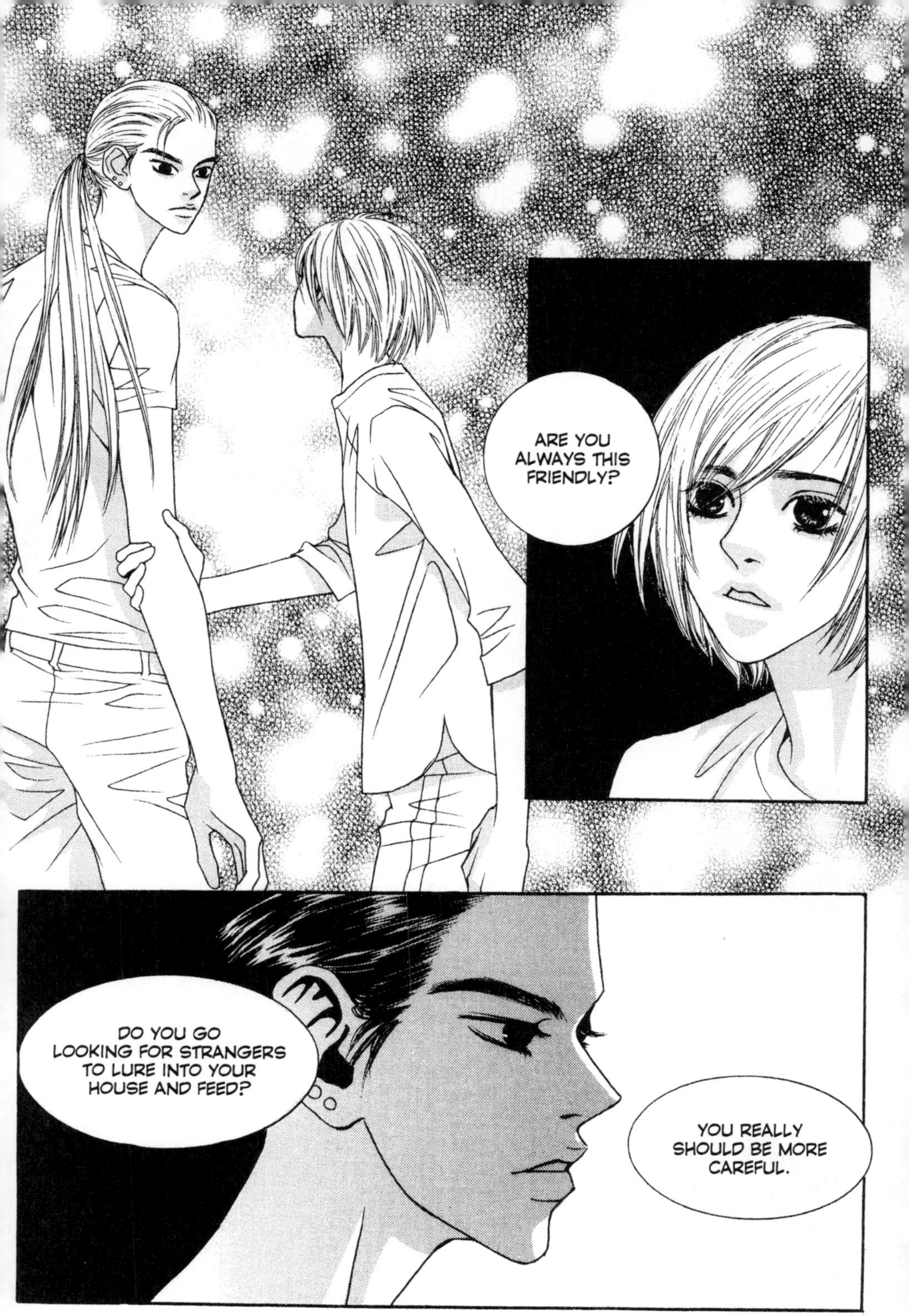
ARE YOU ALWAYS THIS FRIENDLY?
DO YOU GO LOOKING FOR STRANGERS TO LURE INTO YOUR HOUSE AND FEED?
YOU REALLY SHOULD BE MORE CAREFUL.

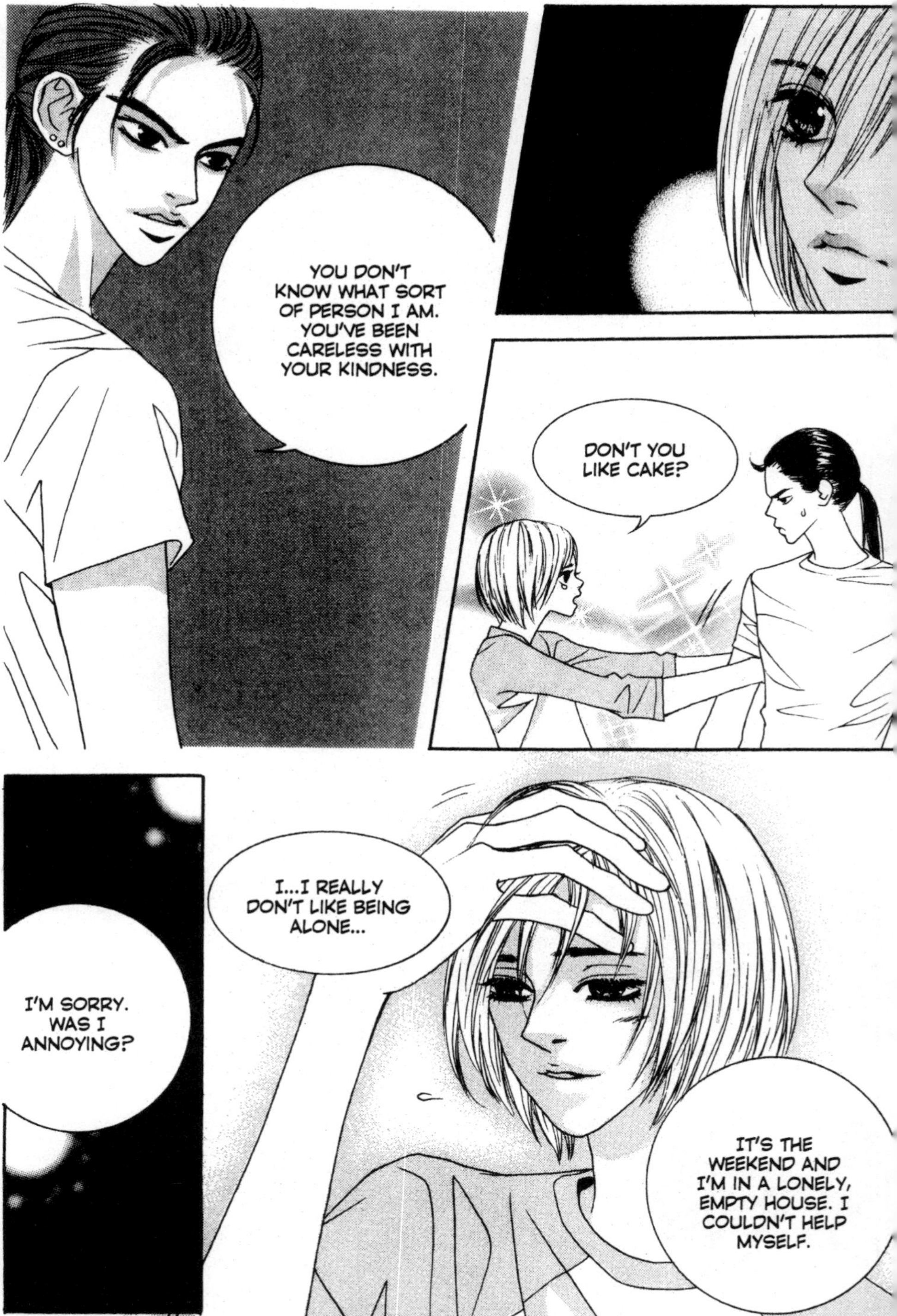
YOU DON'T KNOW WHAT SORT OF PERSON I AM. YOU'VE BEEN CARELESS WITH YOUR KINDNESS.
DON'T YOU LIKE CAKE?
I'M SORRY. WAS I ANNOYING?
I...I REALLY DON'T LIKE BEING ALONE...
IT'S THE WEEKEND AND I'M IN A LONELY, EMPTY HOUSE. I COULDN'T HELP MYSELF.

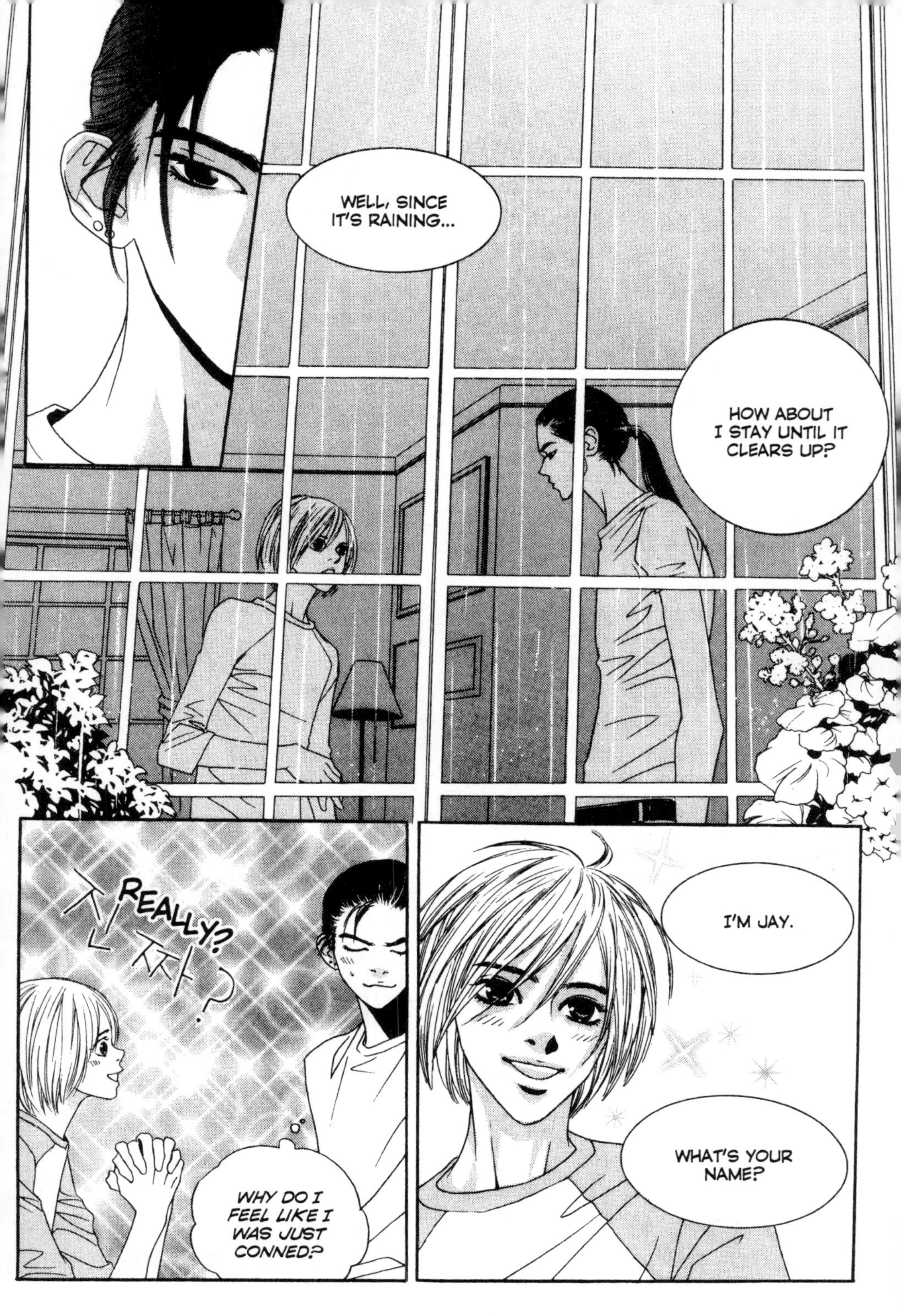
WELL, SINCE IT'S RAINING...
HOW ABOUT I STAY UNTIL IT CLEARS UP?
진짜?
REALLY?
WHY DO I FEEL LIKE I WAS JUST CONNED?
I'M JAY.
WHAT'S YOUR NAME?

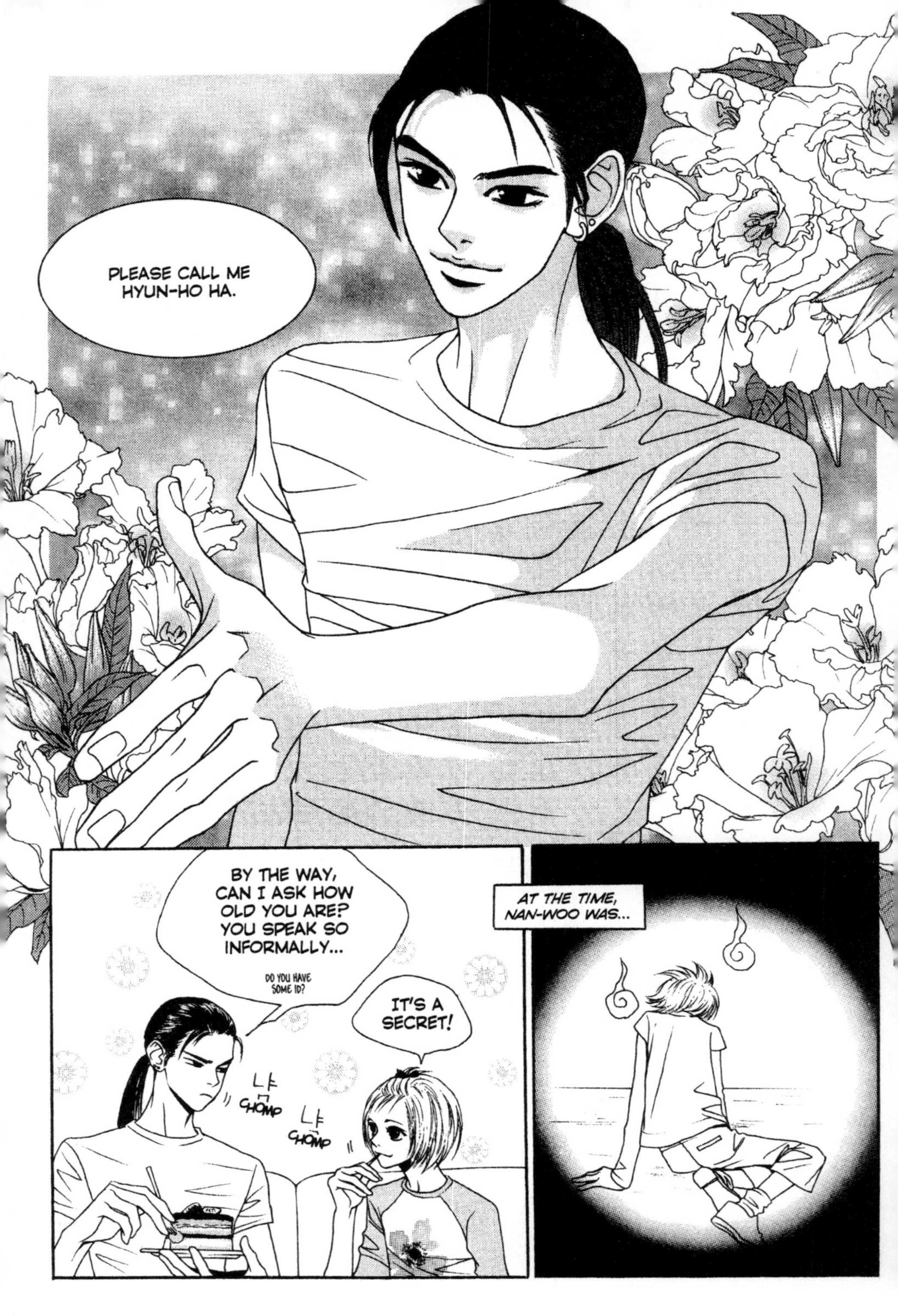
PLEASE CALL ME HYUN-HO HA.
BY THE WAY, CAN I ASK HOW OLD YOU ARE? YOU SPEAK SO INFORMALLY...
DO YOU HAVE SOME ID?
냠 CHOMP
냠 CHOMP
IT'S A SECRET!
AT THE TIME, NAN-WOO WAS...

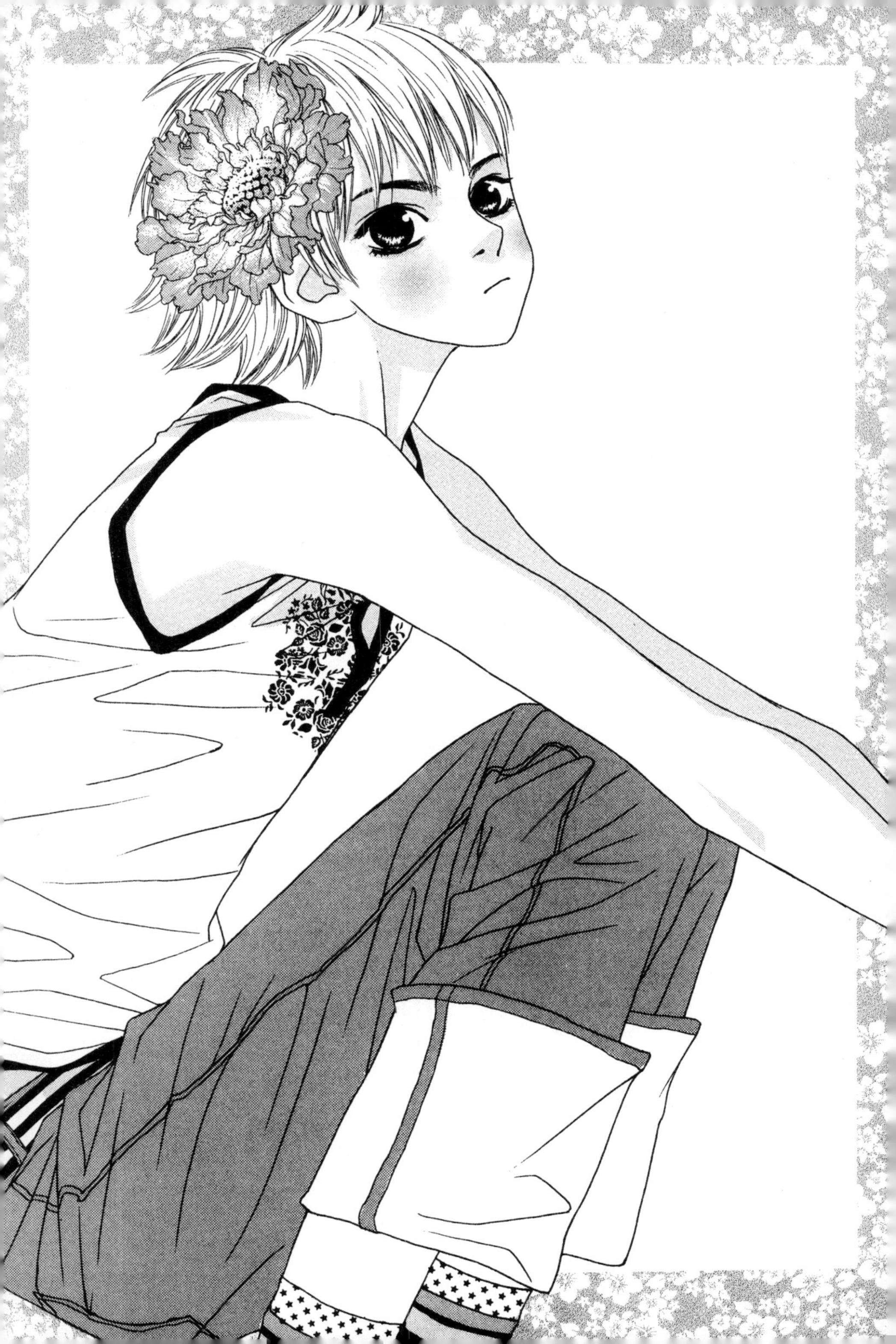

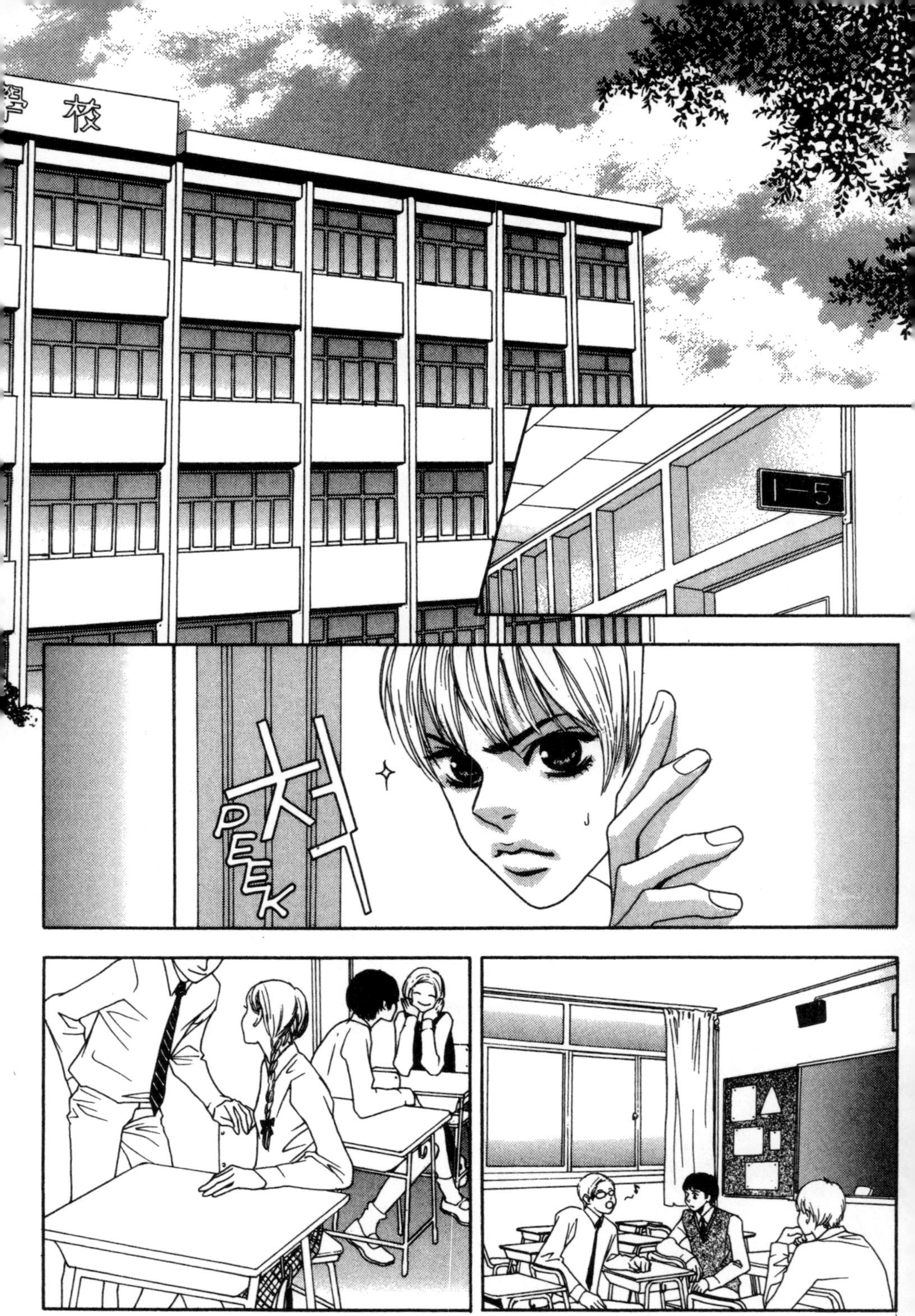

1—5
PEEK

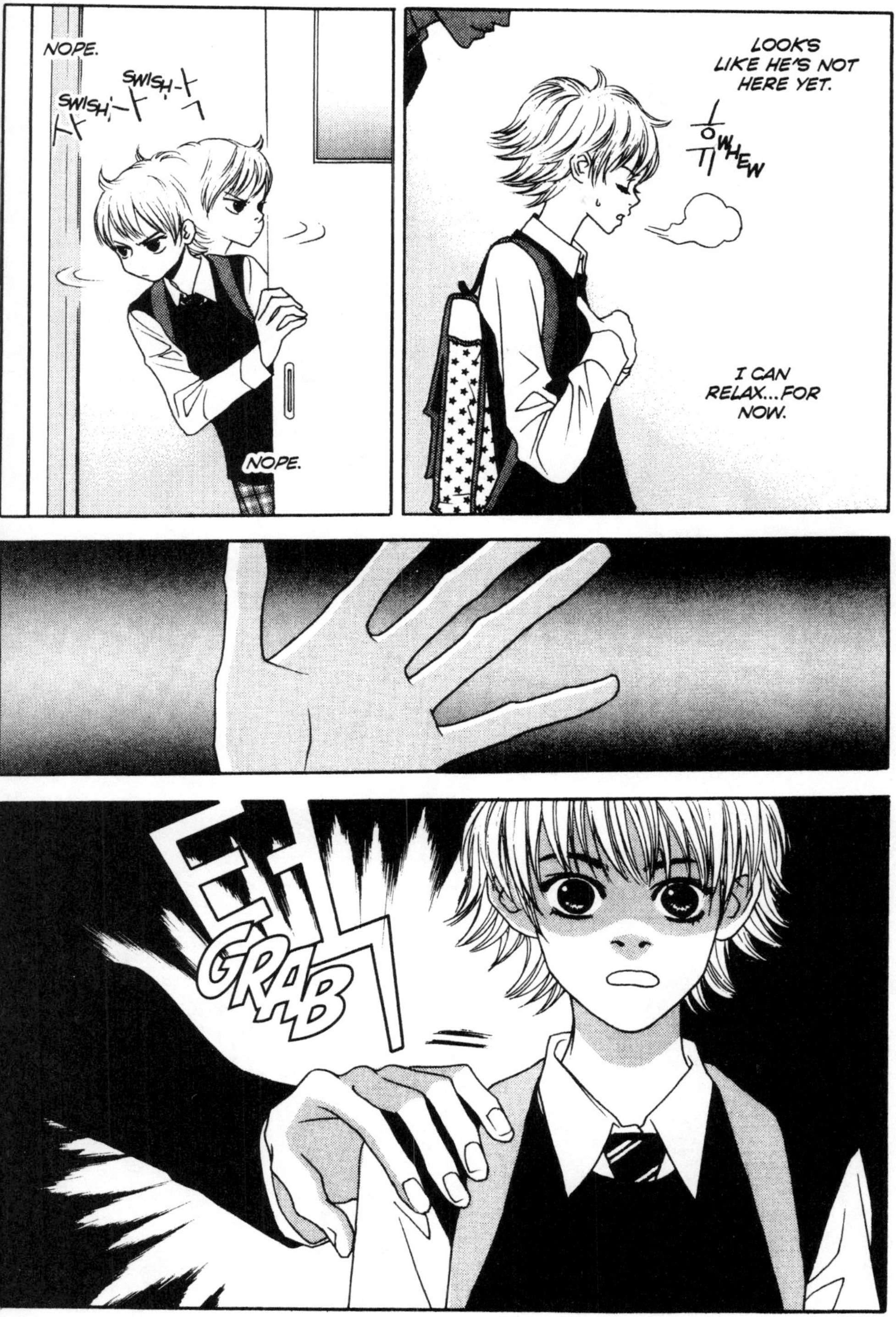
NOPE.
SWISH-
SWISH-
NOPE.
LOOKS LIKE HE'S NOT HERE YET.
WHEW
I CAN RELAX...FOR NOW.
GRAB

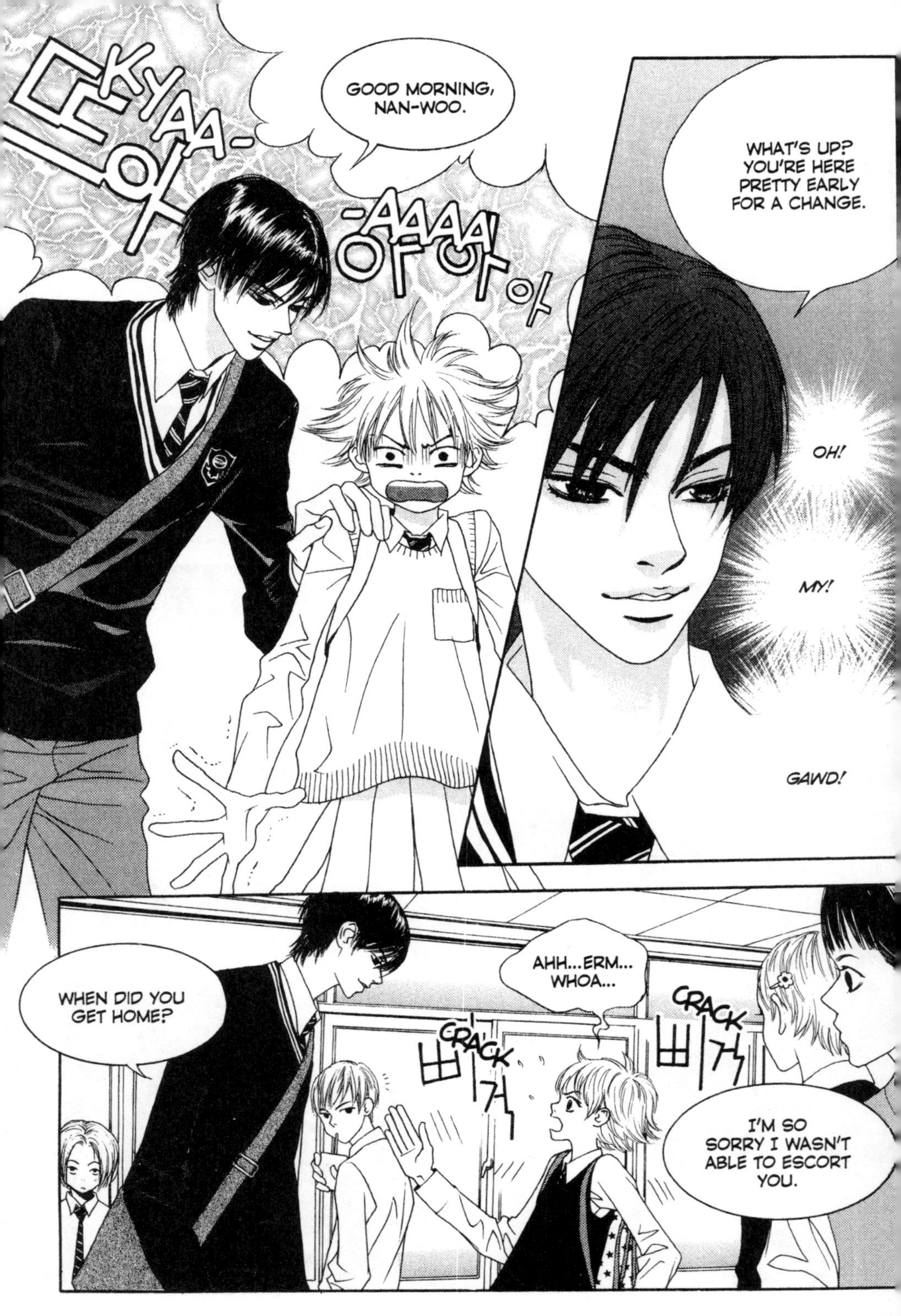
KYAA-
-AAAA!
GOOD MORNING, NAN-WOO.
WHAT'S UP? YOU'RE HERE PRETTY EARLY FOR A CHANGE.
OH!
MY!
GAWD!
WHEN DID YOU GET HOME?
AHH...ERM... WHOA...
CRACK
CRACK
I'M SO SORRY I WASN'T ABLE TO ESCORT YOU.

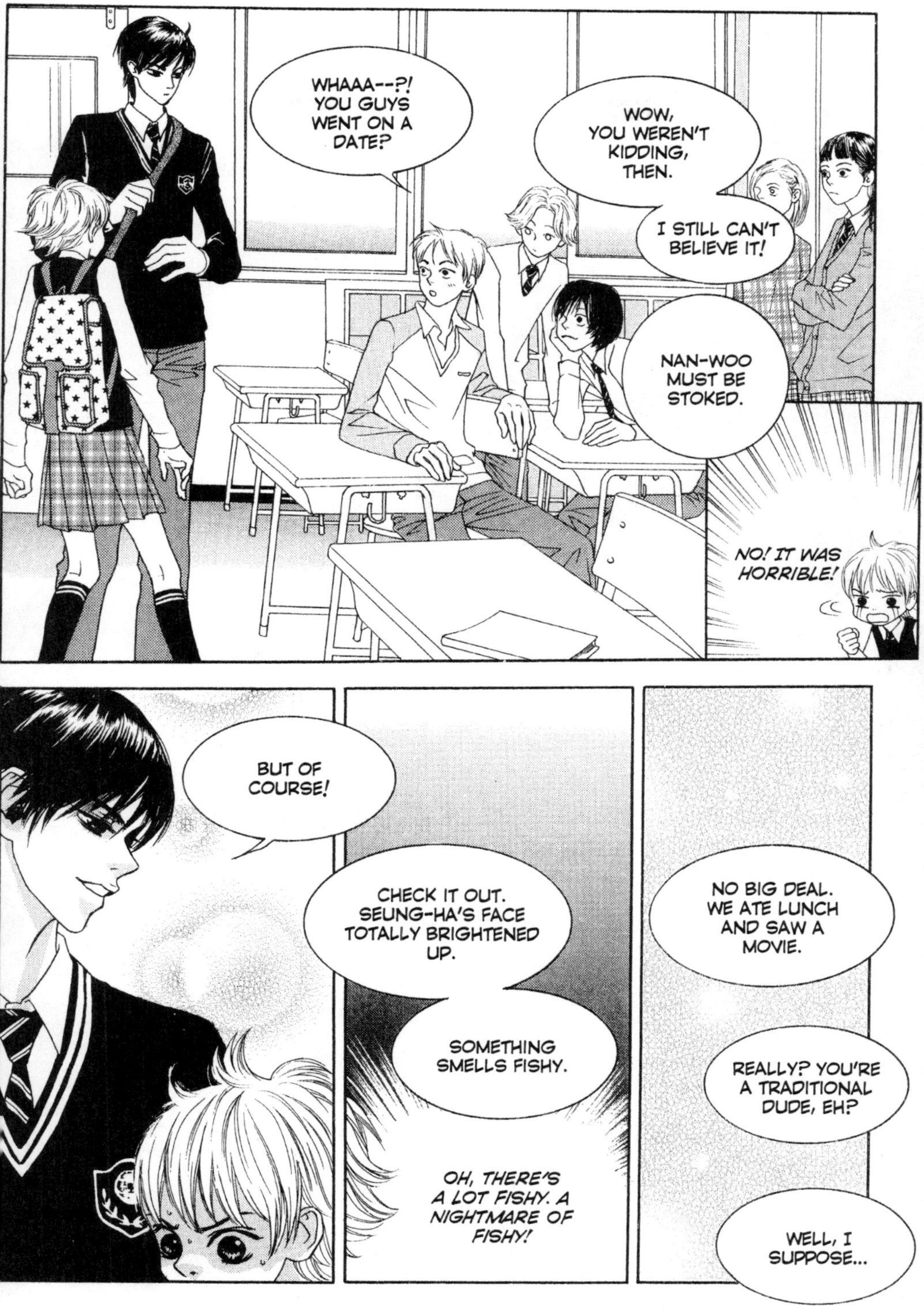

WHAAA--?! YOU GUYS WENT ON A DATE?
WOW, YOU WEREN'T KIDDING, THEN.
I STILL CAN'T BELIEVE IT!
NAN-WOO MUST BE STOKED.
NO! IT WAS HORRIBLE!
BUT OF COURSE!
CHECK IT OUT. SEUNG-HA'S FACE TOTALLY BRIGHTENED UP.
SOMETHING SMELLS FISHY.
OH, THERE'S A LOT FISHY. A NIGHTMARE OF FISHY!
NO BIG DEAL. WE ATE LUNCH AND SAW A MOVIE.
REALLY? YOU'RE A TRADITIONAL DUDE, EH?
WELL, I SUPPOSE...

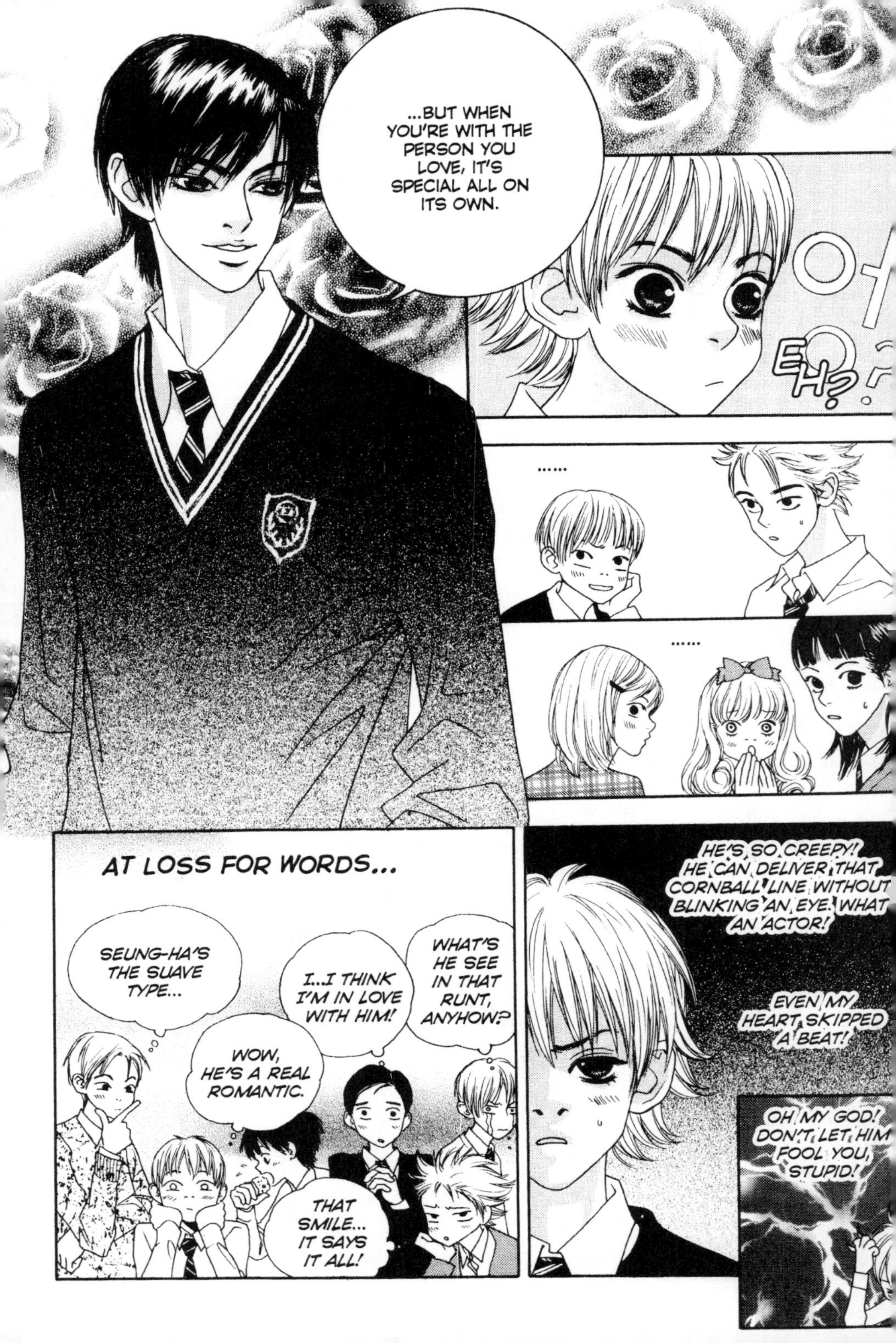
...BUT WHEN YOU'RE WITH THE PERSON YOU LOVE, IT'S SPECIAL ALL ON ITS OWN.
EH?
......
......
AT LOSS FOR WORDS...
SEUNG-HA'S THE SUAVE TYPE...
WOW, HE'S A REAL ROMANTIC.
I..I THINK I'M IN LOVE WITH HIM!
WHAT'S HE SEE IN THAT RUNT, ANYHOW?
THAT SMILE... IT SAYS IT ALL!
HE'S SO CREEPY! HE CAN DELIVER THAT CORNBALL LINE WITHOUT BLINKING AN EYE. WHAT AN ACTOR!
EVEN MY HEART SKIPPED A BEAT!
OH MY GOD! DON'T LET HIM FOOL YOU, STUPID!

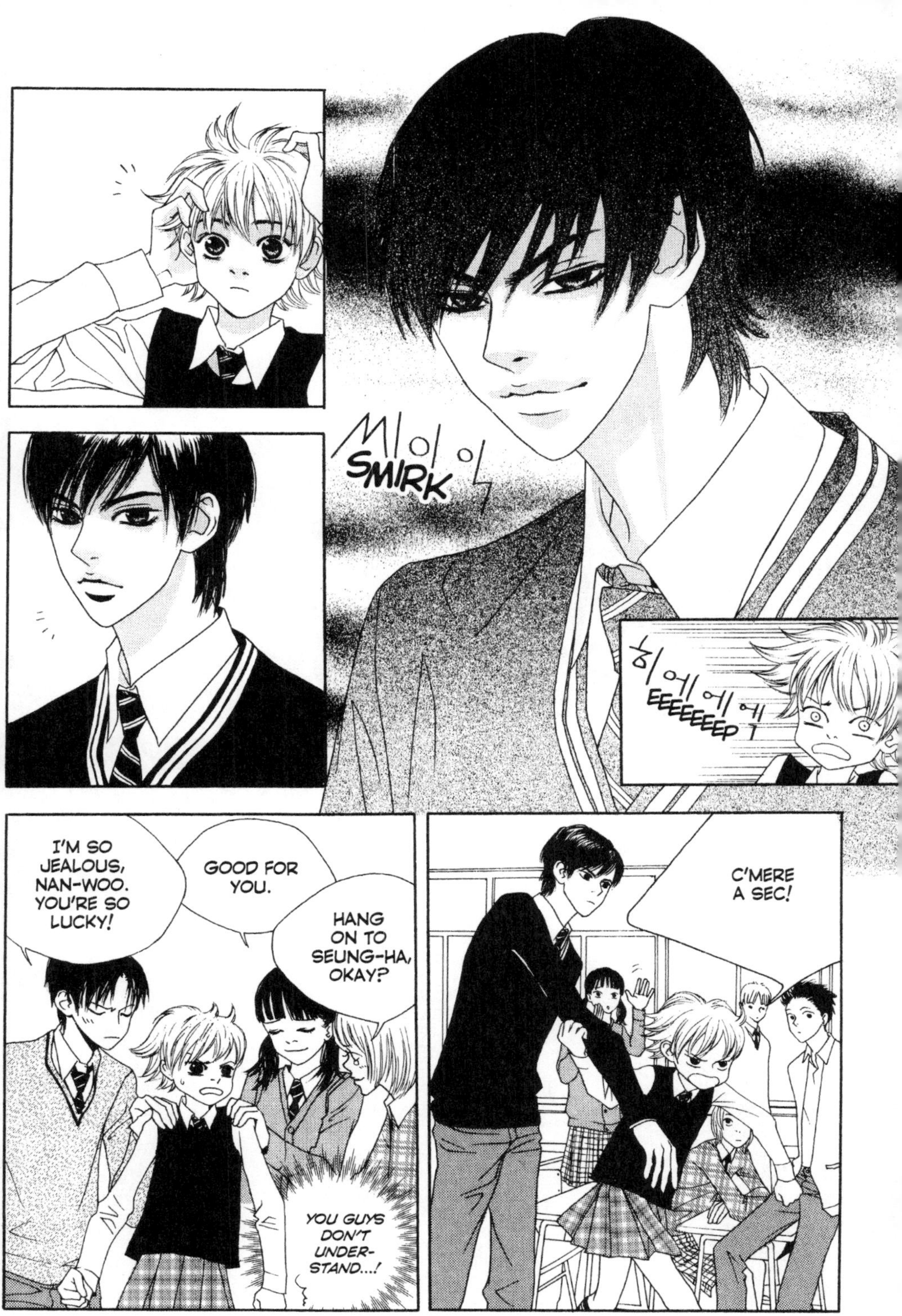
씨이이익
SMIRK
히에에엑
EEEEEEEEP
I'M SO JEALOUS, NAN-WOO. YOU'RE SO LUCKY!
GOOD FOR YOU.
HANG ON TO SEUNG-HA, OKAY?
YOU GUYS DON'T UNDER-STAND...!
C'MERE A SEC!

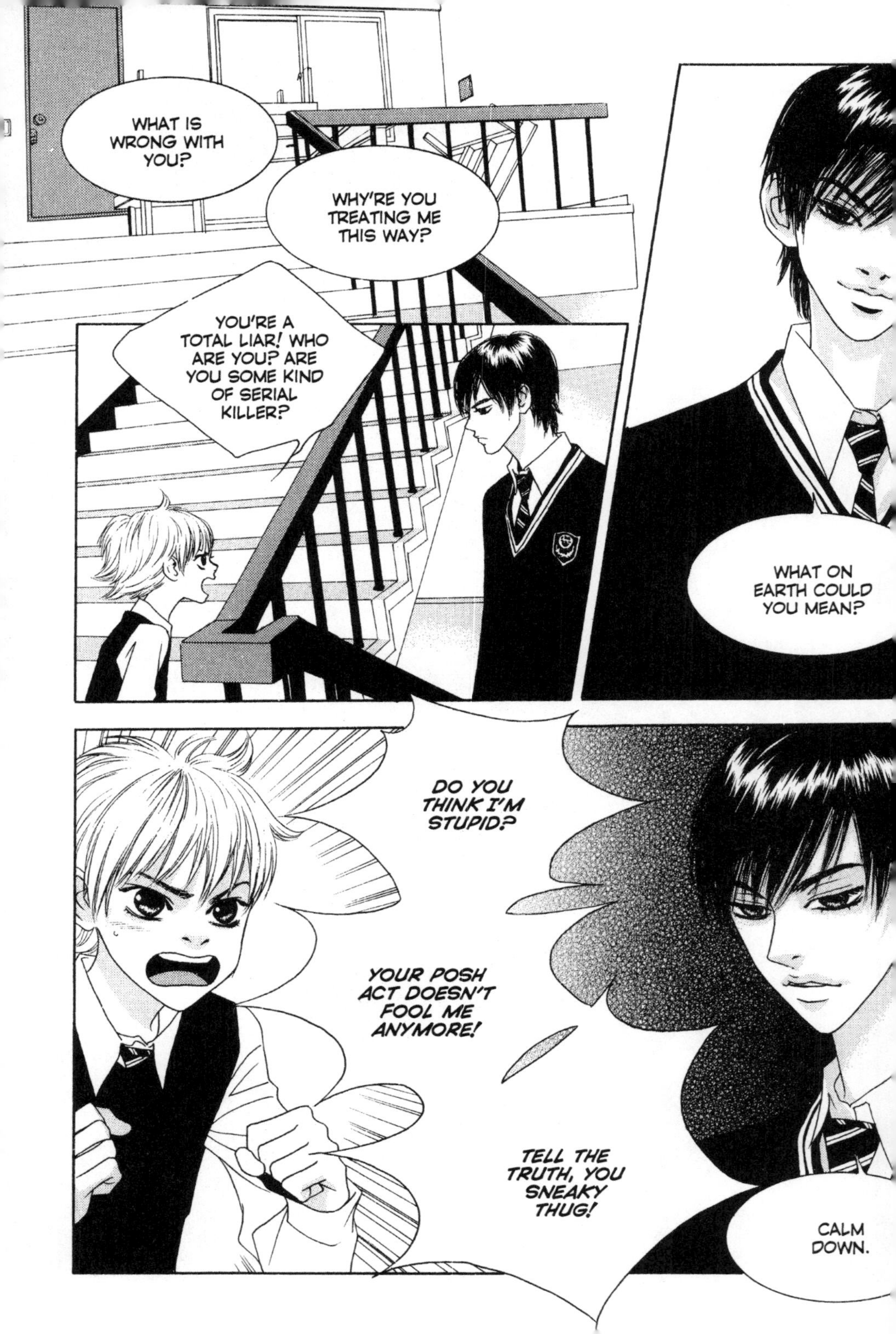
WHAT IS WRONG WITH YOU?
WHY'RE YOU TREATING ME THIS WAY?
YOU'RE A TOTAL LIAR! WHO ARE YOU? ARE YOU SOME KIND OF SERIAL KILLER?
WHAT ON EARTH COULD YOU MEAN?
DO YOU THINK I'M STUPID?
YOUR POSH ACT DOESN'T FOOL ME ANYMORE!
TELL THE TRUTH, YOU SNEAKY THUG!
CALM DOWN.

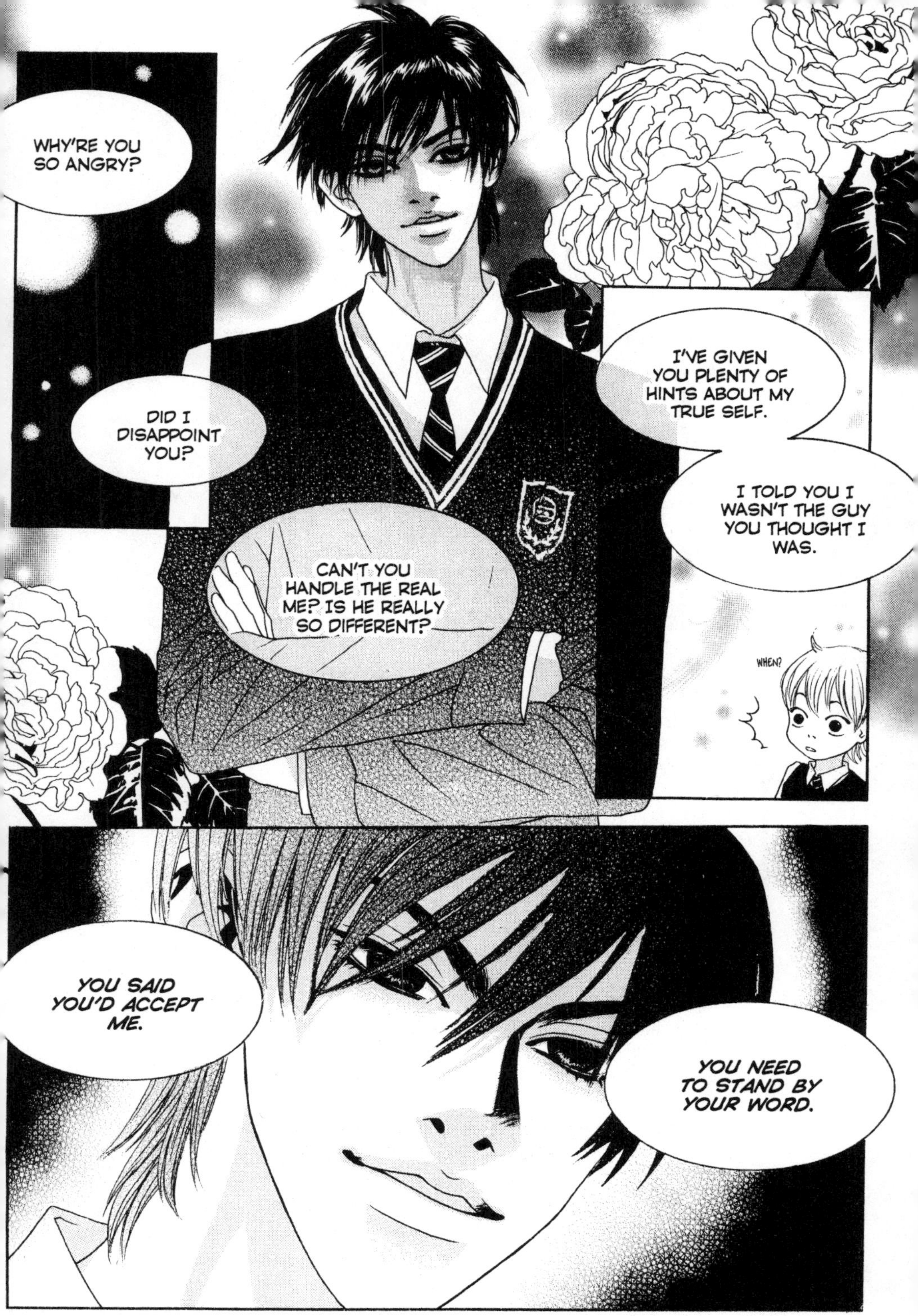
WHY'RE YOU SO ANGRY?
DID I DISAPPOINT YOU?
CAN'T YOU HANDLE THE REAL ME? IS HE REALLY SO DIFFERENT?
I'VE GIVEN YOU PLENTY OF HINTS ABOUT MY TRUE SELF.
I TOLD YOU I WASN'T THE GUY YOU THOUGHT I WAS.
WHEN?
YOU SAID YOU'D ACCEPT ME.
YOU NEED TO STAND BY YOUR WORD.

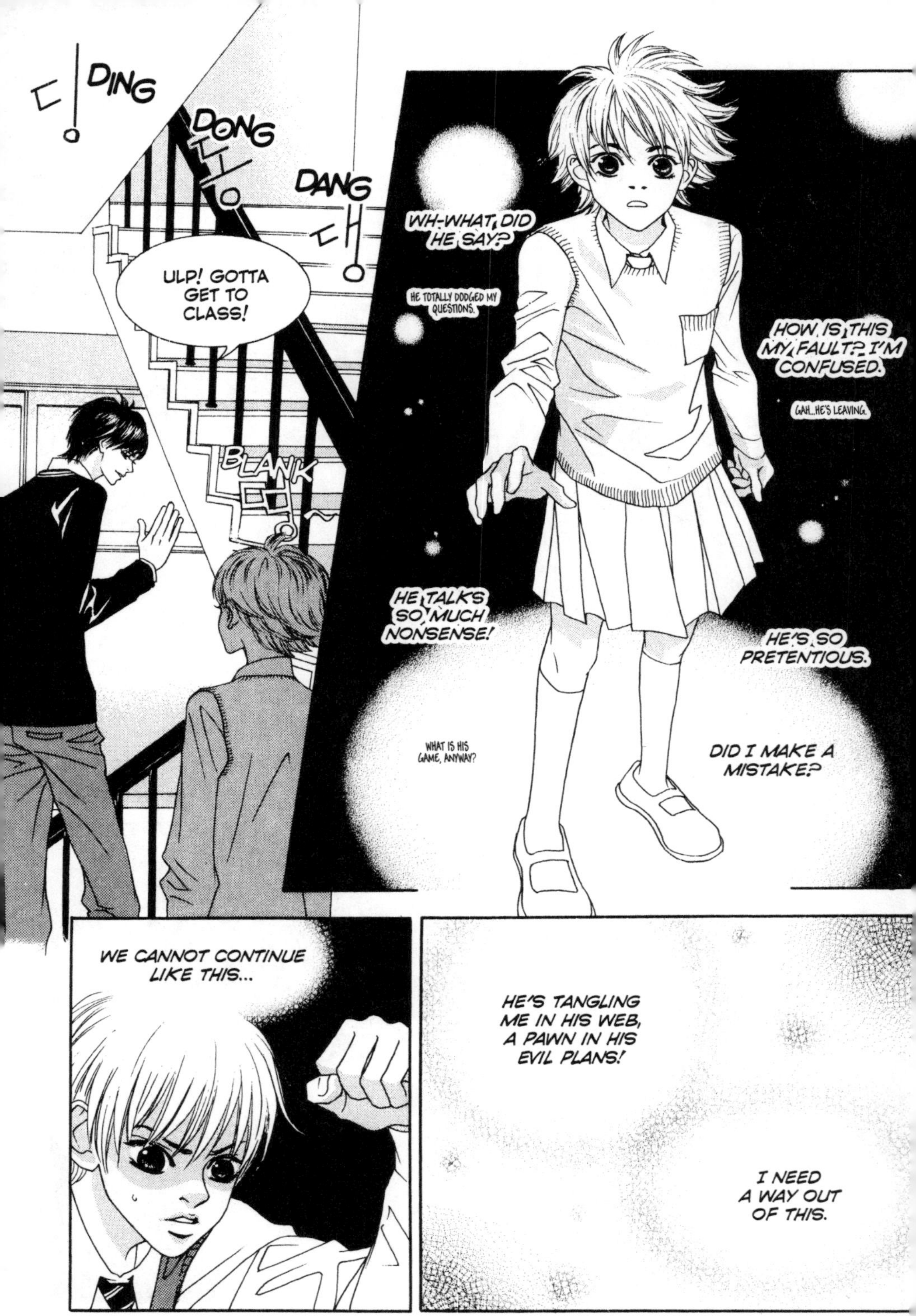
DING
DONG
DANG
ULP! GOTTA GET TO CLASS!
BLANK
WH-WHAT DID HE SAY?
HE TOTALLY DODGED MY QUESTIONS.
HOW IS THIS MY FAULT? I'M CONFUSED.
GAH...HE'S LEAVING.
HE TALKS SO MUCH NONSENSE!
HE'S SO PRETENTIOUS.
WHAT IS HIS GAME, ANYWAY?
DID I MAKE A MISTAKE?
WE CANNOT CONTINUE LIKE THIS...
HE'S TANGLING ME IN HIS WEB, A PAWN IN HIS EVIL PLANS!
I NEED A WAY OUT OF THIS.

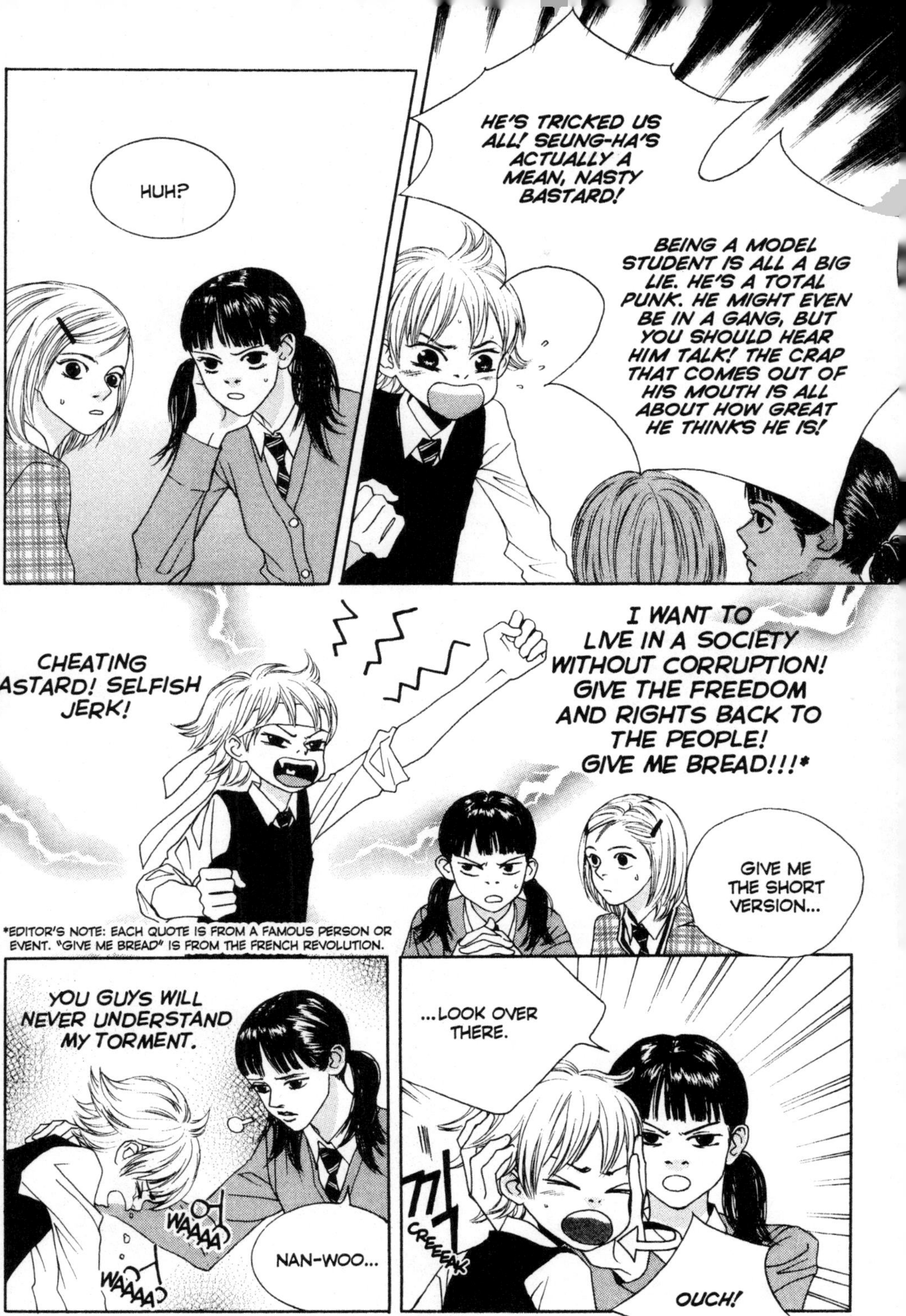
HUH?
HE'S TRICKED US ALL! SEUNG-HA'S ACTUALLY A MEAN, NASTY BASTARD!
BEING A MODEL STUDENT IS ALL A BIG LIE. HE'S A TOTAL PUNK. HE MIGHT EVEN BE IN A GANG, BUT YOU SHOULD HEAR HIM TALK! THE CRAP THAT COMES OUT OF HIS MOUTH IS ALL ABOUT HOW GREAT HE THINKS HE IS!
CHEATING ASTARD! SELFISH JERK!
I WANT TO LIVE IN A SOCIETY WITHOUT CORRUPTION! GIVE THE FREEDOM AND RIGHTS BACK TO THE PEOPLE! GIVE ME BREAD!!!*
GIVE ME THE SHORT VERSION...
YOU GUYS WILL NEVER UNDERSTAND MY TORMENT.
WAAAA
WAAAA
NAN-WOO...
...LOOK OVER THERE.
CREEEEAK
OUCH!

*EDITOR'S NOTE: EACH QUOTE IS FROM A FAMOUS PERSON OR EVENT. "GIVE ME BREAD" IS FROM THE FRENCH REVOLUTION.

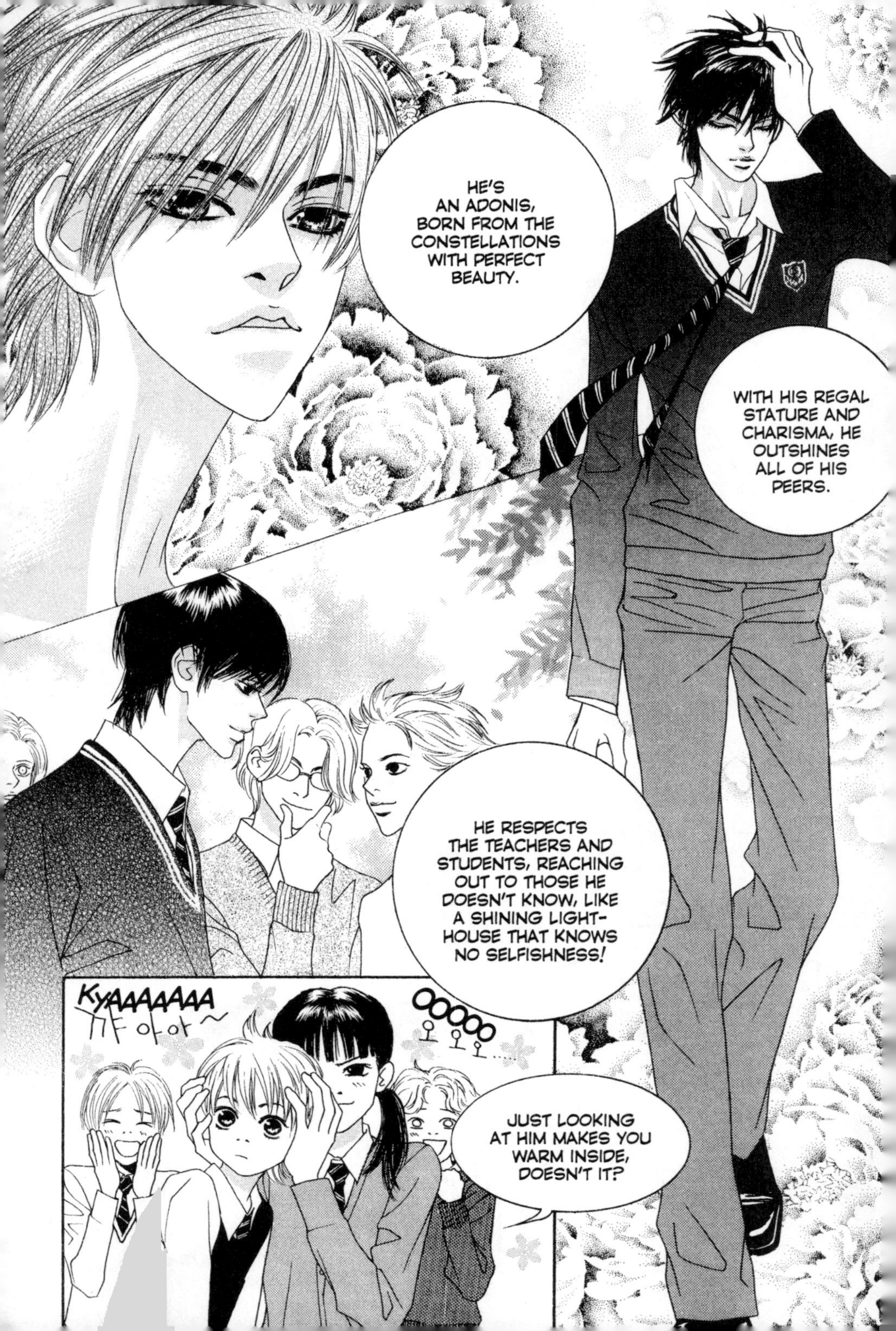
HE'S AN ADONIS, BORN FROM THE CONSTELLATIONS WITH PERFECT BEAUTY.
WITH HIS REGAL STATURE AND CHARISMA, HE OUTSHINES ALL OF HIS PEERS.
HE RESPECTS THE TEACHERS AND STUDENTS, REACHING OUT TO THOSE HE DOESN'T KNOW, LIKE A SHINING LIGHT-HOUSE THAT KNOWS NO SELFISHNESS!
KYAAAAAAA
OOOOO
JUST LOOKING AT HIM MAKES YOU WARM INSIDE, DOESN'T IT?

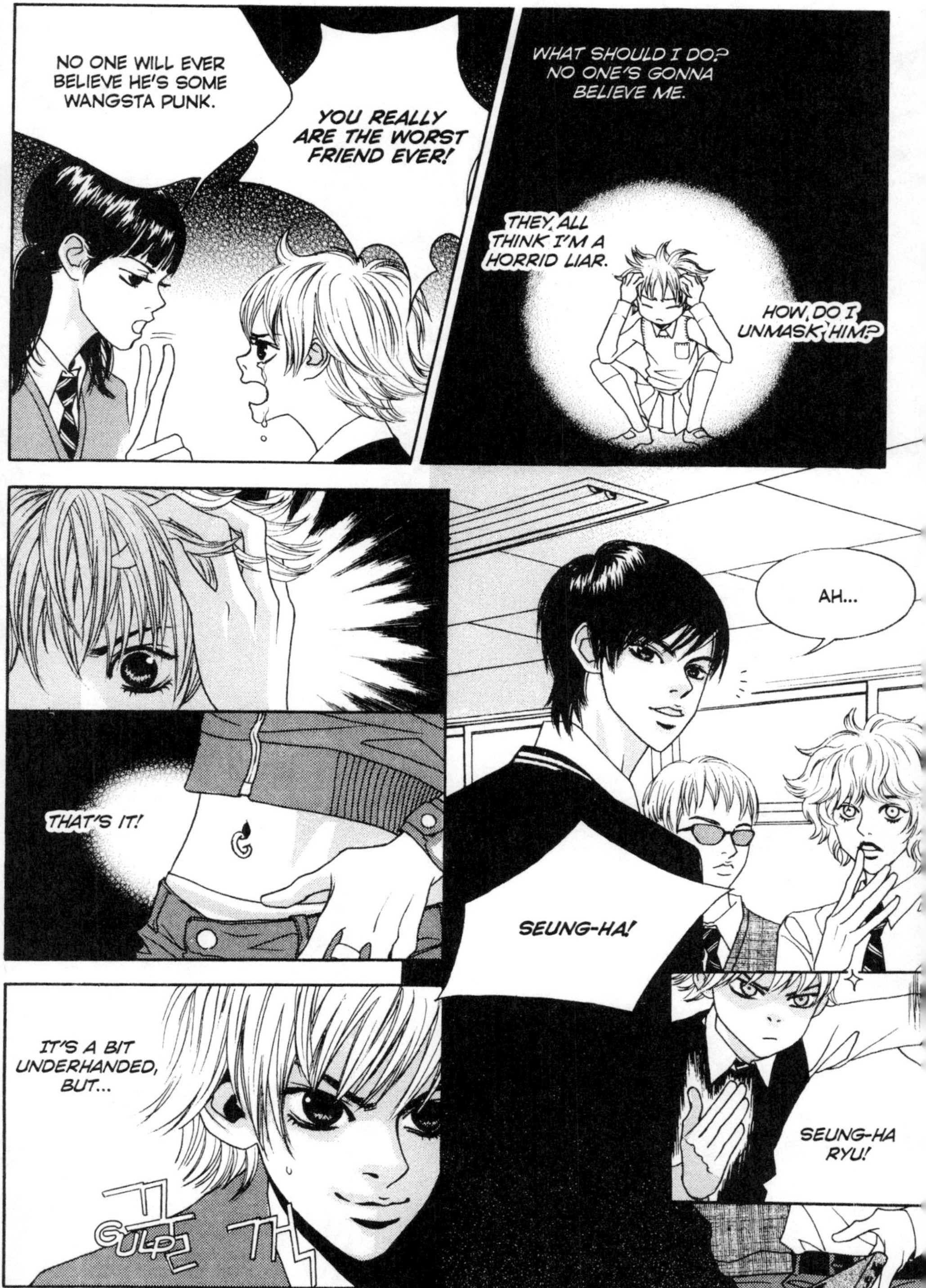
NO ONE WILL EVER BELIEVE HE'S SOME WANGSTA PUNK.
YOU REALLY ARE THE WORST FRIEND EVER!
WHAT SHOULD I DO? NO ONE'S GONNA BELIEVE ME.
THEY ALL THINK I'M A HORRID LIAR.
HOW DO I UNMASK HIM?
THAT'S IT!
AH...
SEUNG-HA!
IT'S A BIT UNDERHANDED, BUT...
GULP
SEUNG-HA RYU!

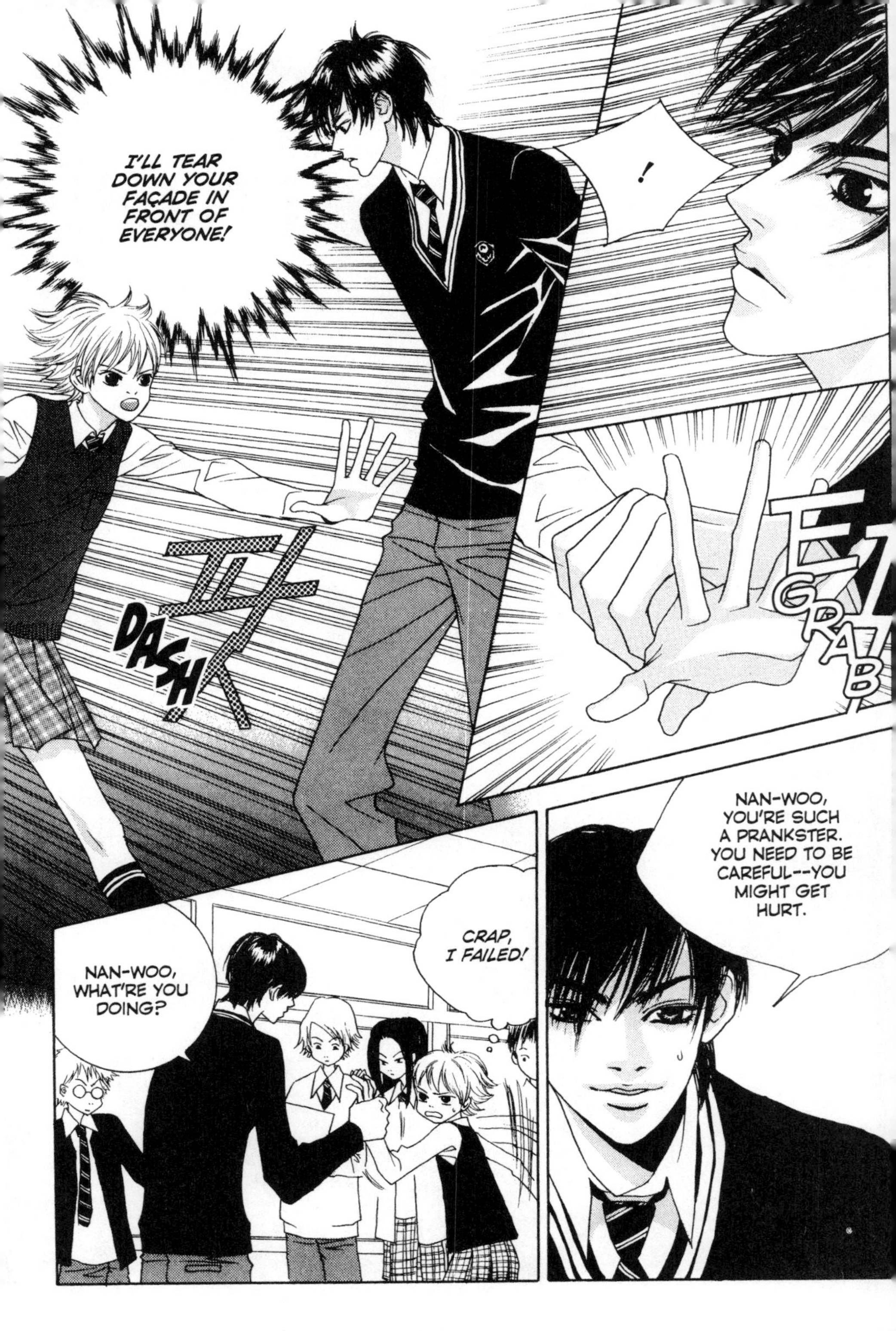
I'LL TEAR DOWN YOUR FAÇADE IN FRONT OF EVERYONE!
DASH
!
GRAB
NAN-WOO, WHAT'RE YOU DOING?
CRAP, I FAILED!
NAN-WOO, YOU'RE SUCH A PRANKSTER. YOU NEED TO BE CAREFUL--YOU MIGHT GET HURT.

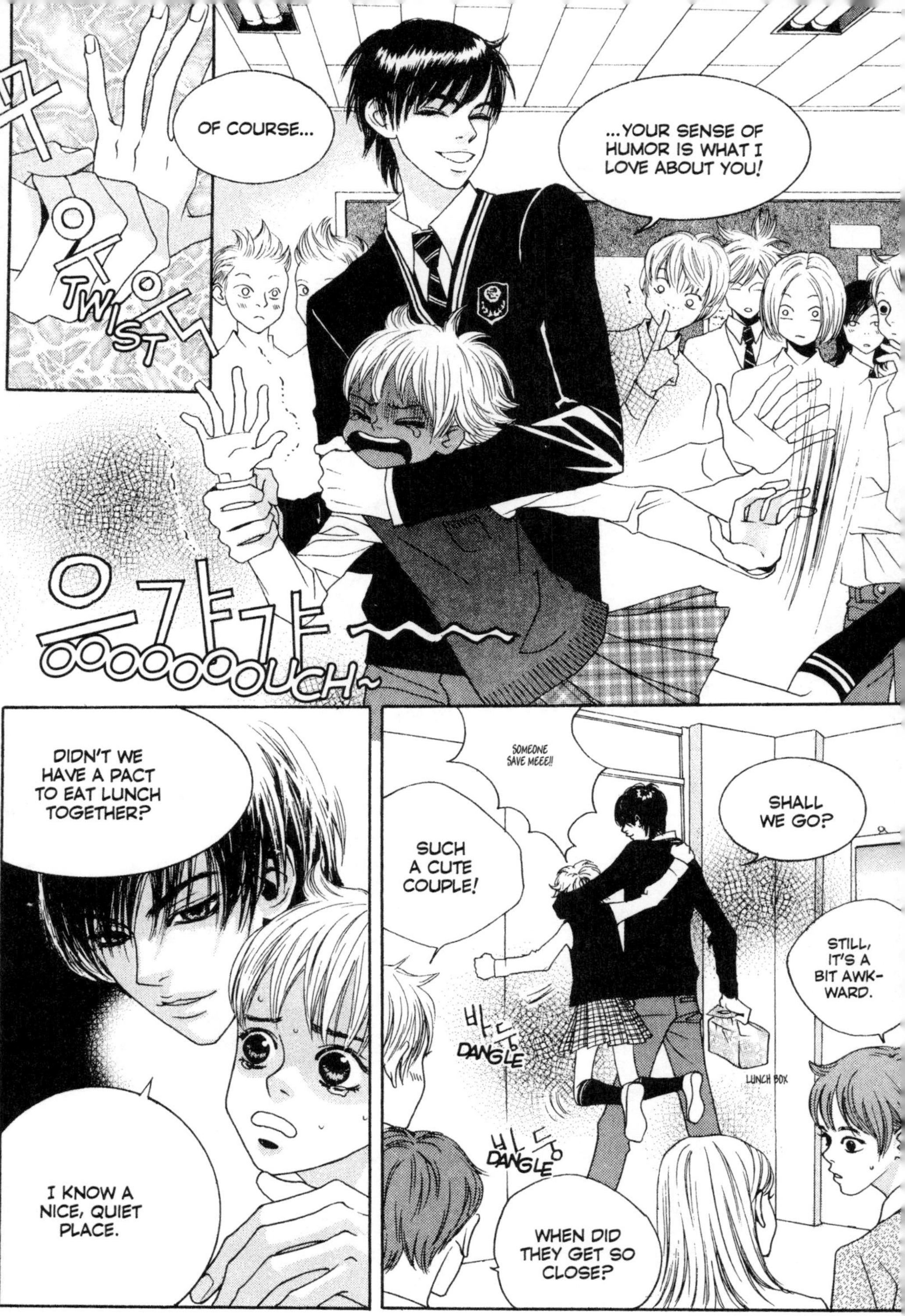
TWIST
OF COURSE...
...YOUR SENSE OF HUMOR IS WHAT I LOVE ABOUT YOU!
으갸갸~
OOOOOOOOOUCH~
DIDN'T WE HAVE A PACT TO EAT LUNCH TOGETHER?
I KNOW A NICE, QUIET PLACE.
SOMEONE SAVE MEEE!!
SUCH A CUTE COUPLE!
SHALL WE GO?
STILL, IT'S A BIT AWK-WARD.
바둥
DANGLE
바둥
DANGLE
LUNCH BOX
WHEN DID THEY GET SO CLOSE?

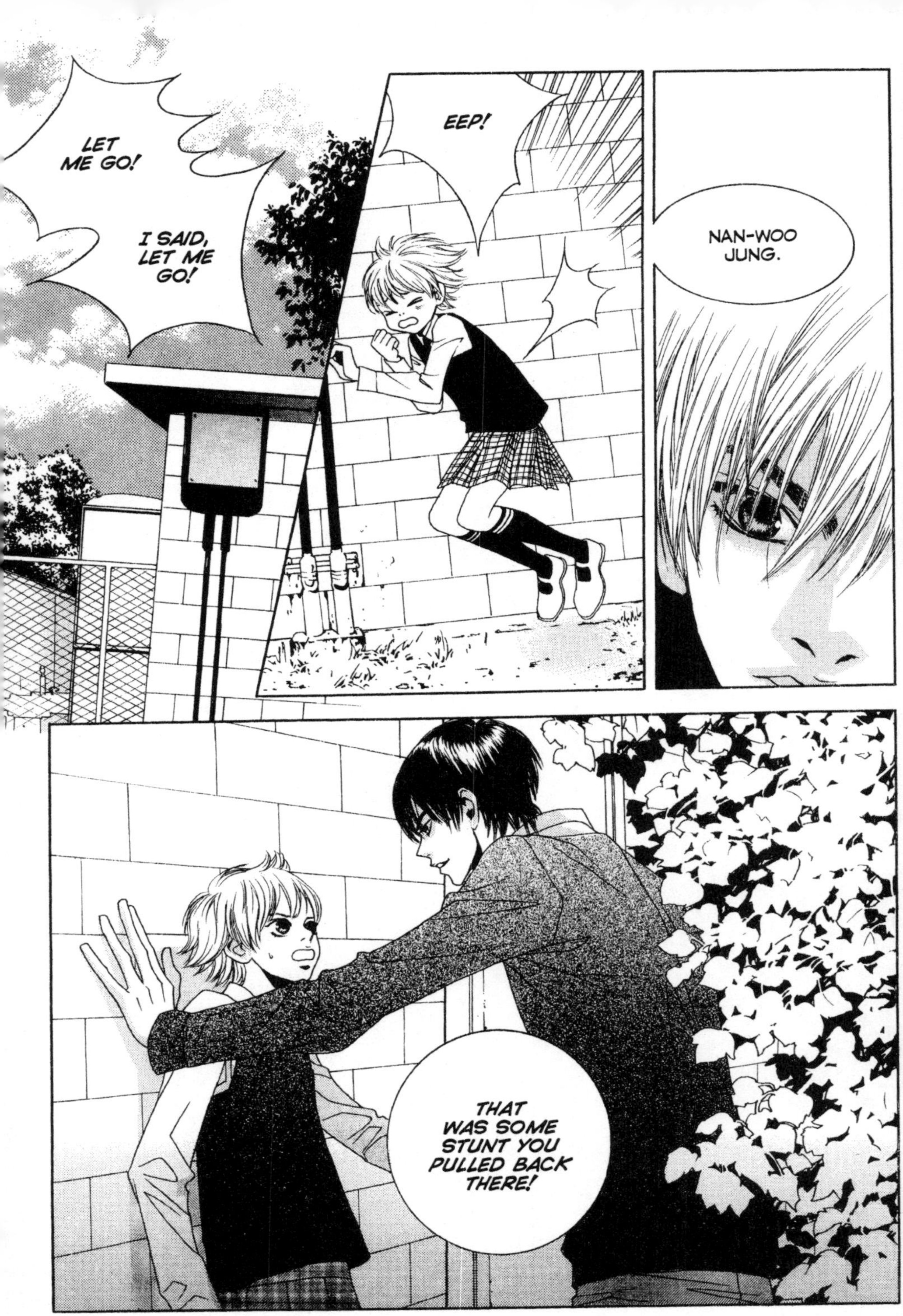
LET ME GO!
I SAID, LET ME GO!
EEP!
NAN-WOO JUNG.
THAT WAS SOME STUNT YOU PULLED BACK THERE!

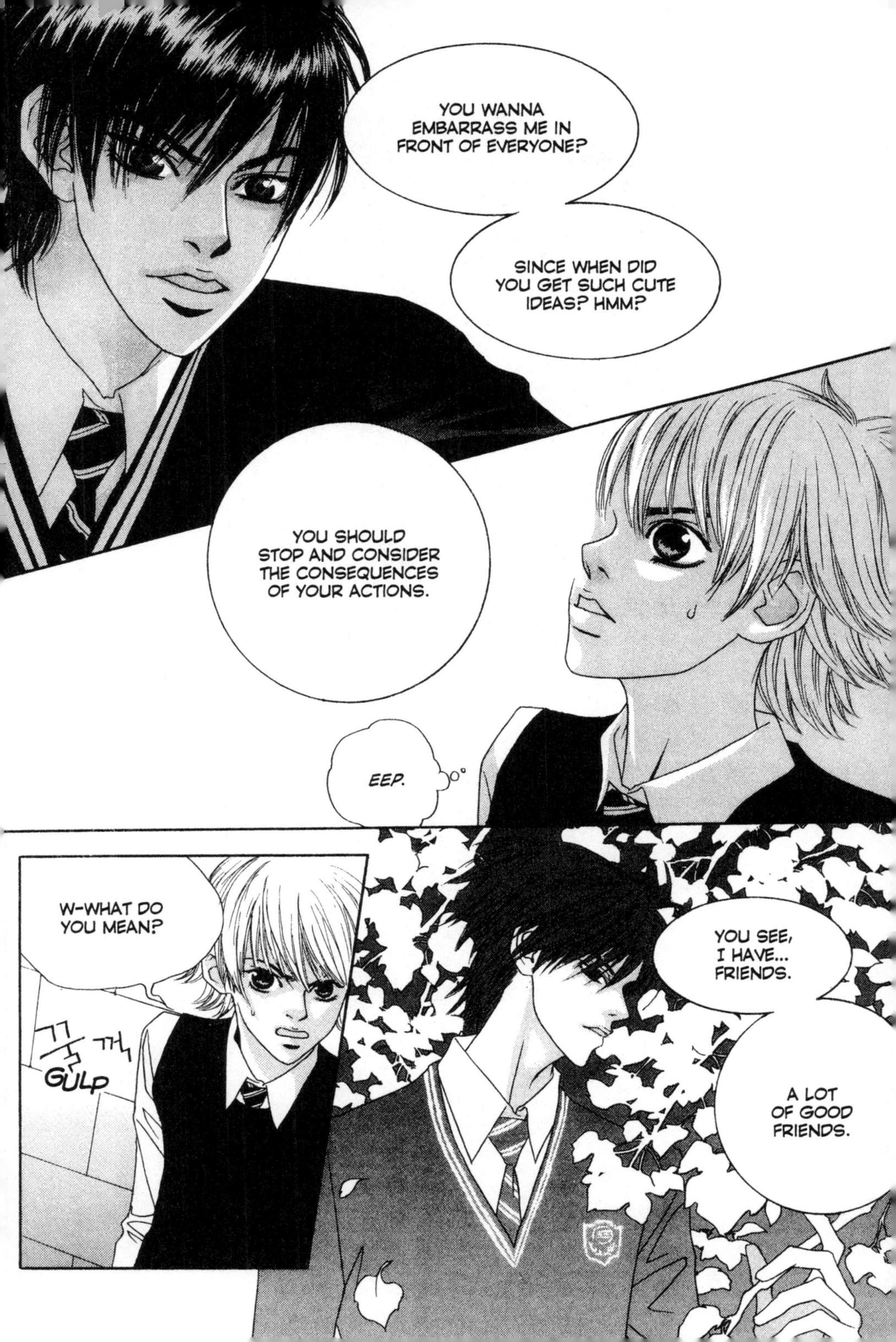
YOU WANNA EMBARRASS ME IN FRONT OF EVERYONE?
SINCE WHEN DID YOU GET SUCH CUTE IDEAS? HMM?
YOU SHOULD STOP AND CONSIDER THE CONSEQUENCES OF YOUR ACTIONS.
EEP.
W-WHAT DO YOU MEAN?
GULP
YOU SEE, I HAVE... FRIENDS.
A LOT OF GOOD FRIENDS.

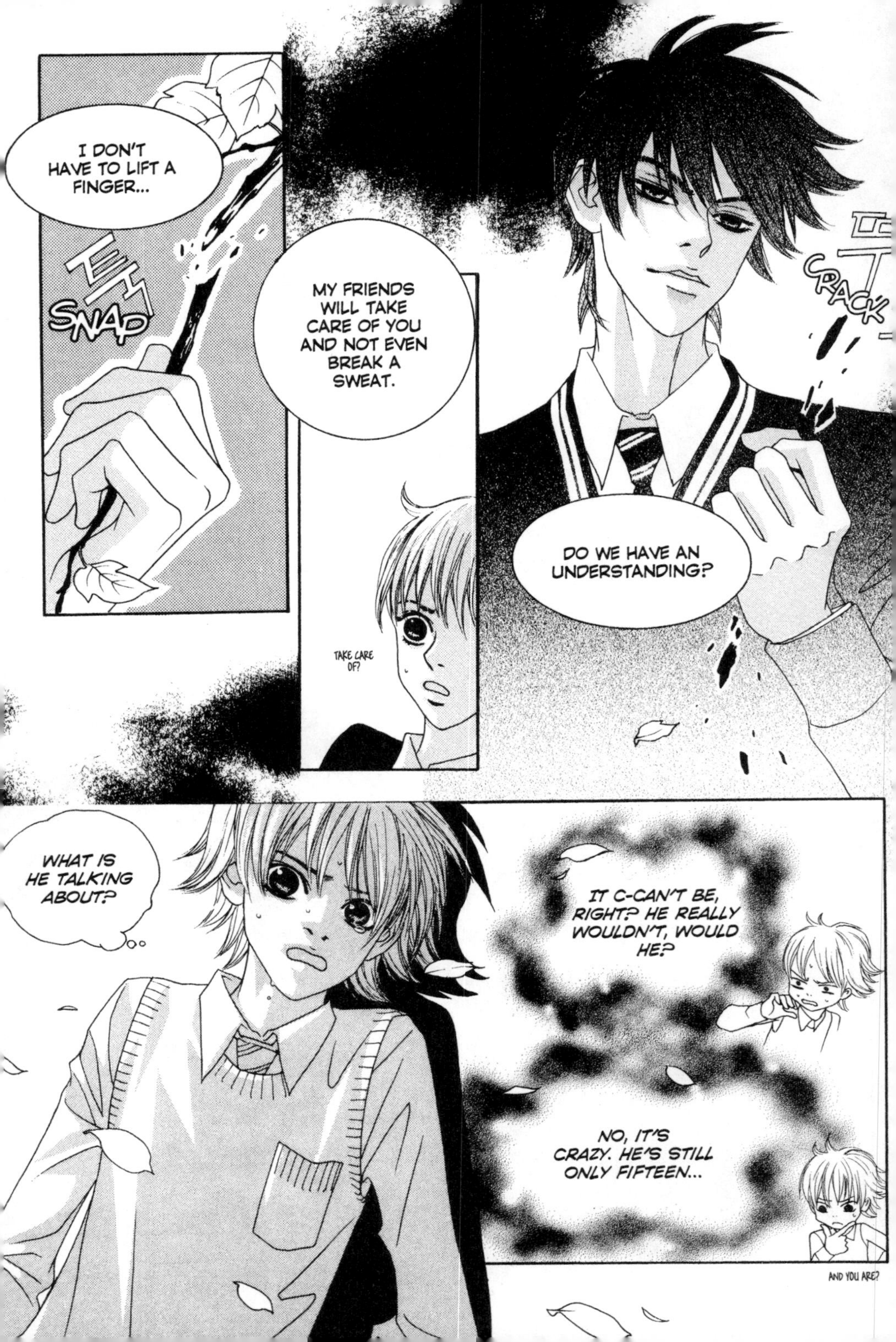
I DON'T HAVE TO LIFT A FINGER...
SNAP
MY FRIENDS WILL TAKE CARE OF YOU AND NOT EVEN BREAK A SWEAT.
TAKE CARE OF?
CRACK
DO WE HAVE AN UNDERSTANDING?
WHAT IS HE TALKING ABOUT?
IT C-CAN'T BE, RIGHT? HE REALLY WOULDN'T, WOULD HE?
NO, IT'S CRAZY. HE'S STILL ONLY FIFTEEN...
AND YOU ARE?

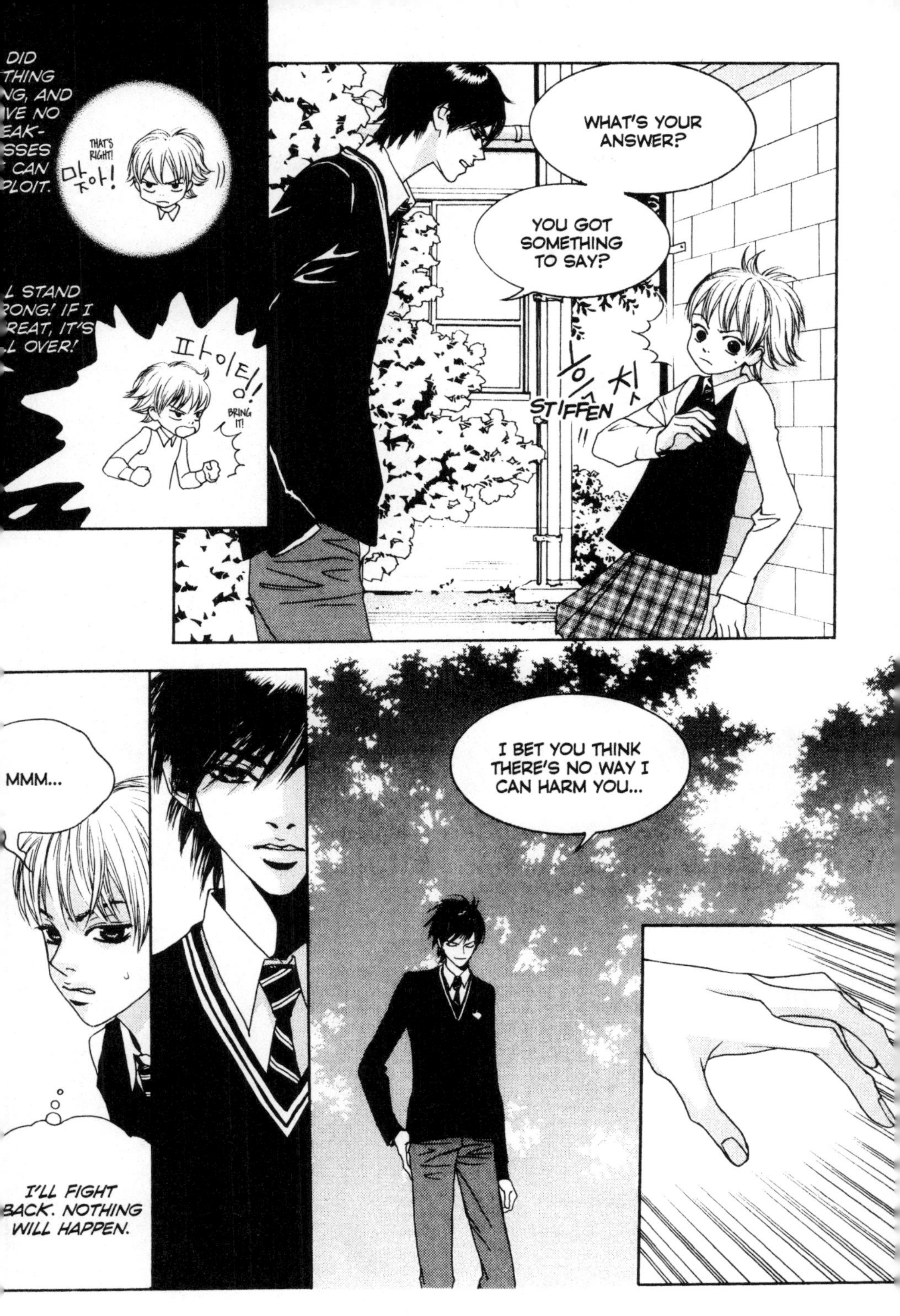
DID
THING
NG, AND
VE NO
EAK-
SSES
CAN
PLOIT.
맞아!
THAT'S RIGHT!
L STAND
RONG! IF I
REAT, IT'S
L OVER!
파이팅!!
BRING IT!
WHAT'S YOUR ANSWER?
YOU GOT SOMETHING TO SAY?
STIFFEN
MMM...
I'LL FIGHT BACK. NOTHING WILL HAPPEN.
I BET YOU THINK THERE'S NO WAY I CAN HARM YOU...

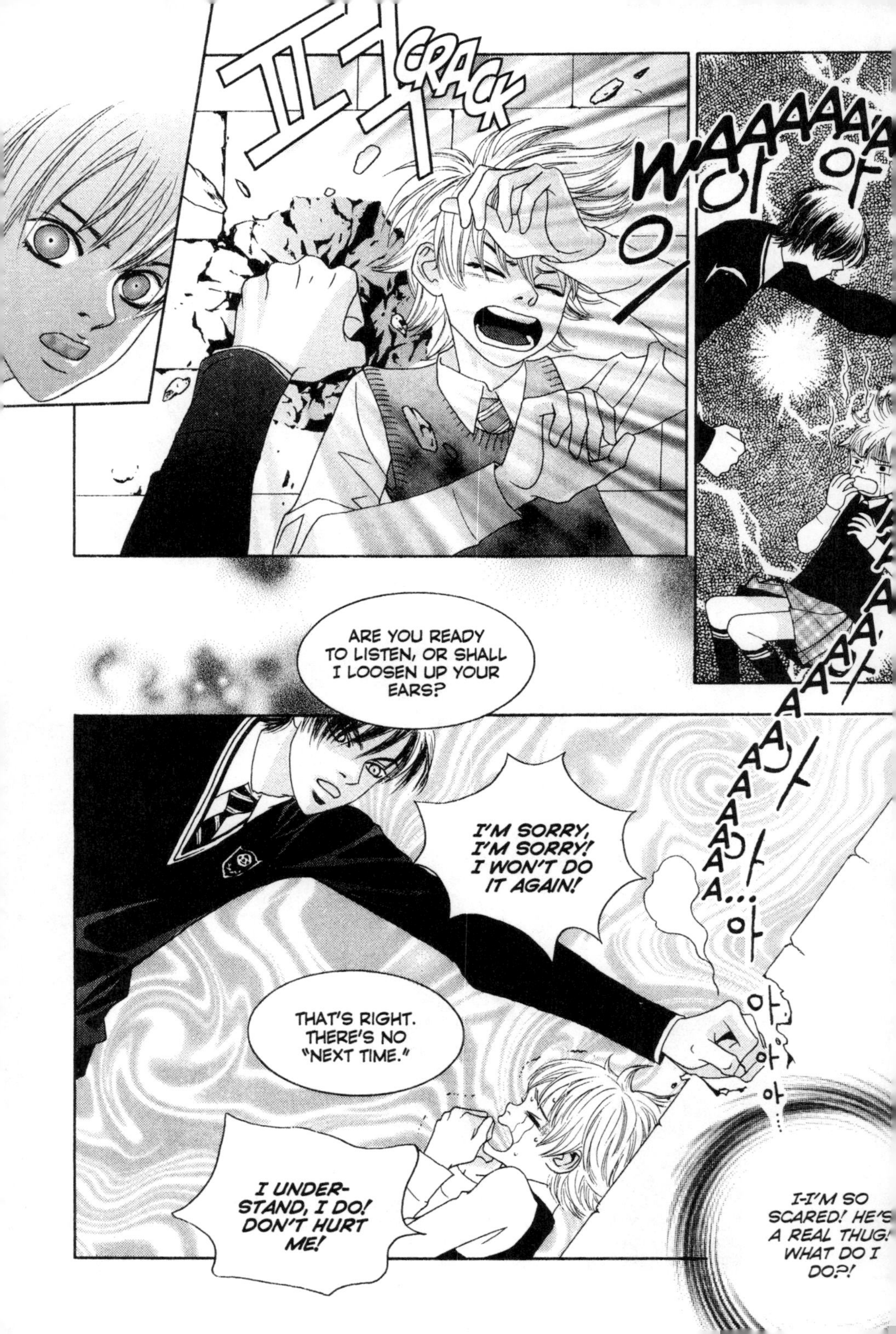
CRACK
WAAAAAAAAAAAAAAAAAAAAAAAA...
ARE YOU READY TO LISTEN, OR SHALL I LOOSEN UP YOUR EARS?
I'M SORRY, I'M SORRY! I WON'T DO IT AGAIN!
THAT'S RIGHT. THERE'S NO "NEXT TIME."
I UNDER-STAND, I DO! DON'T HURT ME!
I-I'M SO SCARED! HE'S A REAL THUG! WHAT DO I DO?!

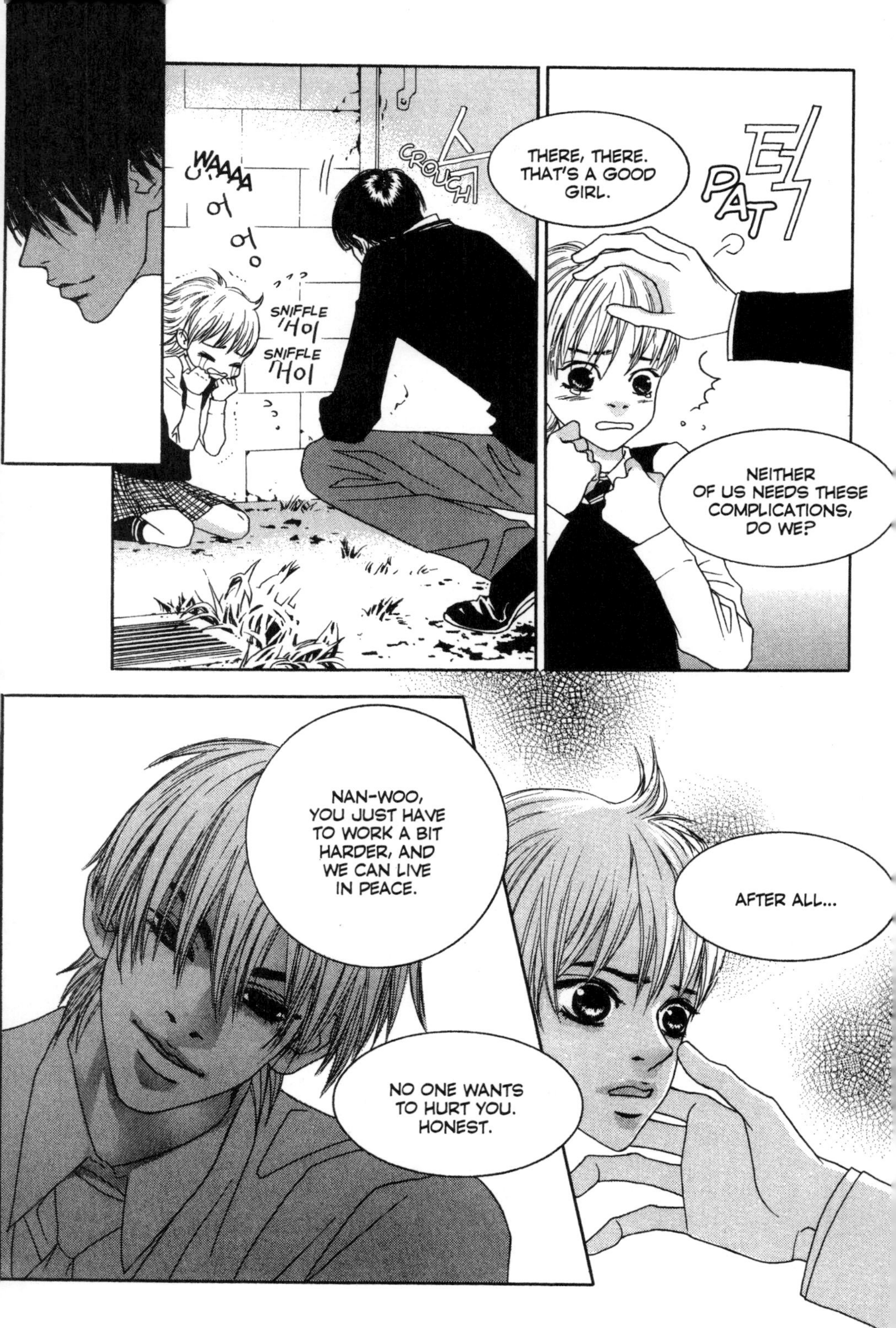
WAAAA
SNIFFLE
SNIFFLE
CROUCH
THERE, THERE. THAT'S A GOOD GIRL.
PAT
NEITHER OF US NEEDS THESE COMPLICATIONS, DO WE?
NAN-WOO, YOU JUST HAVE TO WORK A BIT HARDER, AND WE CAN LIVE IN PEACE.
AFTER ALL...
NO ONE WANTS TO HURT YOU. HONEST.

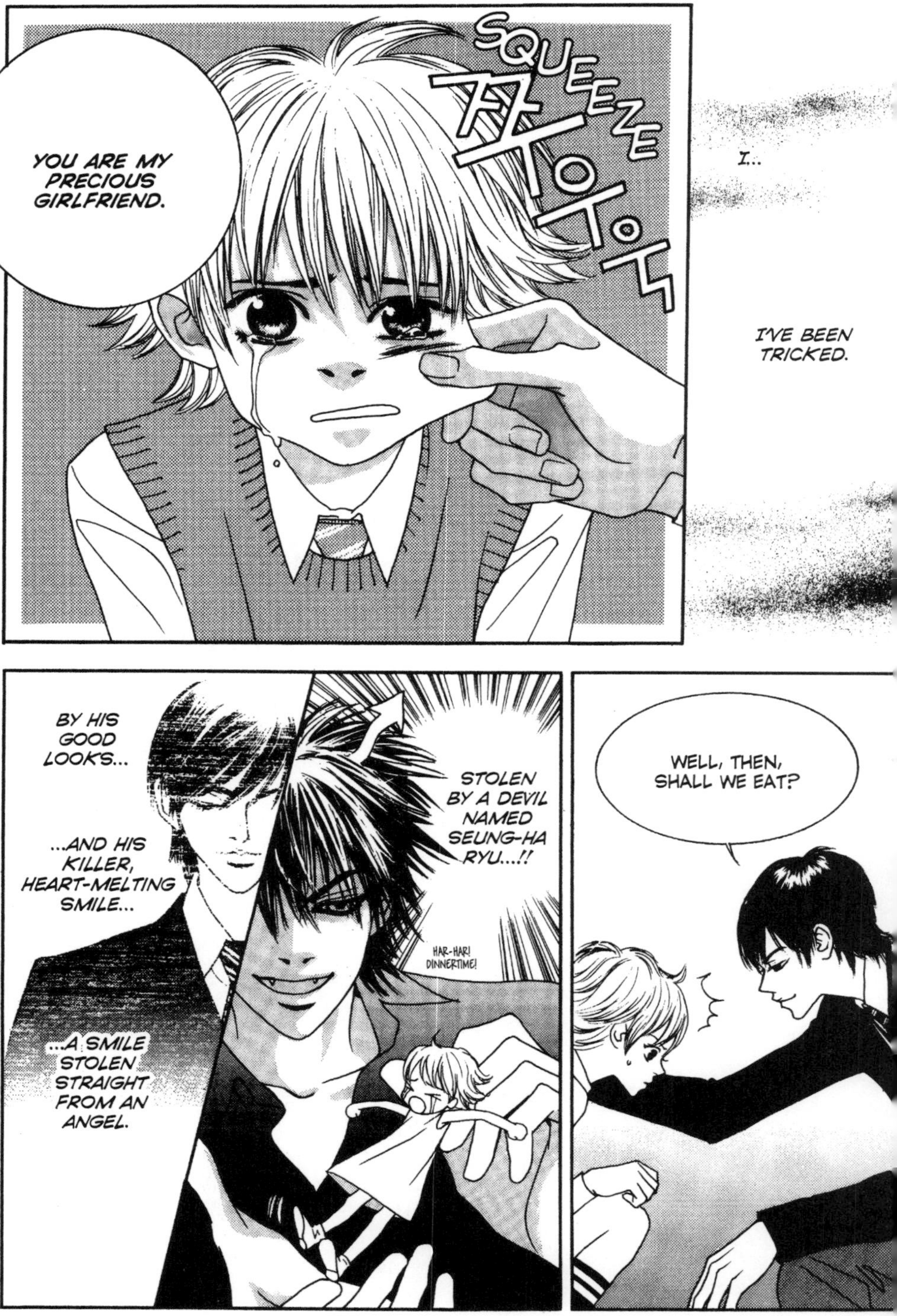
YOU ARE MY PRECIOUS GIRLFRIEND.
SQUEEZE
I...
I'VE BEEN TRICKED.
BY HIS GOOD LOOKS...
...AND HIS KILLER, HEART-MELTING SMILE...
...A SMILE STOLEN STRAIGHT FROM AN ANGEL.
STOLEN BY A DEVIL NAMED SEUNG-HA RYU...!!
HAR-HAR! DINNERTIME!
WELL, THEN, SHALL WE EAT?

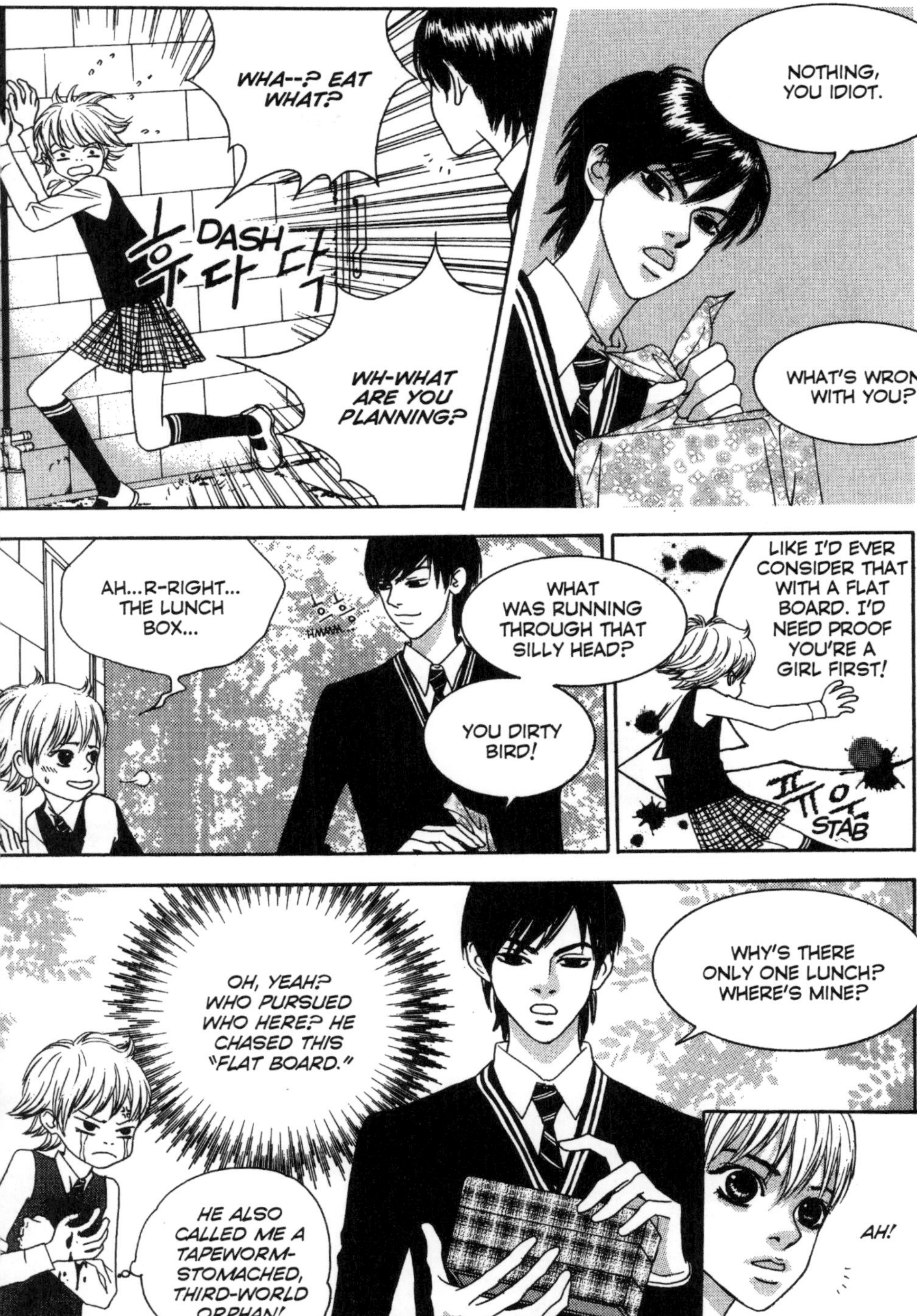

WHA--? EAT WHAT?
DASH
후다닥
WH-WHAT ARE YOU PLANNING?
NOTHING, YOU IDIOT.
WHAT'S WRONG WITH YOU?
AH...R-RIGHT... THE LUNCH BOX...
HMMM...
WHAT WAS RUNNING THROUGH THAT SILLY HEAD?
YOU DIRTY BIRD!
LIKE I'D EVER CONSIDER THAT WITH A FLAT BOARD. I'D NEED PROOF YOU'RE A GIRL FIRST!
STAB
OH, YEAH? WHO PURSUED WHO HERE? HE CHASED THIS "FLAT BOARD."
WHY'S THERE ONLY ONE LUNCH? WHERE'S MINE?
HE ALSO CALLED ME A TAPEWORM-STOMACHED, THIRD-WORLD ORPHAN!
AH!

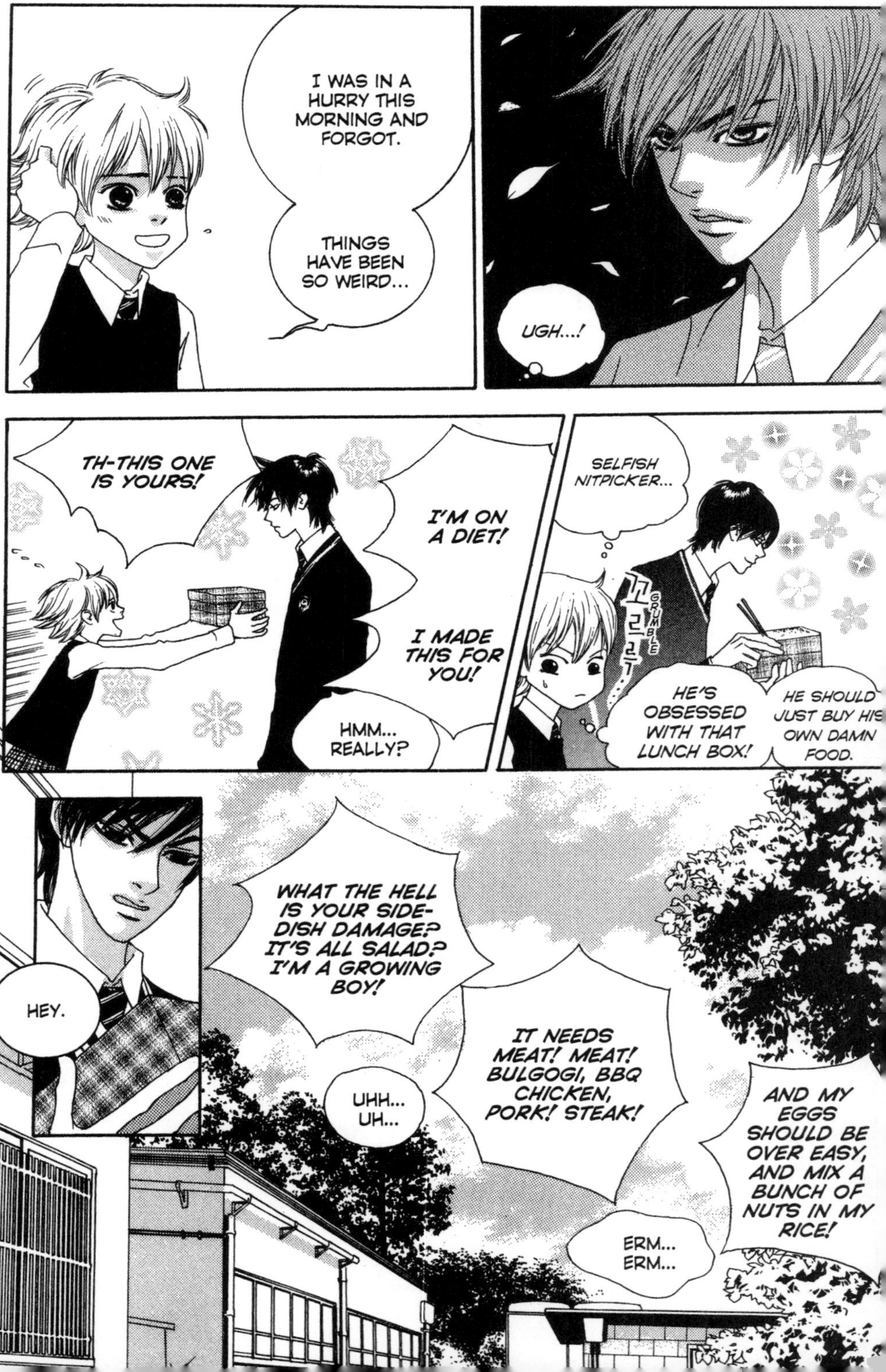
I WAS IN A HURRY THIS MORNING AND FORGOT.
THINGS HAVE BEEN SO WEIRD...
UGH...!
TH-THIS ONE IS YOURS!
I'M ON A DIET!
I MADE THIS FOR YOU!
HMM... REALLY?
SELFISH NITPICKER...
꼬르륵
GRUMBLE
HE'S OBSESSED WITH THAT LUNCH BOX!
HE SHOULD JUST BUY HIS OWN DAMN FOOD.
HEY.
WHAT THE HELL IS YOUR SIDE-DISH DAMAGE? IT'S ALL SALAD? I'M A GROWING BOY!
UHH... UH...
IT NEEDS MEAT! MEAT! BULGOGI, BBQ CHICKEN, PORK! STEAK!
AND MY EGGS SHOULD BE OVER EASY, AND MIX A BUNCH OF NUTS IN MY RICE!
ERM... ERM...

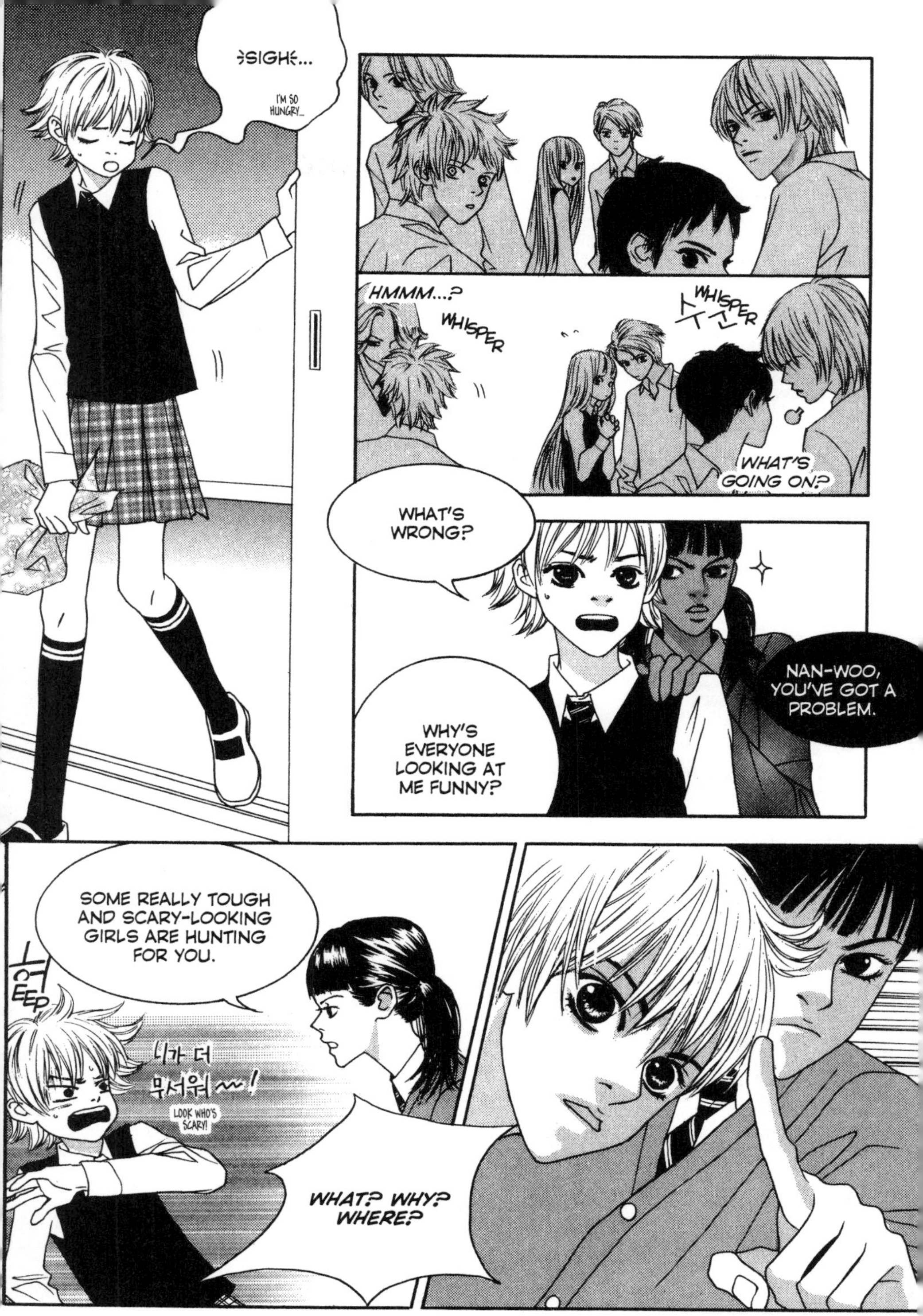

≶SIGH≶...
I'M SO HUNGRY...
HMMM...?
WHISPER
WHISPER
WHAT'S GOING ON?
WHAT'S WRONG?
WHY'S EVERYONE LOOKING AT ME FUNNY?
NAN-WOO, YOU'VE GOT A PROBLEM.
SOME REALLY TOUGH AND SCARY-LOOKING GIRLS ARE HUNTING FOR YOU.
EEEP
니가 더 무서워~!
LOOK WHO'S SCARY!
WHAT? WHY? WHERE?

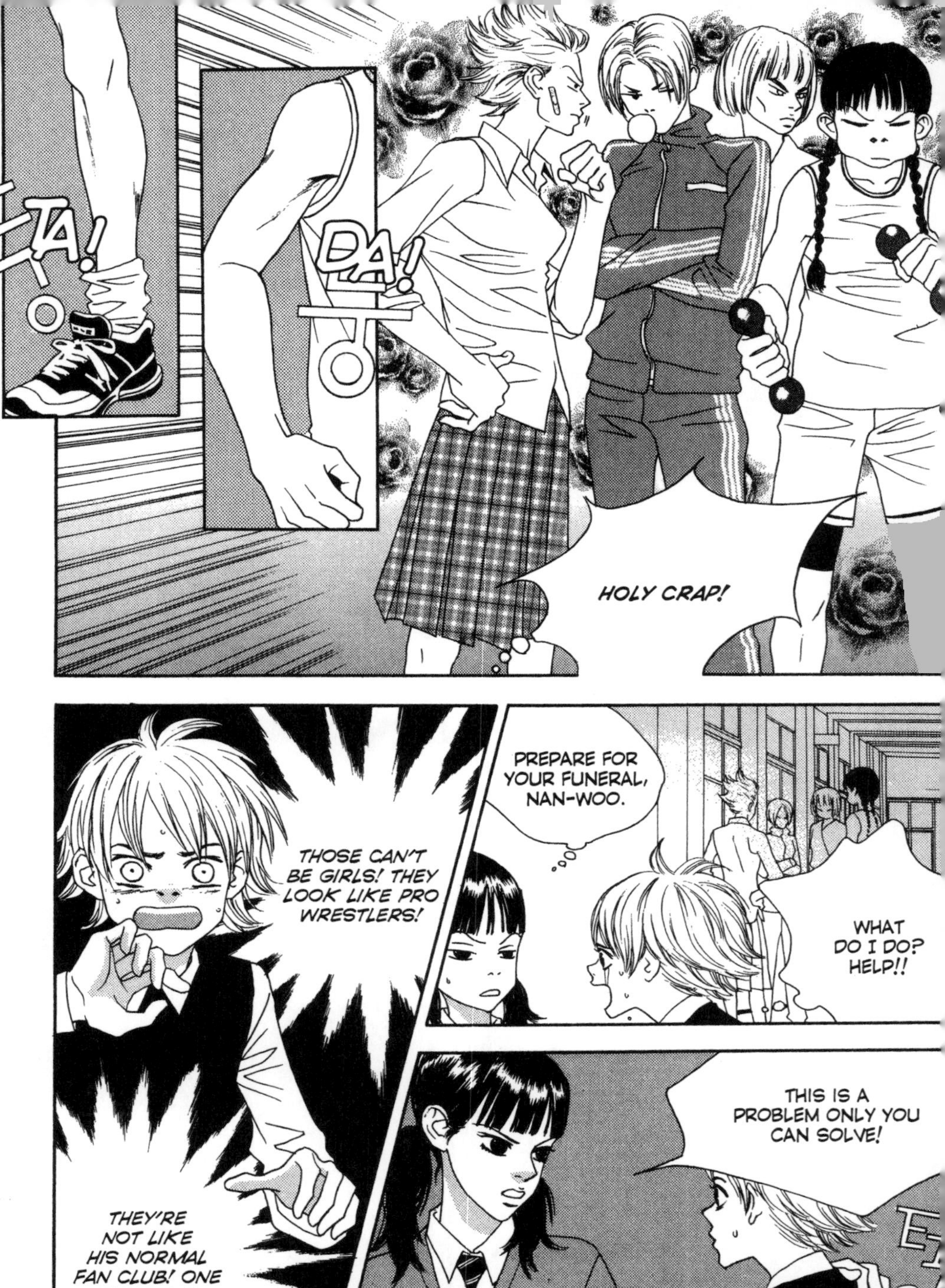
TA!
DA!
HOLY CRAP!
THOSE CAN'T BE GIRLS! THEY LOOK LIKE PRO WRESTLERS!
THEY'RE NOT LIKE HIS NORMAL FAN CLUB! ONE BLOW, AND I'M DEAD!
PREPARE FOR YOUR FUNERAL, NAN-WOO.
WHAT DO I DO? HELP!!
THIS IS A PROBLEM ONLY YOU CAN SOLVE!

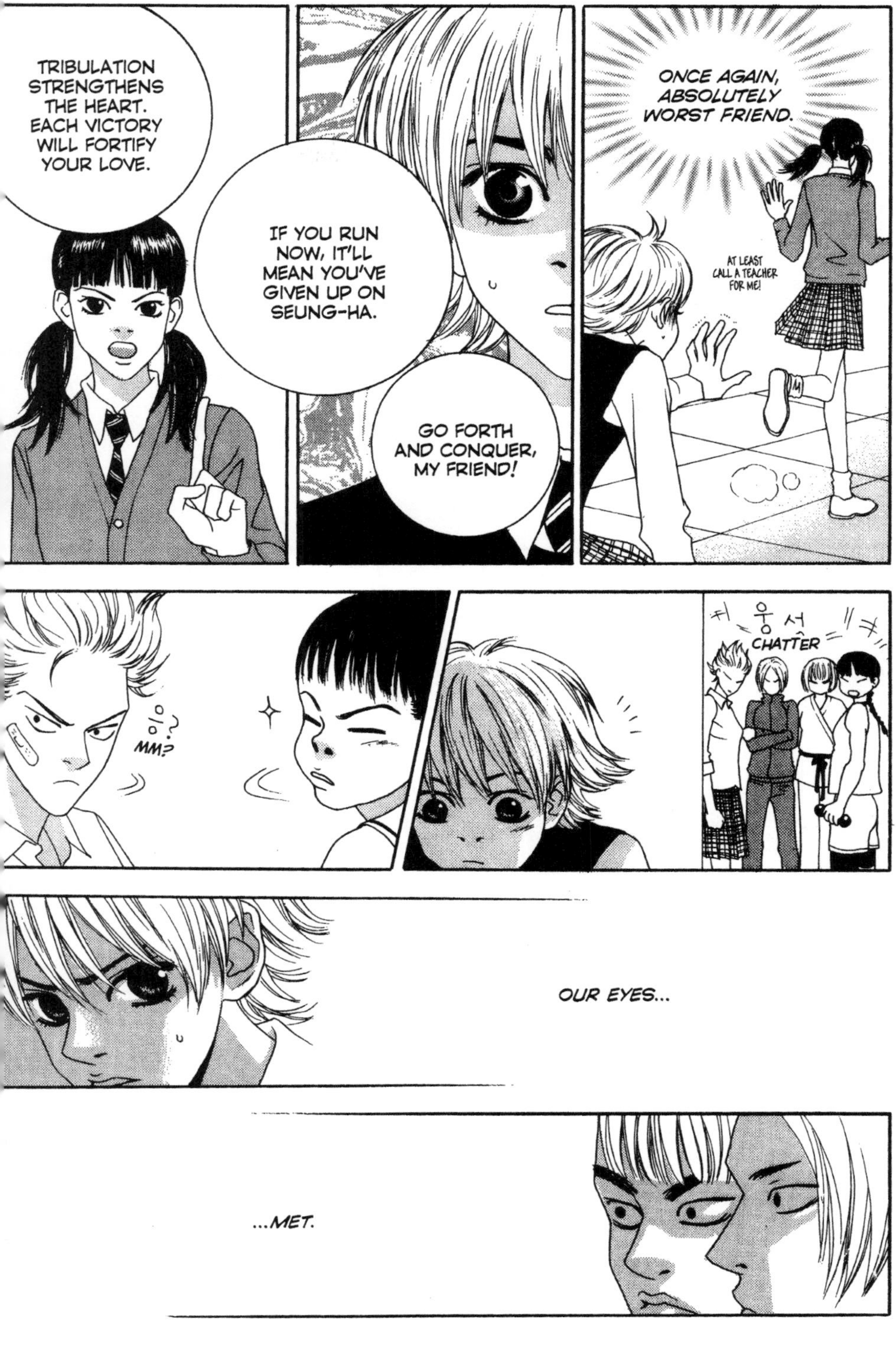
TRIBULATION STRENGTHENS THE HEART. EACH VICTORY WILL FORTIFY YOUR LOVE.
IF YOU RUN NOW, IT'LL MEAN YOU'VE GIVEN UP ON SEUNG-HA.
GO FORTH AND CONQUER, MY FRIEND!
ONCE AGAIN, ABSOLUTELY WORST FRIEND.
AT LEAST CALL A TEACHER FOR ME!
MM?
CHATTER
OUR EYES...
...MET.

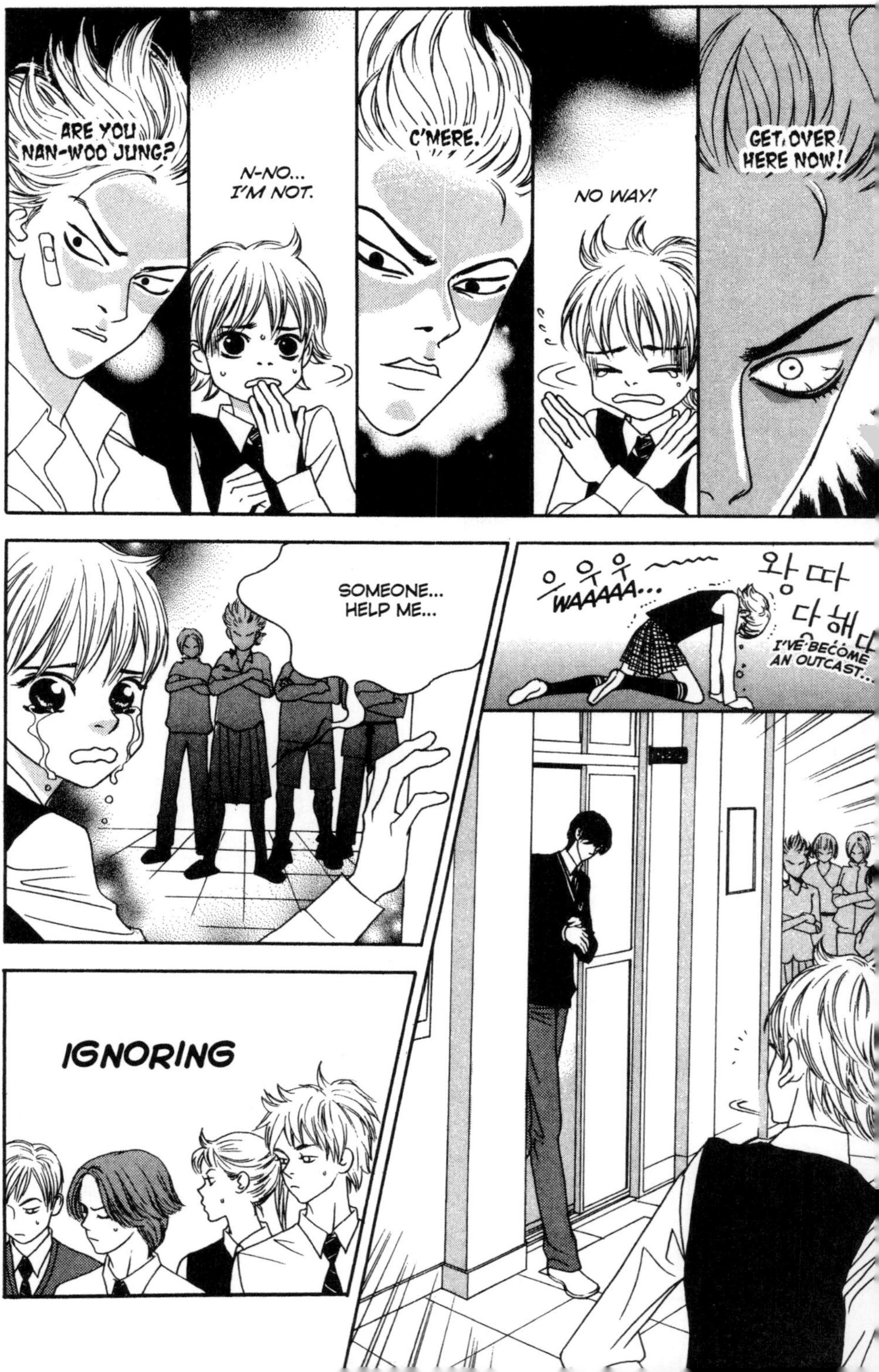
ARE YOU NAN-WOO JUNG?
N-NO... I'M NOT.
C'MERE.
NO WAY!
GET OVER HERE NOW!
SOMEONE... HELP ME...
우우우 ~~~
WAAAAA...
왕따 다 됐다
I'VE BECOME AN OUTCAST...
IGNORING

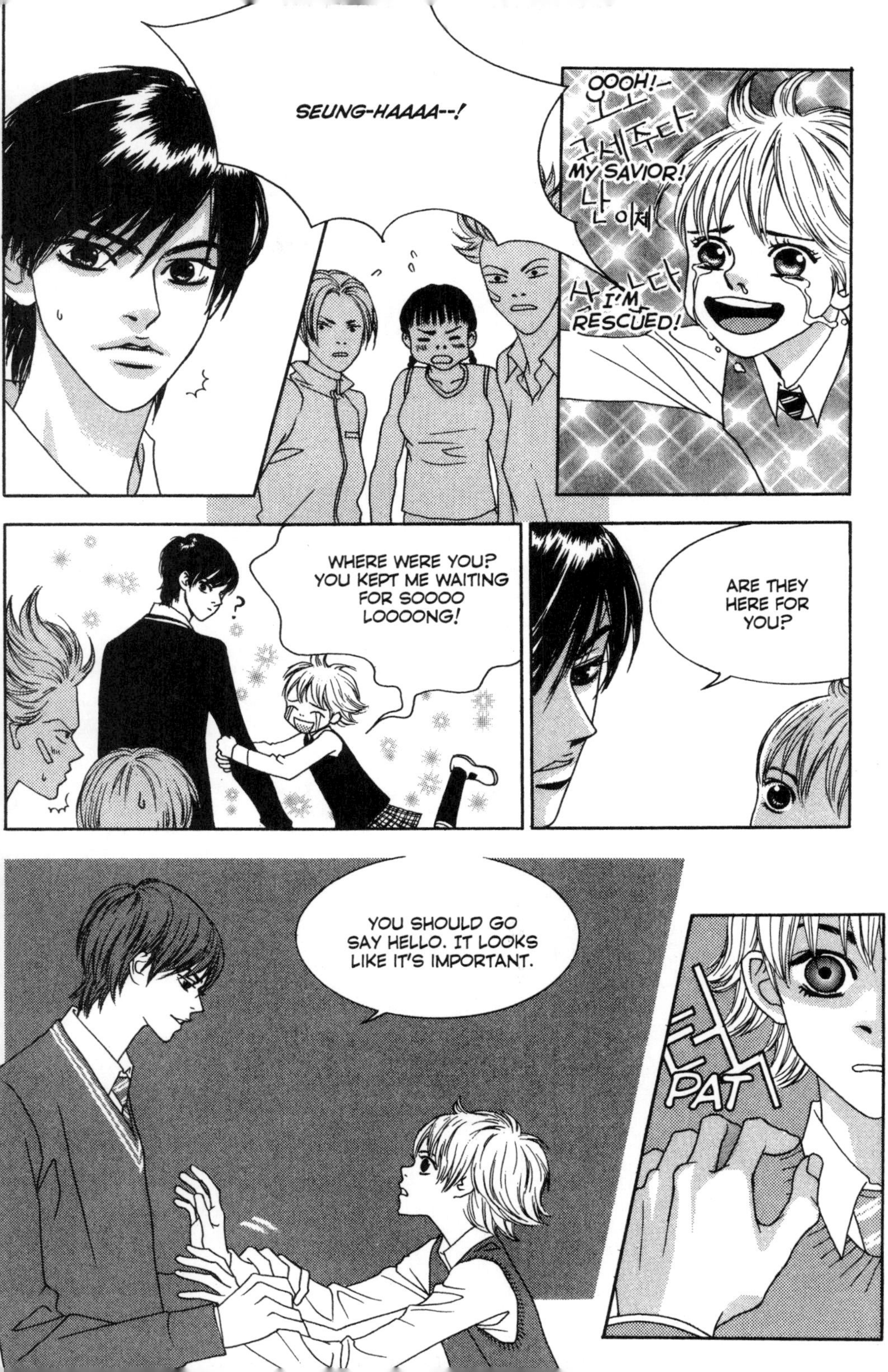
SEUNG-HAAAA--!
OOOH! 오오
구세주다 MY SAVIOR!
난 이제 살았다 I'M RESCUED!
WHERE WERE YOU? YOU KEPT ME WAITING FOR SOOOO LOOOONG!
ARE THEY HERE FOR YOU?
YOU SHOULD GO SAY HELLO. IT LOOKS LIKE IT'S IMPORTANT.
PAT

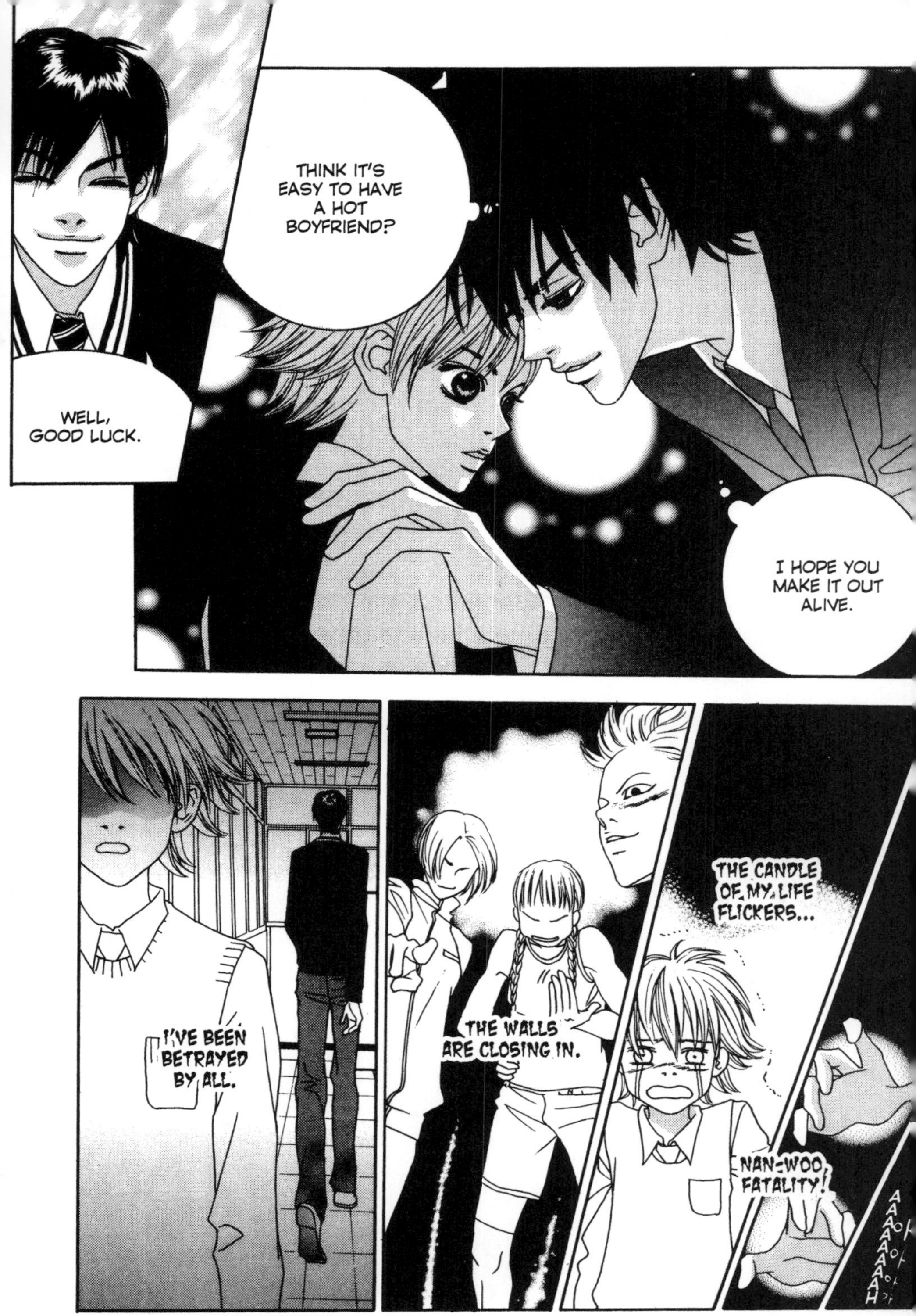

THINK IT'S EASY TO HAVE A HOT BOYFRIEND?
WELL, GOOD LUCK.
I HOPE YOU MAKE IT OUT ALIVE.
I'VE BEEN BETRAYED BY ALL.
THE WALLS ARE CLOSING IN.
THE CANDLE OF MY LIFE FLICKERS...
NAN-WOO, FATALITY!
AAAAAAAAH

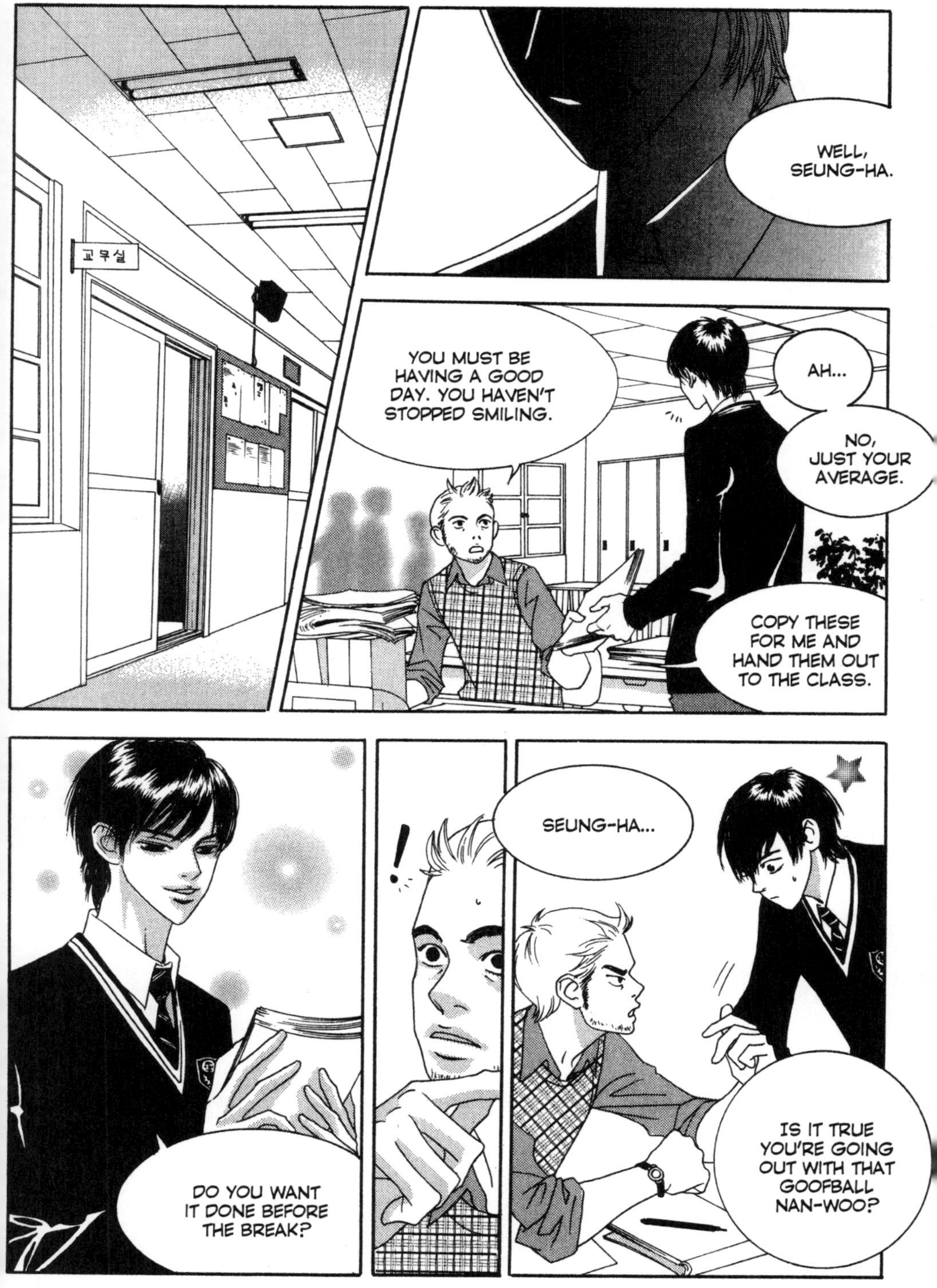
교무실
WELL, SEUNG-HA.
YOU MUST BE HAVING A GOOD DAY. YOU HAVEN'T STOPPED SMILING.
AH...
NO, JUST YOUR AVERAGE.
COPY THESE FOR ME AND HAND THEM OUT TO THE CLASS.
DO YOU WANT IT DONE BEFORE THE BREAK?
SEUNG-HA...
IS IT TRUE YOU'RE GOING OUT WITH THAT GOOFBALL NAN-WOO?

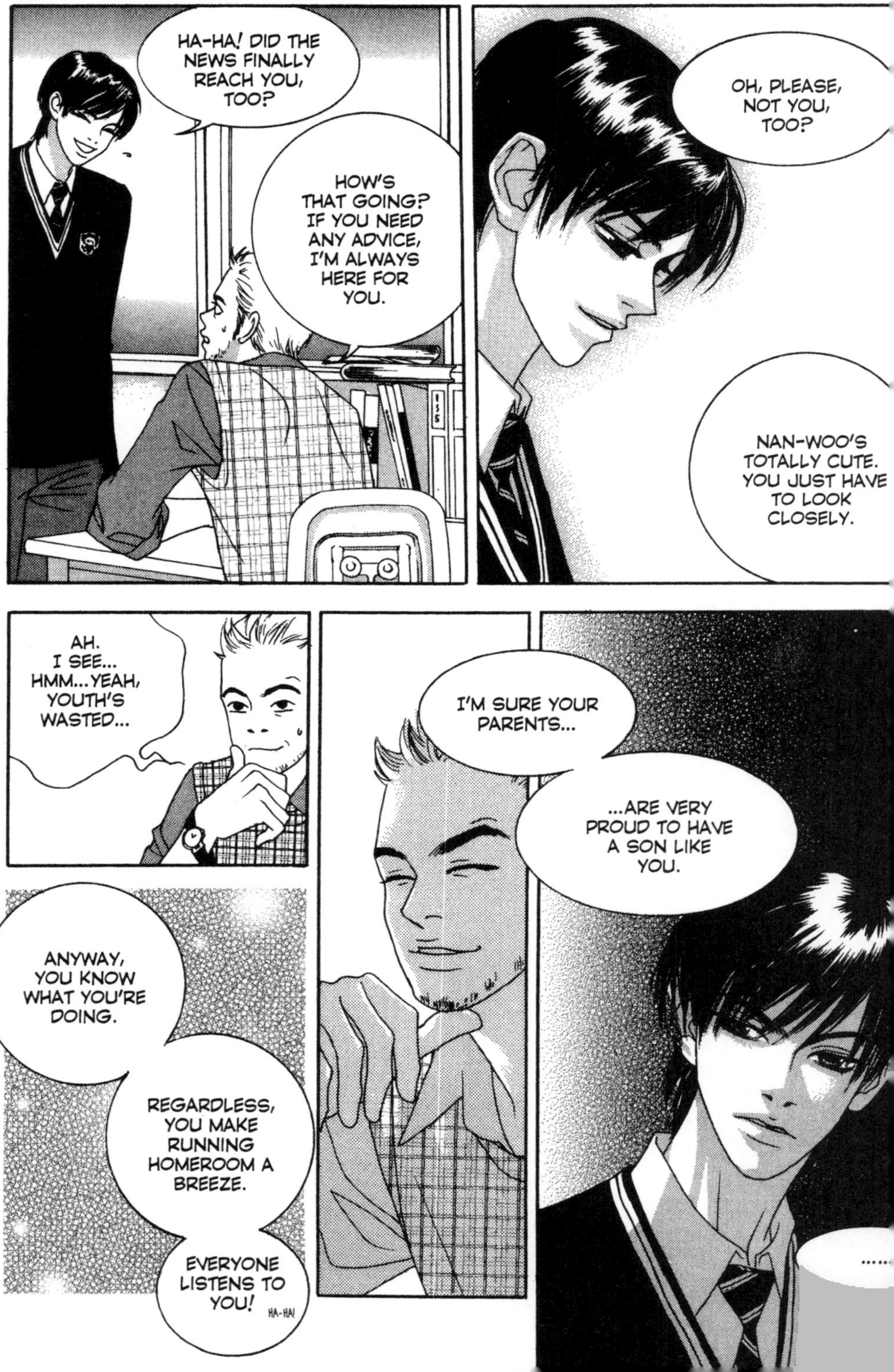
HA-HA! DID THE NEWS FINALLY REACH YOU, TOO?
HOW'S THAT GOING? IF YOU NEED ANY ADVICE, I'M ALWAYS HERE FOR YOU.
OH, PLEASE, NOT YOU, TOO?
NAN-WOO'S TOTALLY CUTE. YOU JUST HAVE TO LOOK CLOSELY.
AH. I SEE... HMM...YEAH, YOUTH'S WASTED...
I'M SURE YOUR PARENTS...
...ARE VERY PROUD TO HAVE A SON LIKE YOU.
ANYWAY, YOU KNOW WHAT YOU'RE DOING.
REGARDLESS, YOU MAKE RUNNING HOMEROOM A BREEZE.
EVERYONE LISTENS TO YOU!
HA-HA!
......

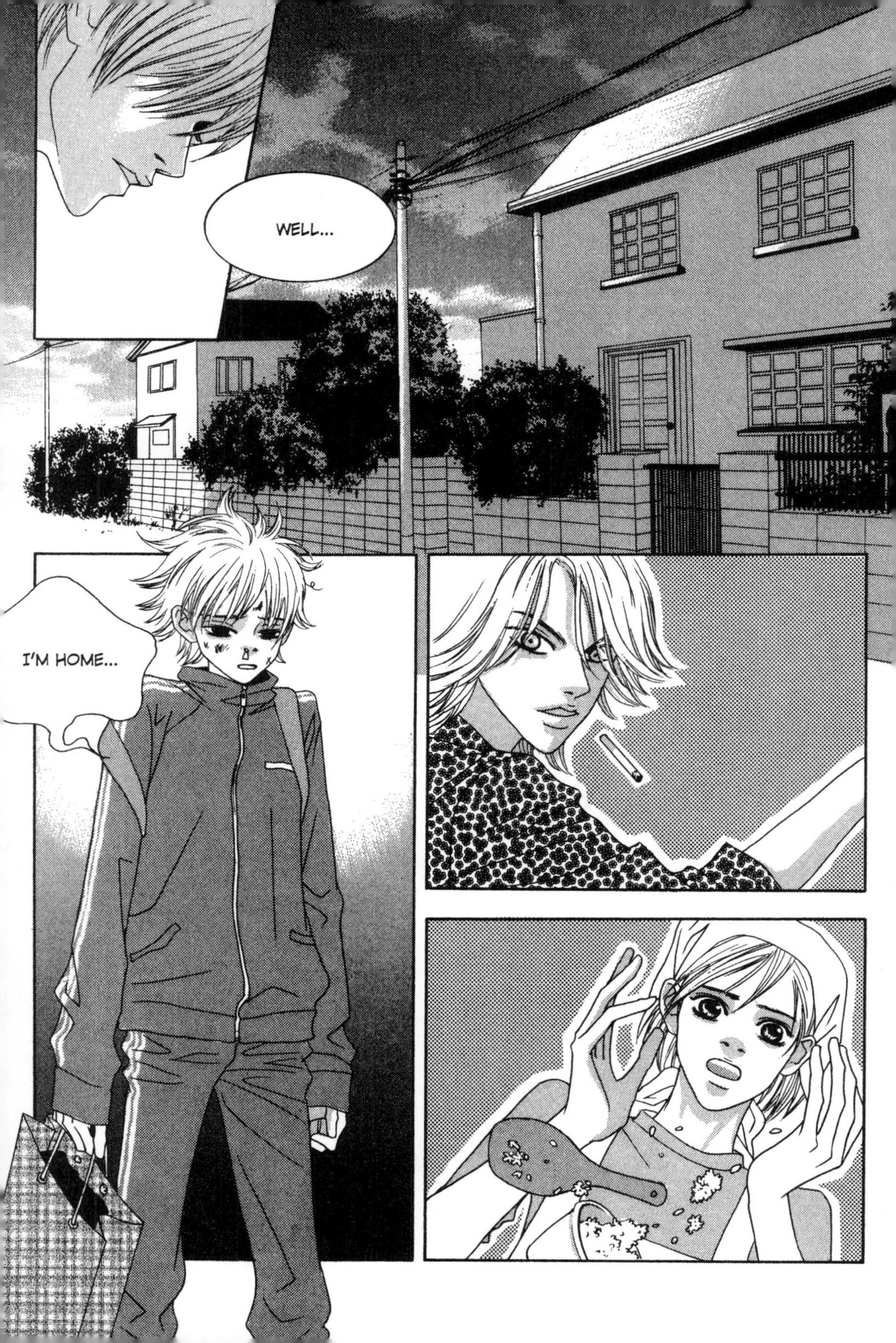
WELL...
I'M HOME...

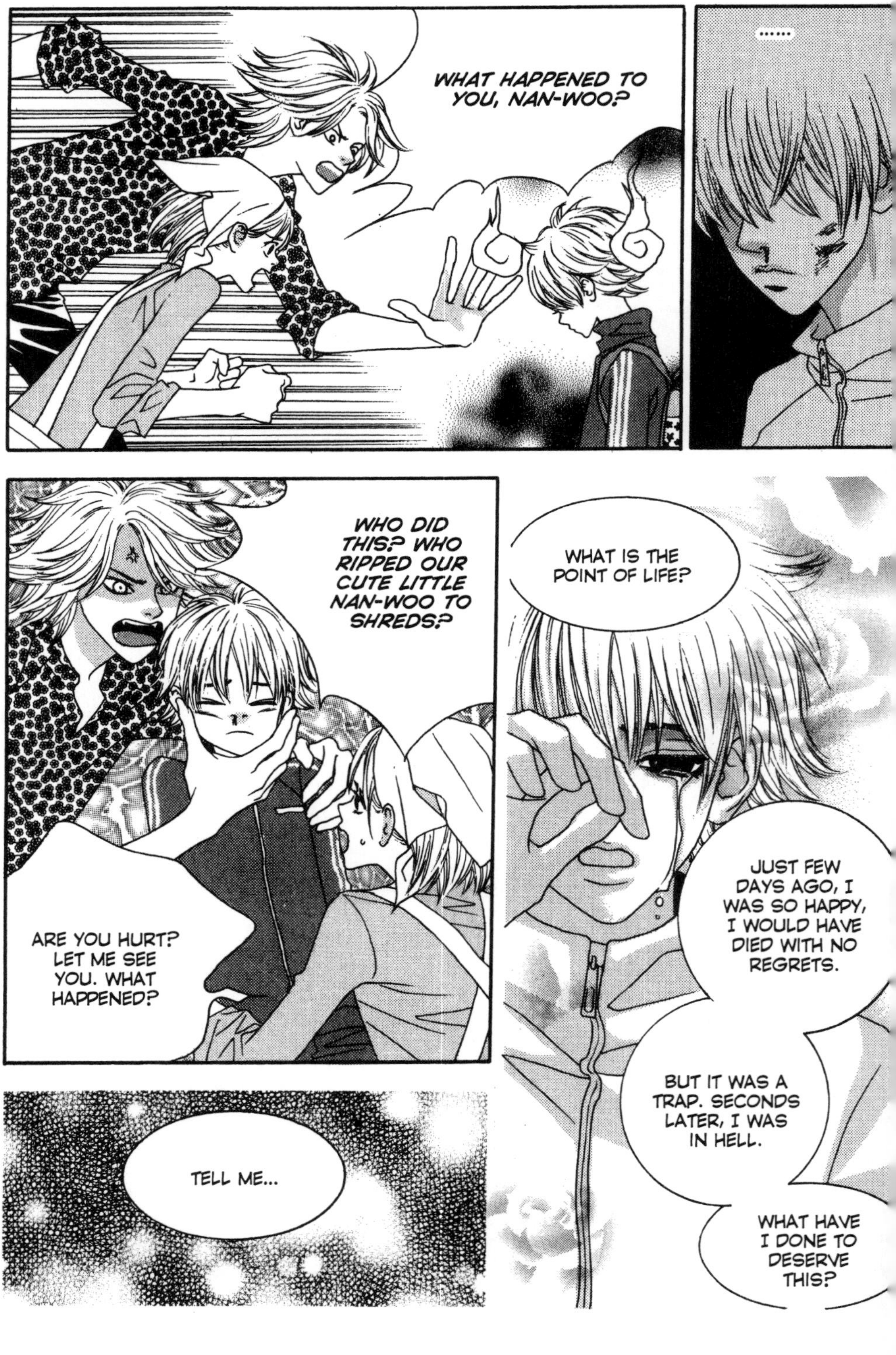
WHAT HAPPENED TO YOU, NAN-WOO?
......
WHO DID THIS? WHO RIPPED OUR CUTE LITTLE NAN-WOO TO SHREDS?
ARE YOU HURT? LET ME SEE YOU. WHAT HAPPENED?
TELL ME...
WHAT IS THE POINT OF LIFE?
JUST FEW DAYS AGO, I WAS SO HAPPY, I WOULD HAVE DIED WITH NO REGRETS.
BUT IT WAS A TRAP. SECONDS LATER, I WAS IN HELL.
WHAT HAVE I DONE TO DESERVE THIS?

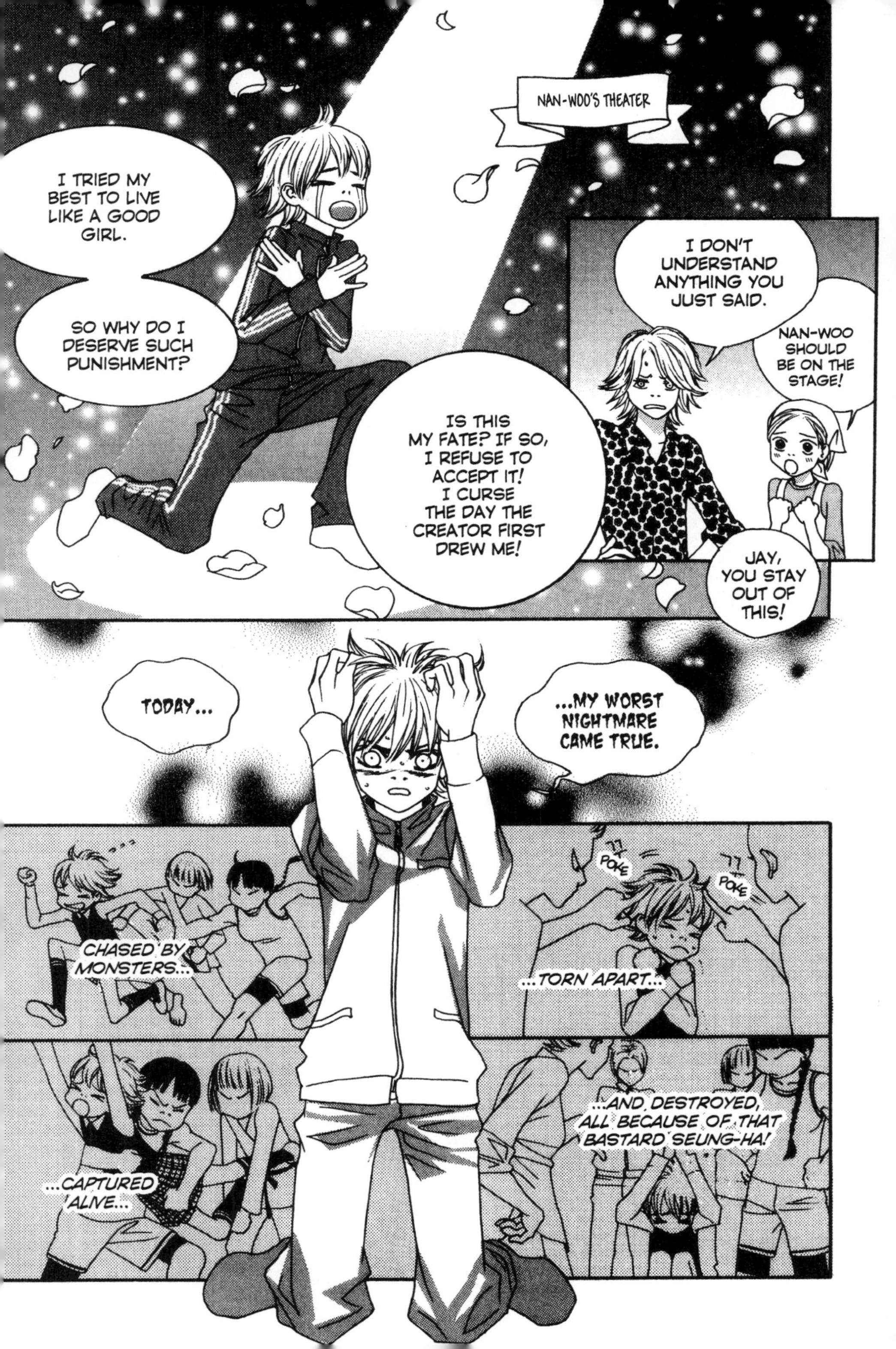
NAN-WOO'S THEATER
I TRIED MY BEST TO LIVE LIKE A GOOD GIRL.
SO WHY DO I DESERVE SUCH PUNISHMENT?
IS THIS MY FATE? IF SO, I REFUSE TO ACCEPT IT! I CURSE THE DAY THE CREATOR FIRST DREW ME!
I DON'T UNDERSTAND ANYTHING YOU JUST SAID.
NAN-WOO SHOULD BE ON THE STAGE!
JAY, YOU STAY OUT OF THIS!
TODAY...
...MY WORST NIGHTMARE CAME TRUE.
CHASED BY MONSTERS...
POKE
POKE
...TORN APART...
...CAPTURED ALIVE...
...AND DESTROYED, ALL BECAUSE OF THAT BASTARD SEUNG-HA!

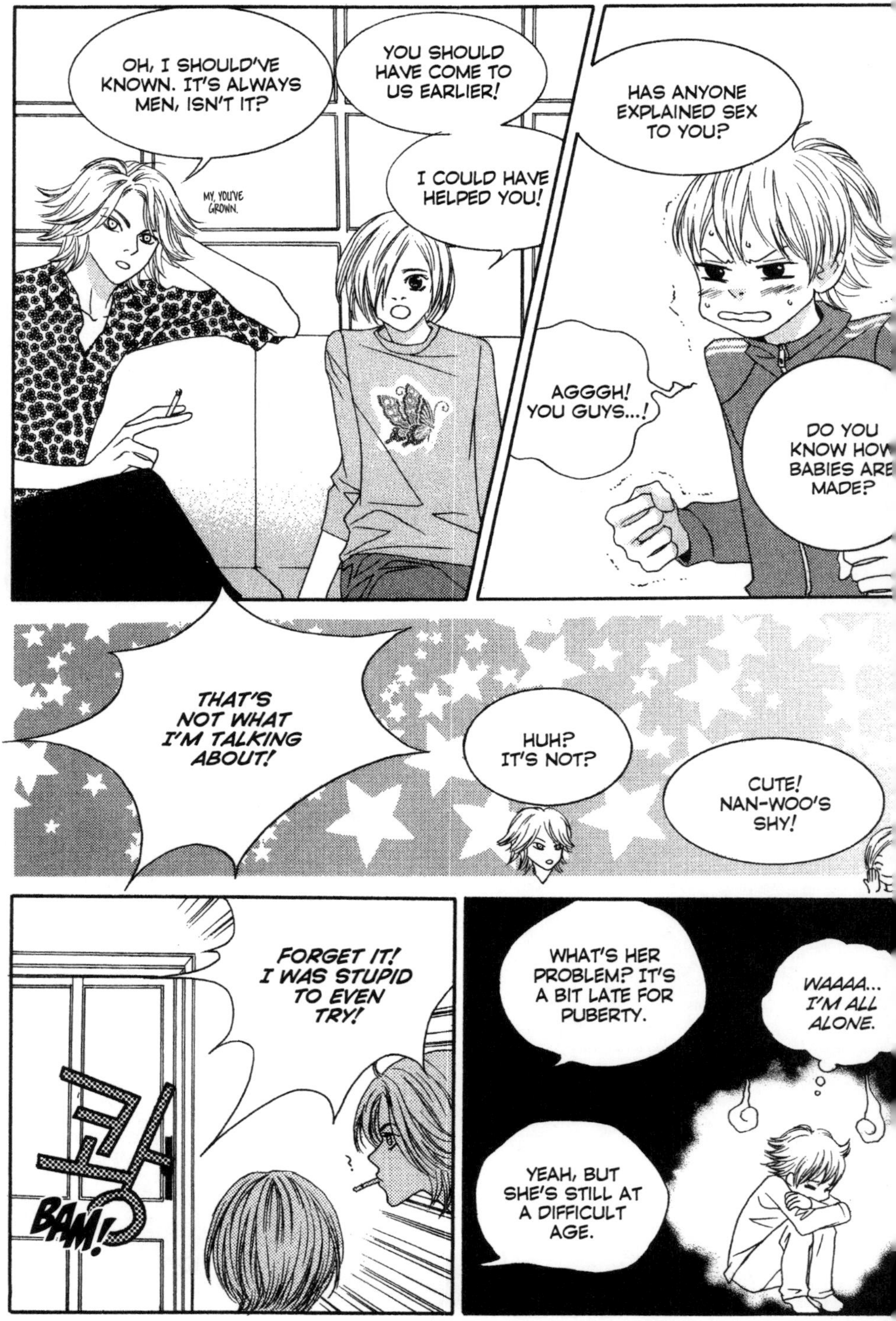
OH, I SHOULD'VE KNOWN. IT'S ALWAYS MEN, ISN'T IT?
MY, YOU'VE GROWN.
YOU SHOULD HAVE COME TO US EARLIER!
I COULD HAVE HELPED YOU!
HAS ANYONE EXPLAINED SEX TO YOU?
AGGGH! YOU GUYS...!
DO YOU KNOW HOW BABIES ARE MADE?
THAT'S NOT WHAT I'M TALKING ABOUT!
HUH? IT'S NOT?
CUTE! NAN-WOO'S SHY!
FORGET IT! I WAS STUPID TO EVEN TRY!
BAM!
WHAT'S HER PROBLEM? IT'S A BIT LATE FOR PUBERTY.
YEAH, BUT SHE'S STILL AT A DIFFICULT AGE.
WAAAA... I'M ALL ALONE.

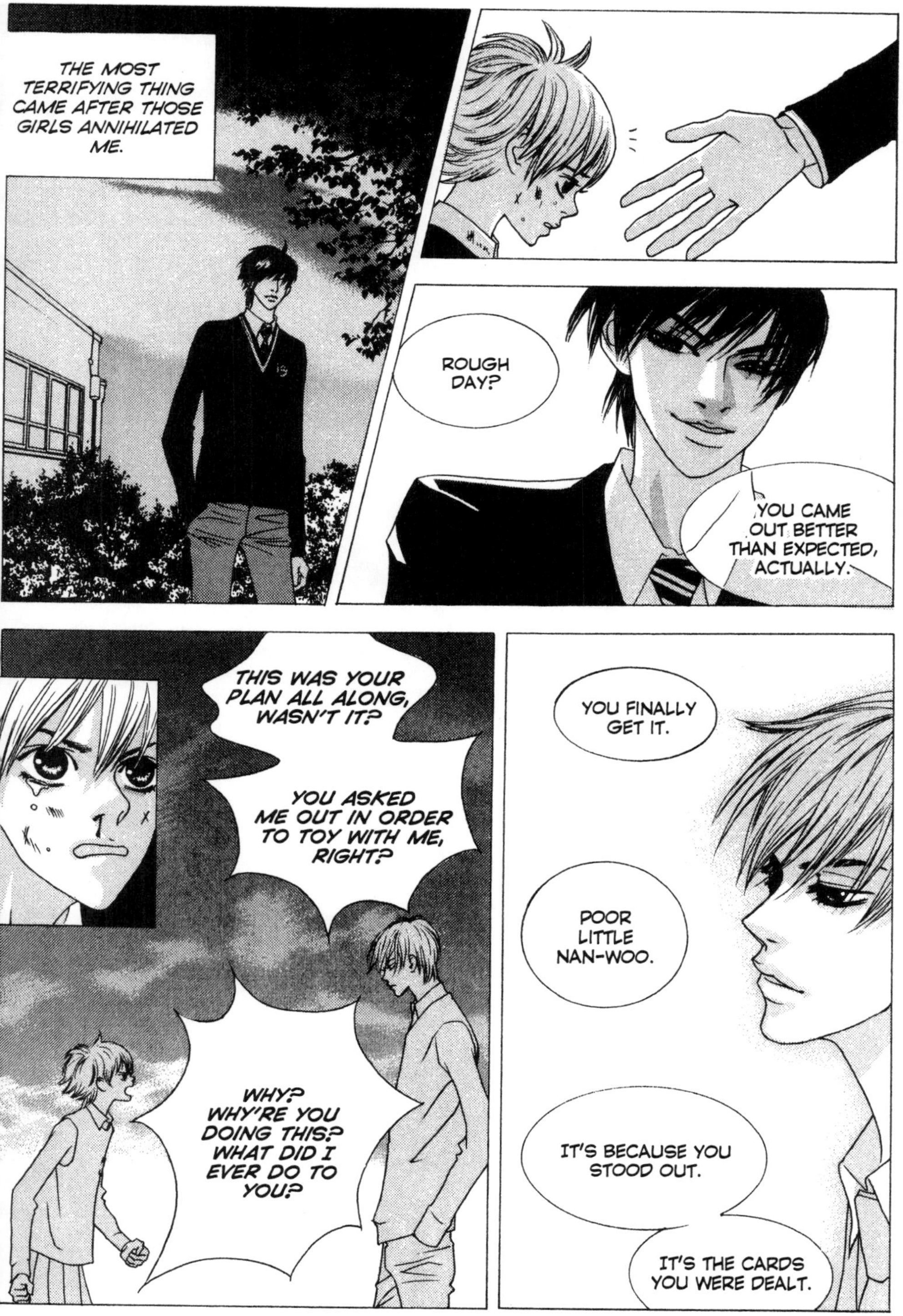
THE MOST TERRIFYING THING CAME AFTER THOSE GIRLS ANNIHILATED ME.
ROUGH DAY?
YOU CAME OUT BETTER THAN EXPECTED, ACTUALLY.
THIS WAS YOUR PLAN ALL ALONG, WASN'T IT?
YOU ASKED ME OUT IN ORDER TO TOY WITH ME, RIGHT?
WHY? WHY'RE YOU DOING THIS? WHAT DID I EVER DO TO YOU?
YOU FINALLY GET IT.
POOR LITTLE NAN-WOO.
IT'S BECAUSE YOU STOOD OUT.
IT'S THE CARDS YOU WERE DEALT.

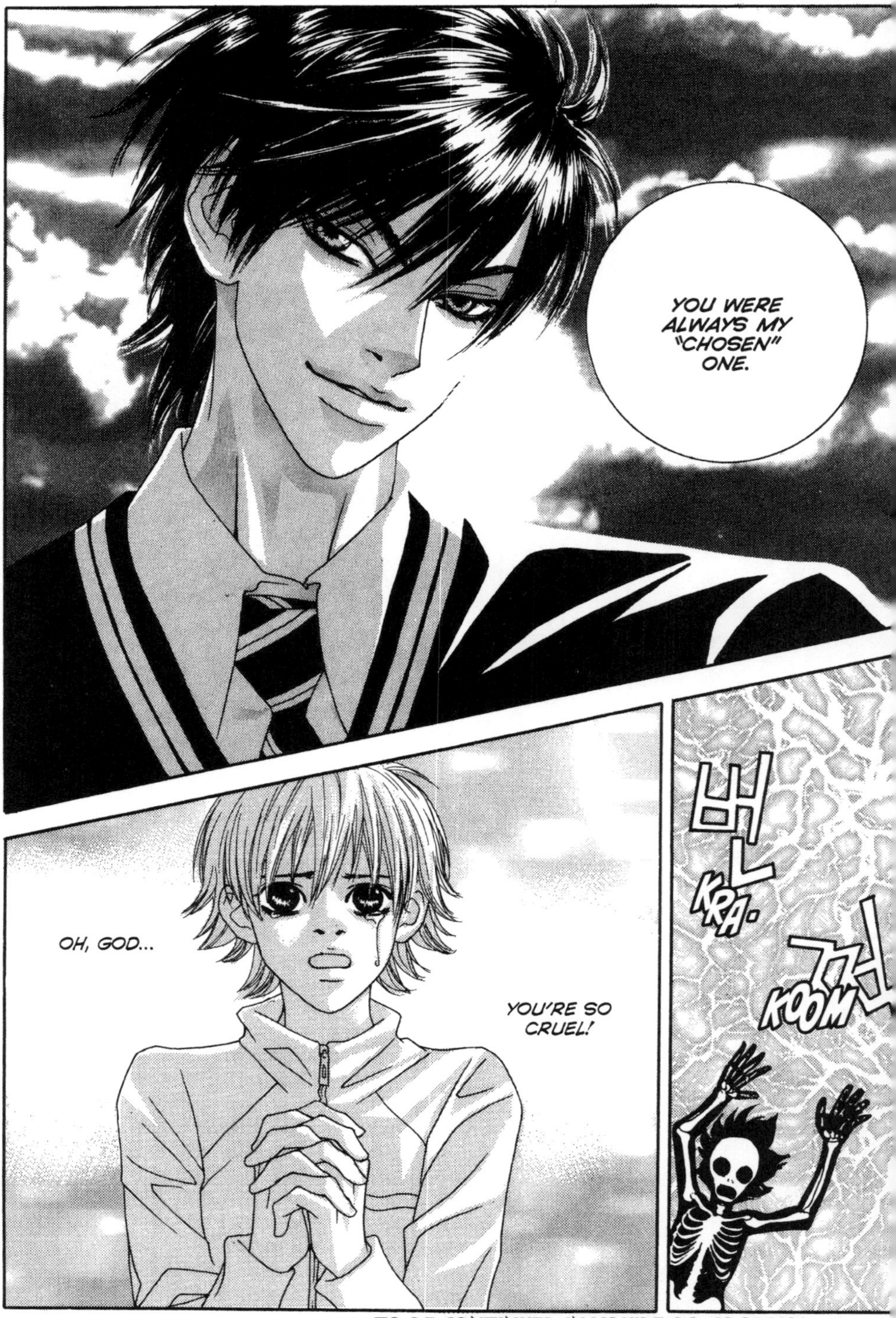
YOU WERE ALWAYS MY "CHOSEN" ONE.
OH, GOD...
YOU'RE SO CRUEL!
KRA-
KOOM

TO BE CONTINUED IN YOU'RE SO COOL VOL. 21

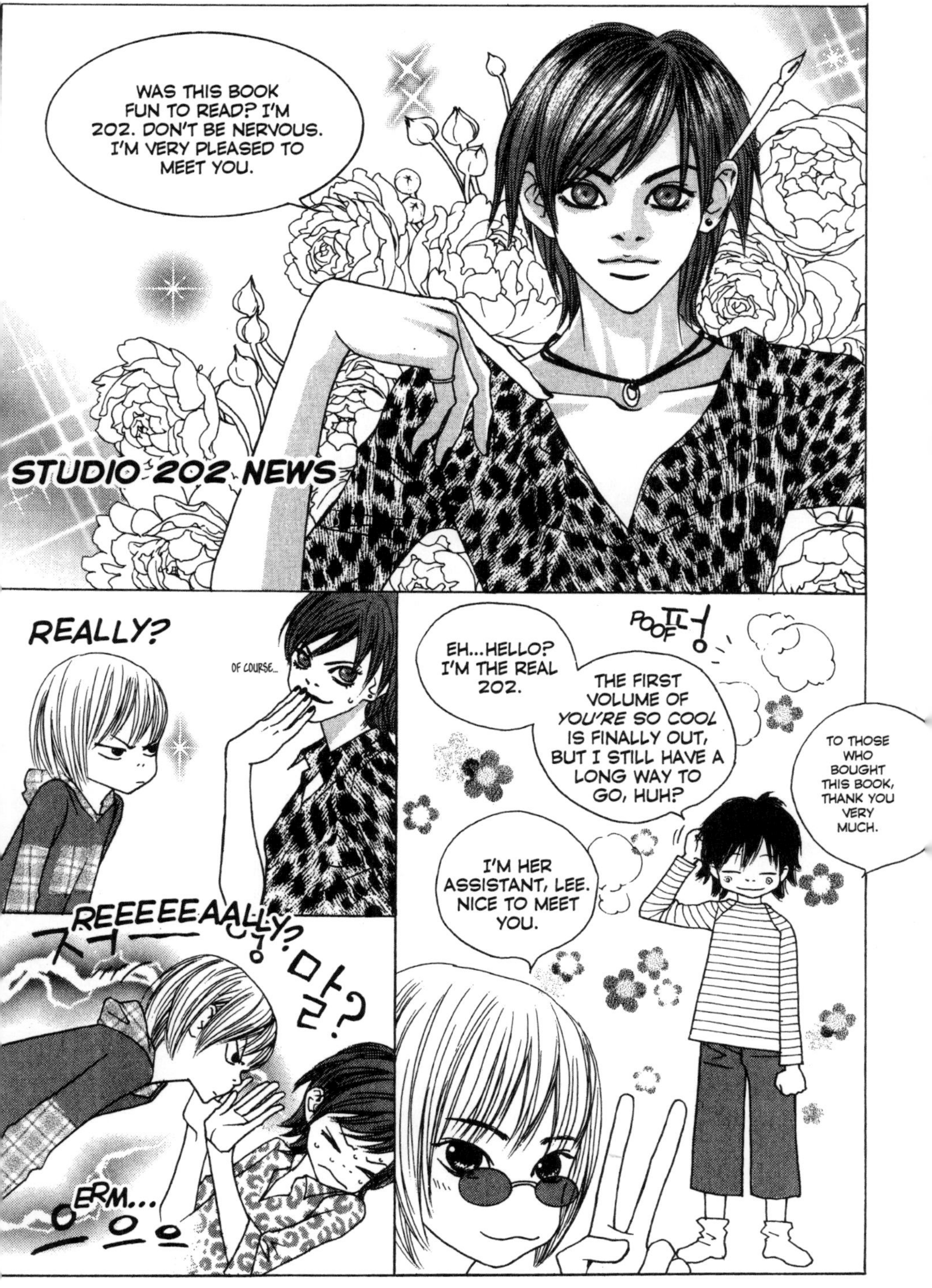
WAS THIS BOOK FUN TO READ? I'M 202. DON'T BE NERVOUS. I'M VERY PLEASED TO MEET YOU.
STUDIO 202 NEWS
REALLY?
OF COURSE...
REEEEEEAALLY?
ERM...
POOF
EH...HELLO? I'M THE REAL 202.
THE FIRST VOLUME OF *YOU'RE SO COOL* IS FINALLY OUT, BUT I STILL HAVE A LONG WAY TO GO, HUH?
TO THOSE WHO BOUGHT THIS BOOK, THANK YOU VERY MUCH.
I'M HER ASSISTANT, LEE. NICE TO MEET YOU.

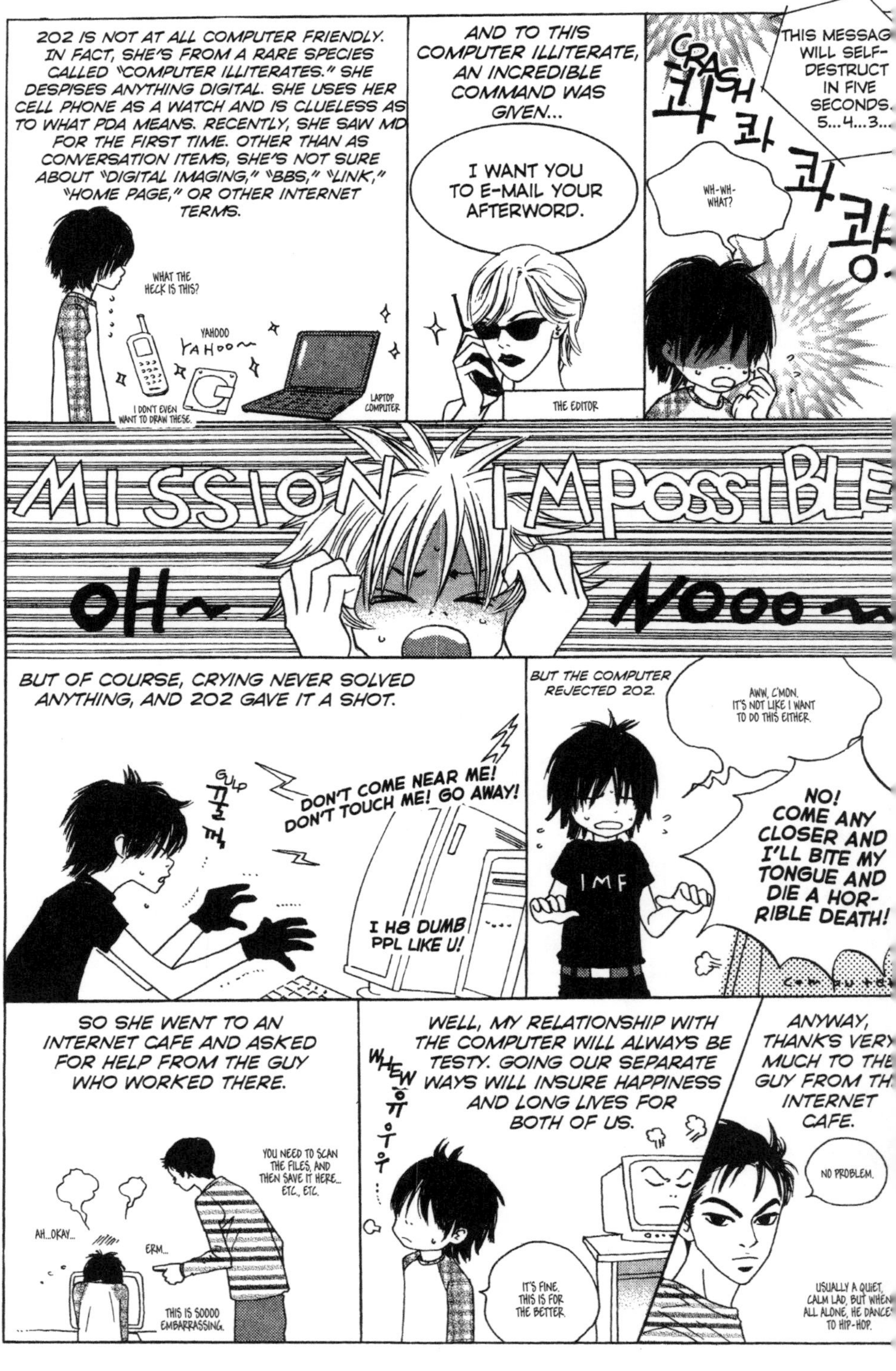

202 IS NOT AT ALL COMPUTER FRIENDLY. IN FACT, SHE'S FROM A RARE SPECIES CALLED "COMPUTER ILLITERATES." SHE DESPISES ANYTHING DIGITAL. SHE USES HER CELL PHONE AS A WATCH AND IS CLUELESS AS TO WHAT PDA MEANS. RECENTLY, SHE SAW MD FOR THE FIRST TIME. OTHER THAN AS CONVERSATION ITEMS, SHE'S NOT SURE ABOUT "DIGITAL IMAGING," "BBS," "LINK," "HOME PAGE," OR OTHER INTERNET TERMS.
WHAT THE HECK IS THIS?
YAHOOO
YAHOO~
I DON'T EVEN WANT TO DRAW THESE.
LAPTOP COMPUTER
AND TO THIS COMPUTER ILLITERATE, AN INCREDIBLE COMMAND WAS GIVEN...
I WANT YOU TO E-MAIL YOUR AFTERWORD.
THE EDITOR
CRASH
콰 콰 콰 쾅
THIS MESSAG WILL SELF-DESTRUCT IN FIVE SECONDS. 5...4...3...
WH-WH-WHAT?
MISSION IMPOSSIBLE
OH~ NOOO~
BUT OF COURSE, CRYING NEVER SOLVED ANYTHING, AND 202 GAVE IT A SHOT.
GULP
DON'T COME NEAR ME! DON'T TOUCH ME! GO AWAY!
I H8 DUMB PPL LIKE U!
BUT THE COMPUTER REJECTED 202.
AWW, C'MON. IT'S NOT LIKE I WANT TO DO THIS EITHER.
NO! COME ANY CLOSER AND I'LL BITE MY TONGUE AND DIE A HORRIBLE DEATH!
IMF
SO SHE WENT TO AN INTERNET CAFE AND ASKED FOR HELP FROM THE GUY WHO WORKED THERE.
YOU NEED TO SCAN THE FILES, AND THEN SAVE IT HERE... ETC., ETC.
AH...OKAY...
ERM...
THIS IS SOOOO EMBARRASSING.
WHEW
WELL, MY RELATIONSHIP WITH THE COMPUTER WILL ALWAYS BE TESTY. GOING OUR SEPARATE WAYS WILL INSURE HAPPINESS AND LONG LIVES FOR BOTH OF US.
IT'S FINE. THIS IS FOR THE BETTER.
ANYWAY, THANKS VERY MUCH TO THE GUY FROM TH INTERNET CAFE.
NO PROBLEM.
USUALLY A QUIET, CALM LAD, BUT WHEN ALL ALONE, HE DANCES TO HIP-HOP.

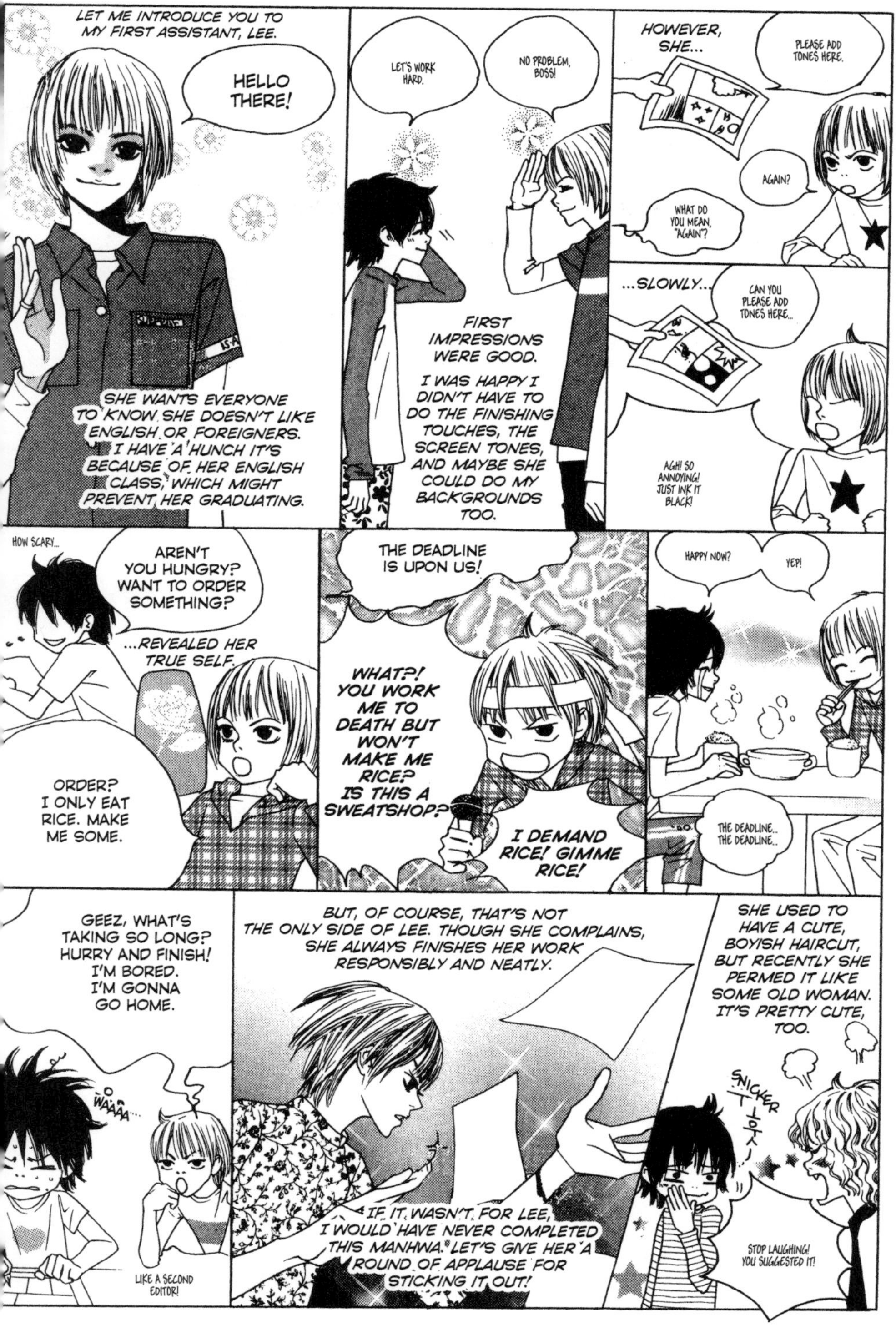
LET ME INTRODUCE YOU TO MY FIRST ASSISTANT, LEE.
HELLO THERE!
SHE WANTS EVERYONE TO KNOW SHE DOESN'T LIKE ENGLISH OR FOREIGNERS. I HAVE A HUNCH IT'S BECAUSE OF HER ENGLISH CLASS, WHICH MIGHT PREVENT HER GRADUATING.
LET'S WORK HARD.
NO PROBLEM, BOSS!
FIRST IMPRESSIONS WERE GOOD.
I WAS HAPPY I DIDN'T HAVE TO DO THE FINISHING TOUCHES, THE SCREEN TONES, AND MAYBE SHE COULD DO MY BACKGROUNDS TOO.
HOWEVER, SHE...
PLEASE ADD TONES HERE.
AGAIN?
WHAT DO YOU MEAN, "AGAIN"?
...SLOWLY...
CAN YOU PLEASE ADD TONES HERE...
AGH! SO ANNOYING! JUST INK IT BLACK!
HOW SCARY...
AREN'T YOU HUNGRY? WANT TO ORDER SOMETHING?
...REVEALED HER TRUE SELF.
ORDER? I ONLY EAT RICE. MAKE ME SOME.
THE DEADLINE IS UPON US!
WHAT?! YOU WORK ME TO DEATH BUT WON'T MAKE ME RICE? IS THIS A SWEATSHOP?
I DEMAND RICE! GIMME RICE!
HAPPY NOW?
YEP!
THE DEADLINE... THE DEADLINE...
GEEZ, WHAT'S TAKING SO LONG? HURRY AND FINISH! I'M BORED. I'M GONNA GO HOME.
WAAAA...
LIKE A SECOND EDITOR!
BUT, OF COURSE, THAT'S NOT THE ONLY SIDE OF LEE. THOUGH SHE COMPLAINS, SHE ALWAYS FINISHES HER WORK RESPONSIBLY AND NEATLY.
IF IT WASN'T FOR LEE, I WOULD HAVE NEVER COMPLETED THIS MANHWA.* LET'S GIVE HER A ROUND OF APPLAUSE FOR STICKING IT OUT!
SHE USED TO HAVE A CUTE, BOYISH HAIRCUT, BUT RECENTLY SHE PERMED IT LIKE SOME OLD WOMAN. IT'S PRETTY CUTE, TOO.
SNICKER
STOP LAUGHING! YOU SUGGESTED IT!

THE CREATOR AND I

BY LEE

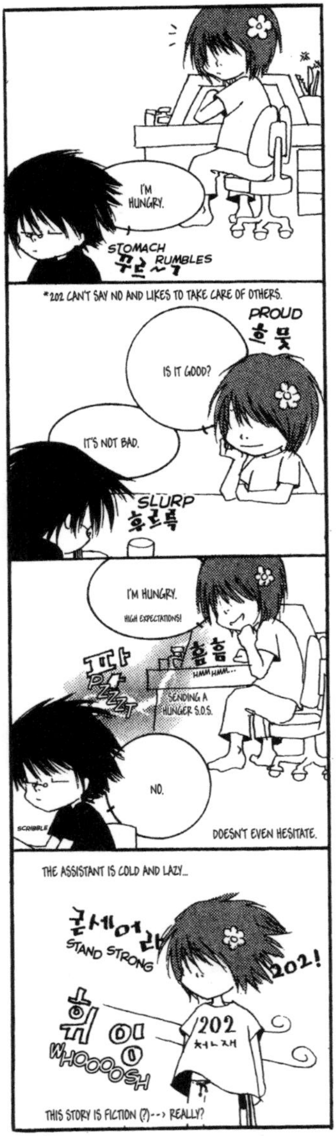
I'M HUNGRY.
STOMACH RUMBLES
*202 CAN'T SAY NO AND LIKES TO TAKE CARE OF OTHERS.
PROUD
흐뭇
IS IT GOOD?
IT'S NOT BAD.
SLURP
후르륵
I'M HUNGRY.
HIGH EXPECTATIONS!
흠흠
HMM HMM...
PZZZT
SENDING A HUNGER S.O.S.
NO.
SCRIBBLE
DOESN'T EVEN HESITATE.
THE ASSISTANT IS COLD AND LAZY...
굳세어라
STAND STRONG
202!
WHOOOOSH
202
THIS STORY IS FICTION (?)--> REALLY?

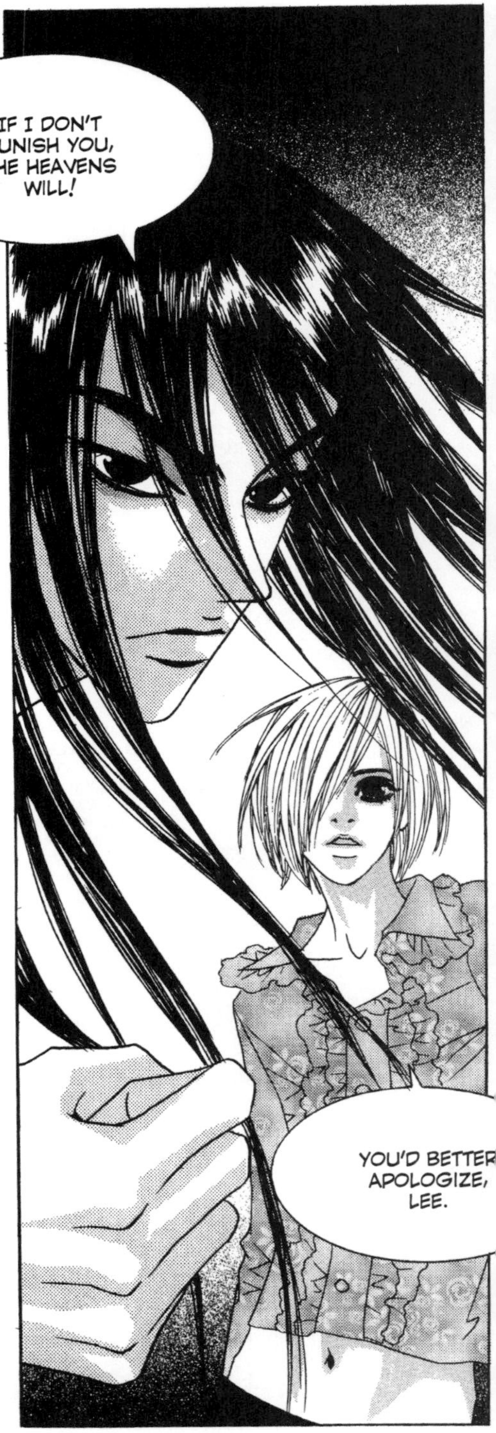
IF I DON'T PUNISH YOU, THE HEAVENS WILL!
YOU'D BETTER APOLOGIZE, LEE.

SPECIAL THANKS TO...

THANKS BE TO GOD, THAT I HAVE ACHIEVED CLOSURE ON THE FIRST VOLUME.
WE TALKED A LOT...AND MADE LOTS OF MISTAKES.
A BIWEEKLY DEADLINE WAS MORE THAN I IMAGINED.
THERE WERE TIMES WHEN I WANTED TO RUN AWAY, TIMES I WANTED TO FAINT...
I RECEIVED A LOT OF SUPPORT AND STRENGTH, AND MY FRIENDS HELPED ME GREATLY.
AND OF COURSE, THANKS TO MY ASSISTANT, LEE, WHO NEVER FAILS TO COME RUNNING IN THE STUDIO TO DUMP MORE OF HER OPINIONS INTO THE ALREADY HELLISH CHAOS WHEN I'M UNDER THE DEADLINE GUN. (WHAP!) I MEAN...YOU ALWAYS LEND A REFRESHING AIR TO THE STUDIO ATMOSPHERE!
AND TO MY HEAD EDITOR, WHO'S BEEN VERY GENTLE WITH ME, AS WELL AS WORRIED FOR ME, AND IN GENERAL, GIVEN ME A LOT OF SUPPORT. I'M SURE SHE LAID IN BED SICK BECAUSE OF ME MANY TIMES. AND TO THE OTHER EDITORS WHO BELIEVED IN ME, THANK YOU VERY MUCH, I'LL WORK HARDER. AND TO THE RESPONSIBLE AND BEAUTIFUL HAE-JIN, YOU'RE JUST TOO PERFECT. AND TO G, LET'S TRY TO EARN A LOT OF MONEY AND BUY OURSELVES A BUILDING. PARADISE ISN'T FAR! LET'S DO IT! AND YOON-SOO, 202'S HEAD CHEERLEADER, WHEN ARE YOU BRINGING THAT KIM-CHI YOU PROMISED?
AND TO THOSE READERS WHO HAVE SUPPORTED ME, I THANK YOU FOR LOVING THIS MANHWA. YOU GUYS ARE THE TRUE STRENGTH THAT KEEPS ME GOING.
THOUGH IT'S A BIT EMBARRASSING TO SAY, THANK YOU, AND I HOPE YOU WILL CONTINUE TO LOVE THIS TITLE. THANK YOU VERY MUCH.

FROM 202

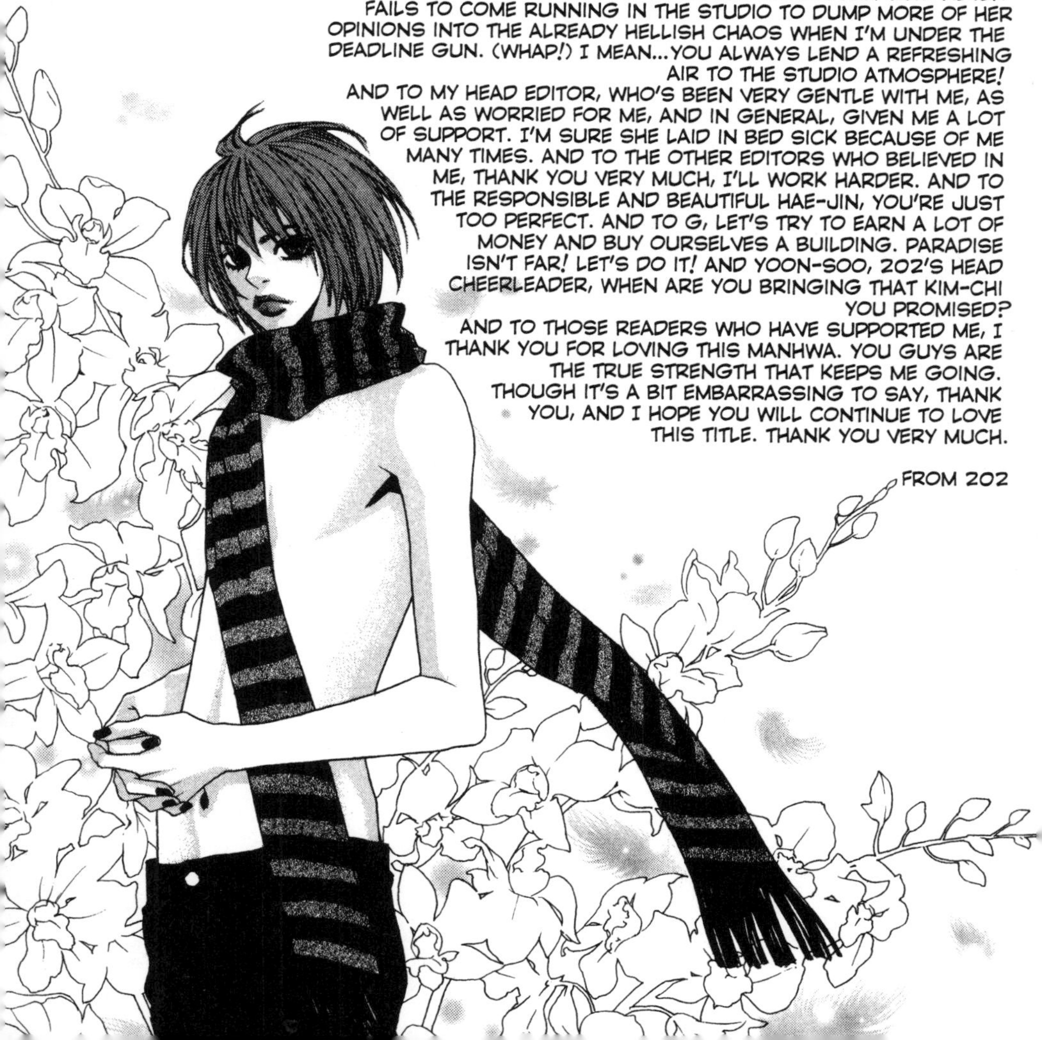

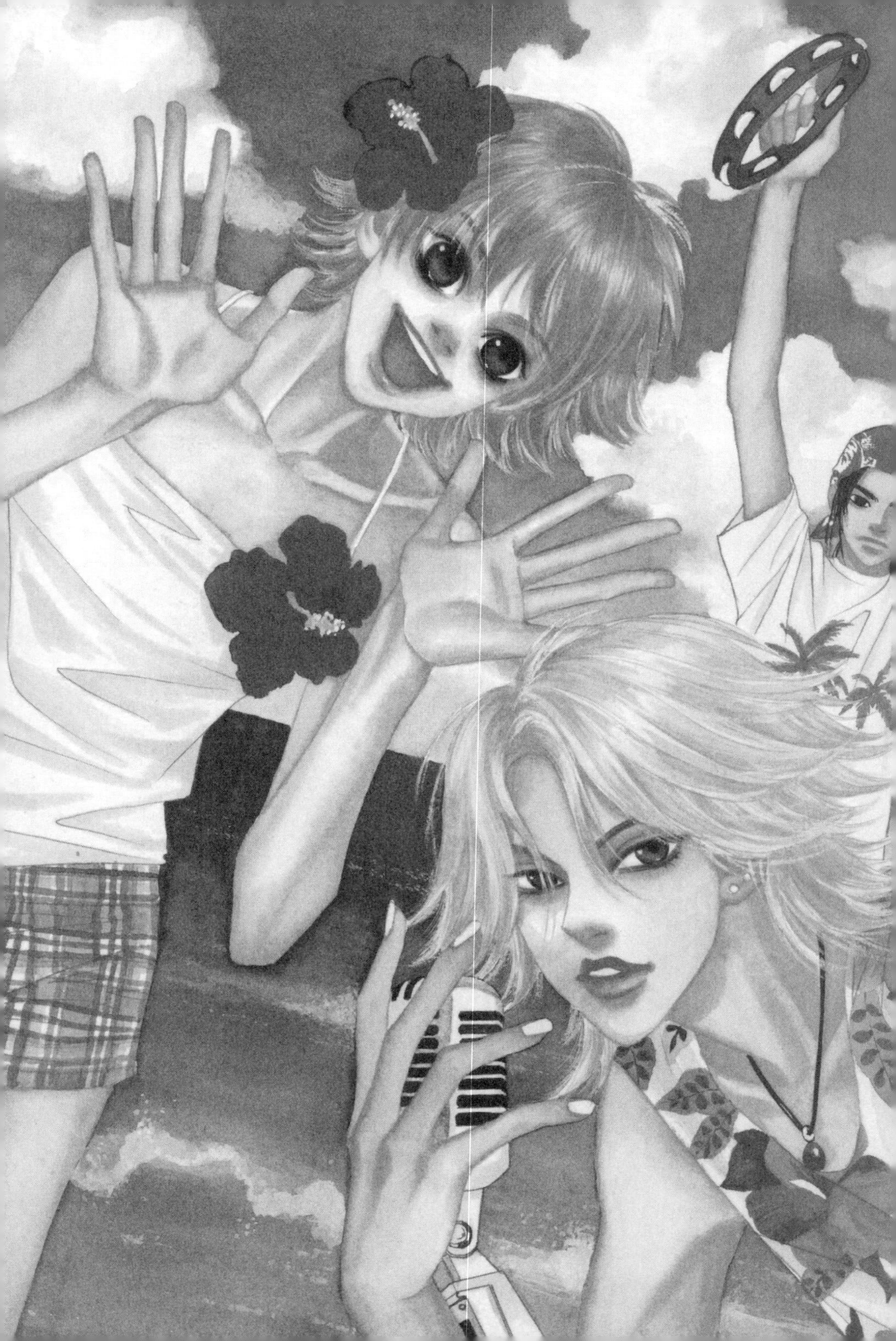

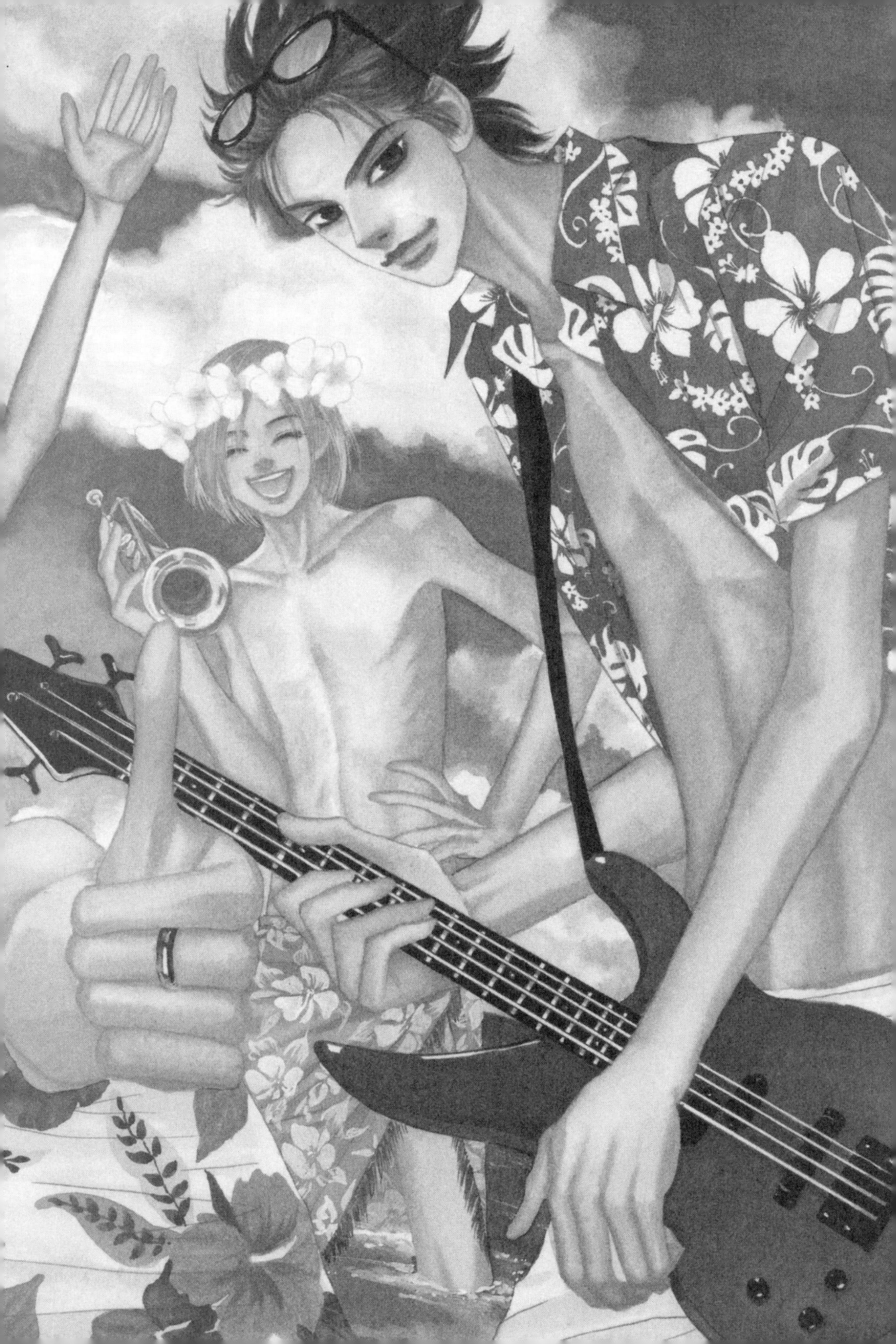

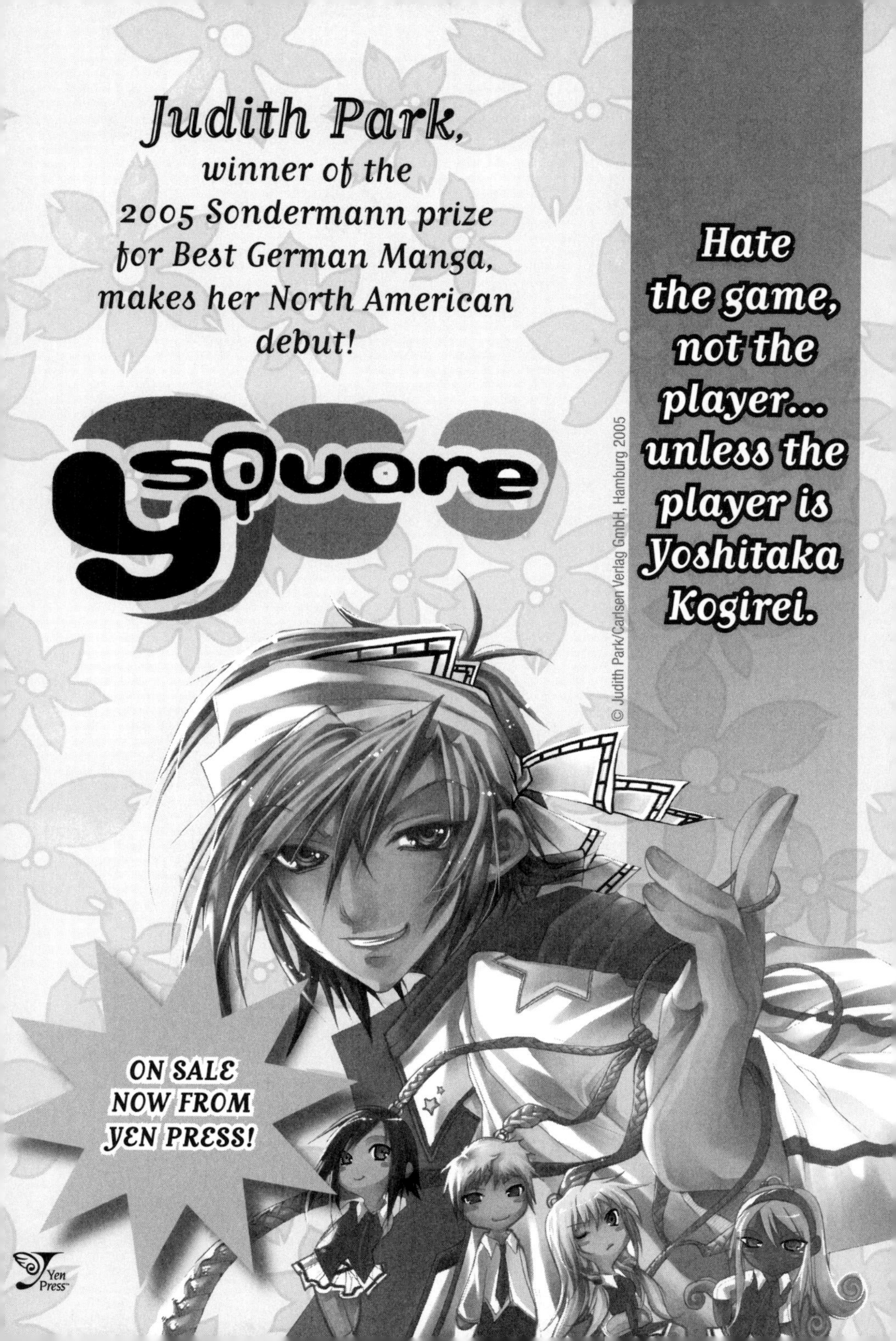
Judith Park,
winner of the
2005 Sondermann prize
for Best German Manga,
makes her North American
debut!
Hate
the game,
not the
player...
unless the
player is
Yoshitaka
Kogirei.
y square
© Judith Park/Carlsen Verlag GmbH, Hamburg 2005
ON SALE
NOW FROM
YEN PRESS!
Yen Press

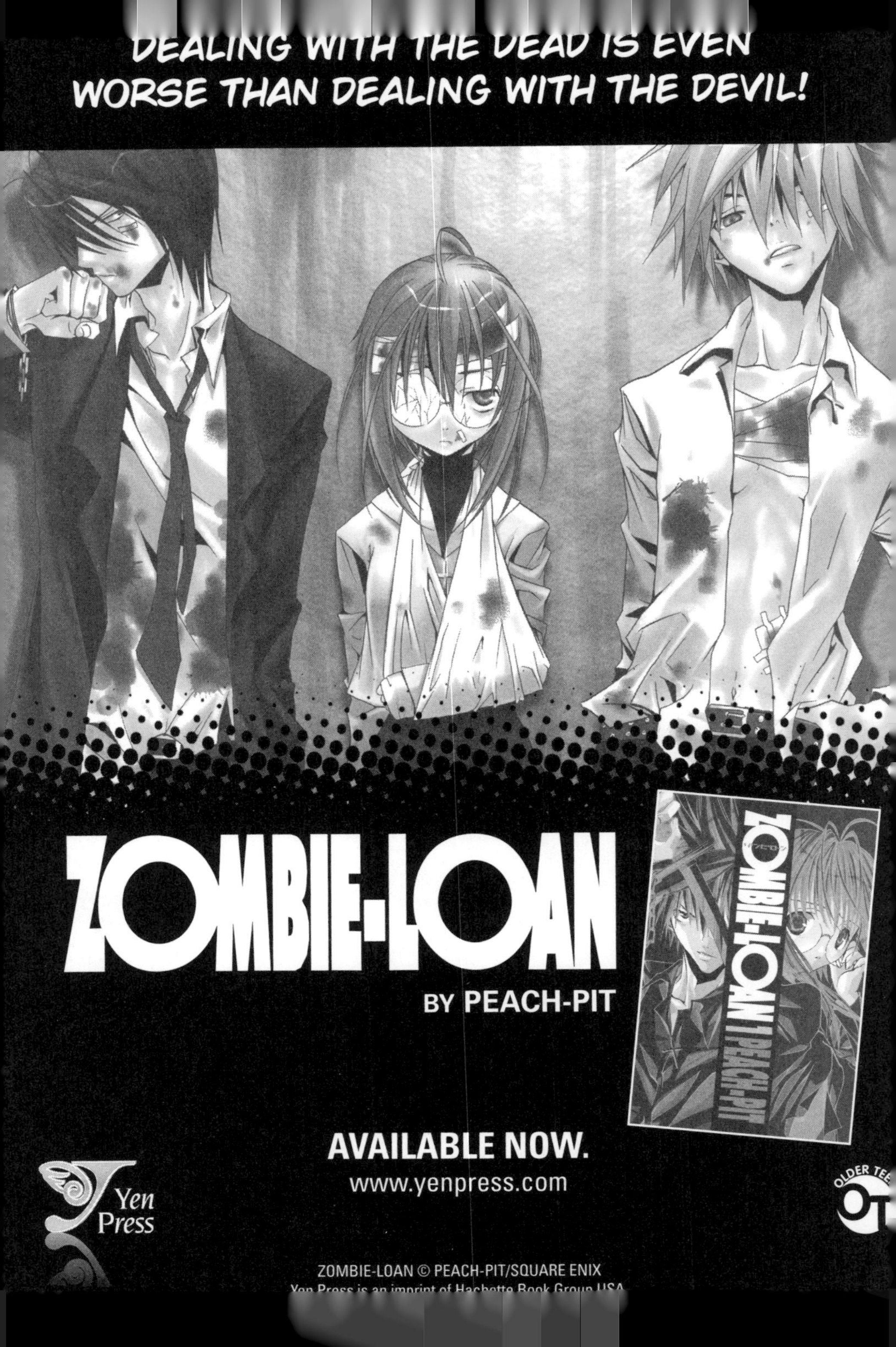
DEALING WITH THE DEAD IS EVEN WORSE THAN DEALING WITH THE DEVIL!
ZOMBIE-LOAN
BY PEACH-PIT
ZOMBIE-LOAN 1 PEACH-PIT
AVAILABLE NOW.
www.yenpress.com
Yen Press
ZOMBIE-LOAN © PEACH-PIT/SQUARE ENIX
Yen Press is an imprint of Hachette Book Group USA

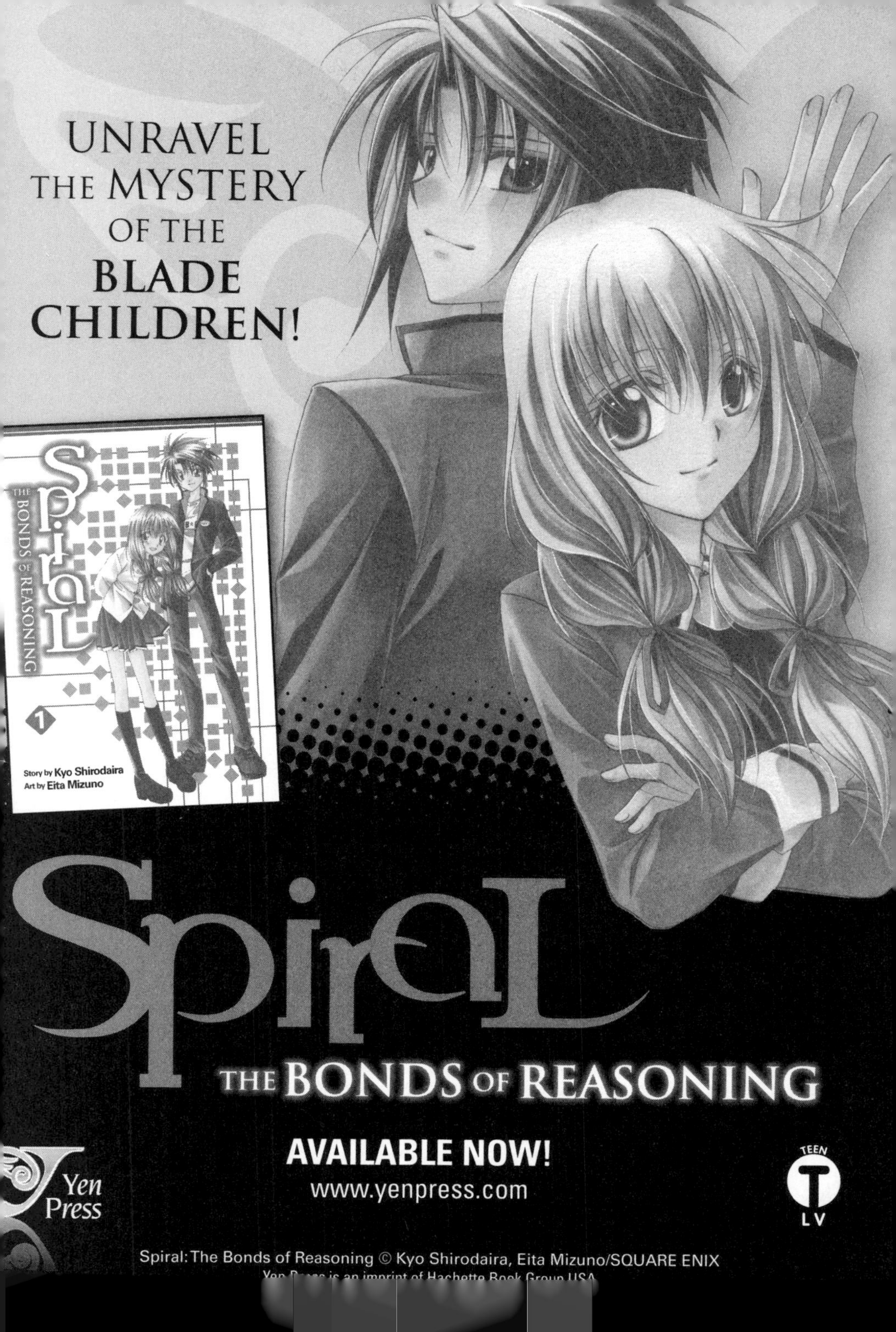
UNRAVEL THE MYSTERY OF THE BLADE CHILDREN!
Spiral
THE BONDS OF REASONING
1
Story by Kyo Shirodaira
Art by Eita Mizuno
Spiral
THE BONDS OF REASONING
AVAILABLE NOW!
www.yenpress.com
Yen Press
TEEN
T
LV
Spiral: The Bonds of Reasoning © Kyo Shirodaira, Eita Mizuno/SQUARE ENIX
Yen Press is an imprint of Hachette Book Group USA

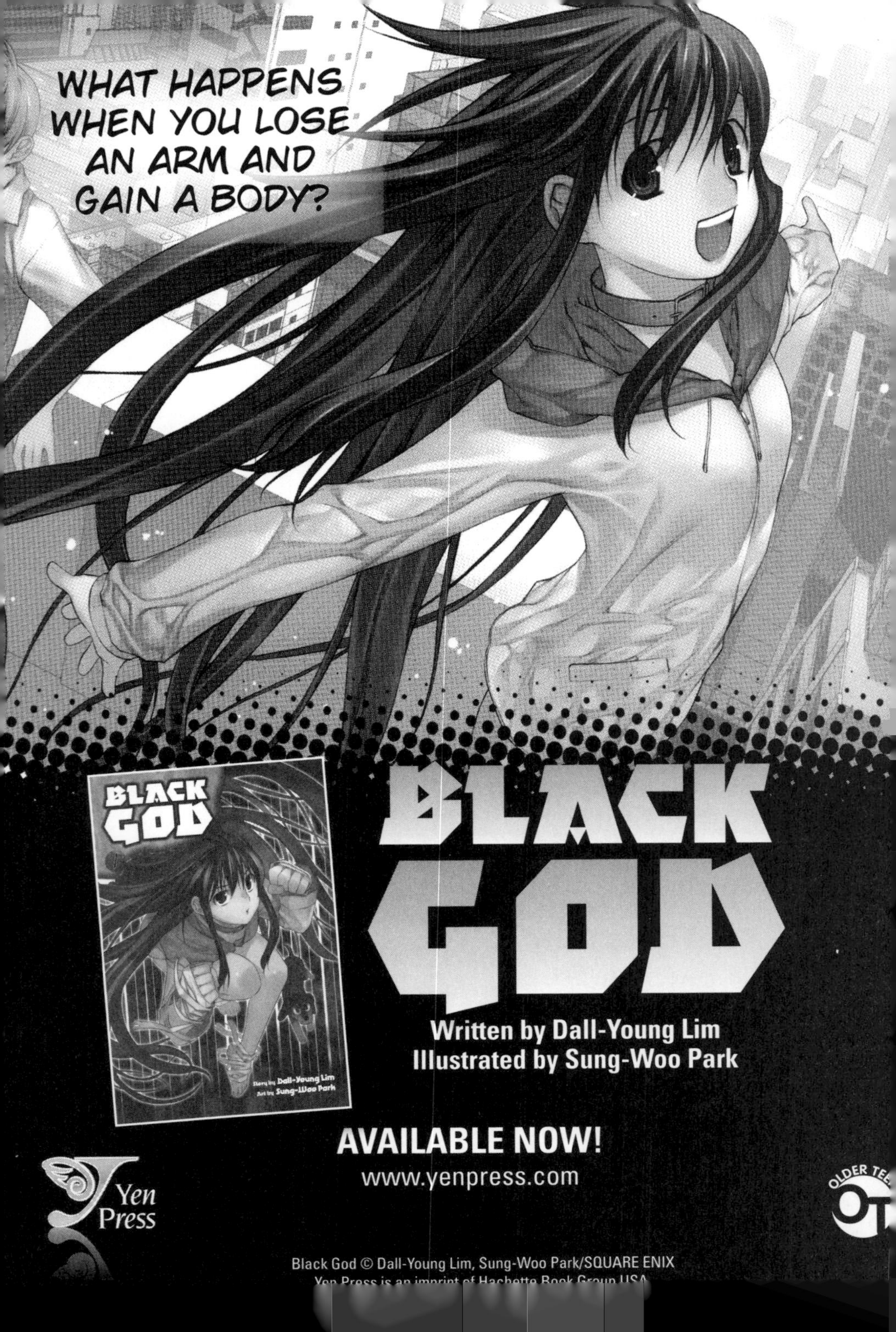
WHAT HAPPENS WHEN YOU LOSE AN ARM AND GAIN A BODY?
BLACK GOD
Story by Dall-Young Lim
Art by Sung-Woo Park
BLACK GOD
Written by Dall-Young Lim
Illustrated by Sung-Woo Park
AVAILABLE NOW!
www.yenpress.com
Yen Press
Black God © Dall-Young Lim, Sung-Woo Park/SQUARE ENIX
Yen Press is an imprint of Hachette Book Group USA